Principles of Change

Principles of Change

How Psychotherapists Implement Research in Practice

Edited by

LOUIS G. CASTONGUAY,
MICHAEL J. CONSTANTINO, AND
LARRY E. BEUTLER

Oxford University Press is a department of the University of Oxford. It furthers
the University's objective of excellence in research, scholarship, and education
by publishing worldwide. Oxford is a registered trade mark of Oxford University
Press in the UK and certain other countries.

Published in the United States of America by Oxford University Press
198 Madison Avenue, New York, NY 10016, United States of America.

© Oxford University Press 2019

All rights reserved. No part of this publication may be reproduced, stored in
a retrieval system, or transmitted, in any form or by any means, without the
prior permission in writing of Oxford University Press, or as expressly permitted
by law, by license, or under terms agreed with the appropriate reproduction
rights organization. Inquiries concerning reproduction outside the scope of the
above should be sent to the Rights Department, Oxford University Press, at the
address above.

You must not circulate this work in any other form
and you must impose this same condition on any acquirer.

CIP data is on file at the Library of Congress
ISBN 978-0-19-932472-9

1 3 5 7 9 8 6 4 2

Printed by Marquis, Canada

Pour ma mere, Gemma, qui a construit des châteaux d'amour sur des échafauds de principes
(For my mother, Gemma, who has built castles of love on scaffolds of principles)
Louis G. Castonguay

For my graduate students and collaborators—your support, inspiration, and dedication fuel my professional pursuits
Michael J. Constantino

For my many colleagues over the past 48 years who have collaborated with me, kept me on track, and informed me of what is real and important. I owe you this and much more. And to my wife Jamie who keeps me together and focused on our goals—bless her.
Larry E. Beutler

The three of us also dedicate this book to Abe Wolf, a man of principles, deep knowledge, clinical wisdom, and a most kind heart. We were honored to have Abe make substantial and insightful contributions to this project, even as he was fighting the recurrence of cancer. Sadly, Abe passed away as the book was going in press. We miss you, friend.
Louis G. Castonguay, Michael J. Constantino, and Larry E. Beutler

Contents

Preface ix
About the Editors xiii
Advisory Board Members xv
Contributors xvii

PART I: INTRODUCTION

1. Implementing Evidence-Based Principles of Therapeutic Change: A Bidirectional Collaboration between Clinicians and Researchers   3
   Louis G. Castonguay, Michael J. Constantino, and Larry E. Beutler

2. An Updated List of Principles of Change That Work   13
   Andrew A. McAleavey, Henry Xiao, Samantha L. Bernecker, Hannah Brunet, Nicholas R. Morrison, Mickey Stein, Soo Jeong Youn, Louis G. Castonguay, Michael J. Constantino, and Larry E. Beutler

PART II: DEPRESSION

3. Depression Cases   41
   Louis G. Castonguay, Michael J. Constantino, and Larry E. Beutler

4. How I Would Apply Change Principles in Psychotherapy with Three Cases of Depression   57
   Benjamin Johnson

5. Empirically Supported Principles of Psychotherapy   97
   Abraham W. Wolf

6. Principles of Therapeutic Change in Treating Depression with an Integrative Application of the Cognitive Behavioral Analysis System of Psychotherapy   129
   Dina Vivian

7. Conceptual, Clinical, and Empirical Perspectives on Principles of Change for Depression   167
   Benjamin Johnson, Dina Vivian, Abraham W. Wolf, Larry E. Beutler, Louis G. Castonguay, and Michael J. Constantino

PART III: ANXIETY DISORDERS

8. Anxiety Disorders Cases 215
   Louis G. Castonguay, Michael J. Constantino, and Larry E. Beutler

9. Principles of Therapeutic Change: A Psychoanalyst's Perspective 231
   Eva D. Papiasvili

10. A Cognitive-Behaviorist's Report from the Trenches 269
    Catherine S. Spayd

11. More Than a Feeling? Application of Principles of Change to Treatment of Anxiety 299
    Igor Weinberg

12. Conceptual, Clinical, and Empirical Perspectives on Principles of Change for Anxiety Disorders 325
    Eva D. Papiasvili, Catherine S. Spayd, Igor Weinberg, Larry E. Beutler, Louis G. Castonguay, and Michael J. Constantino

PART IV: CONCLUSION

13. Harvesting the Fruits of a Clinician-Researcher Collaboration and Planting Seeds for New Partnerships 365
    Louis G. Castonguay, Michael J. Constantino, and Larry E. Beutler

Author Index 377
Subject Index 383

Preface

"You want to know how to become a good therapist? First and foremost, you have to master techniques of treatment protocols that have been found effective in randomized clinical trials."

"How does therapy work? The bottom line: It's all about the therapeutic relationship."

"Techniques? Relationship? Who are we kidding? What really matters is whether the client wants and can change."

It is these kind of comments, frequently heard at conferences and professional gatherings, that led two of us, LGC and LEB, to create a task force in the early 2000s to give credence to an absolutely "brilliant" idea of ours: "Therapeutic change might not be entirely explained by either one of these variables alone; it is more likely related to a complex combination of technical, relational, and participant factors." Brilliant and earth shattering, right? To demonstrate our point (which, of course, was by no mean an original one), we invited 12 groups of influential scholars to review the research literature on the role of these three types of factors in the treatment of diverse clinical problems. From these reviews, we also asked them to derive principles of change that could inform therapists from different theoretical orientations. This led to our book, *Principles of Change That Work*, which Oxford University Press (OUP) published in 2006.

When we were approached to edit a sequel to that book, we agreed—but only under the conditions that we would not do it alone and that the second volume would be more than an updated version of the first one. Rather, we (a trio that now included MJC) wanted to improve the list of principles that resulted from the first book by conducting a new and uniform review of the research and, most important, by addressing the major criticism (as painful to hear as it was fair) that had been voiced about the first volume: "The book tells me what are some of the principles that are linked to outcome, but it does not inform me about how to use them in my day-to-day practice."

We were fortunate to have Andrea Zekus and Sarah Harrington, both at OUP, endorse our self-imposed ambitious goals. As described in the first chapter of the present volume, we have tackled these goals by having graduate students complete a major review of empirical literature and by having six expert clinicians describe, in rich and engaging detail, the implementation of the 38 principles of change that were retained from the review.

By illustrating how, when, and with whom these principles are applied in different treatment approaches, the current book not only addresses a valid critique of the first one, but it also highlights the unique expertise of professionals who are participating in and observing psychotherapy as it is routinely practiced. The book also provides an opportunity for practitioners to delineate convergences and divergences in the implementation of principles, express opinions regarding their clinical helpfulness and validity, and make suggestions for future revisions and research regarding these principles. Ultimately, by presenting complementary knowledge (what do we know about empirically about principles of change, and what are ways to implement them clinically?) and by fostering exchanges between clinicians and researchers, our hope is that this book offers a fresh, broad, and integrative perspective on evidence-based practice.

For allowing us to pursue this collaborative project, we want to thank Sarah and Andrea, not only for their vote of confidence but also for their support and patience. We also want to express our gratitude to Hayley Singer for her help throughout the final phase of publication, as well as to Patricia Santoso for given us permission to use her beautiful art on the cover of our book. We are most grateful for the lengthy literature review conducted by outstanding early-career scientists-practitioners: Samantha Bernecker, Hannah Brunet, Andrew McAleavey, Nicholas Morrison, Mickey Stein, Henry Xiao, and Soo Jeong Youn. A special "thank you" to Andrew, who coordinated this review, as well as to Henry, who aggregated and organized its findings.

We are also thankful to friends on our advisor board: Barry Farber, Charles Gelso, Marvin Goldfried, Gary Groth-Marnat, Laurie Heatherington, Hanna Levenson, Phillip Levendusky, and Heidi Levitt. Their advice has allowed us to recruit exemplary clinicians willing to write about the complex relationship between scientific findings and clinical realities. Our deepest gratitude goes to these authors—six highly gifted and experienced practitioners/scholars: Benjamin Johnson, Eva Papiasvili, Catherine Spayd, Dina Vivian, Igor Weinberg, and Abraham Wolf. We greatly appreciate the time and wisdom they provided in completing each of the many tasks that we asked them to contribute, let alone the kindness and collaborative spirit that they demonstrated in dealing with many waves of feedback and revisions. We are not only grateful for their bold and elegant chapters but also humbled for how much we learned from the insightful, nuanced, and creative ways they each conduct and think about psychotherapy.

Louis G. Castonguay, PhD
State College, Pennsylvania
Michael J. Constantino, PhD
Northampton, Massachusetts
Larry E. Beutler, PhD, ABPP
El Dorado Hills, California

About the Editors

Louis G. Castonguay, PhD, completed his doctorate in Clinical Psychology at SUNY–Stony Brook, a clinical internship at UC Berkeley, and a postdoctorate at Stanford University. He is currently a Liberal Arts Professor of Psychology at Penn State University. With more than 200 publications (including nine co-edited books), his scholarly work and research focus on different aspects of the therapeutic change and training (including variables related to interventions, relationship, client, and therapist), especially within the context of psychotherapy integration. He is also involved in practice-oriented research and the development of Practice Research Networks, both aimed at facilitating the collaboration between clinicians and researchers. In addition, he has been investigating the process and efficacy of new integrative treatments for generalized anxiety disorder and depression. He has received several recognitions, including Distinguished Awards for his lifetime contributions from both the Division of Psychotherapy of the American Psychological Association and the Society for Psychotherapy Research (SPR). He also served as president of SPR and the the North American chapter of SPR.

Michael J. Constantino, PhD, completed his doctoral training in Clinical Psychology at the Pennsylvania State University, a clinical internship at SUNY–Upstate Medical University, and a postdoctoral fellowship at the Stanford University Medical Center. Dr. Constantino is currently a professor in the Department of Psychological and Brain Sciences at the University of Massachusetts–Amherst, where he directs the Psychotherapy Research Lab and serves as Graduate Program Director. Dr. Constantino's professional and research interests center on patient, therapist, and dyadic factors in psychosocial treatments; pantheoretical principles of clinical change (i.e., *common factors*); and measurement-based care. He has authored or co-authored over 140 journal articles and book chapters and over 220 professional presentations. Dr. Constantino's work has been recognized internationally, including with his receipt of the American Psychological Foundation's Early Career Award, the Society for the Exploration of Psychotherapy Integration's New Researcher Award, the Society for Psychotherapy Research's Outstanding Early Career Achievement Award, the American Psychological Association (APA) Division 29 (Society for the Advancement of Psychotherapy) Distinguished Publication of Psychotherapy Research Award, and APA and Division 29 fellow status.

Dr. Constantino is president of APA Division 29 and past president of the North American Society for Psychotherapy Research.

Larry E. Beutler, PhD, is the past Director of the National Center on the Psychology of Terrorism, a multicenter institute sponsored by Stanford University, Palo Alto University, and the Palo Alto Veterans Health Care System. He is the William McInnes Distinguished Professor Emeritus and the former Chair and Director of Training for the Clinical Psychology Program at Palo Alto University's Pacific Graduate School of Psychology in Palo Alto, California. He also holds an appointment as Professor Emeritus at the University of California–Santa Barbara where he established and directed the Clinical/Counseling/School Psychology Program. Dr. Beutler's first positions following his graduation (PhD, Clinical Psychology) from the University of Nebraska–Lincoln (1970) was at Duke University Medical School. This placement was followed by appointments at Stephen F. Austin State University, Baylor College of Medicine, and the University of Arizona. Subsequently, he moved to California. Dr. Beutler is a Diplomate of the American Board of Professional Psychology (ABPP), a two-term past international president of the Society for Psychotherapy Research (SPR), past president of the Society for Clinical Psychology (Division 12, APA), and past president of the Division of Psychotherapy (American Psychological Association, Division 29). He is a recipient of the Distinguished Scientific Achievement Award from the California Psychological Association, the Distinguished Research Career Award from the Society for Psychotherapy Research, International, and a Presidential Citation from the president of the American Psychological Association.

Advisory Board Members

Barry A. Farber, PhD
Charles J. Gelso, PhD
Marvin R. Goldfried, PhD
Gary Groth-Marnat, PhD
Laurie Heatherington, PhD
Hanna Levenson, PhD
Phillip G. Levendusky, PhD
Heidi M. Levitt, PhD

Contributors

Samantha L. Bernecker, PhD
Department of Psychology
Harvard University

Larry E. Beutler, PhD, ABPP
Department of Clinical Psychology
Palo Alto University

Hannah Brunet, PhD
Neurological Institute
Cleveland Clinic Lou Ruvo Center for Brain Health

Louis G. Castonguay, PhD
Department of Psychology
The Pennsylvania State University

Michael J. Constantino, PhD
Department of Psychological and Brain Sciences
University of Massachusetts Amherst

Benjamin Johnson, PhD, ABPP
The Warren Alpert Medical School of Brown University
Rhode Island Center for Cognitive Behavioral Therapy

Andrew A. McAleavey, PhD
Department of Psychiatry
Weill Cornell Medicine

Nicholas R. Morrison, MS
Department of Psychological and Brain Sciences
University of Massachusetts Amherst

Eva D. Papiasvili, PhD, ABPP
Department of Clinical Psychology
Teachers College, Columbia University
Institute of the Postgraduate Psychoanalytic Society, New York

Catherine S. Spayd, PhD
Private practice
Duncansville, Pennsylvania

Mickey Stein, PhD
Clinical Psychologist Back In Motion
Vancouver, Canada

Dina Vivian, PhD
Department of Psychology
Stony Brook University

Igor Weinberg, PhD
Department of Psychiatry
Harvard Medical School

Abraham W. Wolf, PhD
Department of Psychiatry
Case Western Reserve University

Henry Xiao, MS
Department of Psychology
The Pennsylvania State University

Soo Jeong Youn, PhD
Department of Psychiatry
Massachusetts General Hospital/
Harvard Medical School

PART I

INTRODUCTION

1

Implementing Evidence-Based Principles of Therapeutic Change

A Bidirectional Collaboration between Clinicians and Researchers

Louis G. Castonguay, Michael J. Constantino, and Larry E. Beutler

It is well recognized that the links between psychotherapy research and practice are tenuous. This can be attributed, in part, to limited active collaboration and direct communication between researchers and clinicians (Beutler, Williams, Wakefield, & Entwhistle, 1995; Castonguay, Barkham, Lutz, & McAleavey, 2013; McWilliams, 2017). Researchers and practitioners comprise different communities, and their communication pattern largely follows a one-way street (Castonguay, 2011). To avoid perishing, researchers are driven to publish their studies in peer-reviewed scientific journals. Working from the assumption that one function of such journals is to disseminate research results to varied psychotherapy communities, many researchers trust (or at least hope) that clinicians will read these articles and apply the findings to their practice.

However, because of space limitations and an emphasis on methodological details, recommendations about how results can influence practice tend to be brief and unelaborated in most research outlets. Furthermore, because researchers are the ones who, by and large, generate such implications, clinicians may find them as having limited applicability to their practice. Finally, although some data suggest that clinicians find research useful (Beutler et al., 1995), they also report that empirical journals are not their primary source for guiding their clinical practice (e.g., Cohen, Sargent, & Sechrest, 1986; Morrow-Bradley & Elliott, 1986). This finding holds even for clinicians who also conduct research (Safran, Abreu, Ogilvie, & DeMaria, 2011). Thus, the current system for disseminating and applying evidence to practice remains prone to a wide clinician–researcher chasm.

To address this gap, several efforts have been made to describe how research findings, especially when presented without jargon, can be relevant to day-to-day practice (e.g., Castonguay et al., 2010; Cooper, 2008). Although such efforts likely provide useful information to therapists, they nevertheless represent a type of "empirical imperialism" whereby researchers, who generally treat few clients, try to instruct therapists, who treat many, on issues worthy of scientific attention and on the lessons that can be derived from research findings (Castonguay, 2011). In the extreme, this amounts to researchers telling therapists what they should want to know and what they should do, which is hardly an effective way to reduce the research–practice gap.

This top–down approach to the accumulation and dissemination of research evidence has had negative ramifications for the field. As Garland, Hulburt, and Hawley (2006) argued, "clinicians feel disenfranchised by researchers, believing that research often disregards their realities and invalidates their experience as professionals" (p. 32). This subjective experience of practitioners is not without basis. In a survey of both clinicians and researchers, Beutler et al. (1995) found that clinicians reported research as being important more than researchers reported the clinical literature as being important. By not fully recognizing clinicians' perspectives, the psychotherapy research field may have suffered from developmental delays and/or myopic impairment in its effort to understand and improve therapeutic change. As Kazdin (2008) aptly noted, "we are letting the knowledge from practice drip through the holes of a colander" (p. 155). Far from being intrinsically irreconcilable with research findings, we argue that the ideas and observations of many clinicians about psychotherapy (how change is facilitated or hampered, with whom and by whom) can shed light on how research evidence can best be implemented and on what issues should be studied to increase the effectiveness of psychotherapy. We concur with Beutler et al.: "Scientists may be missing important avenues for identifying critical areas of research. They may do a better scientific job if they were more attentive to the writings and ideas of their clinical colleagues" (pp. 989–990).

Goals of the Book

The present book builds on a previous volume, *Principles of Therapeutic Change that Work* (Castonguay & Beutler, 2006), and represents a new collaboration based on direct, two-way communication between researchers and clinicians that relies on their respective and overlapping knowledge and expertise. To us, this synergy holds promise for increasing our understanding and improving our delivery of psychotherapy. Blending knowledge from these sources, however, requires that we acknowledge that psychotherapy is more complex than applying a standard and sequenced package of interventions to classes of clients, with the assumption that these interventions are, above anything else, the primary factors responsible for therapeutic improvement. This assumption, which underlies the method of studying psychotherapy through randomized clinical trials (RCTs) is dated at best and naïve at worst. Whereas comparative RCTs narrowly privilege the contributions of the client's diagnosis and the therapeutic model, a broader evidence-informed and integrative view of psychotherapy emphasizes client factors beyond diagnoses, therapist factors (including between-therapist effects), dyadic processes, and the need to personalize treatment to individuals and contexts (Constantino, Coyne, & Gomez Penedo, 2017). Guided by such an integrative view, this volume is an attempt to create a new avenue toward evidence-based practice that relies on clinicians as active collaborators, rather than as passive recipients, in understanding and implementing research findings.

Castonguay and Beutler's (2006) first volume integrated, in broad brush strokes, research findings on factors that contribute to client improvement either directly (e.g., predictors) or in interaction (e.g., client trait × treatment effects). Influential psychotherapy scholars worked in teams (most of which comprised researchers of different theoretical orientations) to review research on three variable domains (participant characteristics, relationship variables, technical/intervention factors) as they applied to one particular type of clinical problem (dysphoric disorders, anxiety disorders, personality problems, substance use disorders). In addition, the authors translated the research evidence into principles of change that could serve as helpful clinical guidelines without being tied to particular jargon or theoretical models. The work of these 12 teams led to an aggregated list of 61 principles of change.

Although this initial volume succeeded in delineating change principles that cut across different theoretical orientations, we have since determined that it did not adequately inform clinicians (as stated by a review on amazon.com, as well as in comments made to the editors/authors at various conferences) in how to apply them. Accordingly, we restructured the present follow-up volume. Specifically, we (a) provided detailed descriptions of the ways in which empirically based principles of change might be effectively and efficiently implemented within and across major contemporary psychotherapies, (b) gave a direct voice to practicing clinicians by having them describe how, when, and with whom they apply (or do not apply) these principles in their clinical practice, and (c) sought to provide clinicians and researchers with opportunities to link collaboratively clinical knowledge and the empirical literature.

Structure of the Book

The book contains four major sections. The first section provides a general overview of the book (current chapter) and presents a revised list of the 61 principles of change that were delineated in the first volume (Chapter 2). The second chapter also describes the process that led to the revised list that regroups principles into five conceptually cohesive and clinically relevant clusters: client prognostic principles, treatment/provider moderating principles, client process principles, therapy relationship principles, and therapist interventions principles.

The second and third sections of the book focus on depression and anxiety disorders, respectively. We decided not to have specific sections on personality and substance use disorders (the other two disorders covered in the first volume) because relatively few clients come to treatment primarily for these disorders (at least in most practices). However, we still emphasize these clinical problems in the current volume. Specifically, both sections on depression and anxiety begin with a brief chapter (Chapters 3 and 8, respectively), written by the editors, presenting three cases: one with co-morbid substance abuse, one with co-morbid personality disorder, and one without substance-abuse or personality disorder co-morbidity. The cases also incorporate clinical features frequently associated with depression or anxiety (e.g., marital, occupational, health problems). We created these vignettes to provide a range of clinical situations for practitioners to describe when and how different principles of change may be applicable in their work.

The core of both sections on depression and anxiety are three additional chapters (Chapters 4, 5, and 6, and 9, 10, and 11, respectively) written by the contributing clinicians. The clinicians represent different blends of insight-oriented, or exploratory, and behavior change-oriented approaches. In preparing this book, we decided not to select clinicians representing "pure" forms of therapy, as relatively few therapists define themselves as *exclusively* cognitive-behavioral, psychodynamic, humanistic, or systemic. To inform their chapter, the clinicians were provided with the revised list of principles and asked to describe how they might use these principles in their work with each of the three clinical cases in their assigned section (depression or anxiety). As described more fully in the following discussion, we invited the authors to explain in detail how they might apply the principles and to think through (out loud, so to speak) their reasoning behind such implementation (or lack thereof).

The depression and anxiety sections both end with a chapter (Chapters 7 and 12, respectively) co-written by the clinician authors and the editors. The first goal of these chapters is to identify convergences and divergences with respect to how therapists work with empirically based principles. Moreover, these chapters examine therapists' perception of the clinical helpfulness and validity of these principles, as well as their ideas regarding possible combinations of separate principles. Also provided are directions for future research based on principles generated by the clinicians and discrepancies between the current empirical data and some of the therapists' perspectives. Final thoughts are then presented, with an emphasis given to the implications of principles regarding therapist effects (to help understand why some therapists are better than others) and training.

The fourth and final section of the book is a concluding chapter (Chapter 13) written by the editors that summarizes the tasks that were completed, the results that were achieved, and the experience of clinicians and researchers involved in this collaborative project. Suggestions are also offered to enhance our conceptual understanding of principles of change, as well as foster partnerships between clinicians and researchers to examine their validity and impact in day-to-day clinical routine.

Selection of Clinicians

Several criteria guided our selection of the clinical authors who served as proxies for therapists sharing their clinical perspectives and approaches to psychotherapy. First, we invited clinicians who represented a variety of theoretical orientations. To quantify these differences and to ensure diversity, we assessed potential authors' orientation with a brief self-report version of the Therapy Process Rating Scale (TPRS; Kimpara, Regner, Usami, & Beutler, 2015). In addition, the selection criteria included (a) having been trained in accredited graduate or postgraduate mental health programs; (b) having been involved in at least half-time clinical practice for at least two years; (c) recognizing the value of evidence-based and integrative practice, including different types of quantitative and qualitative research; and (d) having previous writing experience, as first author or co-author of professional publications.

To create a pool of potential authors, we drew on our own knowledge of clinicians and created an advisory board of reputable scholars and/or clinicians in the field. Advisory board members were selected based on the following criteria: (a) being known for their publications on the conduct and/or training of psychotherapy; (b) having trained and supervised many clinicians for several years; (c) having maintained a clinical practice for several years; (d) valuing the contributions of a diversity of theoretical orientations (even if being viewed by many in the field as an influential figure of a particular approach);

and (e) recognizing the value not only of evidence-based practice (drawn from both quantitative and qualitative research) but also of other methods of knowledge acquisition. We were fortunate to benefit from the expertise and recommendations of the following advisory board members: Drs. Barry Farber, Charles Gelso, Marvin Goldfried, Gary Groth-Marnat, Laurie Heatherington, Hanna Levenson, Phillip Levendusky, and Heidi Levitt.

Writing Guidelines for the Clinical Chapters

As mentioned, each clinical author was presented with three cases of clients with a primary diagnosis of either depression or anxiety, as well as the list of change principles. As also noted, these principles were clustered in five categories:

1. *Client prognostic principles*: client characteristics that correlate with improvement following treatment.
2. *Client moderating principles*: client characteristics, often present at baseline, that interact with treatment to influence intervention efficacy.
3. *Client process principles*: client during-treatment behaviors that facilitate or interfere with improvement.
4. *Therapy relationship principles*: elements of the client–therapist exchange that facilitate or interfere with improvement.
5. *Therapist intervention principles*: therapist during-treatment behaviors that either facilitate or interfere with improvement.

The main task of the clinical authors was to describe how they may or may not work with these principles if they were to see clients similar to those depicted in their three assigned cases. By consensual decision among the authors and editors, the authors first described their general reactions to the list of principles and their writing task. For example, one author stated that none of the principles are used alone. Another author anticipated that when writing about the principles, he would need to find a way to deal with a tension between his clinical judgment and research results. We believe that these types of gut reactions should be made explicit, as they represent salient knowledge about the clinical relevance of empirically derived principles. We also felt that increasing the authors' awareness of their initial reactions would help them create their own organizational heuristic for discussing the principles vis-à-vis the case material.

Following these introductory self-reflections, the authors wrote a case formulation and a general treatment plan for each of the three cases. For the remainder of the chapter, they described how they would or would not implement the principles. For this primary task, we provided the following general guidelines:

When describing such implementation, we would like you to write as if you were talking to supervisees and/or colleagues about how you conduct therapy. We do not want you to worry about writing a formal, scholarly paper aimed for a peer-review journal. Rather, we urge you to let the elegance, complexity, richness, and rigor of your thinking emerge naturally from making explicit what is implicit in your mind about clinical work (you may even give a try at talking to a voice recorder, as a way to ease the process of bringing alive your ideas about how psychotherapy unfolds with diverse clients). Relatedly, we do not want extensive references to theoretical or empirical literature. Put bluntly, what we want is readers to have access to expertise, knowledge, and wisdom that YOU have acquired and refined over years of extensive clinical work. This is because one of the main goals of the book is to offer a stage to experienced practitioners whose voices, in our opinion, have not received as much attention as those of theoreticians and researchers.

We want you to describe how you would make the principles work, integrating across all domains covered by the list of principles—client characteristics (prognostic predictors, moderators) and experience during sessions, relationship variables, and technical/intervention factors. Three questions should guide the description of your clinical work. For the client prognostic principles, the question is: "When and how do I intervene with these clients?" For the client process principles, the question is: "How do I foster or deal with this?" For the three other sets of principles, the question is: "When and how do I do this?"

Depending on the therapeutic context, we expect that there are many ways that you implement these principles, or choose not to, and we want to hear as many of them as possible! One of the primary reasons that we provided you with three different cases is precisely to provide you with a range of specific clinical situations to illustrate how and under what circumstances principles can be applied to best address the needs, difficulties, and strengths of particular clients. Thus, to help you show your flexible and attuned use of helpful processes of change, as well as to help you bring to life the empirically derived principles, we would like to you to constantly refer to the cases we've provided when answering the questions mentioned above.

In providing instructions to the authors and in editing their chapters, we encouraged them to use writing strategies that they, as individual writers, found to be most fruitful in describing their clinical work. Accordingly, some authors structured the main part of their chapter based on the clinical cases presented to them, describing the implementation of the principles one case at a time. Others chose to structure their chapter using the clusters of principles that we derived, describing the implementation of each principle across three cases simultaneously. Stylistically, some authors depicted their work through a fluid integration of the principles, while others elected to describe the principles separately within each of their respective clusters. We felt that providing a degree of freedom in the structure and narrative style used would help the authors to find their voice and bring the principles to life. We also felt that the readers would enjoy, as we did, the various ways of writing about clinical work.

As a concluding piece of their chapter, the authors briefly stated their experience in writing it. Then, they were asked to complete a few final tasks: To read the chapter written by the other authors in their respective section (depression or anxiety disorders) and identify points of convergences and complementarities across their work, and rate the helpfulness of each of the principles that they referenced (plus a few other principles that were not retained in our list because of insufficient empirical evidence). They were also invited to share thoughts that they might have regarding (a) combining separate principles, (b) implementing others beyond the list, (c) seeing some principles as invalid or unhelpful under certain circumstances, as well as (d) using these empirically based principles to improve training and better understand why some therapists are better than others. These tasks served as the foundation for the concluding chapter for each section.

Moving Beyond a Bridge between Science and Practice

By retaining and updating a list of empirically based change principles, this book maintains the major contributions of the first volume. Building on this work, the present volume not only illustrates how these guidelines can be implemented in day-to-day practice (as well as within and across theoretical orientations), but it also reflects a unique partnership between researchers and practitioners that goes beyond previous attempts to "bridge" science and practice. As noted elsewhere (Castonguay et al., 2013), "rather than trying to connect science and practice, as if they stand on different river banks, we should strive to confound the two activities in order to create a new, unified landscape of knowledge and action" (p. 122). Having researchers and clinicians working together to define and demonstrate how research findings can best improve therapy might be an optimal strategy to build such a landscape.

References

Beutler, L. E., Williams, R. E., Wakefield, P. J., & Entwistle, S. R. (1995). Bridging scientist and practitioner perspectives in clinical psychology. *American Psychologist, 50*, 984–994. doi:10.1037/0003-066X.50.12.984

Castonguay, L. G. (2011). Psychotherapy, psychopathology, research and practice: Pathways of connections and integration. *Psychotherapy Research, 21*, 125–140. doi:10.1080/10503307.2011.563250

Castonguay, L. G., Barkham, M., Lutz, W., & McAleavey, A. A. (2013). Practice-oriented research: Approaches and application. In M. J. Lambert (Ed.). *Bergin and Garfield's handbook of psychotherapy and behavior change* (6th ed., pp. 85–133). New York: Wiley.

Castonguay, L. G., & Beutler, L. E. (Eds.). (2006). *Principles of therapeutic change that work*. New York: Oxford University Press.

Castonguay, L. G., Muran, J. C., Angus, L., Hayes, J. H., Ladany, N., & Anderson, T. (Eds.). (2010). *Bringing psychotherapy research to life: Understanding change through the work of leading clinical researchers*. Washington, DC: American Psychological Association. doi:10.1037/12137-000

Cohen, L. H., Sargent, M. M., & Sechrest, L. B. (1986). Use of psychotherapy research by professional psychologists. *American Psychologist, 41*, 198–206. doi:10.1037/0003-066X.41.2.198

Constantino, M. J., Coyne, A. E., & Gomez Penedo, J. M. (2017). Contextualized integration as a common playing field for clinicians and researchers: Comment on McWilliams. *Journal of Psychotherapy Integration, 27*, 296–303. doi:10.1037/int0000067

Cooper, M. (2008). *Essential research findings in counseling and psychotherapy: The facts are friendly*. London: SAGE.

Garland, A. F., Hurlburt, M. S., & Hawley, K. M. (2006). Examining psychotherapy processes in a services research context. *Clinical Psychology: Science and Practice, 13*, 30–46. doi:10.1111/j.1468-2850.2006.00004.x

Kazdin, A. E. (2008). Evidence-based treatment and practice: New opportunities to bridge clinical research and practice, enhance the knowledge base, and improve patient care. *American Psychologist, 63*, 146–159. doi:10.1037/0003-066X.63.3.146

Kimpara, S., Regner, E., Usami, S., & Beutler, L. E. (2015, August). *Systematic treatment selection (STS): How to monitor therapists' interventions and cross-cultural differences between north America and Argentina*. Paper presented at the Annual Meeting of the American Psychological Association, Toronto.

McWilliams, N. (2017). Integrative research for integrative practice: A plea for respectful collaboration across clinician and researcher roles. *Journal of Psychotherapy Integration, 27,* 283–295. doi:10.1037/int0000054

Morrow-Bradley, C., & Elliott, R. (1986). Utilization of psychotherapy research by practicing psychotherapists. *American Psychologist, Special, 41,* 188–197. doi:10.1037/0003-066X.41.2.188

Safran, J. D., Abreu, I., Ogilvie, J., & DeMaria, A. (2011). Does psychotherapy research influence the clinical practice of researcher-clinicians? *Clinical Psychology: Science and Practice, 18,* 357–371. doi:10.1111/j.1468-2850.2011.01267.x

[handwritten note: Principles of Change, but not just Transtheoretical Model Stages of Change]

2

An Updated List of Principles of Change That Work

*Andrew A. McAleavey, Henry Xiao, Samantha L. Bernecker,
Hannah Brunet, Nicholas R. Morrison, Mickey Stein, Soo Jeong Youn,
Louis G. Castonguay, Michael J. Constantino, and Larry E. Beutler*

This chapter describes the process through which we arrived at the updated list of evidence-based therapeutic change principles that we asked our six exemplary clinician authors to address in the next two sections of the book. The principles retained in this update result from an iterative process that took more than three years to complete. The search and selection task involved in this process required the collaboration of the three book editors, a graduate student project coordinator (the first author of this chapter), and six graduate students who reviewed the empirical literature (the second through seventh authors of this chapter).

As described in Chapter 1, the 61 principles presented in this book's first edition (Castonguay & Beutler, 2006) represented the aggregate output from 12 groups of scholars who reviewed the research on three domains of psychotherapy (client characteristics, relationship variables, and technical factors), as nested within four types of clinical problems (dysphoric, anxiety, substance use, and personality disorders). Although this approach was a practical way to capitalize on different scholars' expertise and to consider principles that might cut across or be specific to certain diagnostic categories, the distinctness of the work groups produced several unintended consequences.

Namely, some principles in the final list were redundant, some were generated with different levels of specificity, and some were based on different interpretations of the literature (e.g., a variable having a direct empirical association with a clinical outcome vs. a variable inferred to have empirical support because it was part of a treatment manual that showed some efficacy). Moreover, given differences in research output associated with particular diagnostic classifications, any determination of pandiagnostic or diagnosis-specific principles could be considered unreliable. They could also be considered invalid given the growing recognition of diagnostic co-morbidity and the reality that many clinicians focus on dimensionality vs. categorization of mental health problems.

Thus, the first step in the revision process consisted of a rational analysis in which we (the editors) aimed to reduce redundancy in the list of principles and to restate them so that they had a similar level of detail. In doing so, we incorporated research updates of which we were aware. Furthermore, we differentiated between direct empirical associations and inferred associations between a participant or process variable and treatment outcome, giving greater weight to research that reflected the former type. Also, we agreed to present principles descriptively and in practical language, as opposed to using diagnostic and technical terminology. Everyday language, we believe, better fits clinical reality and provides a level of abstraction and description that all therapists could share when discussing the clinical change principles. This step led to the combination of several previously separate principles and the deletion of some principles altogether. These changes occurred mostly because these principles as originally written were judged to be too specific to be understood broadly, especially when compared to the general descriptions of some of the other principles. In addition, a number of principles were slightly modified to increase their clarity and/or clinical meaningfulness.

As a second step, the graduate student team was charged with comparing the revised principles (of client characteristics, relationship variables, and technique factors) to those variables covered in the primary references on which their reviews would be based; that is, the second edition of *Psychotherapy Relationships That Work* (Norcross, 2011) and the sixth edition of the *Handbook of Psychotherapy and Behavior Change* (Lambert, 2013). With this comparison, several matching problems were identified and resolved by consensus among the project coordinator and editors. The resolutions involved reformulating some principles, dividing some, and eliminating parts of others, all in the service of better matching the extant research base (as exemplified in the syntheses provided in the Lambert and Norcross volumes). Also at this stage, one principle (related to feedback from routine outcome monitoring) was added based on the presence of a meta-analysis in the Norcross book.

As a third step, the graduate student team was charged with making a formal review of the literature to ensure accuracy of empirical support. For each principle, one student conducted the review (unless a large number of studies required collaboration with a second reviewer). We held conference calls with the project coordinator and the reviewers as needed to address any questions and to maintain consistency in the review process. The following parameters and decision guidelines applied.

1. To make a determination of empirical support, the reviewers first relied on the conclusions reached by the chapter authors in the Norcross (2011) book who conducted original meta-analyses on variable–outcome associations. Arguably, such meta-analyses provide the most comprehensive and definitive state of the research on the degree to which a principle associates with treatment outcomes.
2. For variables not included in the Norcross book, the authors relied on literature reviewed in the Lambert (2013) book, the previous edition of the current book (Castonguay & Beutler, 2006), and/or other recent syntheses published in other outlets since 2006. If such reviews did not exist, the reviewers were asked to derive conclusions based on the preponderance of recent (published after 2006) evidence revealed by their own reviews of individual empirical studies (i.e., a principle was considered empirically *supported* if at least 50% of the studies conducted on this population contained at least one statistically significant relation between the principle and a measure of outcome). We did not set a minimum number of studies that had to have been conducted on a particular principle–outcome relation; rather, we left this determination to the reviewers' judgment, with consensual discussion among all team members as needed.
3. The reviewers were asked to clearly and systematically specify the basis for each of their determinations.
4. The reviewers were encouraged to suggest restating principles to reflect more accurately the evidence.

Once the formal review process was completed, the project coordinator and the editors made final adjustments, including the restatement of certain principles to ensure consistency in wording style, as well as some further additions, deletions, or splitting single principles into multiple principles. With these changes, the final revised list included 38 general principles that were viewed as having sufficient empirical support (see Box 2.1). As mentioned in Chapter 1, the editors categorized the final principle list into five categories: client prognostic principles, treatment/provider moderating principles, client process principles, therapy relationship principles, and therapist intervention principles. The principles in Box 2.1 are those that the clinician authors referenced while writing their chapters. Appendix 2.1 presents a glossary for constructs featured in some of the principles in Box 2.1, whereas Appendix 2.2 presents the references to studies from which each of the 38 retained principles were derived.

Box 2.2 lists nine principles that were deleted based on lack of sufficient evidence. When the clinical authors had completed their respective chapters, they

Box 2.1 List of Empirically Based Principles of Change

Client Prognostic Principles

1. Clients with higher levels of baseline impairment may benefit less from psychotherapy than clients with lower levels of impairment.
2. Clients whose primary presenting problems are complicated by a co-morbid secondary personality disorder (PD) diagnosis may benefit less from psychotherapy than clients without a co-morbid PD diagnosis.
3. Clients with more secure attachment may benefit more from psychotherapy than clients with less secure attachment (i.e., more attachment anxiety).
4. Clients with higher initial expectations for benefiting from psychotherapy may benefit more from it than clients with lower initial outcome expectations.
5. Clients who are more intrinsically (or autonomously) motivated to engage in psychotherapy may benefit more from it than clients who are less intrinsically (or autonomously) motivated (see glossary in Appendix 2.1 for definition of intrinsic [or autonomous] motivation).
6. Clients in advanced stages of change readiness (i.e., they are actively preparing for or currently taking action toward healthy behavior) may benefit more from psychotherapy than clients at lower stages of change readiness (see glossary in Appendix 2.1 for definition of readiness for change).
7. Clients with low socio-economic status and employment problems may benefit less from psychotherapy than clients with higher socio-economic status and no employment problems.
8. Clients who have experienced adverse childhood events may benefit less from psychotherapy than clients who did not experience adverse childhood events.
9. Anxious clients with more negative self-attributions may benefit less from psychotherapy than clients with fewer negative self-attributions.

Treatment/Provider Moderating Principles

10. Clients whose therapist uses interventions consistent with the client's level of problem assimilation may benefit more from psychotherapy than patients whose interventions are not consistent with their assimilation level (see glossary in Appendix 2.1 for definition of level of problem assimilation).

11. Clients with higher levels of resistance may benefit more from psychotherapy that is more nondirective compared to clients with lower levels of resistance who may benefit more from psychotherapy that is more directive (see glossary in Appendix 2.1 for definition of resistance/reactance).
12. Clients with lower motivation for, or higher ambivalence about, change may benefit more from psychotherapy when their therapist is responsive and person-centered versus more directive and change-oriented.
13. Clients who are matched to their preferred therapy role, therapist demographics, or treatment type may benefit more from psychotherapy than clients unmatched on these preferences.
14. Clients whose preference for religiously or spiritually oriented psychotherapy is accommodated may benefit more from treatment than clients whose preference is unmet.
15. Clients who present with poorer interpersonal functioning are likely to benefit less from psychotherapy when their therapist uses a higher versus lower proportion of transference interpretations.
16. Clients higher in baseline impairment may benefit more from psychotherapy that is longer-term and/or more intensive compared to clients lower in baseline impairment who may benefit equally well from psychotherapy that is long- or short-term and/or more or less intensive.
17. Clients with externalizing coping styles may benefit more from psychotherapy that is more focused on behavior change and symptom reduction than fostering insight and self-awareness (see glossary in Appendix 2.1 for more details).
18. Clients with internalizing coping styles may benefit more from psychotherapy that is more focused on fostering insight and self-awareness than behavior change and symptom reduction (see glossary in Appendix 2.1 for more details).
19. Clients with moderate to severe impairment and/or fewer social supports will benefit more from psychotherapy when their therapist helps them address their social or medical needs.
20. Clients with substance use problems may be equally likely to benefit from psychotherapy delivered by a therapist with or without his or her own history of substance use problems.

Client Process Variables

21. Clients who more actively participate in the treatment process may benefit more from psychotherapy than clients who less actively participate (see glossary in Appendix 2.1 for definition of active participation).

22. Clients who are more resistant to the therapist or therapy may benefit less from psychotherapy than clients who are less resistant (see glossary in Appendix 2.1 for definition of resistance/reactance).

Therapy Relationship Principles

23. Clients experiencing a higher quality therapeutic alliance in group psychotherapy (group cohesion) or individual psychotherapy (bonding/collaboration) may benefit more than clients experiencing a lower quality alliance.
24. Clients experiencing more therapist regard and affirmation may benefit more from psychotherapy than clients experiencing less therapist regard and affirmation.
25. Clients experiencing more therapist congruence may benefit more from psychotherapy than clients experiencing less therapist congruence.
26. Clients experiencing more therapist empathy may benefit more from psychotherapy than clients experiencing less therapist empathy.
27. Clients who experience alliance rupture–repair episodes and/or who work with therapists trained to repair alliance ruptures may benefit more from psychotherapy than clients who experience no or unrepaired ruptures and/or work with therapists not trained specifically on rupture–repair interventions.
28. Clients whose therapist uses more supportive self-disclosures may benefit more from psychotherapy than clients whose therapist uses less supportive self-disclosures (or does not disclose at all).

Therapist Intervention Principles

29. Clients whose therapist uses a higher proportion of general psychodynamic interpretations may benefit more from psychotherapy than clients whose therapist uses a lower proportion of general psychodynamic interpretations.
30. Clients whose therapist uses higher quality psychodynamic interpretations may benefit more from psychotherapy than clients whose therapist uses lower quality psychodynamic interpretations (see glossary in Appendix 2.1 for definition of quality of psychodynamic interpretation).
31. Clients whose therapist receives feedback based on a routinely delivered outcome measure may benefit more from psychotherapy than clients whose therapist does not receive feedback.

32. Clients who receive feedback from their therapist on their performance in treatment may benefit more from psychotherapy than clients who do not receive feedback.
33. Clients may benefit more from psychotherapy when their therapist is more versus less flexible in their administration of, or adherence to, a given treatment approach.
34. Clients whose therapist selectively/responsively fosters more adaptive interpersonal changes may benefit more broadly from psychotherapy than those whose therapist fosters fewer adaptive interpersonal changes.
35. Clients whose therapist selectively/responsively fosters more self-understanding may benefit more broadly from psychotherapy than clients whose therapist fosters less self-understanding.
36. Clients whose therapist selectively/responsively fosters more emotional experiencing and/or deepening may benefit more broadly from psychotherapy than clients whose therapist fosters less emotional experiencing and/or deepening.
37. Clients whose therapist selectively/responsively uses nondirective interventions skillfully may benefit more from psychotherapy than clients whose therapist uses nondirective interventions unskillfully.
38. Clients whose therapist selectively/responsively fosters more behavior changes may benefit more broadly from psychotherapy than clients whose therapist fosters fewer behavior changes.

Box 2.2 List of principles deleted based on lack of sufficient evidence

1. The benefits of therapy may be enhanced if the therapist is able to tolerate his or her own negative feelings regarding the patient and the treatment process.
2. The therapist is likely to be more effective if he or she is patient.
3. If psychotherapists are open, informed, and tolerant of various religious views, treatment effects are likely to be enhanced.
4. If patients and therapists come from the same or similar racial/ethnic backgrounds, dropout rates are positively affected and improvement is enhanced.

5. Patients representing underserved ethnic or racial groups achieve fewer benefits from conventional psychotherapy than Anglo-American groups.
6. Positive change is likely if the therapist provides a structured treatment and remains focused in the application of his or her interventions.
7. Therapists working with a specific disorder may increase their effectiveness if they receive specialized training with this population.
8. The positive impact of therapy is likely to be increased if the therapist is comfortable with long-term, emotionally intense relationships.
9. Younger clients may benefit more from psychotherapy than older clients.

were asked to rate these deleted principles in terms of clinical helpfulness. As described in the concluding chapters of the depression and anxiety disorders sections (Chapters 7 and 12, respectively), this was done to get their perspective on whether or not these principles are potentially valid and might thus deserve further empirical attention.

References

Beutler, L. E., Harwood, T. M., Michelson, A., Song, X., & Holman, J. (2011). Reactance/resistance level. In J. C. Norcross (Ed.), *Psychotherapy relationships that work: Evidence-based responsiveness* (2nd ed., pp. 261–278). New York, NY: Oxford University Press. doi:10.1093/acprof:oso/9780199737208.003.0013

Castonguay, L. G., & Beutler, L. E. (Eds.). (2006). *Principles of therapeutic change that work*. New York, NY: Oxford University Press.

Lambert, M. J. (Ed.). (2013). *Bergin and Garfield's handbook of psychotherapy and behavior change* (6th ed.). New York, NY: Wiley.

Norcross, J. C. (2011). *Psychotherapy relationships that work: Evidence-based responsiveness* (2nd ed.). New York, NY: Oxford University Press. doi:10.1093/acprof:oso/9780199737208.001.0001

Stiles, W. B. (2002). Assimilation of problematic experiences. In J. C. Norcross (Ed.), *Psychotherapy relationships that work: Therapist contributions and responsiveness to patients*. (pp. 357–365). New York, NY: Oxford University Press.

Appendix 2.1

Glossary for Box 2.1

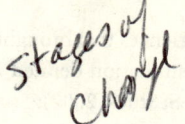
stages of change

Principle 5: Intrinsic (or autonomous) motivation. Motivation is defined as "the general desire or willingness of someone to do something" (Google definition). This refers to a client characteristic, as opposed to a process variable, such as active participation (Principle 21). The two can be related but are distinct, as when a client is compliant to tasks agreed upon with therapist but he or she is extrinsically motivated—he or she is compliant but driven by what the therapist is expecting or asking.

Principle 6: Readiness for change stages. This is an established construct in counseling, and it involves five stages of change (Norcross, Krebs, & Pochaska, 2011):

- Precontemplation: "stage at which there is no intention to change behavior in the foreseeable future. Most patients in this stage are unaware or under-aware of their problems . . . Resistance to recognizing or modifying a problem is the hallmark of pre-contemplation" (p. 279).
- Contemplation: "stage in which are aware that a problem exists and are seriously thinking about overcoming it, but have not yet made a commitment to take action. Contemplators struggle with their positive evaluations of the dysfunctional behavior and the amount of effort, energy, and loss it will cost to overcome it . . . Serious consideration of problem resolution is the central element of contemplation" (pp. 279–280).
- Preparation: "stage that combines intentions and behavioral criteria. Individuals in this stage are intending to take action in the next month, and have unsuccessfully taken action in the past year. As a group, patients prepare for actions, report small behavioral changes, 'baby steps,' so to speak" (p. 280).
- Action: "stage in which individuals modify their behavior, experiences, and/or environment in order to overcome their problem. Action involves the most overt behavioral changes and requires considerable commitment of time and energy . . . Modification of the target behavior to an acceptable criterion and significant overt efforts to change are the hallmarks of action" (p. 280).
- Maintenance: "stage in which people work to prevent relapse and consolidate the gains attained during action . . . Stabilizing behavior change and avoiding relapse are the hallmarks of maintenance" (p. 280).

Globally, readiness for change could be viewed as specific forms of active participation (Principle 5) and motivation (Principle 6).

Principle 10. Level of problem assimilation. This refers to a client's place on a developmental sequence from low to high integration of problematic experiences into his or her dominant sense of self. As argued by Stiles (2002), the assimilation model "suggests that in successful psychotherapy, clients follow a regular developmental sequence of recognizing, reformulating, understanding, and eventually resolving the problematic experiences that brought them in treatment" (p. 357). This sequence involves eight levels of assimilation defined in the following Assimilation of Problematic Experiences Scale (APES; Stiles, 2002):

"0. Warded off/dissociated. Client is unaware of the problem; the problematic voice is silent or dissociated. Affect may be minimal, reflecting successful avoidance.
1. Unwanted thoughts/active avoidance. Client prefers not to think about the experience. Problematic voices emerge in response to therapist interventions or external circumstances and are suppressed or avoided. Affect is intensely negative but episodic and unfocused; the connection with the content may be unclear.
2. Vague awareness/emergence. Client is aware of a problematic experience but cannot formulate the problem clearly. Problematic voice emerges into sustained awareness. Affect includes acute psychological pain or panic associated with the problematic material.
3. Problem statement/clarification. Content includes a clear statement or a problem—something that can be worked on. Opposing voices are differentiated and can talk about each other. Affect is negative but manageable, not panicky.
4. Understanding/insight. The problematic experience is formulated and understood in some way. Voices reach an understanding with each other (a meaning bridge). Affect may be mixed, with some unpleasant recognition but also some pleasant surprise.
5. Application/working through. The understanding is used to work on a problem. Voices work together to address problems of living. Affective tone is positive, optimistic.
6. Resourcefulness/problem solution. The formerly problematic experience has become a resource, used for solving problems. Voices can be used flexibly. Affect is positive, satisfied.
7. Integration/mastery. Client automatically generalizes solutions; voices are fully integrated, serving as resources in new situations. Affect is positive or neutral (that is, this is no longer something to get excited about" (p. 358).

Principles 11 and 22. Resistance/reactance. As defined by Beutler, Harwood, Michelson, Song, and Holman (2011), reactance is a "special expression of resistance that occurs in the form of rebellion and that is situationally induced . . . [It is] affected by one's tolerance for events that limit freedom—it is responsive to traitlike sensitivities as well as state-like properties of the environment" (p. 263). Put in different words, highly reactant individuals do not like to be controlled by other people, and they become oppositional and noncompliant when external demands to comply limit their personal options. Resistance/reactance is related but distinct to the process variable of active participation (Principle 5). A client can have a low level of tolerance toward perceived threat of loss of freedom but can still be fully engaged in the therapy, as when he or she does not perceive the therapist as being directive and controlling (see Principle 14).

Principle 17. Externalizing coping style. Patients whose personalities are characterized by "externalizing" styles (e.g., impulsivity, social gregariousness, emotional liability, and external blame for problems) benefit more from direct behavioral change and symptom reduction efforts, including building new skills and managing impulses, than they do from procedures that are designed to facilitate insight and self-awareness. Therapists should focus on direct change, enhancing external cues to gain emotional control, and developing problem solving and self-control skills. Therapeutic change is likely if therapists help such clients accept, tolerate, and, at times, fully experience their emotions.

Principle 18. Internalizing coping style. Patients whose personalities are characterized by "internalizing" styles (e.g., low levels of impulsivity, indecisiveness, self-inspection, and overcontrol) tend to benefit more from procedures that foster self-inspection, self-understanding, insight, interpersonal attachments, and self-esteem than they do from procedures that aim at directly altering symptoms and building new social skills. The therapist treating such patients should especially focus on cognitive change, emotional expression, and physiological response as a way of modifying behavioral and emotional change.

Principle 21: Active participation. This refers to client's active engagement and collaboration in the tasks of therapy, such as homework completion and treatment compliance. It is a process variable that might be related to but is distinct from client characteristics such as motivation (Principle 5). For example, a client may want (be motivated) to change but not be actively participating in the work required by therapy.

Principle 30. Quality of psychodynamic interpretations. The quality of an interpretation in psychodynamic therapy refers to its accuracy and, more specifically, its focus on "the central interpersonal themes for each patient" (Crits-Christoph & Connolly Gibbons, 2002, p. 298).

Appendix 2.2

References Supporting Retained Principles of Change (Box 2.1)

Client Prognostic Principles

1. Clients with higher levels of baseline impairment may benefit less from psychotherapy than clients with lower levels of impairment.
   Bottlender, R., Strauß, A., & Möller, H. (2000). Impact of duration of symptoms prior to first hospitalization on acute outcome in 998 schizophrenic patients. *Schizophrenia Research, 44*, 145–150. doi:10.1016/s0920-9964(99)00186-3
   Brancu, M., Thompson, N. L., Beckham, J. C., Green, K. T., Calhoun, P. S., Elbogen, E. B., . . . Wagner, H. R. (2014). The impact of social support on psychological distress for U.S. Afghanistan/Iraq era veterans with PTSD and other psychiatric diagnoses. *Psychiatry Research, 217*, 86–92. doi:10.1016/j.psychres.2014.02.025
   Curry, J., Rohde, P., Simons, A., Silva, S., Vitiello, B., Kratochvil, C., . . . March, J. (2006). Predictors and moderators of acute outcome in the Treatment for Adolescents with Depression Study (TADS). *Journal of the American*

Academy of Child & Adolescent Psychiatry, 45, 1427–1439. doi:10.1097/01.chi.0000240838.78984.e2

Forty, L., Smith, D., Jones, L., Jones, I., Caesar, S., Cooper, C., . . . Craddock, N. (2008). Clinical differences between bipolar and unipolar depression. *British Journal of Psychiatry, 192*, 388–389. doi:10.1192/bjp.bp.107.045294

Jaracz, K., Górna, K., Jaracz, J., Kiejda, J., Wilkiewicz, M., & Rybakowski, J. (2012). Long-term evaluation of mental status in schizophrenic patients after a first psychiatric hospitalization according to symptomatic remission criteria. *Neuropsychiatria i Neuropsychologia/Neuropsychiatry and Neuropsychology, 7*, 1–6.

Jonsson, U., Bohman, H., Knorring, L. V., Olsson, G., Paaren, A., & Knorring, A. V. (2011). Mental health outcome of long-term and episodic adolescent depression: 15-year follow-up of a community sample. *Journal of Affective Disorders, 130*, 395–404. doi:10.1016/j.jad.2010.10.046

Krampe, H., Stawicki, S., Wagner, T., Bartels, C., Aust, C., Ruther, E., . . . Ehrenreich, H. (2006). Follow-up of 180 Alcoholic patients for up to 7 years after outpatient treatment: Impact of alcohol deterrents on outcome. *Alcoholism: Clinical and Experimental Research, 30*, 86–95. doi:10.1111/j.1530-0277.2006.00013.x

Someah, K., Stein, M., Edwards, C., & Beutler, L. E. (2015, May). *Meta analysis: Functional impairment*. Poster session presented at the Western Psychological Association, Las Vegas, NV.

Storch, E. A., Larson, M. J., Merlo, L. J., Keeley, M. L., Jacob, M. L., Geffken, G. R., . . . Goodman, W. K. (2007). Comorbidity of pediatric obsessive-compulsive disorder and anxiety disorders: Impact on symptom severity and impairment. *Journal of Psychopathology and Behavioral Assessment, 30*, 111–120. doi:10.1007/s10862-007-9057-x

Zlotnick, C., Rodriguez, B. F., Weisberg, R. B., Bruce, S. E., Spencer, M. A., Culpepper, L., & Keller, M. B. (2004). Chronicity in posttraumatic stress disorder and predictors of the course of posttraumatic stress disorder among primary care patients. *Journal of Nervous and Mental Disease, 192*, 153–159. doi:10.1097/01.nmd.0000110287.16635.8e

2. Clients whose primary presenting problems are complicated by a co-morbid secondary personality disorder diagnosis may benefit less from psychotherapy than clients without a co-morbid personality disorder diagnosis.

Bell, L. (2001). What predicts failure to engage in or drop out from treatment for bulimia nervosa and what implications does this have for treatment? *Clinical Psychology & Psychotherapy, 8*, 424–435. doi:10.1002/cpp.288

Bell, L. (2002). Does concurrent psychopathology at presentation influence response to treatment for bulimia nervosa? *Eating and Weight Disorders, 7*, 168–181.

Beutler, L. E., Blatt, S., Alimohamed, S., Levy, K. N., & Angtuaco, L. (2006). Participant factors in treating dysphoric disorders. In L. G. Castonguay & L. E. Beutler (Eds.), *Principles of therapeutic change that work* (pp. 13–64). New York, NY: Oxford University Press.

Bradizza, C. M., Stasiewicz, P. R., & Paas, N. D. (2006). Relapse to alcohol and drug use among individuals diagnosed with co-occurring mental health and substance use disorders: A review. *Clinical Psychology Review, 26*, 162–178. doi:10.1016/j.cpr.2005.11.005

Bruce, K. R., & Steiger, H. (2005). Treatment implications of Axis-II co-morbidity in eating disorders. *Eating Disorders, 13*, 93–108. doi:10.1080/10640260590893700

Budge, S. L., Moore, J. T., Del Re, A. C., Wampold, B. E., Baardseth, T. P., & Nienhuis, J. B. (2013). The effectiveness of evidence-based treatments for personality disorders when comparing treatment-as-usual and bona fide treatments. *Clinical Psychology Review, 33*, 1057–1066. doi:10.1016/j.cpr.2013.08.003

Comment: Mulder, R. T. (2006). Personality disorder and outcome in depression. *British Journal of Psychiatry, 189*, 186–187. doi:10.1192/bjp.189.2.186b

Crane, A. M., Roberts, M. E., & Treasure, J. (2007). Are obsessive-compulsive personality traits associated with a poor outcome in anorexia nervosa? A systematic review of randomized controlled trials and naturalistic outcome studies. *International Journal of Eating Disorders, 40*, 581–588. doi:10.1002/eat

De Bolle, M., De Fruyt, F., Quilty, L. C., Rolland, J.-P., Decuyper, M., & Bagby, R. M. (2011). Does personality disorder co-morbidity impact treatment outcome for patients with major depression? A multi-level analysis. *Journal of Personality Disorders, 25*, 1–15. doi:10.1521/pedi.2011.25.1.1

Dreessen, L., & Arntz, A. (1998). The impact of personality disorders on treatment outcome of anxiety disorders: Best-evidence synthesis. *Behaviour Research and Therapy, 36*, 483–504.

Eskildsen, A., Hougaard, E., & Rosenberg, N. K. (2010). Pre-treatment patient variables as predictors of drop-out and treatment outcome in cognitive behavioural therapy for social phobia: A systematic review. *Nordic Journal of Psychiatry, 64*, 94–105. doi:10.3109/08039480903426929

Fournier, J. C., DeRubeis, R. J., Shelton, R. C., Gallop, R., Amsterdam, J. D., & Hollon, S. D. (2008). Antidepressant medications v. cognitive therapy in people with depression with or without personality disorder. *British Journal of Psychiatry, 192*, 124–129. doi:10.1192/bjp.bp.107.037234

Haaga, D. A. F., Hall, S. M., & Haas, A. (2006). Participant factors in treating substance use disorders. In L. G. Castonguay & L. E. Beutler (Eds.), *Principles of therapeutic change that work* (pp. 275–292). New York, NY: Oxford University Press.

Keeley, M. L., Storch, E. A., Merlo, L. J., & Geffken, G. R. (2008). Clinical predictors of response to cognitive-behavioral therapy for obsessive-compulsive disorder. *Clinical Psychology Review, 28*, 118–130. doi:10.1016/j.cpr.2007.04.003

Kool, S., Schoevers, R., de Maat, S., Van, R., Molenaar, P., Vink, A., & Dekker, J. (2005). Efficacy of pharmacotherapy in depressed patients with and without personality disorders: A systematic review and meta-analysis. *Journal of Affective Disorders, 88*, 269–278. doi:10.1016/j.jad.2005.05.017

Maddux, R. E., Riso, L. P., Klein, D. N., Markowitz, J. C., Rothbaum, B. O., Arnow, B. A., . . . Thase, M. E. (2009). Select co-morbid personality disorders and the treatment of chronic depression with nefazodone, targeted psychotherapy, or their combination. *Journal of Affective Disorders, 117,* 174–179. doi:10.1016/j.jad.2009.01.010

Modesto-Lowe, V., & Kranzler, H. (1999). Diagnosis and treatment of alcohol-dependent patients with co-morbid psychiatric disorders. *Alcohol Research and Health, 23,* 144–149.

Mulder, R. T. (2002). Personality pathology and treatment outcome in major depression: A review. *American Journal of Psychiatry, 159,* 359–371.

Newman, M. G., Crits-Christoph, P., Connolly Gibbons, M. B., & Erickson, T. M. (2006). Participant factors in treating anxiety disorders. In L. G. Castonguay & L. E. Beutler (Eds.), *Principles of therapeutic change that work* (pp. 121–154). New York, NY: Oxford University Press.

Newton-Howes, G., Tyrer, P., & Johnson, T. (2006). Personality disorder and the outcome of depression: Meta-analysis of published studies. *British Journal of Psychiatry, 188,* 13–20. doi:10.1192/bjp.188.1.13

Pompili, M., Venturini, P., Palermo, M., Stefani, H., Seretti, M. E., Lamis, D. A., . . . Girardi, P. (2013). Mood disorders medications: Predictors of nonadherence: Review of the current literature. *Expert Review of Neurotherapeutics, 13,* 809–825.

Shea, M. T., Pilkonis, P. A., Beckham, E., Collins, J. F., Elkin, I., Sotsky, S. M., & Docherty, J. P. (1990). Personality disorders and treatment outcome in the NIMH Treatment of Depression Collaborative Research Program. *American Journal of Psychiatry, 147,* 711–718.

Swift, J. K., & Greenberg, R. P. (2012). Premature discontinuation in adult psychotherapy: A meta-analysis. *Journal of Consulting and Clinical Psychology, 80,* 547–559. doi:10.1037/a0028226

Tyrer, P., Seivewright, N., Ferguson, B., Murphy, S., & Johnson, A. L. (1993). The Nottingham Study of Neurotic Disorder: Effect of personality status on response to drug treatment, cognitive therapy and self-help over two years. *British Journal of Psychiatry, 162,* 219–226. doi:10.1192/bjp.162.2.219

3. Clients with more secure attachment may benefit more from psychotherapy than clients with less secure attachment (i.e., more attachment anxiety).

Levy, K. N., Ellison, W. D., Scott, L. N., & Bernecker, S. L. (2011). Attachment style. In J. C. Norcross (Ed.), *Psychotherapy relationships that work: Evidence-based responsiveness* (2nd ed., pp. 377–401). New York, NY: Oxford University Press. doi:10.1093/acprof:oso/9780199737208.003.0019

4. Clients with higher initial expectations for benefitting from psychotherapy may benefit more from it than clients with lower initial outcome expectations.

Constantino, M. J., Glass, C. R., Arnkoff, D. B., Ametrano, R. M., & Smith, J. Z. (2011). Expectations. In J. C. Norcross (Ed.), *Psychotherapy relationships that work: Evidence-based responsiveness* (2nd ed., pp. 354–376). New York, NY: Oxford University Press. doi:10.1093/acprof:oso/9780199737208.003.0018

5. Clients who are more intrinsically (or autonomously) motivated to engage in psychotherapy may benefit more from it than clients who are less intrinsically (or

autonomously) motivated (see glossary in Appendix 2.1 for definition of intrinsic [or autonomous] motivation).

Holdsworth, E., Bowen, E., Brown, S., & Howat, D. (2014). Client engagement in psychotherapeutic treatment and associations with client characteristics, therapist characteristics, and treatment factors. *Clinical Psychology Review, 34,* 428–450. doi:10.1016/j.cpr.2014.06.004

Mausbach, B. T., Moore, R., Roesch, S., Cardenas, V., & Patterson, T. L. (2010). The relationship between homework compliance and therapy outcomes: An updated meta-analysis. *Cognitive Therapy and Research, 34,* 429–438. doi:10.1007/s10608-010-9297-z

Parhar, K. K., Wormith, J. S., Derkzen, D. M., & Beauregard, A. M. (2008). Offender coercion in treatment: A meta-analysis of effectiveness. *Criminal Justice and Behavior, 35,* 1109–1135. doi:10.1177/0093854808320169

6. Clients in advanced stages of change readiness (i.e., they are actively preparing for or currently taking action toward healthy behavior) may benefit more from psychotherapy than clients at lower stages of change readiness (see glossary in Appendix 2.1 for definition of readiness for change).

Norcross, J. C., Krebs, P. M., & Prochaska, J. O. (2011). Stages of change. In J. C. Norcross (Ed.), *Psychotherapy relationships that work: Evidence-based responsiveness* (2nd ed., pp. 279–300). New York, NY: Oxford University Press. doi:10.1093/acprof:oso/9780199737208.001.0001

7. Clients with low socio-economic status and employment problems may benefit less from psychotherapy than clients with higher socioeconomic status and no employment problems.

Adamson, S. J., Sellman, J. D., & Frampton, C. M. A. (2009). Patient predictors of alcohol treatment outcome: A systematic review. *Journal of Substance Abuse Treatment, 36,* 75–86. doi:10.1016/j.jsat.2008.05.007

Littlejohn, C. (2006). Does socio-economic status influence the acceptability of, attendance for, and outcome of, screening and brief interventions for alcohol misuse: A review. *Alcohol and Alcoholism, 41,* 540–545. doi:10.1093/alcalc/agl053

Swift, J. K., & Greenberg, R. P. (2012). Premature discontinuation in adult psychotherapy: A meta-analysis. *Journal of Consulting and Clinical Psychology, 80,* 547–559. doi:10.1037/a0028226

Wierzbicki, M., & Pekarik, G. (1993). A meta-analysis of psychotherapy dropout. *Professional Psychology: Research and Practice, 24,* 190–195. doi:10.1037//0735-7028.24.2.190

8. Clients who have experienced adverse childhood events may benefit less from psychotherapy than clients who did not experience adverse childhood events.

Bachelor, A., Meunier, G., Laverdiére, O., & Gamache, D. (2010). Client attachment to therapist: Relation to client personality and symptomatology, and their contributions to the therapeutic alliance. *Psychotherapy: Theory, Research, Practice, Training, 47,* 454–468. doi:10.1037/a0022079

Carter, J. D., Luty, S. E., Mckenzie, J. M., Mulder, R. T., Frampton, C. M., & Joyce, P. R. (2011). Patient predictors of response to cognitive behaviour therapy and interpersonal psychotherapy in a randomised clinical trial for depression. *Journal of Affective Disorders, 128,* 252–261. doi:10.1016/j.jad.2010.07.002

Diener, M. J., & Monroe, J. M. (2011). The relationship between adult attachment style and therapeutic alliance in individual psychotherapy: A meta-analytic review. *Psychotherapy, 48,* 237–248. doi:10.1037/a0022425

Levy, K. N., Ellison, W. D., Scott, L. N., & Bernecker, S. L. (2011). Attachment style. In J. C Norcross (Ed.), *Psychotherapy relationships that work: Evidence-based responsiveness* (2nd ed., pp. 377–401). New York, NY: Oxford University Press. doi:10.1093/acprof:oso/9780199737208.003.0019

Nanni, V., Uher, R., & Danese, A. (2012). Childhood maltreatment predicts unfavorable course of illness and treatment outcome in depression: A meta-analysis. *American Journal of Psychiatry, 169,* 141–151. doi:10.1176/appi.ajp.2011.11020335

Obegi, J. H., & Berant, E. (2010). *Attachment theory and research in clinical work with adults.* New York, NY: Guilford.

Perry, J. C., Bond, M., & Roy, C. (2007). Predictors of treatment duration and retention in a study of long-term dynamic psychotherapy: Childhood adversity, adult personality, and diagnosis. *Journal of Psychiatric Practice, 13,* 221–232. doi:10.1097/01.pra.0000281482.11946.fc

Saypol, E., & Farber, B. A. (2010). Attachment style and patient disclosure in psychotherapy. *Psychotherapy Research, 20,* 462–471. doi:10.1080/10503301003796821

Strauss, B., Kirchmann, H., Eckert, J., Lobo-Drost, A., Marquet, A., Papenhausen, R., . . . Höger, D. (2006). Attachment characteristics and treatment outcome following inpatient psychotherapy: Results of a multisite study. *Psychotherapy Research, 16,* 579–594. doi:10.1080/10503300600608322

9. Anxious clients with more negative self-attributions may benefit less from psychotherapy than clients with fewer negative self-attributions.

Beutler, L. E., Harwood, T. M., Kimpara, S., Verdirame, D., & Blau, K. (2011). Coping style. In J. C. Norcross (Ed.), *Psychotherapy relationships that work: Evidence-based responsiveness* (2nd ed., pp. 336–353). New York, NY: Oxford University Press. doi:10.1093/acprof:oso/9780199737208.003.0017

Beutler, L. E., Machado, P. P. P., Engle, D., & Mohr, D. (1993). Differential patient × treatment maintenance among cognitive, experiential, and self-directed psychotherapies. *Journal of Psychotherapy Integration, 3*(1), 15–31. doi:10.1037/h0101191.

Beutler, L. E., Moleiro, C., Malik, M., Harwood, T. M., Romanelli, R., Gallagher-Thompson, D., & Thompson, L. (2003). A comparison of the dodo, EST, and ATI factors among co-morbid stimulant-dependent, depressed patients. *Clinical Psychology & Psychotherapy, 10*(2), 69–85. doi:10.1002/cpp.354.

Calvert, S. J., Beutler, L. E., & Crago, M. (1988). Psychotherapy outcome as a function of therapist–patient matching on selected variables. *Journal of Social and Clinical Psychology, 6*(1), 104–117. doi:10.1521/jscp.1988.6.1.104.

Karno, M. P, Beutler, L. E., & Harwood, T. M. (2002). Interactions between psychotherapy procedures and patient attributes that predict alcohol treatment effectiveness. *Addictive Behaviors, 27*(5), 779–797. doi:10.1016/s0306-4603(01)00209-x.

Knekt, P., Lindfors, O, Härkänen, T., Välikoski, M., Virtala, E., Laaksonen, M. A., Marttunen, M. . . . Helsinki Psychotherapy Study Group. (2007). Randomized trial on the effectiveness of long-and short-term psychodynamic psychotherapy and solution-focused therapy on psychiatric symptoms during a 3-year follow-up. *Psychological Medicine, 38,* 689–703. doi:10.1017/s003329170700164x.

Litt, M. D. (1991). Matching alcoholics to coping skills or interactional therapies. *Pharmacology Biochemistry and Behavior, 39,* 239. doi:10.1016/0091-3057(91)90492-k.

Litt, M. D. (1992). Types of alcoholics, II. *Archives of General Psychiatry, 49,* 609. doi:10.1001/archpsyc.1992.01820080017003.

Milrod, B. (2007). A randomized controlled clinical trial of psychoanalytic psychotherapy for panic disorder. *American Journal of Psychiatry, 164,* 265. doi:10.1176/appi.ajp.164.2.265.

Treatment/Provider Moderating Principles

10. Clients whose therapist uses interventions consistent with the client's level of problem assimilation may benefit more from psychotherapy than patients whose interventions are not consistent with their assimilation level (see glossary in Appendix 2.1 for definition of level of problem assimilation).

    Detert, N. B., Llewelyn, S., Hardy, G. E., Barkham, M., & Stiles, W. B. (2006). Assimilation in good- and poor-outcome cases of very brief psychotherapy for mild depression: An initial comparison. *Psychotherapy Research, 16,* 393–407. doi:10.1080/10503300500294728

    Osatuke, K., & Stiles, W. B. (2011). Numbers in assimilation research. *Theory & Psychology, 21,* 200–219. doi:10.1177/0959354310391352

11. Clients with higher levels of resistance may benefit more from psychotherapy that is more nondirective compared to clients with lower levels of resistance who may benefit more from psychotherapy that is more directive (see glossary in Appendix 2.1 for definition of resistance/reactance).

    Beutler, L. E., Harwood, T. M., Michelson, A., Song, X., & Holman, J. (2011). Reactance/resistance level. In J. C. Norcross (Ed.), *Psychotherapy relationships that work: Evidence-based responsiveness* (2nd ed., pp. 261–278). New York, NY: Oxford University Press. doi:10.1093/acprof:oso/9780199737208.003.0013

12. Clients with lower motivation for, or higher ambivalence about, change may benefit more from psychotherapy when their therapist is responsive and person-centered versus more directive and change-oriented.

Hall, K. L., & Rossi, J. S. (2008). Meta-analytic examination of the strong and weak principles across 48 health behaviors. *Preventive Medicine, 46,* 266–274. doi:10.1016/j.ypmed.2007.11.006

Hettema, J., Steele, J., & Miller, W. R. (2005). Motivational interviewing. *Annual Review of Clinical Psychology, 1,* 91–111. doi:10.1146/annurev.clinpsy.1.102803.143833

Lundahl, B., & Burke, B. L. (2009). The effectiveness and applicability of motivational interviewing: A practice-friendly review of four meta-analyses. *Journal of Clinical Psychology, 65,* 1232–1245. doi:10.1002/jclp.20638

Lundahl, B. W., Kunz, C., Brownell, C., Tollefson, D., & Burke, B. L. (2010). A meta-analysis of motivational interviewing: twenty-five years of empirical studies. *Research on Social Work Practice, 20,* 137–160. doi:10.1177/1049731509347850

Miller, W. R., & Rollnick, S. (2013). *Motivational interviewing: Helping people change.* New York, NY: Guilford.

Norcross, J. C., Krebs, P. M., & Prochaska, J. O. (2011). Stages of change. In J. C. Norcross (Ed.), *Psychotherapy relationships that work: Evidence-based responsiveness* (2nd ed., pp. 279–300). New York, NY: Oxford University Press. doi:10.1093/acprof:oso/9780199737208.003.0014

Rollnick, S., & Miller, W. R. (1995). What is motivational interviewing? *Behavioural and Cognitive Psychotherapy, 23,* 325–334. doi:10.1017/s135246580001643x

13. Clients who are matched to their preferred therapy role, therapist demographics, or treatment type may benefit more from psychotherapy than clients unmatched on these preferences.

Swift, J. K., Callahan, J. L., & Vollmer, B. M. (2011). Preferences. In J. C. Norcross (Ed.), *Psychotherapy relationships that work: Evidence-based responsiveness* (2nd ed., pp. 301–315). New York, NY: Oxford University Press. doi:10.1093/acprof:oso/9780199737208.003.0015

14. Clients whose preference for religiously or spiritually oriented psychotherapy is accommodated may benefit more from treatment than clients whose preference is unmet.

Worthington, E. L., Jr., Hook, J. N., Davis, D. E., & McDaniel M. A. (2011). Religion and spirituality. In J. C. Norcross (Ed.), *Psychotherapy relationships that work: Evidence-based responsiveness* (2nd ed., pp. 402–422). New York, NY: Oxford University Press. doi:10.1093/acprof:oso/9780199737208.003.0020

15. Clients who present with poorer interpersonal functioning are likely to benefit less from psychotherapy when their therapist uses a higher versus lower proportion of transference interpretations.

Crits-Christoph, P., & Gibbons, M. B. C. (2002). Relational interpretations. In J. C. Norcross (Ed.) *Psychotherapy relationships that work: Therapist contributions and responsiveness to patients* (pp. 285–302). New York, NY: Oxford University Press.

Crits-Christoph, P., Gibbons, M. B. C., & Mukherjee, D. (2013). Psychotherapy process-outcome research. In M. J. Lambert (Ed.), *Bergin and Garfield's handbook of psychotherapy and behavior change* (6th ed., pp. 298–340). New York, NY: Wiley.

16. Clients higher in baseline impairment may benefit more from psychotherapy that is longer-term and/or more intensive compared to clients lower in baseline impairment who may benefit equally well from psychotherapy that is long- or short-term and/or more or less intensive.

    Beail, N., Kellett, S., Newman, D. W., & Warden, S. (2007). The dose-effect relationship in psychodynamic psychotherapy with people with intellectual disabilities. *Journal of Applied Research in Intellectual Disabilities, 20*, 448–454. doi:10.1111/j.1468-3148.2007.00385.x

    Deckersbach, T., Peters, A. T., Sylvia, L., Urdahl, A., Magalhães, P. V., Otto, M. W., . . . Nierenberg, A. (2014). Do co-morbid anxiety disorders moderate the effects of psychotherapy for bipolar disorder? Results from STEP-BD. *American Journal of Psychiatry, 171*, 178–186. doi:10.1176/appi.ajp.2013.13020225

    Katon, W., Unützer, J., & Russo, J. (2010). Major depression: The importance of clinical characteristics and treatment response to prognosis. *Depression and Anxiety, 27*, 19–26. doi:10.1002/da.20613

    Milos, G. F., Spindler, A. M., Buddeberg, C., & Crameri, A. (2003). Axes I and II co-morbidity and treatment experiences in eating disorder subjects. *Psychotherapy and Psychosomatics, 72*, 276–285. doi:10.1159/000071899

    Thompson-Brenner, H., & Westen, D. (2005). A naturalistic study of psychotherapy for bulimia nervosa, Part 1. *Journal of Nervous and Mental Disease, 193*, 573–584. doi:10.1097/01.nmd.0000178843.81100.eb

17. Clients with externalizing coping styles may benefit more from psychotherapy that is more focused on behavior change and symptom reduction than fostering insight and self-awareness (see glossary in Appendix 2.1 for more details).

    Beutler, L. E., Harwood, T. M., Kimpara, S., Verdirame, D., & Blau, K. (2011). Coping style. In J. C. Norcross (Ed.), *Psychotherapy relationships that work: Evidence-based responsiveness* (2nd ed., pp. 336–353). New York, NY: Oxford University Press. doi:10.1093/acprof:oso/9780199737208.003.0017

18. Clients with internalizing coping styles may benefit more from psychotherapy that is more focused on fostering insight and self-awareness than behavior change and symptom reduction (see glossary in Appendix 2.1 for more details).

    Beutler, L. E., Harwood, T. M., Kimpara, S., Verdirame, D., & Blau, K. (2011). Coping style. In J. C. Norcross (Ed.), *Psychotherapy relationships that work: Evidence-based responsiveness* (2nd ed., pp. 336–353). New York, NY: Oxford University Press. doi:10.1093/acprof:oso/9780199737208.003.0017

19. Clients with moderate to severe impairment and/or fewer social supports will benefit more from psychotherapy when their therapist helps them address their social or medical needs.

    Goldschmidt, A. B., Best, J. R., Stein, R. I., Saelens, B. E., Epstein, L. H., & Wilfley, D. E. (2014). Predictors of child weight loss and maintenance among family-based treatment completers. *Journal of Consulting and Clinical Psychology, 82*, 1140–1150. doi:10.1037/a0037169

Hatfield, J. P., Hirsch, J. K., & Lyness, J. M. (2012). Functional impairment, illness burden, and depressive symptoms in older adults: Does type of social relationship matter? *International Journal of Geriatric Psychiatry, 28*, 190–198. doi:10.1002/gps.3808

Lindfors, O., Ojanen, S., Jääskeläinen, T., & Knekt, P. (2014). Social support as a predictor of the outcome of depressive and anxiety disorder in short-term and long-term psychotherapy. *Psychiatry Research, 216*, 44–51. doi:10.1016/j.psychres.2013.12.050

Norman, R., Manchanda, R., Northcott, S., Harricharan, R., & Windell, D. (2012). P-1279: Social support and five year functional outcomes in an early intervention program for psychosis. *European Psychiatry, 27*, 1. doi:10.1016/s0924-9338(12)75446-9

Sherbourne, C. D., Hays, R. D., & Wells, K. B. (1995). Personal and psychosocial risk factors for physical and mental health outcomes and course of depression among depressed patients. *Journal of Consulting and Clinical Psychology, 63*, 345–355. doi:10.1037//0022-006x.63.3.345

Thrasher, S., Power, M., Morant, N., Marks, I., & Dalgleish, T. (2010). Social support moderates outcome in a randomized controlled trial of exposure therapy and (or) cognitive restructuring for chronic posttraumatic stress disorder. *Canadian Journal of Psychiatry, 55*, 187–190. doi:10.1177/070674371005500311

Young, J. F., Mufson, L., & Davies, M. (2006). Impact of co-morbid anxiety in an effectiveness study of interpersonal psychotherapy for depressed adolescents. *Journal of the American Academy of Child & Adolescent Psychiatry, 45*, 904–912. doi:10.1097/01.chi.0000222791.23927.5f

20. Clients with substance use problems may be equally likely to benefit from psychotherapy delivered by a therapist with or without his or her own history of substance use problems.

    McCrady, B. S., Haaga, D. A. F., Lebow, J. (2006). Treatment factors in treating substance use disorders. In L. G. Castonguay & L. E. Beutler (Eds.), *Principles of therapeutic change that work* (pp. 319–341). New York, NY: Oxford University Press.

Client Process Variables

21. Clients who more actively participate in the treatment process may benefit more from psychotherapy than clients who less actively participate (see glossary in Appendix 2.1 for definition of active participation).

    Holdsworth, E., Bowen, E., Brown, S., & Howat, D. (2014). Client engagement in psychotherapeutic treatment and associations with client characteristics, therapist characteristics, and treatment factors. *Clinical Psychology Review, 34*, 428–450. doi:10.1016/j.cpr.2014.06.004

    Mausbach, B. T., Moore, R., Roesch, S., Cardenas, V., & Patterson, T. L. (2010). The relationship between homework compliance and therapy outcomes: An updated meta-analysis. *Cognitive Therapy and Research, 34*, 429–438. doi:10.1007/s10608-010-9297-z

Parhar, K. K., Wormith, J. S., Derkzen, D. M., & Beauregard, A. M. (2008). Offender coercion in treatment: A meta-analysis of effectiveness. *Criminal Justice and Behavior, 35*, 1109–1135. doi:10.1177/0093854808320169

Tryon, G. S., & Winograd, G. (2011). Goal consensus and collaboration. In J. C. Norcross (Ed.), *Psychotherapy relationships that work: Evidence-based responsiveness* (2nd ed., pp. 153–167). New York, NY: Oxford University Press. doi:10.1093/acprof:oso/9780199737208.003.0007

22. Clients who are more resistant to the therapist or therapy may benefit less from psychotherapy than clients who are less resistant (see glossary in Appendix 2.1 for definition of resistance/reactance).

    Beutler, L. E., Harwood, T. M., Michelson, A., Song, X., & Holman, J. (2011). Reactance/resistance level. In J. C. Norcross (Ed.), *Psychotherapy relationships that work: Evidence-based responsiveness* (2nd ed., pp. 261–278). New York, NY: Oxford University Press. doi:10.1093/acprof:oso/9780199737208.003.001

Therapy Relationship Principles

23. Clients experiencing a higher quality therapeutic alliance in group psychotherapy (group cohesion) or individual psychotherapy (bonding/collaboration) may benefit more than clients experiencing a lower quality alliance.

    Burlingame, G. M., McClendon, D. T., & Alonso, J. (2011). Cohesion in group therapy. In J. C. Norcross (Ed.), *Psychotherapy relationships that work: Evidence-based responsiveness* (2nd ed., pp. 110–131). New York, NY: Oxford University Press. doi:10.1093/acprof:oso/9780199737208.003.0005

    Flückiger, C., Del Re, A. C., Horvath, A. O., Symonds, D., Ackert, M., & Wampold, B. E. (2013). Substance use disorders and racial/ethnic minorities matter: A meta-analytic examination of the relation between alliance and outcome. *Journal of Counseling Psychology, 60*, 610–616. doi:10.1037/a0033161

    Horvath, A. O., Del Re, A. C., Flückiger, C., & Symonds, D. (2011). Alliance in individual psychotherapy. In J. C. Norcross (Ed.), *Psychotherapy relationships that work: Evidence-based responsiveness* (2nd ed., pp. 25–69). New York, NY: Oxford University Press.

24. Clients experiencing more therapist regard and affirmation may benefit more from psychotherapy than clients experiencing less therapist regard and affirmation.

    Farber, B. A., & Doolin, E. M. (2011). Positive regard and affirmation. In J. C. Norcross (Ed.), *Psychotherapy relationships that work: Evidence-based responsiveness* (2nd ed., pp. 168–186). New York, NY: Oxford University Press. doi:10.1093/acprof:oso/9780199737208.003.0008

25. Clients experiencing more therapist congruence may benefit more from psychotherapy than clients experiencing less therapist congruence.

    Kolden, G. G., Klein, M. H., Wang, C., & Austin, S. B. (2011). Congruence/genuineness. In J. C. Norcross (Ed.), *Psychotherapy relationships that work: Evidence-based responsiveness* (2nd ed., pp. 187–202). New York, NY: Oxford University Press. doi:10.1093/acprof:oso/9780199737208.003.0009

26. Clients experiencing more therapist empathy may benefit more from psychotherapy than clients experiencing less therapist empathy.
    Elliott, R., Bohart, A. C., Watson, J. C., & Greenberg, L. S. (2011). Empathy. In J. C. Norcross (Ed.), *Psychotherapy relationships that work: Evidence-based responsiveness* (2nd ed., pp. 132–152). New York, NY: Oxford University Press. doi:10.1093/acprof:oso/9780199737208.003.0006

27. Clients who experience alliance rupture–repair episodes and/or who work with therapists trained to repair alliance ruptures may benefit more from psychotherapy than clients who experience no or unrepaired ruptures and/or work with therapists not trained specifically on rupture–repair interventions.
    Safran, J. D., Muran, J. C., & Eubanks-Carter, C. (2011). Repairing alliance ruptures. In J. C. Norcross (Ed.), *Psychotherapy relationships that work: Evidence-based responsiveness* (2nd ed., pp. 224–238). New York, NY: Oxford University Press. doi:10.1093/acprof:oso/9780199737208.003.0011

28. Clients whose therapist uses more supportive self-disclosures may benefit more from psychotherapy than clients whose therapist uses less supportive self-disclosures (or does not disclose at all).
    Hill, C. E., & Knox, S. (2002). Self-disclosure. In J. C. Norcross (Ed.) *Psychotherapy relationships that work: Therapist contributions and responsiveness to patients* (pp. 255–266). New York, NY: Oxford University Press.

Therapist Intervention Principles

29. Clients whose therapist uses a higher proportion of general psychodynamic interpretations may benefit more from psychotherapy than clients whose therapist uses a lower proportion of general psychodynamic interpretations.
    Crits-Christoph, P., & Gibbons, M. B. C. (2002). Relational interpretations. In J. C. Norcross (Ed.) *Psychotherapy relationships that work: Therapist contributions and responsiveness to patients* (pp. 285–302). New York, NY: Oxford University Press.
    Crits-Christoph, P., Gibbons, M. B. C., & Mukherjee, D. (2013). Psychotherapy process-outcome research. In M. J. Lambert (Ed.), *Bergin and Garfield's handbook of psychotherapy and behavior change* (6th ed., pp. 298–340). New York, NY: Wiley.

30. Clients whose therapist uses higher quality psychodynamic interpretations may benefit more from psychotherapy than clients whose therapist uses lower quality psychodynamic interpretations (see glossary in Appendix 2.1 for definition of quality of psychodynamic interpretation).
    Crits-Christoph, P., & Gibbons, M. B. C. (2002). Relational interpretations. In J. C. Norcross (Ed.) *Psychotherapy relationships that work: Therapist contributions and responsiveness to patients* (pp. 285–302). New York, NY: Oxford University Press.
    Crits-Christoph, P., Gibbons, M. B. C., & Mukherjee, D. (2013). Psychotherapy process-outcome research. In M. J. Lambert (Ed.), *Bergin and Garfield's*

handbook of psychotherapy and behavior change (6th ed., pp. 298–340). New York, NY: Wiley.

31. Clients whose therapist receives feedback based on a routinely delivered outcome measure may benefit more from psychotherapy than clients whose therapist does not receive feedback.

    Lambert, M. J., and Shimokawa, K. (2011). Collecting client feedback. In J. C. Norcross (Ed.), *Psychotherapy relationships that work: Evidence-based responsiveness* (2nd ed., pp. 203–223). New York, NY: Oxford University Press. doi:10.1093/acprof:oso/9780199737208.003.0010

32. Clients who receive feedback from their therapist on their performance in treatment may benefit more from psychotherapy than clients who do not receive feedback.

    Claiborn, C. D., Goodyear, R. K., & Horner, P. A. (2002). Feedback. In J. C. Norcross (Ed.), *Psychotherapy relationships that work: Therapist contributions and responsiveness to patients* (pp. 217–234). New York, NY: Oxford University Press.

    Newman, M. G., Stiles, W. B., Janeck, A., & Woody, S. R. (2006). Integration of therapeutic factors in anxiety disorders. In L. G. Castonguay & L. E. Beutler (Eds.), *Principles of therapeutic change that work* (pp. 187–202). New York, NY: Oxford University Press.

33. Clients may benefit more from psychotherapy when their therapist is more versus less flexible in their administration of, or adherence to, a given treatment approach.

    Owen, J., & Hilsenroth, M. J. (2014). Treatment adherence: The importance of therapist flexibility in relation to therapy outcomes. *Journal of Counseling Psychology, 61,* 280–288. doi:10.1037/a0035753

34. Clients whose therapist selectively/responsively fosters more adaptive interpersonal changes may benefit more broadly from psychotherapy than those whose therapist fosters fewer adaptive interpersonal changes.

    Bressi, C., Porcellana, M., Marinaccio, P. M., Nocito, E. P., & Magri, L. (2010). Short-term psychodynamic psychotherapy versus treatment as usual for depressive and anxiety disorders. *Journal of Nervous and Mental Disease, 198,* 647–652. doi:10.1097/nmd.0b013e3181ef3ebb

    Crits-Christoph, P., Gibbons, M. B., Narducci, J., Schamberger, M., & Gallop, R. (2005). Interpersonal problems and the outcome of interpersonally oriented psychodynamic treatment of GAD. *Psychotherapy: Theory, Research, Practice, Training, 42,* 211–224. doi:10.1037/0033-3204.42.2.211

    Puschner, B., Kraft, S., & Bauer, S. (2004). Interpersonal problems and outcome in outpatient psychotherapy: Findings from a long-term longitudinal study in Germany. *Journal of Personality Assessment, 83,* 223–234. doi:10.1207/s15327752jpa8303_06

    Quilty, L. C., Mainland, B. J., Mcbride, C., & Bagby, R. (2013). Interpersonal problems and impacts: Further evidence for the role of interpersonal functioning in treatment outcome in major depressive disorder. *Journal of Affective Disorders, 150,* 393–400. doi:10.1016/j.jad.2013.04.030

Renner, F., Jarrett, R. B., Vittengl, J. R., Barrett, M. S., Clark, L. A., & Thase, M. E. (2012). Interpersonal problems as predictors of therapeutic alliance and symptom improvement in cognitive therapy for depression. *Journal of Affective Disorders, 138,* 458–467. doi:10.1016/j.jad.2011.12.044

Vittengl, J. R., Clark, L. A., & Jarrett, R. B. (2003). Interpersonal problems, personality pathology, and social adjustment after cognitive therapy for depression. *Psychological Assessment, 15,* 29–40. doi:10.1037/1040-3590.15.1.29

35. Clients whose therapist selectively/responsively fosters more self-understanding may benefit more broadly from psychotherapy than clients whose therapist fosters less self-understanding.

    Crits-Christoph, P., Gibbons, M. B. C., & Mukherjee, D. (2013). Psychotherapy process-outcome research. In M. J. Lambert (Ed.), *Bergin and Garfield's handbook of psychotherapy and behavior change* (6th ed., pp. 298–340). New York, NY: Wiley.

36. Clients whose therapist selectively/responsively fosters more emotional experiencing and/or deepening may benefit more broadly from psychotherapy than clients whose therapist fosters less emotional experiencing and/or deepening.

    Elliott, R., Greenberg, L. S., Watson, J., Timulak, L., & Freire, E. (2013). Humanistic-experiential psychotherapies. In M. J. Lambert (Ed.), *Bergin and Garfield's handbook of psychotherapy and behavior change* (6th ed., pp. 495–538). New York, NY: Wiley.

37. Clients whose therapist selectively/responsively uses nondirective interventions skillfully may benefit more from psychotherapy than clients whose therapist uses nondirective interventions unskillfully.

    Elliott, R., Greenberg, L. S., Watson, J., Timulak, L., & Freire, E. (2013). Humanistic-experiential psychotherapies. In M. J. Lambert (Ed.), *Bergin and Garfield's handbook of psychotherapy and behavior change* (6th ed., pp. 495–538). New York, NY: Wiley.

    Greenberg, L. S., & Pascual-Leone, A. (2006). Emotion in psychotherapy: A practice-friendly research review. *Journal of Clinical Psychology, 62,* 611–630. doi:10.1002/jclp.20252

38. Clients whose therapist selectively/responsively fosters more behavior changes may benefit more broadly from psychotherapy than clients whose therapist fosters fewer behavior changes.

    Butler, A., Chapman, J., Forman, E., & Beck, A. (2006). The empirical status of cognitive-behavioral therapy: A review of meta-analyses. *Clinical Psychology Review, 26,* 17–31. doi:10.1016/j.cpr.2005.07.003

    Dimidjian, S., Hollon, S. D., Dobson, K. S., Schmaling, K. B., Kohlenberg, R. J., Addis, M. E., . . . Jacobson, N. S. (2006). Randomized trial of behavioral activation, cognitive therapy, and antidepressant medication in the acute treatment of adults with major depression. *Journal of Consulting and Clinical Psychology, 74,* 658–670. doi:10.1037/0022-006x.74.4.658

Dutra, L., Stathopoulou, G., Basden, S. L., Leyro, T. M., Powers, M. B., & Otto, M. W. (2008). A meta-analytic review of psychosocial interventions for substance use disorders. *American Journal of Psychiatry, 165,* 179–187. doi:10.1176/appi.ajp.2007.06111851

Hoffman, S. G., & Smits, J. A. (2008). Cognitive-behavioral therapy for adult anxiety disorders. *Journal of Clinical Psychiatry, 69,* 621–632. doi:10.4088/jcp.v69n0415

Kliem, S., Kröger, C., & Kosfelder, J. (2010). Dialectical behavior therapy for borderline personality disorder: A meta-analysis using mixed-effects modeling. *Journal of Consulting and Clinical Psychology, 78,* 936–951. doi:10.1037/a0021015

Ougrin, D. (2011). Efficacy of exposure versus cognitive therapy in anxiety disorders: Systematic review and meta-analysis. *BMC Psychiatry, 11.* doi:10.1186/1471-244x-11-200

PART II

DEPRESSION

PART II

DEPRESSION

3
Depression Cases

Louis G. Castonguay, Michael J. Constantino, and Larry E. Beutler

This chapter describes three cases of depression. We provided these cases and the principles list delineated in Chapter 2 to the clinician authors prior to them writing their chapters in the present section. The three clinicians who read and wrote about the depression cases are Benjamin Johnson (Chapter 4), Abraham W. Wolf (Chapter 5), and Dina Vivian (Chapter 6).

Aside from the primary symptom, the depression cases described in this chapter were designed to be almost identical to the anxiety cases presented in Chapter 8. As elaborated in the following discussion, "Victor," our first case, is depicted as meeting the criteria for major depressive disorder. In contrast to the other two, however, he does not present with co-morbidity of either substance abuse or personality disorder. In addition to depression, "Brian" (the second case) presents with the co-morbid disorder of alcohol abuse, and Anne (the third case) demonstrates marked co-morbid symptoms of personality disorder (i.e., borderline personality disorder). Additionally, a number of clinically relevant phenomena have been integrated across the three cases. In addition to the editors' practical and theoretical knowledge, these phenomena have been derived from two sources.

The first source includes a wealth of findings from psychopathology research related to symptomatology, clinical features, course, co-morbidity, prevalence, and etiology of depression (LeMoulth, Castonguay, Joorman, & McAleavey, 2013). We relied on this knowledge from basic science to construct broad and in-depth pictures of various aspects of the phenomenology and determinants of depression. The second source is the revised list of principles presented in Chapter 2, which we used to provide clinical material, across the three cases, pertinent to the principles provided to the clinical authors. To make sure that we covered these principles accurately and comprehensively, all cases were rated (and then slightly modified accordingly) using the Innerlife STS (http://www.innerlife.com)—a well-researched and psychometrically sound client self-report measure that yields 22 symptom scales and a host of personality traits and dispositions that relate directly to most of the 38 principles of change described in this volume. The principle list with relevant notations on the three depression cases is provided in Appendix 3.1.

Finally, we have also included Appendix 3.2, which presents a profile of therapy style for each of the three contributing therapists. These profiles were derived from the self-report version of the Therapy Process Rating Scale (TPRS; Kimpara, Regner, Usami, & Beutler, 2015). The TPRS provides information about what the therapist does in psychotherapy. We focused on therapist actions rather than beliefs or theories because these appear to be better predictors of outcomes (Beutler, Clarkin, & Bongar, 2000). Using therapist actions, the TPRS lends itself to determining the degree to which the therapist's behaviors and interventions are compatible with patient preferences, demographic characteristics, coping styles, resistance levels, and other qualities that are embedded in the principles that were presented in Chapter 2 (e.g., principles 1, 2, 6, 7, 11, 13, 15–19, 22, 29, 35, and 37). The authors completed the TPRS before they wrote their respective chapter, and we used these profiles to divide therapists between the depression and anxiety cases to balance the assignments in terms of therapeutic styles. We also used these profiles when discussing convergences and divergences among therapists' implementation of principles of change in the last chapters of the depression and anxiety sections of this book.

The Depression Cases

Case 1: Victor (Depression without Substance Abuse and Personality Disorder Comorbidity)

Victor is a 41-year-old Hispanic man who has been experiencing feelings of sadness and despair for the last six months. He also reports being bothered during this period by anhedonia, psychomotor agitation, hypersomnia, weight loss, chronic fatigue, and loss of energy and concentration. He has been feeling both guilty and worthless and has on several occasions thought about suicide to end what he described as his "miserable life." He reports shame at being a weak, unsuccessful man who has no major accomplishments in his personal or professional life. In addition, Victor meets criteria for generalized anxiety disorder (GAD) and agoraphobia. Although Victor is currently more distressed by his depression, he has experienced anxiety symptoms (especially uncontrollable worry and self-criticism) for many years before experiencing depressive symptoms.

Victor has been married for 20 years to Leonora, a Latina two years his junior, with whom he has been best friends since he was 15 years old. They met when they were in high school and married six years later, soon after they found out that she was pregnant. They have two children, a girl aged 21 and a boy aged 18. Victor and Leonora share many values, including the importance of family relationships, hard work, their children's education, and their religious faith (Roman Catholic). Their relationship has been very close and intense. While the first several years of their marriage were harmonious, over the past four years they have argued frequently and have grown more distant from each other, both emotionally and sexually. The main topics of discord are about what Leonora perceived as Victor's lack of engagement in carrying out his responsibilities regarding home and children, as well as Victor's perception of Leonora's lack of support and validation. Financial difficulties and the couple's social isolation have also contributed to marital distress. While both Victor and Leonora are working (full-time and half-time, respectively), they are living in an expensive part of the United States, many miles away from each other's parents and siblings.

Like Leonora, Victor was born in the United States following his parents' immigration from Central America. He described conflicted feelings about his youth. He respects the fact that both of his parents had to work very long hours at nongratifying jobs to survive in a country where, for many years, they did not speak the prevalent language. He remembers fondly the nurturing ways his mother would relate to him when he was young. He is also grateful for the inspiration he got from both of his parents to work hard and to be personally disciplined (especially in choosing "the right" friends and avoiding risky situations involving sex, drugs, alcohol, and gang-related activities). At the same time, he regrets the fact that, as a child, he had to spend many hours alone and many more hours caretaking his three younger siblings while his parents were working. With painful emotions, he also remembers how demanding, critical, and emotionally unavailable his father was during Victor's youth.

After completing high school, Victor went straight to work. He began community college when he was 20 years old, but he had to drop out after a year when he found that Leonora was pregnant with his daughter. He returned to work to take on the increasing responsibilities required by his job. Victor is now manager of a small business, which imposes long hours six days a week. Although his advancement in the company has led to some modest salary increases, they have always lived on the edge financially. His job also comes with constant stress between the demands from his employers and the expectations of the workers (and former peers) that he now supervises. Victor feels that he has little control or power over the pressures that he faces at work. He also finds that the organizational and managerial challenges that he has to address on a daily basis are neither stimulating nor gratifying. He feels stuck in a static and unsatisfying occupational position that he cannot leave because of the revenue it provides (although it is not nearly sufficient for him and his family to be financially comfortable).

Victor had a strong connection with his siblings and several of his cousins as a child. Although he was not as close with them as he was with Leonora, he always had male friends in and outside of schools. He was involved in many sports as a teenager and maintained regular contact with several male friends until the birth of his son. For the last several years, he has not made time to pursue sports or other hobbies nor to enjoy the company of friends. Thus, now and even before he became depressed, Victor has not been involved in any activities that bring him pleasure and personal satisfaction. His agoraphobia (fear of going to large public events) has also imposed restriction to the couple's social life.

Victor also reports a number of issues that have had an impact on his interpersonal relationships, both at work and at home. Since becoming depressed, he has found himself easily irritated and angry, and he has noted that his frustration and hostility has made both Leonora and his co-workers annoyed and frustrated with him. Their negative feelings and criticism toward him, as well as their occasional avoidance of him, have been quite hurtful (especially considering that Victor has always felt the desire to be close to others). In fact, Leonora has told him several times that she wishes he was less needy of her reassurance and that he was more assertive at work. Victor recognizes that he has always been insecure, which has made him frequently rely on advice from others. He also admits that his tendency to seek guidance and reassurance from others has limited his ability to develop and exercise leadership at work. Leonora complains that he lets others, both bosses and supervisees, control him. Victor agrees and feels that since he has been depressed, he has become particularly uncomfortable when others rely on him for support and expect him to take initiative and control over situations at work or at home.

Indeed, his tendency to let others control him, if not dominate him, has become a major cause of painful ruminations for Victor and arguments with his wife. Although he has always showed a tendency to blame himself for problems and failures, for the last several months, Victor has been stuck in a constant and uncontrollable cycle of trying to assert himself, failing, and then spiraling down to a process of worry, shame, anger, and sadness about his unwillingness or inability to be more autonomous, decisive, and assertive, both at work and at home. He is convinced that these traits reflect an immutable weakness of his personality, which he uses to explain to himself why he has not been able to succeed personally and professionally. He is also convinced that he cannot change this core aspect of who he is and that it will always preclude him from achieving meaningful accomplishments and gaining genuine affection and respect from others.

Case 2: Brian (Depression and Substance Abuse)

Brian is a 45-year-old White man who is hesitantly seeking help for his depression and alcohol problems after repeated urging of friends and family. Brian completed high school and has been working in the construction business for the last 28 years. He has been dysthymic since his teenage years, and he has struggled with two episodes of mild to moderate major depression (superimposed on his dysthymia) between the age of 24 and 26 and one in his 30s. He saw a therapist during the third episode but terminated after two sessions without benefit. About a year before his current consultation, he began experiencing intense depressive symptoms that became severe to their current level. In addition to marked dysphoria and anhedonia, Brian is suffering from insomnia, psychomotor retardation, and concentration. He has also gained weight and feels fatigued most of the time. Most concerning to those close to him, Brian has talked about killing himself on numerous occasions in the last few months.

Brian's alcohol problems have also been a serious concern. He began drinking with peers as a teenager but progressively began to drink alone, which has contributed to social isolation (he still has friends from high school and work but sees them rather infrequently). Brian has been drinking nightly since the age of 21, and while he used to restrain himself to two beers during most of his 20s, he gradually increased his consumption and now drinks an average of five per evening. He also smokes marijuana but only occasionally. He admits that his drinking has led him to engage in dangerous behaviors, such as driving while impaired on several occasions. Brian has tried several times to reduce his alcohol consumption, but he has been unsuccessful in part because he feels strongly that alcohol helps him relax and tolerate his stress. He also felt anxious and physically uncomfortable when attempting to drink less.

Brian's substance use has numerous negative consequences. In addition to the increased social isolation, his ability to show up on time to work and to meet the physical demands of his job have suffered (this was true even before his chronic depression became severe). His boss has complained to him several times about his work performance and recently warned him that he might be fired. His last girlfriend, like the one before her, told him that his alcohol problems and his unwillingness to address them were the main reasons for her terminating their two-year relationship. She complained that his drinking made him lethargic, irritable, and difficult to get along with. She also complained of his low level of sexual drive or ability, as well as his lack of interest in activities, social or otherwise, outside of his apartment. Although Brian claimed that he never physically abused the current or previous girlfriends, he acknowledged that another reason for their separation was that she became afraid of his violent temper when he was heavily intoxicated.

Brian recognizes that he drinks too much, but he claims that most of his problems at work and with his former girlfriends were not his fault. Likewise, he attributes his work problems to his boss being stressed out all the time and thus being too demanding. He also complains that his boss has different standards and favors some other employees over him, including some who drink at least as much as he does. He also says that his former girlfriend had never been happy about what he was doing for her or their relationship and was always looking for a fight. Furthermore, he states that his boss and former girlfriend are/were both critical and controlling of him, making him feel upset and angry. He feels that neither of them can/could trust and accept him as he is, give him the space and the right to make his own decision, do what he wants to do and how he wants to do it, and be who he wants to be. He also believes that over the last few years the unrealistic demands from his boss and the constant critics of his former girlfriend are the main reasons for his increased and excessive alcohol use. Nevertheless, he recognizes that her leaving him, as well as his threat of losing his job, are two stressful events that have contributed to his current and most serious depression episode. He also admits that his anger, distrust of others, and poor impulse control will make it difficult for him to find, let alone keep, another girlfriend and job. He is, however, not convinced that therapy will be helpful for his problems.

Brian also feels alone more than at any time in his life. He maintains that he has never been good at meeting new people. He also feels that it would be difficult for him to find a new job. He describes himself as having poor "people skills." He does not participate in community activities (social and/or athletic) and does not belong to a church (his parents were Protestant, but religion was not emphasized at home, and he neither paid attention to nor rejected the Christian faith). Highly demoralized, he feels stuck in his current life, without prospect for major changes or positive things, personally and professionally; not surprisingly, he describes his life as unfulfilling and lacking in meaning.

In terms of family history, Brian reports that he had a difficult upbringing. His father was frequently unemployed and drank heavily. His father also had a violent temper and was both verbally and physically abusive with him and his two brothers. His father passed away when Brian was 20, and he never really talked about his conflicted feelings. These feelings consist both of profound sadness and, equally, intense resentment for the loss of his father. Brian's mother was depressed most of the time during his upbringing. She was not only disappointed and stressed out about her husband's occupational failures but also afraid of him. Brian recalls that she spent most days doing very little (she did not have a job outside of the house) and barely had energy for cooking and basic house chores. Brian felt distant from both parents during his childhood and adolescence and seldom sees or talks to his mother even to this day. He fought a lot with his brothers when they were young, but he also feels that they ultimately developed a strong bond, especially around doing and watching sports. Like with his friends from high school, Brian has not had regular contact with his brothers. He feels that it is mostly they who have failed to maintain their connections. Although he feels grateful that both of them have reached out to him in difficult times, especially recently, he also has wished that they would contact him in times other than when they feel that he is depressed.

Case 3: Anne (Depression and Personality Disorder)

Anne is 24-year-old White woman struggling with strong feelings of sadness and self-loathing for the last six months. Her depression is currently related to the end of a romantic relationship with a man of her age, Peter, with whom she is still deeply in love. They were together for three years by her report, but the last two were characterized by a cycle of break-ups and make-ups. She had a number of brief affairs with other young men during the last two years that she was with Peter, but none of them created for her the same wishes for closeness and intimacy as she has been longing for with Peter. Before meeting Peter, she had experienced a few sexual relationships with men that she had found exciting (a musician, ski instructor, drug dealer), but she never considered them "a boyfriend." Neither does she have many close relationships with women, with the exception of a friend from high school. She has had infrequent contacts with this woman. At the time of therapy, Anne was taking two classes at the university and was working part-time in a library. She was also living at her parents' house.

Anne has never felt that she fit in with peers. Being introverted, she spends a lot of time reading novels, listening to music, and doing outdoors activities on her own. Yet she has rarely felt at peace or happy to be alone. While always feeling a yearning to be with others, she has viewed herself as not being strong, interesting, and socially skilled enough to develop and maintain close relationships. The only time she did not feel socially isolated was when she was part of a small group of high school students who had counter-culture social and political values and consumed hard drugs, including heroin together.

Extremely smart, Anne did well in school until college. Having been an avid reader of classic literature, she majored in both English and philosophy. Although she excelled in her first year, getting recognition from several of her teachers for the creativity and insightfulness of her writing, she started having difficulty completing and passing her courses in her second year. These increasing difficulties followed an abortion she had early in the fall semester. She admits that this event may also have had an impact on her relationship with Peter; she became dependent on him, but at the same time she was fearful of closeness and reluctant to engage in sexual intimacy. After several months, Peter began to be less engaged in the relationship, which made Anne cling to him even more. She progressively withdrew from others, as most of her social contacts at that time were with Peter's friends. Her academic difficulties became exacerbated, in part because of her difficulty concentrating but also because of her avoidance of anxiety-provoking issues (exams, deadlines) and her preoccupation with possible ways to cope with them (e.g., contacting advising resources). She never quite followed through with these plans, however. Attempts to separate, always initiated by Peter, triggered depressive episodes and suicidal gestures. A serious suicide attempt led to a brief psychiatric hospitalization.

Even when she and Peter re-established their relationship, Anne remained constantly insecure, emotional unstable (especially vacillating among periods sadness, anger, and anxiety), jealous of any time he spent with others, and periodically engaged in self-harm (cutting). She also occasionally resumed her consumption of hard drugs, which she had stopped after meeting Peter. The relationship with Peter finally ended, according to Anne, when she spent the summer alone at her parents' country house, during which time she had an affair. Although they both agreed that the separation was inevitable, almost immediately afterward she became seriously depressed and sought psychotherapy.

During the intake, which took two sessions, Anne revealed persistent patterns of fluctuation in both her self-confidence and her sense of having a direction in her life. She also reported being frequently impulsive and "irresponsible." She remembered several moments of excitement and motivation in her life, including periods when she became very focused on one or another potential career choices. Ultimately, all of these interests and moments of motivation rapidly extinguished into a general state of disinterest, boredom, frustration, depression, anxiety, and self-doubt. She complained of not having a clear sense of what she wants and who she is. She also reported that her self-esteem and life choices were frequently based on others' opinions or her expectations of such opinions. Yet, despite her being drawn to others, most of Anne's relationships with others have been emotionally draining and disappointing. She explained that it takes time to let others get close to her but that once she feels attached, friends usually stop being interested in being around her. She believes that what she views as her being a real friend, others view as her as being too needy, dependent, and even clingy; which not only has made her frequently and extremely angry at others but also resentful of her own tendency to let her hopes build up and her fears to lessen, thus opening the door to another cycle of disappointment. People have been hard to trust throughout her life, and personal relationships always seem to turn sour and painful. This was certainly the case with Peter, whom she described at different times during the intake with a mixture of opposing emotions. She describes him, even now, as being gentle, loving, romantic, and inspiring but also selfish, manipulative, shallow, and untrustworthy.

Anne was reluctant to confide information about her parents and her childhood. She described her mother as having been controlling and constantly involved in activities to avoid being lonely and depressed. She was particularly vague about her relationship with her father, presenting him, glowingly, in terms of his personality (hard-working, highly intelligent, no-nonsense) but also noting his frequent absences from home—either for his job or for selfishly taking time alone to build and enjoy the country house. Anne has not had a close connection with her siblings. She described her older brother as distant, dismissive, and extremely mean (verbally and physically). She also acknowledged having been envious and jealous of her younger sister, whom she described as always being happy, bubbly, carefree, and popular among her peers and adults. Although she recognized having felt alone and as having been treated as an outcast, attempts to clarify her history or to explore remaining feelings and thoughts toward her childhood and family were met with resistance.

During the intake sessions, Anne also seemed conflicted about entering therapy. Although she appreciated the therapist's desire to listen, she communicated subtle annoyance at some of the therapist's questions about her goals for therapy and evinced noticeable frustration at some of therapist's questions when suggesting topics to be explored during therapy. Anne seemed to have low expectations about treatment, feeling that no one is likely to be able to change her life for the better. Yet, she admitted to needing therapy, not only because of her distress level but also because of how unfulfilling, meaningless, lonely, and hopeless her life has become following the end of her relationship with Peter and her academic drifting. She described having dwelled in thought for at least six months on what she views as lifelong failures in relationships and in school and especially her frustration at being stuck in patterns of rumination, regret, and sadness about what she could have done better in all areas of her life.

References

Beutler, L. E., Clarkin, J. E., & Bongar, B. (2000). *Guidelines for the systematic treatment of the depressed patient.* New York, NY: Oxford University Press.

Kimpara, S., Regner, E., Usami, S., & Beutler, L. E. (2015, August). *Systematic Treatment Selection (STS): How to monitor therapists' interventions and cross-cultural differences between north America and Argentina.* Paper presented at the Annual Meeting of the American Psychological Association, Toronto.

LeMoult, J., Castonguay, L. G., Joormann, J., & McAleavey, A. (2013). Depression. In L. G. Castonguay & T. F. Oltmanns (Eds.), *Psychopathology: From science to clinical practice* (pp. 17–61). New York, NY: Guilford.

Appendix 3.1

List of Principles of Change with Notations for Authors Working on Depression Cases

Client Prognostic Principles

1. Clients with higher levels of baseline impairment may benefit less from psychotherapy than clients with lower levels of impairment.

   As outlined in the following text, all three cases show impairment in terms of depressive symptoms, co-morbidity, global functioning, and interpersonal functioning. In general, Case 2 (with substance use problems) has higher level of impairment and distress, followed by Case 3 (with personality disorder) and Case 1. Although varying in terms of intensity, some features of impairment are shared either by two or three of them. Other clinical features, however, are specific to one of the three cases.

Depression

- Severity of depressive symptoms: severe (Case 2); moderate (Case 3); mild (Case 1)
- Early onset (Cases 2 and 3)
- Increase risk of suicide with acute and negative mood (Cases 2 and 3)
- Genetic factors/family history (Cases 2 and 3)
- Chronicity (Case 2)
- Recurrence/relapse (Case 2)
- Not fully recover from previous treatment (Case 2)
- Sexual dysfunction (Case 2)

- Somatic symptoms:
  - psychomotor agitation (Case 1)/retardation (Case 2); weigh loss (Case 1)/gain (Case 2); insomnia (Case 2)/hypersomnia (Case 1)

Co-Morbidity

- Generalized anxiety disorder (Case 1), dysthymia (Case 2), and agoraphobia (Case 1)

Global Functioning

- Quality of life (Cases 1–3)
- Stressful events and inadequate or lack of coping skills to deal with them:
  - Occupational failure/difficulties (Cases 1–3); social difficulties (humiliation, rejection, loss, social exclusion; Cases 1–3)
- Reduce work performance (Cases 1–3)
- Behavioral avoidance (Cases 2 and 3)

Interpersonal Functioning

- Lack of support (Cases 1–3)
- Isolation/loneliness—personal and professional (Cases 1–3)
- Romantic dissatisfaction/discord/difficulties (Cases 1–3)
- Anger and annoying to others (Cases 1–3)
- Social skill deficit (Cases 2 and 3)
- Loss of parent (Case 2)
- Seeking reassurance (Cases 1 and 3)
- Seeking for confirmation (Case 1)

2. Clients whose primary presenting problems are complicated by a co-morbid secondary personality disorder (PD) diagnosis may benefit less from psychotherapy than clients without a co-morbid PD diagnosis.
   - Case 3
3. Clients with more secure attachment may benefit more from psychotherapy than clients with less secure attachment (namely, more attachment anxiety).
   - Parental problems potentially related to attachment insecurity are present in all three cases.
4. Clients with higher initial expectations for benefitting from psychotherapy may benefit more from it than clients with lower initial outcome expectations.
   - Low or mixed expectations about therapy (Cases 2 and 3)

5. Clients who are more intrinsically (or autonomously) motivated to engage in psychotherapy may benefit more from it than clients who are less intrinsically (or autonomously) motivated.
   - Low motivation about therapy (Case 2)

6. Clients in advanced stages of change readiness (i.e., they are actively preparing for or currently taking action toward healthy behavior) may benefit more from psychotherapy than clients at lower stages of change readiness.
   - The three cases show different levels of readiness for change, with Case 1 being the most advanced and Case 2, the least.

7. Clients with low socio-economic status and employment problems may benefit less from psychotherapy than clients with higher socioeconomic status and no employment problems
   - Socio-economic status: low-mid (Case 2); mid (Cases 1 and 3)
   - Education: high school (Case 2); some college (Cases 1 and 3)

8. Clients who have experienced adverse childhood events may benefit less from psychotherapy than clients who did not experience adverse childhood events.
   - Inadequate parenting: neglect (inattention, withdraw, emotional unresponsiveness, lack of reinforcement; Cases 1–3); abuse (verbal/physical, Cases 2 and 3)

9. Anxious clients with more negative self-attributions may benefit less from psychotherapy than clients with fewer negative self-attributions.
   - Case 1

Treatment/Provider Moderating Principles

10. Clients whose therapist uses interventions consistent with the client's level of problem assimilation may benefit more from psychotherapy than patients whose interventions are not consistent with their assimilation level.
    - Case 1 may show signs of higher level of problem assimilation than Cases 2 and 3

11. Clients with higher levels of resistance may benefit more from psychotherapy that is more nondirective compared to clients with lower levels of resistance who may benefit more from psychotherapy that is more directive.
    - Resistance/reactance: low (Case 1); high (Case 2); mixed (Case 3)

12. Clients with lower motivation for, or higher ambivalence about, change may benefit more from psychotherapy when their therapist is responsive and person-centered versus more directive and change-oriented.
    - Cases 2 and 3

13. Clients who are matched to their preferred therapy role, therapist demographics, or treatment type may benefit more from psychotherapy than clients unmatched on these preferences.
    - This could be relevant to all three cases.

14. Clients whose preference for religiously or spiritually oriented psychotherapy is accommodated may benefit more from treatment than clients whose preference is unmet.
    - Strong Catholic faith (Case 1); no commitment to Protestant faith (Case 2)
15. Clients who present with poorer interpersonal functioning are likely to benefit less from psychotherapy when their therapist uses a higher versus lower proportion of transference interpretations.
    - Cases 2 and 3
16. Clients higher in baseline impairment may benefit more from psychotherapy that is longer-term and/or more intensive compared to clients lower in baseline impairment who may benefit equally well from psychotherapy that is long- or short-term and/or more or less intensive
    - Cases 2 and 3
17. Clients with externalizing coping styles may benefit more from psychotherapy that is more focused on behavior change and symptom reduction than fostering insight and self-awareness.
    - Externalizer (Case 2); mixed externalizer and internalizer (Case 3)
18. Clients with internalizing coping styles may benefit more from psychotherapy that is more focused on fostering insight and self-awareness than behavior change and symptom reduction.
    - Internalizer (Case 1); mixed externalizer and internalizer (Case 3)
19. Clients with moderate to severe impairment and/or fewer social supports will benefit more from psychotherapy when their therapist helps them address their social or medical needs.
    - Cases 2 and 3
20. Clients with substance use problems may be equally likely to benefit from psychotherapy delivered by a therapist with or without his or her own history of substance use problems.
    - Case 2

Client Process Variables

21. Clients who more actively participate in the treatment process may benefit more from psychotherapy than clients who less actively participate.
    - Potential difficulty of engagement in therapy (Cases 2 and 3)
22. Clients who are more resistant to the therapist or therapy may benefit less from psychotherapy than clients who are less resistant.
    - Resistance/reactance: low (Case 1); high (Case 2); mixed (Case 3)

Therapy Relationship Principles

23. Clients experiencing a higher quality therapeutic alliance in group psychotherapy (group cohesion) or individual psychotherapy (bonding/collaboration) may benefit more than clients experiencing a lower quality alliance.
24. Clients experiencing more therapist regard and affirmation may benefit more from psychotherapy than clients experiencing less therapist regard and affirmation.
25. Clients experiencing more therapist congruence may benefit more from psychotherapy than clients experiencing less therapist congruence.
26. Clients experiencing more therapist empathy may benefit more from psychotherapy than clients experiencing less therapist empathy.
27. Clients who experience alliance rupture–repair episodes and/or who work with therapists trained to repair alliance ruptures may benefit more from psychotherapy than clients who experience no or unrepaired ruptures and/or work with therapists not trained specifically on rupture–repair interventions.
28. Clients whose therapist uses more supportive self-disclosures may benefit more from psychotherapy than clients whose therapist uses less supportive self-disclosures (or does not disclose at all).

Therapist Intervention Principles

29. Clients whose therapist uses a higher proportion of general psychodynamic interpretations may benefit more from psychotherapy than clients whose therapist uses a lower proportion of general psychodynamic interpretations.
30. Clients whose therapist uses higher quality psychodynamic interpretations may benefit more from psychotherapy than clients whose therapist uses lower quality psychodynamic interpretations.
31. Clients whose therapist receives feedback based on a routinely delivered outcome measure may benefit more from psychotherapy than clients whose therapist does not receive feedback.
32. Clients who receive feedback from their therapist on their performance in treatment may benefit more from psychotherapy than clients who do not receive feedback.
33. Clients may benefit more from psychotherapy when their therapist is more versus less flexible in their administration of, or adherence to, a given treatment approach.
34. Clients whose therapist selectively/responsively fosters more adaptive interpersonal changes may benefit more broadly from psychotherapy than those whose therapist fosters fewer adaptive interpersonal changes.
35. Clients whose therapist selectively/responsively fosters more self-understanding may benefit more broadly from psychotherapy than clients whose therapist fosters less self-understanding.

36. Clients whose therapist selectively/responsively fosters more emotional experiencing and/or deepening may benefit more broadly from psychotherapy than clients whose therapist fosters less emotional experiencing and/or deepening.
37. Clients whose therapist selectively/responsively uses nondirective interventions skillfully may benefit more from psychotherapy than clients whose therapist uses nondirective interventions unskillfully.
38. Clients whose therapist selectively/responsively fosters more behavior changes may benefit more broadly from psychotherapy than clients whose therapist fosters fewer behavior changes.

Appendix 3.2

Therapists' TPRS Profile

Following is a brief description of each therapist in terms of their Therapy Process Rating Scale (TPRS) profile and how they are likely to behave in psychotherapy.

Benjamin Johnson

Dr. Johnson is very self-confident; he holds high expectations for himself and feels capable of achieving these goals. He is not a directive therapist, preferring instead to elicit patient responses and to follow the patient's lead. In so doing, he uses interventions to help arouse and clarify the patient's feelings and to follow these feelings to working material. In so doing, he does not seek maximal arousal but, rather, seeks to locate and maintain a moderate level of arousal in provoking change. Finally, Dr. Johnson has a strong behavioral focus but not exclusively so. He also seeks to achieve change through insight but seems to see direct behavior change as a means to gaining insight.

Dina Vivian

Dr. Vivian rates herself as using all classes on interventions except directiveness at a very high rate. She considers herself to be skillful. She is self-confident, but she does not present herself as having as high level of self-confidence as some of the other therapists participating in this project. She presents herself as a therapist who confronts the patient to achieve levels of arousal that are motivating. Indeed, this is a central part of her interventions. But even more frequently, she works to achieve insight in this process. From her description, Dr. Vivian is a therapist that operates within a framework of theoretical integration, combining dynamic concepts and principles with behavioral assignments. She focuses on external behaviors, monitors them, and assesses the consequences of these behaviors. Concomitantly, while she seeks to enhance patient insight, she is not particularly concerned with the resurrection of historical connections to understand the patient's insights or emotional experiences and looks more for understanding than "insight" in the classical sense of "uncovering" unconscious material.

Abraham W. Wolf

Like most of the other therapists, Dr. Wolf has strong confidence in his skills in facilitating change. This is sufficiently high as to suggest confidence and consistency with the level attributed to him and not so high as to suggest rigidity and willfulness. He presents himself as an evocative rather than a directive therapist and as being about equally concerned with achieving insight and direct behavior change. While he values the role of arousal as a motivator for change and as a guide to productive insights, he seems able to produce the arousal without high levels of direction or confrontation.

4
How I Would Apply Change Principles in Psychotherapy with Three Cases of Depression

Benjamin Johnson

This chapter references the three different cases of depression presented in Chapter 3. For each, I present my case formulation and general treatment plan. I then review more specifically how I would implement the principles in each category of the list—patient prognostic, treatment/provider moderating, patient process, therapeutic relationship, and therapist intervention. I highlight similarities and differences in how I would apply the change principles to the different cases, providing a range of relevant clinical examples of how I typically intervene. Throughout, I put phrases in quotes to indicate the language I might use to express an idea to a patient; vibrant, memorable words help patients remember and internalize concepts. Finally, I offer several general recommendations for how clinicians might let the principles influence their psychotherapeutic work. Indeed, these principles feel part and parcel of much of what I do to try to help people grow as individuals and improve their lives.

My General Reactions to the Task of Writing this Chapter

I am very upbeat about reflecting on how I apply research-derived therapeutic principles to my work in psychotherapy in general and to these cases specifically. I have based much of my approach to clinical work on these principles, as I was exposed to them early in my development by attending the Society for Psychotherapy Research (SPR) conferences and perusing books like *Garfield and Bergin's Handbook of Psychotherapy and Behavior Change* (Lambert, 2013). I practice in a flexible, principle-guided way. I love the work that I do with patients, and I generally feel effective. However, I think that there are large differences in how I, as now an experienced clinician, implement therapeutic principles compared to how graduate students first studying psychotherapy might implement them. I am eager to talk about the stance and style I have developed over almost 30 years of studying and practicing psychology.

Case 1: The Case of Victor

Case Formulation and Treatment Plan

Prominent Clinical Features of Victor's Problems
Victor struggles with depression, hopelessness, and irritability. He has conflict with his wife, Leonora, turns to her for reassurance, but feels unsupported. He lacks social support outside of his wife, with little support available from other family members and few current friends. His work life is stressful, as he avoids fully assuming the leadership role he is in, fearing the reactions of his subordinates if he were to manage more forcefully. Outside of work, he does little for pleasure or relaxation. He has had periods of intense worry and anxiety and has avoided large social activities because of anxiety. His self-esteem is extremely poor, and he can ruminate about being worthless.

Variables Most Likely Related to the Etiology or Maintenance of His Problems
Victor's mother was nurturing during his early childhood. However, his parents worked long hours and were often unavailable. Victor's father was critical, demanding, and distant emotionally during his childhood. Though Victor developed male friendships and found a romantic partner in Leonora, he left childhood with a core sense of longing for more connection from others, a limited sense of his power to develop these connections, and a fragile sense of self-worth.

It seems that Victor's insecurities have led him to develop several problematic patterns. He works long hours and leaves little energy for enjoyable activities and male friendships. His worry and anxiety have led him to avoid opportunities for fun and getting further involved with the world. He turns to others at work for reassurance, which makes it harder to be perceived as a strong leader. This, in turn, leaves him feeling worse about himself. He spirals into feeling helpless and hopeless, making his depressive symptoms worse.

Central Points of Focus for Treatment and General Treatment Directions

My treatment of Victor will target his depressive symptoms. I will help him increase his self-care, building activities that give him some pleasure and sense of accomplishment. I will examine his interpersonal patterns at work and help him find a way of interacting with his co-workers that balances his affiliative personality with his desire to feel respected. We will strengthen his marriage, helping him to communicate effectively with Leonora, both seeking support and engaging in positive activities that help them bond as a couple. As he avoids less and improves his interpersonal patterns, his self-esteem should improve. We will also explore his understanding of childhood, helping him make peace with his early life story.

Applying the Change Principles

Patient Prognostic Principles

The patient prognostic principles inform my predictions about how a patient's treatment might unfold. My experience, combined with these principles, lead me to feel optimistic and motivated beginning treatment with Victor. Consistent with Principle 1, Victor has relatively low baseline impairment, as he has reasonably stable employment, housing, and a functioning marriage. Victor has had high levels of worry and agoraphobia; however, these symptoms are not central right now. Once he feels less depressed and has an improved self-esteem, they may resurface as important targets. For now, I am more concerned with his depression, self-esteem, and interpersonal patterns. If Victor had higher baseline impairment (as in the cases of Brian and Anne that I discuss later), I might worry more about his tendency to be irritable and off-putting to others. Here, though, I am optimistic that therapy will reduce his frustration and agitation with others, leading him to be closer to his true affiliative self that wants to connect positively with others.

Victor does not seem to have a personality disorder, so Principle 2 is not in play. He has interpersonal patterns that impact his life, but he connects with others at times and can maintain meaningful relationships. Thus, I expect to be able to form a positive therapeutic relationship with him early in treatment. I will certainly work to make him feel like I accurately and empathically appreciate his struggles. I am hopeful, though, that I will also be able to help him improve some of the ways he deals with people. If he had more significant personality pathology like Anne, I might not be able to work on his patterns as early in treatment and as directly.

It is unclear how secure Victor's attachment style is (Principle 3), but he did have good relationships earlier in life with his siblings, cousins, male friends, and Leonora (unlike Brian, who had few positive connections). To the extent that he does have insecurities in relationships, it will certainly be important for us to address them. I expect that by forming a deep and meaningful connection with Victor in treatment, I may be able to further meet his needs for support and caring. His case recalls the work of Carl Rogers; under the right conditions, I am hopeful that he will naturally move toward personal growth.

Similar to Anne, Victor feels quite defective and like he won't ever be able to succeed and be respected. Thus, he may not assume that he will get better quickly and easily with treatment; Principle 4 suggests that this might reduce the chance of a positive treatment outcome. I need to demonstrate to him at the outset of treatment that it can be helpful. Indeed, I strive to identify small steps in the right direction that patients can make as early as the end of the initial evaluation. I want him to see that making changes in his approach to how he manages himself and his relationships will lead to different results, such as an improved mood and more confidence. For example, I might work with him to identify a few things he would do differently if he were going to prioritize his recovery, perhaps reaching out to old friends or investigating new leisure activities. We would negotiate concrete things to try between sessions and have him log the emotional result. He will hopefully see that more awareness and wise, strategic choices can promote significantly different results in his life. These strategies will hopefully mitigate the risk of low initial outcome expectation.

It is unclear how intrinsically motivated Victor will be to engage in therapy (Principle 5). At least we don't have evidence that he is being forced into it by others, like Brian, or is deeply conflicted about it, like Anne. I will work to make therapy feel like something Victor wants to do and encourage him to own the choice of engaging in it. I work to strengthen intrinsic motivation by planting certain seeds. I sometimes tell people that I generally take a personal growth metaphor to the work and that I hope to help people both reduce symptoms and increase thriving. With a patient who readily admits not knowing how to cope with difficulties, I might emphasize a skill-building metaphor to increase intrinsic motivation, hoping to get the person excited about adding items to their toolbox. I like the aims of therapy to be ambitious, where the patient and I seek high levels of functioning. I talk with some patients about becoming emotional leaders in their families. I hope Victor may come to enjoy treatment and even take satisfaction on sharing things he is learning with others, such as his wife. If I sensed that Victor felt pressured to continue treatment at any point, I would underline how we can be flexible about our relationship in a way that feels right to him. For instance, I could share that we can reduce session frequency at any point and that I will remain here for him. I tell patients that

I also adopt a "primary care" stance, where I see people more frequently when they are symptomatic and less frequently as they improve. However, I generally remain available to people even after an episode of active treatment has ended. I even welcome annual check-ups to support progress if patients are interested.

Victor's misery is high. He is aware that something doesn't work well in his relationships and that his mood is depressed. He tries to make changes at work, attempting to be assertive, even though he is unable to maintain a stance he feels good about. I will capitalize on his relatively high levels of change readiness (Principle 6) by intervening actively in treatment. We will help him see that therapeutic strategies can enable him to make meaningful changes.

Victor doesn't enjoy aspects of his work, and he feels trapped there financially. However, he has enough money and job security that these basic safety concerns shouldn't distract us from the symptom reduction and personal growth work that he desires. Thus, I am not concerned about the impact of Principle 7. As I will discuss, I am much more concerned about Brian's job stability.

Principle 8 warns about the impact of adverse childhood events. Victor felt mistreated by his father and burdened by caring for his siblings. However, he does not report the same level of dysfunction in his childhood as described in the cases of Brian and Anne. Thus, I expect to be able to devote more attention to his current concerns, aiming for rapid symptom relief.

Victor has had periods of significant worry and rumination, and he has noteworthy feelings of low self-worth. He is preoccupied with feeling weak and unworthy of respect and success. Consistent with Principle 9 (warning of worse outcomes for anxious patients with negative self-attributions), I will work to contextualize and depersonalize his problems. I will help him understand that his work difficulties don't mean that he is inherently inferior. Instead, we will examine his attitudes and behaviors, both at work and at home, that relate to his problems. We will also explore how his personality aligns with his current role and find ways to capitalize better on his personal strengths as a leader. Hopefully, his self-acceptance will grow over treatment.

Treatment/Provider Moderating Principles
I will aim to make my treatment consistent with Victor's level of problem assimilation (Principle 10). For example, Victor believes he has little control or power over the pressures he faces at work. Thus, I will avoid launching right into problem-solving about how to cope better there. I need to empathize and perhaps pull for exceptions to the rule. "Have you ever noticed times in which you feel more effective at work or times when you feel happy and relaxed there?"

Despite some hopelessness, Victor doesn't seem particularly resistant (Principle 11), so I can be relatively directive. After plenty of exploration and validation, I will offer many directive strategies. As an extended example of such strategies, I might take in this case, let's consider Victor's pattern of feeling dominated and controlled by others, as well as when he resists being assertive and taking a leadership position.

There is much to do to dismantle this pattern. First, I need to understand the terrain with targeted questions. Note that I tend toward an assimilative form of therapy integration, in which I assimilate contributions from different theories into my preferred theoretical lens, which is based in social learning theory and cognitive-behavioral therapy. "What is the best most recent example of the pattern?" "What was a recent situation in which you were aware of feeling controlled by others?" I would deconstruct this example and identify how it started and the mood the patient was in beforehand. If it was a work situation and he felt pushed to do something, I would ask him what he feared would happen if he pushed back. I would also help him identify an interior voice that wanted to be heard. I might try to access this voice by asking, "What would you have liked to say in this situation? Your boss wanted you to do X—were you aware of your own opinion in the moment? If I were in your head, what would I have heard you saying? If I were there—invisible and on your shoulder—and said, 'Time out, pause, slow down'—what do you think about this situation? If you had full power, what would you want?" Likely, Victor's preferences and instincts are buried under layers of fear. I want to help him identify his core need in the situation; he might want to feel power or self-respect or that other people will see his feelings as important. I might also ask Victor whether he ever feels dominated or controlled by me in therapy. We could use the safety of our relationship to explore times he feels this way and to meta-communicate about the pattern, perhaps providing an opportunity for me to use therapeutic disclosures (Principle 28) about my experience in these moments. These discussions can be powerful, memorable, and transformative; emotional experiencing levels (see Principle 36) are high when discussing relationship patterns in real time.

However, I think it can be a therapeutic error to push too forcefully for a parallel in the therapeutic relationship if either the relationship isn't ready, the patient doesn't actually feel like the pattern occurs in the therapeutic relationship in any significant way, or if it will be too uncomfortable or shame-inducing for the patient. Indeed, my sense is that more inexperienced therapists may insist that there is a similar interpersonal cycle in the therapeutic relationship in a way that feels awkward to the patient.

To further understand the cycle, I would ask for the figurative "video recordings" of what Victor does in these situations. Does he at first resist and then give in? Does he act passive-aggressively? Does he avoid asking subordinates at work to do their jobs? Once I understand his behavior, we can trace the short- and long-term consequences. In the short run, his behavior may reduce his perception of the likelihood of conflict and give him a whiff of approval and acceptance. In the long run, he may feel resentful and victimized inside, while also teaching people not to respect his needs. I will help Victor understand the "deal" he is making and begin to see if he thinks it is a "good deal"—whether the short-term bargain for reduced conflict and more acceptance is paying off. Often, we find that the behavior doesn't work "as advertised."

I want to help Victor build a more virtuous cycle; there are many ways to break the pattern. For one, I can help him explore what he would do if he was "filled with courage" and didn't need anyone else's approval. This would help us to operationalize empowered behavior. What consequences would Victor fear if he was assertive? By getting language on these fears, they tend to be easier to weaken. Sometimes, I push these fears to the extreme, helping the patient to hear the words, "I completely and totally disapprove of you" or "I no longer like you or accept you." These worst-case scenarios can help patients laugh about what seemed so powerful and inevitable before.

I explain that gradual exposure can be the "royal road" to progress. Victor and I would identify a range of ways he could stand his ground or express his needs. We would role-play assertive responses in session, have him practice between sessions, and then process the results in the next meeting. In a reverse role play, I could demonstrate strong responses while he lodged demands like his coworkers do. This exercise could also loosen his perspective on the situation. If we identified ways he feels controlled by me in therapy, we could have him practice being more direct in treatment and help him get used to more transparent conversations and interpersonal negotiations.

I might also help Victor be more self-accepting about his difficulty setting limits with his employees and others. People come in all different types of personalities and strength/vulnerability packages. It may be that setting limits with others will never be a core strength. This doesn't make him weak and unmanly. Indeed, it is likely the flip side of his strength. He may be more wired to get along with people, to empathize, and to connect. Lots of people find that they don't like managing others and are not very good at it. I would likely share that I find helping and connecting with others comes more easily than leading and directing them. I can help Victor take stock of his current job and see if there might be other roles that play to his strengths.

Principle 12 speaks to times when the patient has lower motivation or higher ambivalence for change. As I view Victor as significantly motivated (unlike Brian), I can deprioritize this principle. Sessions will involve a mix of responsive, person-centered interventions and directive, change-oriented strategies, as they usually do in my work. Victor doesn't emphasize strong preferences about his role in therapy, therapist demographics, treatment type (Principle 13), for spiritually-oriented psychotherapy (Principle 14), or for a clinician with a substance-abuse background (Principle 20). Thus, I will not focus on these variables. Indeed, I encourage trainees to "do the work of therapy," as opposed to talking about therapy and what it will entail. I prefer to demonstrate my approach rather than present a theoretical rationale that can be debated, pulling the patient into a different mode of relating. Principle 15 suggests that using too many transference interpretations with patients with poorer interpersonal functioning can be problematic. Victor has decent interpersonal functioning, despite his issues. I might use this principle to give myself the "green light" to reference our relationship when trying to help him. For instance, I might brainstorm with him situations in which he might need to be assertive with me, as his clinician, and explore what might happen if he were to express his needs and preferences. If he were able to ask for something from me, I might notice that and reinforce his efforts.

When patients have higher baseline impairment, Principle 16 suggests they might benefit from longer-term, more intensive treatment. As Victor is in moderate distress, I can use this principle to feel good about offering to see him twice weekly to start. I sometimes express to trainees that there is nothing magic about once weekly psychotherapy. Frequency is an important variable to examine with patients, as is session length. If Victor thought seeing me once per week was fine, I would accept that preference and underline my flexibility were his needs to change. In our group practice, clinicians have occasionally seen patients three or four times per week if they are helping someone avoid hospitalization.

Victor has more of an internalizing than externalizing coping style. Thus, as per Principles 17 and 18, I will work to foster Victor's awareness and understanding of his problem patterns. I will feel free to promote symptom reduction and behavioral change, too. Over the course of several months, I hope to see improvement in all these realms. As discussed previously, I hope to help him understand that he is not defective, even though he may have been caught in patterns of thinking and relating that maintain his difficulties with assertiveness at work and at home.

Like Brian and Anne, Victor's social support has been lacking. I will help him identify old or new activities that might meet some of his social needs (Principle 19). I will also identify whether there are people who used to be in his life who he might reach out to again. I may need to reframe this issue as being a crucial responsibility that he has been neglecting. "We can't expect you to do well at home and at work if your core needs for fun and connection aren't being met." I want him to feel an increased sense of duty to increase his self-care.

Patient Process Variables

Principle 21 fits well with my typical style of engaging patients actively in the treatment process. Here, I will make sure that Victor is highly engaged in treatment both during and between sessions. I will make sure, for instance, that I am in no way "lecturing" him as a primary treatment mode. Indeed, I generally have an instinct for when to follow and when to lead. If something in the dynamic between the patient and me feels "off," or if the patient seems less engaged, I notice this, slow down, check on the patient's motivation for treatment (Principle 5), resistance level (Principle 22), problem assimilation level (Principle 10), change readiness (Principle 6), or whether there was an alliance rupture (Principle 27).

My sessions typically have a flow to them. I start with updates, clarify a focus, work the focus, set collaborative goals for the week, and then do an alliance and learning check—making sure the patient feels good about what we did and can summarize their key takeaways. Early in treatment, I want Victor to know what he needs to do to make small, meaningful progress. Indeed, we will collaboratively generate ideas for possible steps in the right direction; I usually ask patients what they think would help first, then share my ideas, and go back and forth as naturally as possible. If Victor responds negatively or defensively to my ideas, I might shift to more of a motivational interviewing stance, promoting his autonomy to explore steps he has considered. Ideally, I want Victor to focus on "direction and effort," taking positive steps in the direction of his goals. I then want him to take credit for any efforts he made, as it is his effort that is most controllable.

By the end of the evaluation session, I will be asking myself and Victor to discuss where to start and what to prioritize. I might bias a patient to starting on what is bothering them the most. Or, I may start where they can pick up an "easy win" and build momentum. These strategies are consistent with the principle of active patient engagement.

Because patients who are more resistant to the therapist or therapy may benefit less than if they are less resistant (Principle 22), I will try to avoid provoking resistance. Indeed, I will not "push" Victor to do things. Instead, I will listen carefully and help him draw connections and contemplate next steps. On occasion, I might make him a proposal or give him an invitation to try things. I don't expect my typical interventions will generate much resistance with Victor, given his presentation, as they might with Brian or Anne.

Therapy Relationship Principles

I derive much of my treatment philosophy, stance, and style from the literature on therapy relationship principles. Indeed, I describe my approach as "alliance-focused, cognitive-behavioral therapy." There are numerous ways

I would attempt to develop a high-quality alliance with Victor (Principle 23). When I begin treatment with a new patient, I organize the patient's problems into themes that feel accurate and clarifying to both of us. At first, I don't struggle to make these themes completely independent from one another or to identify causal chains among them. Instead, I try to capture the main concerns expressed by patients and to reflect their emotional priority to them using language that helps to simplify and make them feel understood (Principle 26). I want Victor to say, "Yes! Exactly—that's it."

After exploring his concerns and taking his full history, I would ask Victor if it was OK for me to summarize his most salient treatment targets as I see them. I want Victor to feel like, "OK, I have nine problems and targets for treatment, but they can be organized and summarized. And there aren't 50 of them—there are 9." Note that I tend to start the summarizing, rather than putting it on the patient to do so, as this is part of how I deeply empathize with the patient's concerns. After summarizing, I check for fit and invite the patient to summarize as well, especially if they see things differently.

Patients often begin therapy feeling bothered by an overwhelming cloud of problems. I want to help the clouds part and for them to see manageable "piles." In the case of Victor, these issues include depressive symptoms; social isolation; conflict with his wife; yearning for more support and validation from Leonora and others; making peace with his painful memories of his unavailable and critical father; occasional irritability, frustration, and hostility toward others; insecurity and tendency to let himself be passive and dominated by others; shame, self-criticism, and emotional downward spiral when he fails at being more assertive; and his core belief, and resulting shame, that he is unsuccessful, unloved, and unaccepted. By listening carefully and organizing the issues the patient presents to me, I hope to rapidly build a sense that we can see targets and we are going to work together to hit them. As treatment unfolds, we can also address his motivation to make changes on these different targets (Principle 12). Also connected with the establishment of a good alliance is the collaborative work in identifying what goals, or themes, to prioritize early in therapy and what steps to take toward progress (see Principle 21).

Principle 24 emphasizes the importance of therapist regard and affirmation. I try to show regard in the first contacts with the patient. I shake hands, make sure that the patient found the office OK, and point out where the bathrooms are. I direct the patient where to sit (on a comfortable couch) to reduce anxiety and uncertainty in the situation. I train students to clarify names explicitly, making sure I call the patient what they wish to be called—I use "Ben" and not Benjamin, as I would find using my full name off-putting and a marker of relationship distance. By giving patients an overview of how I tend to run sessions (e.g., reviewing steps in the right direction and then choosing a central focus), I am also conveying respect, socializing them to the process of therapy directly and helping them feel like they are in competent hands.

Later in treatment, I might show respect and regard for the patient's needs by emphasizing my flexibility about the frequency of meetings. I might make it clear to Victor that we can move to meeting every two or four weeks, as he sees fit, and also that we can return to meeting weekly, if needed. I also try to convey affirmation of the patient's importance to me, to treat as valid their feelings, preferences, and needs, and to respect their inherent worth and value. In Victor's case, I can listen and reflect his personality traits and natural interpersonal tendencies (e.g., being more affiliative) and help him see these as valid. I could use self-disclosure (Principle 28) and share that some high-conflict work cultures would be a bad match for me. I might also affirm Victor's need and desire to feel genuine affection and respect from others; we are social creatures and this need is valid and understandable. I will try to build hope that this need can be met and help him build skills and make changes to his environment to allow him to feel more successful.

Principle 25 identifies the utility of therapist congruence. I take this as a calling to be authentic with patients—revealing my true personality rather than trying to "play a role" (such as the expert role) or have a façade with patients (like I am aloof or disinterested). I suspect this principle comes into play in many ways in my work. I dress in a way that feels right to me in my professional work (neither too casual or too formal—I am professional, but comfortable). I have chosen the colors, furniture, and fabrics in my office carefully, in a way that I hope feels warm and inviting. I greet people with a smile and I am not shy about looking like I am happy to see them and eager for diving into the work; I am almost always eager to hear the updates and to help people move forward in their lives. I suppose that I love the role of therapist and love helping people with their personal growth; this part of life is a natural fit for me. With Victor, I can convey authenticity by giving him honest feedback when the situation calls for it, such as if he avoided a situation that called for assertiveness, and helping him identify ways to be more courageous next time. I might be funny or tell a relevant story if I felt so inclined. I sometimes use the language, "So I am not distracted by it, I would like to offer a suggestion about what you could say in this interaction"—underlying my own desire to contribute something in particular. I am usually quite present and invested, and I hope this shows. As another example of how I can be genuine with Victor, if he clings to a powerless, victim-oriented stance regarding his work life, I can challenge that directly. After sufficient empathy and validation, I can own my stance strongly if need be, "Victor, I would like to offer you my perspective on your work life, and I think we can find you a lot more power to express yourself than you experience now." Later in treatment, I might convey authenticity by sharing how happy I am that he is feeling so much better or is proud of the changes he has made.

Principle 26 underlines the facilitative role that therapist empathy plays in treatment. I will meet each situation Victor presents with a typical flow. This includes exploration, empathy, and validation. I train students to always validate feelings and to seek what makes sense about someone's perspective before challenging thoughts and filters on a situation. I will try to put myself in Victor's shoes and make sure I deeply understand his perspective before doing or saying anything else. Indeed, I hope my patients feel more thoroughly understood by me than they have almost ever felt before. I can show Victor empathy in a number of different ways. I can acknowledge how painful it is when he feels disconnected from his wife or that I understand how frustrating it can be to feel like you are emotionally drowning and yet have people pushing you to go against your interpersonal nature. I would validate how his reactions make sense; his strong dislike of conflict makes it so much easier to avoid pressing his views on his employees. I can convey that his emotions—the way he feels about his life—are important and worth prioritizing.

He has been so miserable lately, having "painful ruminations," and he is sick of this emotional cycle. I can empathize with how powerless he feels to stop other people from controlling him, acknowledging that he feels both powerless and frustrated by his inability to change this state. I can empathize with his core needs for love, respect, and support, as well as to feel good about himself. These are all common human needs, and many people struggle if they don't feel like these needs are well met. Normalizing his feelings and outlook is part of conveying my appreciation for his perspective.

Principle 27 concerns alliance ruptures and the power of rupture-repair cycles to help people grow. To promote the prevention and resolution of alliance tears, I will tell Victor at the beginning of treatment to "have a big mouth" and let me know if I don't seem to be understanding him. I make a deal, usually in first sessions: "Relationships are a lot about communication. I will give it to you straight every step of the way, and I will ask you to do the same." I explain that I am not a mind reader, but I am flexible, so "please communicate." I hope these moves prevent alliance ruptures and guide him if he does feel misunderstood by me. Because he is prone to feeling controlled and dominated by others, I will ask him periodically if there have been ways in which he has felt controlled by me. I hope he gets better at expressing his needs in the moment, slowing things down when he gets the first glimpse he feels controlled. If he does convey even a hint of reluctance about something, I will reinforce it and appreciate the difficulty of this move for him.

As I alluded to earlier (when mentioning that I prefer to help rather than direct people), there are numerous times when I would make use of Principle

28 regarding supportive self-disclosures. I will try to tell Victor many memorable, meaningful stories, being careful that they are for his benefit, not mine. A good story can stick with us forever. Recently, when helping a patient explore a growing recognition of what he wanted in life, I told him a story about how someone I know has traded cars numerous times and how this struck me as a powerful example of how some people are able to be very in touch with their wants and feel empowered to act upon them. If Victor needed to fire someone at work, I might offer my own upset at the few times I have needed to do the same. Recently, I normalized someone feeling overwhelmed by responsibilities by saying ways I related to that feeling—and how important it can be for me and most of us to learn what to do when overwhelmed and how to resist urges to procrastinate and avoid.

Therapist Intervention Principles

Principle 29 notes the utility of general psychodynamic interpretations. As a cognitive-behaviorally oriented clinician, I don't typically use this language; I do, however, work with patients to identify the origins of core beliefs and to identify how repetitive interpersonal patterns have evolved over time. I might also help people explore the function of a behavior in their lives. I might work with Victor to explore the origins of his insecurities and how avoiding asserting himself may work to protect him from feared consequences. I believe that a patient's learning history is important and that identifying how an "old pattern" developed can help people "depersonalize" it a bit, seeing that the problem isn't inherently "them" but developed out of experience and necessary (though now dated) ways of coping.

Principle 30 emphasizes that the quality of an interpretation matters. Indeed, I will address with Victor his most central interpersonal patterns, picking the right battles to fight and leaving less central patterns alone. His tendency to feel dominated and controlled is central to his distress, thus deserving of the most focus. Note that I say more in the following discussion about the implementation of both Principles 29 and 30 when discussing how I would explore Victor's relationship with his father.

Principle 31 recommends the utility of clinician's receiving feedback on a routinely delivered outcome measure. However, people see me for so many different reasons and their central concerns differ. I worry that giving all of my patients a paper-and-pencil measure each session may reduce the sense of personalization I work so hard to convey. There are also practical barriers that make it cumbersome in routine practice to implement, such as how to administer and record scores. Thus, I will use an interview-based approach to gather regular feedback from Victor. I will assess his functional and emotional progress most sessions. I can ask about his efforts to implement the changes we have agreed upon, perhaps in how he is managing tensions with his wife or co-workers. I will get a sense of his mood on average and at his best and worst in the week. I will have him compare his overall mood to the prior week and to months before as treatment progressed. If he reports little change in mood or has trouble following through on goals, I will address this directly.

I will also give Victor credit for the efforts and changes I hear in his reports, consistent with Principle 32 regarding the importance of giving patients feedback about their progress. If I truly believe he has managed a situation far differently and better than he would have prior to treatment, I want to make sure to acknowledge this. I want him to strive for progress, notice progress, and celebrate progress. My acknowledgement is crucial.

I convey my flexibility toward treatment in many ways, consistent with Principle 33. I give people "multiple choice" questions. If I ask Victor what he wants to work on, and he says he isn't sure, I don't leave him stranded. I might say, "Well, we left off last time talking about how stressful it was giving out new schedules to people at work. I am happy to hear more about how that is going. Or, we could talk more about your marriage or other career options." I very consciously try to convey flexibility within organization. There are topics, targets, strategies, and themes. More generally, I recommend working on whatever feels most emotionally salient to the patient on a given day and weave in strategies and connect themes in the context of that issue. I also convey flexibility by being willing to change when we meet, how frequently we meet, or even in which of my offices we meet. If a reliable patient needs to miss an occasional session because of a last-minute change to his work schedule, I would likely forgive the cancellation fee; if missed sessions become a routine issue, I will address it directly. There are, of course, limits to my flexibility. If, for example, a patient just wants to talk and clearly expresses no desire to make changes in their lives, it isn't a good match for me and I will refer out. If a patient is aggressive with front-desk staff, and I can't help them communicate with respect, I might also need to set a clear limit and recommend other options.

My work with Victor would use Principle 35, emphasizing the value of promoting self-understanding, and Principle 34, on the importance of fostering adaptive interpersonal changes, quite directly. As mentioned in my discussion of Principle 9 about negative self-attribution, I would help him revisit his interpretation of his interpersonal problems (being inherently inferior), as well as identifying, accepting, and making use of his own personal leadership strengths. As also previously discussed in detail (see Principle 11), I would help him to examine the drivers of his interpersonal behavior and try to build new patterns. He would hopefully become much more flexible and self-aware in his high-risk situations, especially when he is likely to feel bowled over by others.

There are numerous ways in which I would help Victor deepen his emotional experiences in sessions, consistent with Principle 36. This happens easily, as I slow him down to unpack difficult situations, looking at what he was feeling in his heart and body—as when I described helping him finding his needs and preferences that have been buried under layers of fear (see Principle 11). By engaging in role plays, I also increase emotional processing and make the learning multimodal. Rehearsing new behavior is a powerful way of learning.

I would certainly be using Principle 38 predominantly; that is, trying to help Victor experiment with numerous behavior changes. I do this by encouraging several mindsets. For one, I emphasize "no commitment—try things on that we discuss." I explain that we want to lower the "barrier to entry" for new behavior—no pressure to keep at a change we are first making. I will make some direct suggestions to try out new behaviors if I believe that our relationship is solid enough for it to be well received. For example, if Victor wanted to give feedback to an employee who was frequently late for work, I might ask him if I could make a suggestion and then offer him something that I say in such situations. As these interventions (as well as many other previously described) show, the implementation of Principle 38 frequently fosters adaptive interpersonal changes highlighted by Principle 34.

How I will address Victor's depressive symptoms of anhedonia, low energy, and avoidance provides another example of how I promote behavioral changes. One strategy is to build a menu of positive activities that might eventually bring him a sense of pleasure or accomplishment. Indeed, I take the cognitive-behavioral view that if I can help patients engage in new, positive behaviors, their thinking, and, ultimately, their feelings are interconnected and will likely shift, too. I can take an index card and have Victor write on one side as a title "Menu of pleasurable, relaxing activities" and on the other side, "Menu of possible accomplishments." We would brainstorm activities first for one side and then the other. I might ask him about what he used to enjoy, what he would do if he were feeling better, and things he has vaguely considered doing. To identify accomplishments, I would take inventory of things he avoids. I would identify activities that he could do independently and accomplishments that would be more social. Also as a way to foster self-understanding (Principle 35), I would educate him that an accomplishment when someone is depressed may be very different from an accomplishment when they are not depressed. In addition, I would try to interrupt any tendency toward comparisons—what is an accomplishment for one person might not be an accomplishment for another. Comparisons are not relevant. When someone is highly depressed, having a shower or going to a local coffee shop can be huge victories. It is my job to help the patient appreciate these victories. Note that there may be some patients who are more resistant to these interventions or for whom they would not be well-received (see Principles 11 and 22). I will comment more with the subsequent case about how I manage clients who are not as trusting and receptive as Victor is likely to be. However, it can be said that, generally, if a patient responded negatively to my framing their efforts as victories, I would be sensitive to this perception and perhaps take more of a following stance. I would let them know what felt like progress to me and then use empathic reflections about their frustration with my misperceptions.

I would also encourage Victor to use the line I use to encapsulate much research—"Motivation follows action." I would help him realize that if he is waiting to feel better before acting, he will be waiting a long time. I would train him to override his motivational system and to use his "frontal cortex" to direct him to engage, despite not feeling like it. I might self-disclose (again, consistent with Principle 28) my love of my own couch (with a sense of humor) and normalize for him that "nothing is easier than my couch." I would explain that I am often conscious of not asking myself whether I feel like or "want" to do something; I let my values guide me, or my sense that "my future self will thank me." The motivation may follow eventually. I also train people in the principle, "If it is healthy, you will get used to it." I discuss with people how a major life challenge is that we get desensitized to "our own junk." We get used to avoiding things and not doing things. This creates a challenge. We can train ourselves to take action despite not feeling like it and not being used to it.

To further promote behavioral changes, early in treatment I will discuss the concept of avoidance.

As in anxiety disorders, I find patients with depression are often engaged in extensive avoidance patterns. I will discuss with Victor the things he tends to avoid, both small and large. Does he avoid returning phone calls or responding to text messages? Does he avoid paying his taxes or scheduling doctor visits. I will help him appreciate the subtle and not so subtle emotional consequences of avoidance. As avoided tasks pile up, he is likely to feel more overwhelmed and more like a failure. This pattern reinforces a very disempowered view of himself.

I will also pair the discussion of avoidance with the central role of approach behavior. I will try to interest him in "living a life of approach." This means I want him relentlessly strengthening approach behavior even when he doesn't feel like it. Every time he approaches something, he gets to feel victorious. I am also normalizing the urge to avoid. If I see someone in a grocery store, I could have an urge to run to the produce aisle. It takes some frontal cortex work to step back, question and laugh at this instinct, and then do what I value—being friendly. Note that I am conscious of trying to make sure patients are attempting changes because they make sense to them and not mainly because they are seeking my approval or fearing my disapproval. I will occasionally feel the need to make sure a given patient is owning the choice to run an experiment and has bought in to the rationale, especially if I sense hesitancy. I sometimes use the strategy of asking the patients to feed it back to me—to challenge them to explain why they would bother expending the energy or taking the risk we are discussing. I have acknowledged that patients may not be ready or interested in making a given change yet. I hope to convey that I will care about and respect the patient whether or not they are ready to attempt any changes at all (see Principles 24 and 26).

Returning to Principle 29, regarding the proportion of general psychodynamic interpretations—or links to the central interpersonal themes of the patient—it will probably be helpful to discuss Victor's childhood and his feelings around his father, especially because he emphasized in his presenting problems how he is still preoccupied by memories of how critical, demanding, and unavailable his father was. I might begin by asking him to tell me more about what his father was like, eliciting some examples. What set your father off? What would you do that would trigger him? How did you feel? What sense did you make of it? I want to help Victor draw connections—between his father's style and behavior and the way the patient experienced and filtered it. I want to help him get much clearer on the conclusions he drew from his father's domineering, yet emotionally unavailable way. Perhaps Victor developed a view of himself as inferior, inadequate, and incompetent, given the messages that were conveyed. His core need for validation and connection were not well met. It seems that Victor felt unsupported on the one hand and given the message that he was flawed and inferior on the other. If this model fit for Victor—and my interpretations were high quality (Principle 30)—I would help him to consider how it influenced his behavior and style in situations as his life unfolded. I might explain how we "find what we scan for" and how if Victor learned to scan for signs he was inferior and unaccepted, he would be much more likely to put things "in this bucket."

As I discuss Victor's past with him, I am proposing that he and all children have core needs. His desire to feel loved, respected, and seen as worthy and competent is common and natural. His needs were not the problem. I might explore how his father's style developed. I might ask Victor, "How did your father learn to look at the world in this way and end up with such a critical style?" Usually patients make the link to the ways their own parents were raised. This doesn't excuse parental behavior; however, we "are pulled to make sense of our experiences" and to find a narrative that is believable and fitting. If his father's father was frequently hit and berated, or grew up in otherwise desperate circumstances, it might help Victor to "depersonalize" his father's behavior.

Alternatively, it may be that Victor's father appears to have been "wired" to be very stoic and negative. Again, I am building an alternative perspective with

Victor—that his father's behavior is not evidence of Victor's own inadequacy but may have emerged from other places. Victor "survived the past" and has much more power as an adult to shape his narrative. This discussion may lead to emotional experiencing and deeper exploration and self-reflection in the session (Principles 35 and 36). More generally, my work with patients is characterized by working over time in a number of different ways and on a range of targets. Sometimes I am pulled to work on symptoms directly—especially when they are highly distressing—and at other times I am pulled to work on deeper themes and patterns. I tend to stick with the typically "top–down" approach of cognitive-behavioral therapy, focusing first on improving coping around current problems and gradually moving toward interventions that target core beliefs and deeper schemas. If a patient is more ambivalent about change, I stay longer in a following mode (Principle 12); if they are more externalizing, I head more quickly to suggestions for behavior change and symptom reduction (Principle 17) whereas if they have a more internalizing coping style, I focus on building self-awareness (Principle 18).

Throughout my work with Victor, I will attempt to use nondirective interventions skillfully (Principle 37). For example, I might slow Victor down in a moment to reflect what I am hearing and which piece of his story seems most emotionally salient. If he seemed to be reflecting deeply on his feelings about his father, I will stay in a following mode, making sure not to disrupt his processing. If I am successful, it will all feel very natural for Victor and he won't feel "on the spot." Again, I want him to feel better understood than he has ever felt in his life.

Case 2: The Case of Brian

Case Formulation and Treatment Plan

Prominent Clinical Features of Brian's Problems

Brian struggles with serious depressive symptoms in the context of significant alcohol dependence. He is often angry and impulsive. He is socially isolated and lacks activities and social support outside of work. He feels that his life lacks meaning and is unfulfilling. Brian can be suicidal.

Variables Most Likely Related to the Etiology or Maintenance of his Problems

Brian grew up in difficult circumstances. His father was alcoholic, frequently angry, had a violent temper, and was verbally and physically abusive. His mother was depressed and emotionally unavailable. He didn't receive much nurturance. Perhaps because of this early interpersonal learning, Brian finds it difficult to forge bonds with new people. He expects criticism and mistreatment from others. He doesn't appreciate the impact of his moods and behaviors on his relationships. He makes little effort to leave his apartment and engage in social activities, despite wishing he had more support. His alcohol use further compounds his difficulties with romantic partners and dampens his motivation for change. His patterns render him isolated, lonely, and with few things that promote positive mood.

Central Points of Focus for Treatment and General Treatment Directions
I will target Brian's depressed mood and help him increase positive activities. His alcohol use, especially at night, needs to be addressed, despite his low level of change-readiness around it. Brian needs much work on his interpersonal relationships. I will try to teach him social skills to increase positive interactions and decrease negative interactions and roll with his readiness to learn such skills and his readiness for change. He will need skills to reduce impulsive behavior when he gets in conflict or frustrated. As he develops more interpersonal skills and engages more successfully with others, he will gain social support and other outlets, which should improve his mood and optimism about life.

Applying the Change Principles

Patient Prognostic Principles
Brian has significantly more baseline impairment than Victor; Principle 1 suggests this may lead him to benefit less from psychotherapy. Thus, I will manage my expectations and the therapeutic relationship carefully. I will be practical and aim to make a positive impact on Brian's life. I will try to form a good relationship with him, convey deep acceptance, and accept that I can't change him overnight.

Principle 2 suggests that when patients have a co-morbid secondary personality disorder, treatment is less likely to be effective. Brian has had significant difficulties with trust, anger, and impulsivity for many years, in addition to the substance use issues. Whether or not he will meet criteria for a personality disorder once he is sober, his entrenched interpersonal patterns may make treatment challenging. I will encourage flexibility in him and be alert to ways that I need to modify the treatment and manage the relationship given his personality and interpersonal patterns.

It seems that Brian has not had as many positive relationships as Victor and that he may need more help to form healthy and trusting relationships. Brian also doesn't benefit from a secure attachment history (Principle 3) or particularly positive expectations about treatment (Principle 4). When these factors are present, one of my goals is to help the patient have a positive experience with a mental health professional. It is important that I don't convey frustration with him or disapproval. I don't want to overpromise; indeed, I may work to keep Brian's expectations low. Our goals are just to understand what's going on and to make things a bit better. Yet, to reduce Brian's skepticism about therapy, I can explain why working together may be helpful. Basic ideas may build a useful framework. "People do better with support." "It can help to talk things through." "Simple communication tools can prevent conflicts."

I won't press the idea that treatment will be helpful; I will try to demonstrate that to him. I will convey attitudes like "I'll accept you where you are" and "Let's take it one step at a time." I will roll with his doubts, not try to eliminate them. It would be fabulous if, over time, Brian's intrinsic motivation to engage in psychotherapy increased, making him more likely to benefit (Principle 5). To support the growth of his intrinsic motivation, I might help him notice the positive consequences of small changes he makes and how others respond to him when he makes a positive effort. I will also encourage him to feel a sense of accomplishment when he makes even small changes in his habits, such as delaying the start of a drinking episode. Note that Victor blames himself for his problems much more than Brian does and needs less work to support his intrinsic motivation.

Whereas Victor was almost desperate to make changes in his patterns, Brian is not eager to change his alcohol-related behavior; Principle 6 suggests his lower level of change-readiness may make it less likely he will make progress here. Thus, I will tread softly, reflecting his own mixed feelings and curiosity about the impact of alcohol on his life. I will tell him that we can work to make drinking more of a choice than an ingrained pattern.

Principle 7 notes that when patients have financial and employment problems, treatment may be less effective. Victor's work situation was much more stable than Brian's situation. Indeed, Brian's job is crucial to his well-being and functioning. If he loses his job, his circumstances will be precarious, and it would be even harder to make progress, especially as he might need to devote his mental energy to a job search. I will emphasize the treatment priority of protecting his job and effectively managing his behavior at work. I would be as practical as possible around this topic, asking him about his lateness and what it takes to do a "good-enough" job and what would be unacceptable to his boss (thus encouraging adaptive behavioral changes; Principle 38).

I will offer basic principles of human nature, such as "People respond poorly when they feel disrespected," hoping to increase his skillfulness in work relationships. There is a similarity across these the cases of Victor and Brian in that they both need to rescript interactions with co-workers to function more effectively.

Though Victor felt his father was critical and unavailable, he had some positive family connections. Brian grew up with a father who drank and had a violent temper and a mother who was depressed and withdrawn; these adverse childhood events may hamper his progress in therapy (Principle 8), as his interpersonal foundation is poor. I can normalize for him that people with such foundations often struggle to "see the glass as half full." His family didn't help him to develop all the "people-skills" he needed. Everyone's journey is unique. Some people had it easier than he did, whereas others had it rougher. What matters is that he survived and can keep growing. At least he is not particularly focused on negative self-attributions (Principle 9) like Victor is; however, his externalizing style will present a different challenge.

Treatment/Provider Moderating Principles
Principle 10 stresses the importance of using interventions consistent with the patient's level of problem assimilation. There is some indication that Brian acknowledges that he has poor interpersonal skills, much like Victor is aware that he struggles with relationships at work. This level of awareness is vital. Relatively early in treatment I would teach him ways of preventing and repairing conflict and how to solve relational problems. Brian seems to want more connection with his brothers. As he deals more with them, he will have the chance to work on interpersonal skills. As we discuss his interactions with his brothers, I will make connections to his central interpersonal themes (Principle 30), such as mistrust, and give him feedback (Principle 32) on his communication style, for example, and support for making prosocial efforts (Principle 24).

Brian's level of problem assimilation (Principle 10) is low regarding his drinking and romantic relationships. I will tread lightly in these areas, trying to increase his readiness to work on them. I would gently offer him language, as the topics naturally emerge, to get "titles" on these problems. For example, I might suggest that though he isn't ready for a healthy relationship yet, we could make achieving this readiness a goal. Regarding his drinking, I can reframe it from he "doesn't have strategies that work" to reduce his drinking to he is "contemplating the benefits of alcohol abstinence."

Principle 11 suggests that patients with higher versus lower levels of resistance may benefit more from psychotherapy that is relatively nondirective. In contrast with Victor, this principle is highly relevant to Brian. Indeed, I would be careful not to push too much and to get buy-in on what he wants to discuss and how he wants to make progress. I would ask his permission before teaching him a strategy. I would also undersell the strategy, saying that "this might help a tiny bit." I will work hard to avoid pulling a "yes, but . . ." response out of him. I have seen clinicians try to go into an unhelpful "teaching mode" with resistant patients. I will avoid this counterproductive stance.

Principle 12 recommends that the therapist be more responsive and person-centered when the patient has lower motivation for, or higher ambivalence about, change. I would implement this principle by taking a highly collaborative stance with Brian. I will treat him as an individual—and not like an "alcoholic" or another stereotype. Toward this goal, I make sure that I know the names and details of patients' family members. Here, I will get the details of his brothers' lives, including what they do for work and what their personalities are like. The more I know about the key players involved, the more I can personalize my interventions and comments.

Brian has not expressed preferences about his role in therapy, therapist demographics, treatment type (Principle 13), or for spiritually oriented therapy (Principle 14). Thus, I won't focus much energy on these variables. There are enough other issues to overcome. If he at some point does express preferences for, or concerns about, any of these variables, I will be responsive and provide options.

Principle 15 warns that for patients like Brian, with worse interpersonal functioning, pushing transference interpretations won't be very effective. With Victor I can profitably explore times he feels controlled by me. Here, I want Brian to experience how good it can feel to be supported and accepted and also to feel how helpful it can be to get "words on feelings" and to receive some gentle suggestions. I would be careful not to scare him out of treatment by making him feel awkward about our relationship. If he did something positive toward me, I could underline that. For example, if he thanked me for helping him to feel better on a given day, I might reflect how much I enjoy his appreciation. I want him to deepen his awareness of how most relationships work, without upsetting him.

Principle 16 emphasizes the utility of longer-term and more intensive psychotherapy when baseline impairment is high. Indeed, I would see Brian twice weekly at the outset of treatment, if he was willing. I will also accept that progress may be slow with him. This is different than the way I would likely work with Victor, whom I might see weekly at first and expect rapid improvement.

Also unlike Victor, Brian clearly has a very externalized coping style. Consistent with Principles 17 and 18, I would be very concrete with him, focusing on behavior change and symptom reduction, instead of on developing insight and self-awareness. I need to help Brian save his job. If he is late or says the wrong thing to his boss or a customer, it could cost him dearly. I often explain to trainees that the goal of psychotherapy is for people to "feel better and function better." I want to make the targets of psychotherapy very understandable for Brian. We need to work to reduce dangerous behaviors, such as driving while impaired, and help him feel more relaxed and content in ways that don't involve substances.

My work with Brian will try to build social support into his life, as per Principle 19. I would propose that he bring family members to sessions on occasion. If he were resistant to this idea, I wouldn't push it; instead, I will listen for shifts in his readiness (see Principle 6). I will review current and past people and activities to see if we can help him re-engage. I sometimes work with patients to develop two menus: one of people they might like to see more, and the other of activities they might enjoy. I then connect these people and activities. "Is there anyone who might be interested in going to the gym with you?" "What activities did you use to do with your brothers for fun?" I might even see if I could find a safe way to reconnect Brian with his mother. Perhaps by setting the stage carefully, I could help him have a successful lunch with her, as one step toward repairing that relationship and helping him to get what emotional benefit he can from it. Note that if I thought a patient did not have the skills to make outings with relatives successful, I would adapt the intervention. I have seen patients for whom it was the right step to practice going to a coffee shop alone or for whom joining a pick-up soccer game would be a better match than going on a dinner date requiring hours of extended conversation.

I am glad that Principle 20 suggests that a therapist without a substance abuse problem can still be effective. If Brian asked directly whether I am in recovery or had been to AA, I would have a sensitive discussion with him and ultimately tell the truth. I will emphasize that I will do all I that can to understand his experience and ask him to tell me if I seem to not understand his experience at any point.

Patient Process Variables
Consistent with Principle 21, I will encourage Brian to participate actively in the treatment process. I make sure to identify what patients can do to make progress outside of sessions. For example, I might negotiate with Brian a plan to resume exercise, as physical activity tends to boost mood, and he has a history of enjoying sports. If he agreed to go to the gym, I could ask him to call and leave me a message about how it went. I want to increase his activity level and have him feel accountable for progress. I also hope that he enjoys sharing his victories with me. Similar to my work with Victor, I can keep him active in sessions by rehearsing new ways of communicating. We might identify a typical situation that leads to conflict, discuss new ways of handling it, and then

role-play the encounter. This would help him to be stimulated during the session and to see ways of following through afterward.

If pursuing therapeutic directions in sessions often led to significant resistance or pushback with a patient, I would be alert to this and avoid power-struggles. I may need to accept, as Principle 22 suggests, that therapy won't be quite as beneficial or transformative for a more versus less resistant patient. Also, as per Principle 11, for therapy to beneficial for a sometimes-resistant patient, I may need to be less directive and more supportive of the patient's autonomy in the face of any such resistances. With Brian, I will be alert to when to follow and when to lead. There may be days on which I will relax into a very supportive mode, acknowledging his feelings that other people are responsible for making life difficult for him. What matters most is that the person in front of me is progressing on their own yardstick of progress. Moreover, comparisons with others' rates of progress aren't relevant.

Therapy Relationship Principles
So much of my approach with patients derives from early training in Principle 23—that when the patient's experience of alliance quality is high, they may experience greater progress in treatment. I use numerous strategies to increase the chance that my patients will feel a strong connection to me as their therapist, as well as to the goals of therapy and the ways we work to achieve the goals. Like with Victor and Anne, to facilitate our relational bond, I will work extremely hard to make sure that Brian feels understood by me and, as I previously mentioned, that he feels deeply accepted by me. I will aim for many accurate empathic reflections—I want him to feel like I really do understand what the world looks like in his boots. I will try to be what Arnold Lazarus called "an authentic chameleon" and speak his language—using metaphors to which he relates and common terms he uses (Lazarus 1993). This may be one way of showing him regard and affirmation (Principle 24). I would also help Brian to realize that he does have goals, even if they aren't clearly formulated. We might link the tasks and goals together by agreeing to work on his people-skills to protect his job and to build better relationships at work.

I generally try to communicate significant positive regard and affirmation to my patients, consistent with Principle 24, and tons of empathy, as per Principle 26. With Brian, I will point out his strengths whenever possible, perhaps emphasizing his ability to be independent. I will give him credit and congratulations for his victories and be patient and kind when he makes a mistake and gets in a conflict. Drawing on Principle 25, I would also be genuine and congruent. If he handled something in a problematic way, I will make sure he takes some helpful lesson from it and learns some alternative way of handling the situation in the future. I want him to know that I am giving it straight to him every step of the way—and that I am not being phony. His greater issues with mistrust may make him more sensitive to people being phony than Victor.

In the spirit of Principle 27, on the importance of repairing alliance ruptures, I would be alert to signs that Brian felt misunderstood or invalidated and attempt to repair quickly. On numerous occasions in therapy, I recognize that "everything is easier said than done," to make it clear that patients don't have to feel embarrassed if they fail a task. At the beginning of treatment, I may request that people let me know if they think that they aren't getting anywhere in therapy. I let them know that although I am not a mind reader, I am flexible and have many ways of working on issues. Principle 28 notes the benefit of supportive self-disclosures. With Brian, I can use stories to validate how hard it can be to get along with other people, how easy it is to find yourself in a rut, and to normalize his mixed feelings about his father. I might share times where I used the strategies that I am offering him to help change my own habits.

As with the case of Victor, and referring again to Principle 23, I will also try to build the alliance by organizing and clarifying the issues he identifies at the outset of treatment. In Brian's case, I could see if these issues capture what he wants to address: serious depression; significant alcohol use, especially at night; social isolation; anger and impulsivity; lack of positive activities and social and family support; poor people skills; and feeling like his life is lacking in meaning and is unfulfilling. I will see if this recounting feels right to him and then work to prioritize the targets. If Brian asked me for guidance about where to start, I would determine which issue felt most bothersome to him; Brian is much more resistant (Principle 11) and more ambivalent about change (Principle 12) than Victor, so I need to be cautious about being directive with him. In all likelihood, it would not be his drinking behavior that Brian would identify. However, I would float the idea of addressing alcohol use first and note the response. I would explore the option of 12-step meetings with him and see if he had ever considered them. If he would be willing to try a meeting, I would expect it to be helpful, especially given his isolation. I wouldn't push it with him, though, as he clearly doesn't like to be controlled by others (see Principle 22); with Victor's style I could take more of a lead. I would gently give Brian the alert up front that we can try to make things better, but that if we don't get anywhere, we may need to have him try a formal substance abuse program.

Therapist Intervention Principles

Principle 32 suggests it can be helpful to give patients feedback on their performance in treatment. Brian needs much affirmation and encouragement. I would be explicit when I thought he did a good job in session, such as when he considered another person's point of view and demonstrated open-mindedness. If I thought he was doing a good job following through on out-of-session agreements, I would tell him so. If he wasn't following through, I would be clear about that and explore the barriers as well.

I find it easy and important to be flexible about how I deliver treatment, consistent with Principle 33. I would use the word *flexible* many times with Brian. Indeed, I might tell him my standard joke—that flexible is my favorite "F-word." We would be open on a given day to change our topic for discussion and be creative about how to make changes. I won't be shy about giving him options. "We've been working on exercise, conflicts at work, and what you do on the weekend. Would you like to follow up on any of those topics, or are there other places we should go today?" I would also notice whether more cognitive or more behavioral strategies seemed to work better with the patient. If he didn't seem to like the metaphor of being a scientist about his thoughts, demonstrated by his comments or nonverbal messages, I would drop it and head in another direction.

As with Victor, much of my work with Brian would be about fostering adaptive interpersonal and behavioral changes, as Principles 34 and 38 encourage. Relying on Principle 35 (increase of self-understanding), we would first help him to become more aware of his behavior toward others, both when things are calm and during conflict. I would then help him to learn and rehearse new ways of communicating and interacting with others to prevent and resolve relational problems. For example, I would help him increase his positive behaviors toward others, like giving more compliments and expressing appreciation. I would also help him reduce negative behaviors toward others, such as being irritable or rude. As I described in addressing Principles 7, 17, and 21, I would implement several interventions aimed at interpersonal and behavioral changes to help Brian save his job, increase his level of activity, and reduce dangerous behaviors associated with drinking.

By processing his feelings toward his father and other family members, I would help Brian deepen his emotional experiences in treatment. Principle 36 reflects the positive benefit of helping patients have powerful emotional experiences in sessions. I might also help him to slow down and really notice moments that he felt better and how good it can be to have some relief or hope. With a patient like Brian, with so many obvious problematic behaviors, it may be especially important to keep asking him about how he *feels*. By talking about emotions more, I hope to increase his general self-awareness of his internal state. I might need to get him used to slowing down, looking inward, and finding words for some of the emotional subtleties he has been numbing. As he is more aware of his feelings, his self-understanding may also increase (Principle 35).

If Brian expresses resistance about tackling the substance issue and he is passive about what else to work on, I would propose that we start reducing depressive symptoms. I would explore activities that could give him pleasure, peace, or energy. I would certainly include exercise on the list and see if we could interest him in getting back in touch with his athletic roots and engaging in something else physical. I would suggest ways he could get going by walking, weight lifting, or jogging—emphasizing those he had tried before. When people are down, it is better to start by proposing behaviors already in their repertoire, as opposed to completely unfamiliar activities. These interventions would be used not only to encourage behavioral changes (Principle 38) but also to foster patient engagement in treatment (Principle 22). If he were unable to overcome his depressive inertia and continued to do little outside of drinking in his house, we would discuss this directly and problem-solve. This might include me accepting that he is not ready for doing more activities out of the house.

I would look to increase the number of supportive people in Brian's life any way that I could, and as quickly as possible (fostering adaptive interpersonal changes and new behavior; Principles 34 and 38). As previously mentioned (see Principle 19), I would propose a family meeting, bringing his brothers or mother into session. Engaging in basic activities together would likely improve his mood. I would be practical with them and figure out what they could do together that all would enjoy and be willing to do. To improve the chance of success, I would suggest they save difficult topics for sessions.

Though I wish Brian would go to a full-fledged substance abuse program, I might very well find myself helping Brian modify his drinking behavior myself, as he seems to minimize the importance of the issue and blame external factors. I prefer to do patients like this some good, seeing it as a precious opportunity to engage with them in mental health treatment, rather than drawing a hard line and sending them away, where it may be years before they are ready to seek substance help. To work on his drinking problem, to the extent he is willing and interested to do so, I would identify alternative activities for him to do after work and on the weekends. I want to help him find things that compete with drinking and help him to delay the onset of it—and hopefully ultimately reduce the quantity. I would identify places that he could go before going home, like the grocery or home improvement store. There may be projects around the house he has been meaning to do. Are there things he can do that, as I mentioned before, would make him feel relaxed and content without having to drink (see Principle 17)? Are there people he can call, text, or visit instead of drinking? We can survey his brothers about what they do when they are not working. I can help Brian identify how he finally decides to go to bed at night. Can I work with him to make it easier to end a drinking episode and go to bed? I might use a solution-focused idea and help him scan for exceptions (i.e., times he doesn't drink at all). I can teach him about cravings and urges and help him learn to surf them better, seeing that with delay and distraction, his urges will often go down on their own. I would help him learn that no single urge to drink lasts forever. I can also explore the function drinking serves in his life and help him more clearly understand the value he is placing on it. When successful, the combination of these interventions aimed at adaptive behavioral and interpersonal changes show how patients with substance abuse can be helped by psychotherapy, even when it is provided by therapists without history of substance problem (Principle 20).

As another major treatment target, I would help Brian track relationship conflicts and teach him ways of being more effective with others (again, see Principles 34 and 38). If he seems uninterested in improving his relationships with others, that will become a point of exploration. If he is willing, I would gather examples of times he gets frustrated or angry, understand the patterns, and build more effective communication and coping skills. Many of the strategies discussed in the case of Victor would be relevant. I suspect that Brian and I would have many discussions about episodes of work stress. I will help him to "get in front" of conflict episodes, communicating his needs clearly and preventatively. He will get better at giving others the benefit of the doubt and experiment with expressing more appreciation, compliments, and respect to others. In line with Principle 35 (fostering self-understanding), I would underline helpful mindsets and attitudes for him to consider, such as "Try to understand where people are coming from," as people often misperceive intentions. I would also try to increase Brian's awareness of how he appears to other people and help him to more carefully consider how he wants to be seen. I hope to strengthen his motivation to get along well with others. Maybe, over time, we will increase his understanding of his central interpersonal themes (Principles 29 and 30).

If Brian can feel a little less depressed, moderate his substance abuse, reduce his conflict episodes at work, and relate better to his family members, it would help a lot. Later in treatment, and consistent with Principles 19 and 34, I might also work to build more communities around him. Can I find one or more social groups that he finds rewarding and supportive? Softball teams, hiking groups, or fitness places? We need some group outside of work to which he can belong. Note that I wouldn't encourage dating until most of these other targets were improved. We need to increase his readiness for a healthy romantic relationship. Eventually, this can become a focus.

Principle 37 focuses on the importance of using nondirective interventions skillfully. With Brian, much more than with Victor, given his distress level and self-blame, it will take a lot of skill to keep him engaged in treatment. In particular, and directly related to nondirective interventions, I would want to be alert to Brian's reactions to empathic reflections. Some patients may be reactive to the idea of having feelings, not wanting to appear weak. The belief that having and displaying feelings makes someone weak and vulnerable may need to be directly examined. Nondirective interventions, such as supportive and validating statements, would also be crucial tools in working with Brian's expected high level of resistance (see Principle 22).

Case 3: The Case of Anne

Case Formulation and Treatment Plan

Prominent Clinical Features of Anne's Problems
Anne currently struggles with sadness and despair, and an extremely poor view of herself. She is preoccupied with her failures in relationships and in finding a life path, and she gets frustrated with being unable to make changes. She has trouble being alone and wants to connect to others. However, when she tries to get close to others, she has trouble maintaining the relationship. She usually ends up disappointed. Her outlook on life is bleak, as she feels lonely, unfulfilled, and hopeless.

Variables Most Likely Related to the Etiology or Maintenance of Her Problems
Anne offers a limited view of her childhood. She describes her father in positive terms yet gives the sense he was not very interested in her. Her mother seems to have struggled with mood and self-esteem problems; their relationship also lacked warmth and closeness. She describes her older brother as extremely mean, and she felt jealous of her highly social younger sister. Thus, Anne left childhood without a firm sense of connection and self-worth. Anne's insecure sense of self seems to contribute to a feeling of drifting in life and a focus on gaining others' approval. Her neediness promotes difficulties staying connected and building relationships, as other people don't provide the level of support, security, and self-worth that she wishes they did. Her lack of self-awareness of her role in these relationship patterns further hampers her ability to get her needs met and to have healthy boundaries.

Central Points of Focus for Treatment and General Treatment Directions
Forming a good working therapeutic relationship will be a key focus of treatment with Anne. We will need to patiently work to help her build self-awareness, without feeling intensely defective as she sees her role in problems. Treatment will involve establishing healthy therapeutic boundaries, letting her feel supported, while also tolerating the limitations of a therapeutic

relationship. I hope to strengthen her sense of self and her core abilities. I want to decrease her need for approval from others and build more capacity for independence. As her self-worth improves, she will be in a better place to tolerate the ambiguities of forming and retaining relationships with others. She will hopefully learn that she can have a whole social support network, filled with imperfect people, and yet end up getting many of her needs met. Later in treatment, we can identify what she needs in a primary romantic relationship and how to navigate the strong emotions involved. After some progress, we will weave in and out of her early life story, developing a narrative around her childhood that helps her to have more peace and closure—and that helps her know how to move forward with her family members.

Applying the Change Principles

Patient Prognostic Principles

Many of the prognostic principles suggest that Anne may have difficulty in treatment and be less likely to benefit from it. She has high baseline impairment (Principle 1) like Brian, significant and enduring relationship and personality issues (Principle 2; more than as evidenced by Victor and quite different in nature than Brian); an insecure attachment style (Principle 3), whereas Brian had a more avoidant style; and mixed feelings about whether therapy will be helpful (Principle 4). Like Victor, she also makes many negative self-attributions for her problems (Principle 9). The goal is to use these principles to benefit the treatment and manage expectations of the process, not to reduce hope. I maintain hope by keeping an open mind about how treatment will unfold and trusting that there is plenty of room for progress, despite the personality issues. Indeed, even small improvements in how Anne feels about herself and how she interacts with others may lead to tremendous improvements in her quality of life.

Principle 5 suggests that patients who are more intrinsically motivated to engage in therapy (like Victor and unlike Brian) may benefit more from it. Perhaps I can reinforce Anne's interest in the process of therapy and support her curiosity about what might happen in working together. There have been times I have tried to demonstrate to patients that though they may have engaged in therapy before, each treatment relationship is unique and may lead to surprising differences. Indeed, I will try to get her to see me as a unique individual and not "just another therapist."

Though Anne has some significant hopelessness about change, she is also sick of how she is feeling, much like Victor. Where is her level of change-readiness (Principle 6)? Perhaps I will be able to use her misery as dynamite to propel experiments with new behavior. "What do you have to lose?" may be a relevant angle as we are discussing new approaches. I can also use this principle by identifying domains of her life in which she is most ready to make changes. For instance, she is so lonely that discussions of a group-based activity to try, such as a yoga or exercise class, might be met with more acceptance. She doesn't have Brian's level of significant substance abuse, which makes it harder for him to feel motivated to leave the home.

Anne is working part-time in a public library. It seems that her socioeconomic status and her employment won't be key barriers to treatment (Principle 7), similar to Victor. I am eager to explore her occupational history and future options with her at some point. Even working in the library may be an important outlet we can build on. Does she have co-workers she likes there? Maybe I can identify parts of the experience that reflect genuine interests or strengths she has. Does she relate better to the younger children, the teens, or maybe the senior citizens? I want Anne to notice the parts of her life that are working. I am always looking to shrink a patient's sense of their problem areas. I use the language of "capabilities" frequently in therapy. I might notice that she is capable of going to work, having a good shift, and being friendly to her co-workers.

Will Anne's adverse childhood events make progress in treatment less likely (Principle 8)? As she wasn't open to discussing her childhood much, it isn't clear how severe her experiences were. As she feels more comfortable with me, I hope to better gauge her level of pain in her childhood. I suspect her relationships with her siblings will be important in understanding her life story.

Treatment/Provider Moderating Principles

I can employ Principle 10, using interventions consistent with Anne's assimilation level, by starting with concerns with which she is clearly aware. For instance, she seems to focus on failure and inadequacy, much as Victor does. I could discuss the failures on which she ruminates and help her develop accurate and helpful ways of understanding them. I would encourage her to be kinder and more compassionate with herself if she did perceive failures. It can be useful to help patients list many factors outside of themselves that contributed to a negative outcome.

How directive or nondirective to be with Anne? Principle 11 notes that patients with higher levels of resistance may benefit from less directive psychotherapy. I would be very conscious of this dynamic in my work with her. There may be problems and topics around which she would be open to more direct suggestions and tools. For instance, she may be receptive to making a list of her strengths and accomplishments, which hopefully won't be too threatening. On the other hand, if she seemed highly reactive talking about her relationship with Peter, I might need to follow more, reflecting her intense mixed feelings about him. When supervising beginning therapists, I explain that my sessions would look extremely different depending on the patient. Sometimes I am sensitively following—perhaps pursuing what Leslie Greenberg and Jeremy Safran have called "the poignancy track"—noticing the soft underlying feelings experienced by the patient (Greenberg & Safran, 1987). In other moments, I take a "coaching" or encouraging stance around new behavior. I can ask a patient to experiment with an assertive way to express herself. This kind of session would involve much role-playing and switching of roles. I want Anne to know that I am capable of being both directive and nondirective—and that we can collaboratively decide what she needs on a given day.

Anne may have more ambivalence when it comes to working on building relationships with others (both male and female, friends and romantic interests). Thus, in line with Principle 12, I may need to be more responsive and person-centered with her around this topic. With some patients, I just notice and underline for them the specific individuals they seem to like. I try to weaken their generalizations (e.g., that they don't like or trust anyone), by discussing more pointedly, the people with whom they do seem to connect. Maybe I will help her to notice that some people in her life are consistent and stable. She works in a library; chances are good that there are a few such people working there. I might listen in her stories for people who seem to like and accept her or to whom she relates.

As with Victor and Brian, Anne has not expressed preferences about a preferred therapy role, therapist demographics, or treatment type or for spiritually oriented therapy (Principles 13 and 14). I will march forward attempting to work with her flexibly and genuinely, demonstrating a sincere interest in getting to know her unique life story.

In patients with more significant relationship difficulties, transference interpretations can be risky (Principle 15). Indeed, forming a solid, trusting working relationship with Anne (which can withstand tears in the therapeutic alliance) will be an ongoing task throughout much of treatment. Like with Brian, I will be sparing in how much I reference her behavior toward me as her therapist. It might play best if I focus on how her positive behavior impacts me, rather than how her negative behavior pushes me away. If she thanks me for something, I will make sure to be appreciative and emphasize our good teamwork and my appreciation for her efforts toward "making our team successful." For some patients, the notion that they are part of a "therapeutic team" can be very new and something that takes time to integrate. As they do, it can be tremendously helpful for them, as they feel better supported than they have been in past relationships.

Because of Anne's long history of relationship and self-esteem difficulties, I would prefer to see her frequently, especially early in treatment, and I will expect an ongoing, long-term relationship (Principle 16). She might be someone for whom I would make an extra effort to reschedule for another day during a week I have a conference, rather than skip a week. I might make an extra effort to negotiate a recurring appointment or two in my schedule each week (e.g., Mondays and Thursdays) so that we can both count on those visits. This is another practical way of strengthening consistence and trust in our relationship.

Principles 17 and 18 discuss how patients with internalizing (like Victor) versus externalizing (like Brian) coping styles may benefit more from psychotherapy that builds insight and self-awareness, rather than psychotherapy focused on behavior change and symptom reduction. I picture doing much work to increase Anne's self-awareness and self-acceptance, as she has a mostly internalizing style. I need to help her understand who she is in relationships, as well as who she is as an individual. I can also help her make sense of her rocky experiences with men, as well as with friends and family members. We will work patiently to discuss her "life story" and how things fit together. I hope to weave together a new narrative that reduces her sense of defectiveness and increases a "growth mindset" in her, such as is described in Carol Dweck's work (Dweck, 2007). Eventually, we will talk about her family-of-origin and her corresponding mixed feelings, what she learned from those relationships, and how she may indeed have "vulnerabilities" that I need to help her manage. Like Brian, I would also help Anne find new ways to get her social needs met (Principle 19). Given her college majors, I could work with her to find a book group. I've found that some patients can engage in and enjoy structured activities, like a pick-up soccer league, even if they aren't ready for much one-on-one engagement.

Anne has used hard drugs in the past. Fortunately, Principle 20 suggests I can be useful to her despite not having a history of substance abuse problems, as discussed in Brian's case. I will work to develop her ability to use a range of skills to cope with her thoughts, feelings, and circumstances to further reduce her risk of substance abuse.

Patient Process Variables

I will have to work to make sure Anne stays a very active participant in the therapeutic process (Principle 21). She may be at risk of being too passive in treatment. As with the other cases, I would work with her to build clarity about what progress might look like and how she can make progress between sessions. With most of my patients, I use many "positive accountability" strategies, such as having them journal or call me after they have had victories. If I felt Anne were drifting toward passivity in treatment, I would bring this up with her directly, yet sensitively. Occasionally I have patients with a habit of very passively and repetitively complaining; if Anne developed this tendency, I would try hard to interrupt it.

I need to be careful not to engage in power struggles with Anne. If a clinician pushed her to join social activities before she was ready (and feeling better about herself, perhaps), she might be resistant like Brian. Principle 22 warns that patients who are more resistant are likely to benefit less from treatment. I need to find targets that feel right to her. As always, she and I need to agree on the goals and tasks of therapy. I will help Anne "own her choices" as much as possible, making sure she feels ready to run whatever experiments we design.

Therapy Relationship Principles

As previously mentioned, the formation and consolidation of a trusting relationship will be a central principle in the treatment for Anne. Consequently, I will do all that I can to develop a high-quality alliance with her (Principle 23), promoting an emotional bond and agreement on the goals of therapy and the tasks necessary to get there. As with many patients with personality issues, Anne will benefit from copious validation and compassionate understanding (Principle 26), perhaps even more than Victor or Brian would need. I will try to convey understanding of how hard her life experiences have been and that there are good reasons she has felt and acted as she has. I also need to validate that she needs life to feel better, despite how hard it is to make that happen. I will point out Anne's strengths as they emerge and show her positive regard and affirmation (Principle 24). Much of my alliance-building work with patients is expressed in my general stance and style. I try to be relaxed, warm, and genuine (in line with Principle 25). I use the "real relationship" freely, disclosing appropriately (Principle 28) and modeling balanced boundaries in relationships. I take a humble, down-to-earth stance with patients. I try not to make people feel one-down or in a low-power position. Anne will know that I am highly engaged with her and that I truly care about her progress. There are many ways this manifests in my clinical practice. For example, I am highly accessible with people, and if there is something important going on in their treatment, I would stay in touch more frequently between sessions (text, email, calls, and more frequent visits—with some safeguards and limits around these). Much of this style would be similar across the three cases.

Relating to Principle 27, there may be alliance tears or ruptures that occur with Anne, given her exquisite sensitivity to relationship dynamics. To prevent tears, I might follow more and promote self-awareness rather than focusing her on making behavioral changes (Principle 18). If alliance issues did arise, I would take plenty of time to address them, acknowledging my role and apologizing, if necessary. In addition, I've learned over many years of practice that every once in a while, we just need to accept someone is having a very bad day and that there isn't much one can do to help. In addition to keeping the "therapeutic ship" steady, I might demonstrate to Anne that I will be there for her, week in and week out, even though she has been negative, passive, or even hostile. I've seen patients re-stabilize and re-engage with treatment, even after they acted like (or said) they would never be back.

Therapist Intervention Principles
Anne has several key interpersonal themes that therapy needs to address. For instance, she can be dependent, needy, and approval-seeking. Thus, I will help her link problematic episodes with people to her core interpersonal themes (Principles 29 and 30), as frequently and accurately as I can, making sure the links fit her experience. I hope that by helping her see how her desire for approval can lead her to do things that push people away, she will eventually feel more in control and empowered to interrupt old patterns. Indeed, I have greatly enjoyed having patients comment to me how much more successful they have become in not impulsively and destructively yielding to old hostile patterns when they feel hurt by their romantic partners, for instance.

Even if I don't use a formal outcome measure, as discussed earlier, I would be sure to monitor Anne's mood and functioning. Hopefully, by reviewing her progress as concretely as I can, she will make greater progress (see Principle 31). I might track her feelings in a variety of ways and in a range of contexts. I could ask her to rate her mood before, during, and after her shifts at work, for instance. I can help her log the number of times in a week she feels she becomes highly distressed and feels out of control. I could ask her to keep track of how many minutes a day she ruminates about Peter. The targets I track with patients change as treatment priorities change.

I will also give Anne feedback about her efforts and performance in treatment (Principle 32). I might comment that I notice how hard she is working to "catch problems early" or to "edit her words" when she is upset. I help patients notice shifts in how they are feeling and in how they are responding to the inevitable curve balls life throws at us.

I tend to conceptualize patients using broad-based social learning and cognitive-behavioral concepts. That said, I express flexibility in treatment at every turn, rather than rigidly adhere to a treatment approach (Principle 33). As an example, I might find an opportunity to educate Anne about typical cognitive distortions. Like Victor, her thoughts may be all-or-nothing and overgeneralized when it comes to her failures (see Principle 10). If she was upset on a particular day, though, about a mistake she made, I might stick with validation as opposed to pointing out distortions.

Consistent with Principles 34, 35, and 38, I will attempt to increase Anne's self-understanding and to help her make positive changes in how she manages relationships and her behavior. As I previously mentioned, I would be using, as responsively as possible, both challenging and validating interventions to help her gain more awareness and new knowledge about herself. Hopefully, as she knows her strengths, interests, tendencies, and personal vulnerabilities more (see Principle 7), it will be easier to make an effort with others and yet remain independent. In addition of having her consider group-based activities (see Principles 6 and 19), I picture helping Anne to attempt some of my favorite interpersonal skills, such as inviting others to do something with you and giving deserved compliments freely. As described in Principle 10, a coaching approach and the use of role playing can be beneficial to increase adaptive social assertiveness and relatedness. I might also help her to design an "independent Saturday," where she does a range of positive activities on her own. In addition, I have found that some patients benefit from identifying types of individuals with whom they get along well. Can I help Anne find even a few people with whom she feels good, even before I help her do better with individuals she finds more threatening? For example, I've had patients who are highly triggered by co-workers but relate well to people in their running club. Some individuals look so much lower functioning in their dealings with their spouse than they do with colleagues.

I hope to promote a significant depth of exploration and emotional experiencing in my work with Anne (Principle 36). I will listen closely to signs of underlying feelings and needs. If she discusses how upsetting her relationship with Peter was, I might try to elicit the hurt, pain, and longing for connection "underneath" the anger. I can try to deepen emotional experiencing with a "timeline" exercise, in which I ask her to identify key moments in her life, perhaps moments where she learned that relationships could hurt her. Putting them on paper may help us gradually approach more sensitive and emotionally loaded stories. Needless to say, the exploration of such emotional and painful stories, including with her parents and siblings, would also be a way to gain a new understanding of her self and her life (Principles 8, 18, and 35).

The use of nondirective or person-centered technique (following, noticing, reflecting) would be particularly indicated when addressing emotional and interpersonal issues with Anne (see examples described for Principles 11 and 12). I hope to use nondirective interventions skillfully with her (Principle 37). In a way that is quite different than Victor, she is highly sensitive; I need to be very alert to what she needs on a given day. There may even be times where we end sessions early, if it is clear she doesn't want to be there on a given day. Sometimes, patients seem receptive to only validating comments and are in no mood for one of my therapeutic stories. With some patients, I can tell on the walk to the waiting room that they are in a dark place and I need to be working at my highest levels of attunement.

As with Victor and Brian, I will try to further the therapeutic relationship by organizing Anne's presenting complaints and seeing if I have heard the full list of her concerns. In her case, I will reflect her difficulties as follows: sadness and low mood, self-loathing and a highly critical view of herself, unstable romantic relationships and difficulty getting over Peter, difficulty with friendships and generally feeling socially isolated, feeling directionless in her life and having an unclear sense of identity, mixed relationships with family members and difficulty talking about the past, and some hopelessness about treatment and life. I will make sure to monitor her response to this list and make sure she is up for hearing it communicated back to her.

Comments across the Three Cases

Victor, Brian, and Anne are all very different individuals. There are similarities and differences in how I might apply the change principles to their treatment. Most broadly, there are interpersonal patterns at play in each case that are contributing to emotional pain and life problems. They will benefit from increased understanding of the triggers for problematic episodes and from learning new ways to respond to others when triggered. Victor will be working on how he responds when he feels dominated by others. Brian will work on how he deals with authority figures. Anne will be developing better boundaries in relationships.

As discussed, it will likely be relatively easy to establish a good working relationship with Victor. With Brian, it will be key to be practical and behavioral and look for opportunities to reduce the impact of substances. With Anne, where trust issues are key and her mixed feelings about relationships are intense, much of the work of therapy will be in navigating the closeness of the therapeutic relationship. She will hopefully build better feelings about herself and learn how to gradually build closeness with others.

There were not strong preferences expressed by these patients about the type of therapy or the nature of the therapist. Thus, the principles about patient choice didn't seem as relevant. There is an art to managing patient preferences when it isn't easy to make a change in provider. Most of the time I find sound clinical skills lead these issues to recede into the background. Sometimes I find it helpful to encourage clinicians not to doubt themselves when working with an individual who sounds like a poor match when talking to intake staff on the phone. Usually, I hear clinicians are pleasantly surprised by how much good the work can do for their patients, regardless of the individual differences.

Conclusions

I find the cases of Victor, Brian, and Anne to be familiar and "real-world." I have seen patients like all three. I tried to illustrate how I would conduct therapy with these individuals, as well as how I would directly and indirectly apply research-derived change principles. The following are a few additional suggestions for how to implement the change principles in your practice.

1. In terms of patient prognostic principles, when a patient appears more hopeless, I encourage you to get treatment moving quickly—working to identify what the "video" of progress would be. I don't encourage trainees to spend much time giving intellectually oriented rationales about why treatment will help. Do the treatment—don't talk about it. Be practical whenever possible.
2. Regarding treatment/provider moderating principles, be as flexible as you can in how you work with patients and directly express flexibility. Make sure the patient knows you are going to work hard to understand their unique experiences and that you will make proposals about what you think might help but that successful therapy requires great teamwork.
3. Relating to principles about patient process variables, I encourage you to help your patients actively participate in treatment in creative ways—before, during, and after sessions. I believe that even senior clinicians often overlook the strategy of bringing family members and other supports into sessions to work on issues at the systems level. Even bringing a spouse into sessions a few times in a course of treatment can help energize the work and facilitate changes in interactional patterns. The patient knows you know the players directly and will often reference this over the course of your work. Also, consider using photographs in therapy. Having patients take pictures of their disorganized desk or completed term paper might enliven the work.
4. The therapy relationship principles are so important to making the work of therapy transformative. Sometimes training can lead newer therapists to be less genuine, affirming, and empathic than they otherwise would be. Make sure that you are not so technical that you lose your humanity and warmth!

5. Therapist intervention principles include the core idea that flexibility in treatment delivery is essential. I learned about this research early in my development as a therapist, and it has been in my mind ever since. I encourage supervisees, for instance, to have the broad game plan in mind but to be highly responsive to what is emotionally "hot" for a patient on a given day. Work on what is hot and generalize from there. In addition, help patients experiment with all sorts of new behavior. Ultimately, we grow by trying on new approaches to living, knowing your therapist has your back regardless of what happens.

Comments on Writing this Chapter and the Change Principles

I greatly enjoyed writing this chapter. At first, I read the principles rather generally, as broad themes. As I worked on the manuscript, I reflected more systematically on each principle and the specific point it was referencing. This did increase my appreciation for each principle and inspired me to think about ways I could employ the principle clinically and creatively. I have already noticed how much more aware I am in my clinical work when these change principles are relevant and when I am using them. I also appreciate the categories of change principles and how this helps organize and clarify my thinking. When I start with a new patient, I will be more acutely aware of the patient prognostic principles and think about how I can develop realistic hopefulness in the patient. As I begin to intervene, I will be thinking about how to adjust the treatment approach in line with the treatment/provider moderating principles. I already am acutely aware of the centrality of the patient process principles, encouraging active engagement in the treatment process and being trying to avoid provoking resistance to the therapy or the therapist. Indeed, I find it natural to speak in a "low-control" way, anyway. I probably go overboard to "invite," "offer," and "encourage," rather than to give people a sense that they must submit. The therapy relationship principles form the core of my work with people. I will continue to prioritize deep listening, noticing strengths in my patients and normalizing and disclosing when appropriate. The therapist intervention principles contain so many important ideas. We need to identify the core interpersonal themes of patients, promote adaptive interpersonal behavior, and deepen the work so it hits at the emotional level. We need to know when to follow and when to lead; both stances can be crucial at the right moment. More broadly, we can't let our theories lead us to be stilted or inhumane when someone is in pain. We need to be flexible and not rigidly adherent.

I hope this chapter helps clinicians increase their confidence and competence working with their patients. I find these principles both reassuring and instructive. We can use them to provide a solid foundation, as we listen to the patient in front of us and flexibly and innovatively apply the change principles.

References

Dweck, C. (2007). *Mindset: The new psychology of success.* New York, NY: Ballentine Books.

Greenberg, L. S., & Safran, J. D. (1987). *Emotion in psychotherapy: Affect, cognition, and the process of change.* New York, NY: Guilford.

Lambert, M. J. (Ed.). (2013). *Bergin and Garfield's handbook of psychotherapy and behavior change* (6th ed.). New York, NY: Wiley.

Lazarus, A. (1993). Tailoring the therapeutic relationship, or being an authentic chameleon. *Psychotherapy, 30*(3), 404–407.

5
Empirically Supported Principles of Psychotherapy

Abraham W. Wolf

My Reaction to the List of Principles

The list of 38 principles represents the summary of systematic reviews and meta-analyses of psychotherapy process and outcome research. For psychotherapy to have credibility in the healthcare community, we need to demonstrate that our practices are grounded in an evidence base comparable to other healthcare practices. Yet, there are challenges in applying principles that are statements of aggregates drawn from research conclusions to individual cases. The 38 principles cover a wide range of topics, including client prognostic factors, guidelines for establishing the therapeutic alliance, and the application of interventions. My challenge is how to map these principles to my clinical judgment in terms of not only how they apply to a case formulation, but also how I will respond in the moment to an individual sitting in front of me. In other words, how do I make the 38 principles actionable.

The best metaphor I have for summarizing these principles is how one learns to play a game. I used to play chess, and after learning how the pieces move, I learned some basic principles like controlling the center of the board, developing pieces early, not crowding your pieces, and so forth. Playing the game, though, means knowing how to respond to the specific moves of your opponent. Psychotherapy, like chess, demands that one responds in a very specific context with a move, a therapeutic move. How the principles can provide a heuristic that informs appropriate contextual responsiveness represents the bridge from science to practice.

My Reaction to the Invitation

In clinical practice, I am rarely given the case summary as complete as the three provided. Even if I were, I would still want to interview the client myself.

Hearing a client's narrative is not just listening for content, it involves attending to the client's voice and other nonverbal behaviors. Furthermore, a case formulation is never static but changes from one session to the next. The patient's voice in telling their story is just as important as the content of that speech. The editors of this volume have done an admirable job culling a set of principles and organizing them into five categories. As a clinician, responding to the challenge of applying the principles to working with a client involves bridging those abstract principles to specific responses. To make the clinical material come alive, I have created dialogues between the three clients and a therapist to illustrate the use of the principles. If we are to make these principles actionable, they have to be illustrated at the level of specific responses and not just to abstract clinical formulations.

A Note on Depression

What does it mean to call someone depressed? Referencing current diagnostic criteria is one approach, but a set of criteria provides little help in understanding the complex and differentiated psychological experience of depression. Prior to applying a set of therapeutic principles, it is necessary to understand just what pathological processes those principles are supposed to treat.

Depression is an experiential state that can be differentiated as a mood, a symptom and a syndrome with both psychological and biological components. Individuals may experience depression as temporary fluctuations of mood in response to disappointments and losses. Depressive symptoms manifest in the context of more severe states such as chronic pain, anxiety, or trauma. Finally, as a syndrome, depression represents a disorder of the central nervous system. As a phenomena amenable to psychological intervention, depression is a symptom best understood in terms of a learned helplessness model with the features of *permanence*, the belief that negative events and their causes are permanent; *pervasiveness*, the tendency to generalize that negative features of one situation to others; and *personalization*, the tendency to attribute negative events to one's own flaws or external circumstances (Seligman, 1998). These features characterize the affective, cognitive, and behavioral aspects of the depressive state. As such, there is a close relationship between experience of depression and anxiety where anxiety is a state in response to the experience of threat and depression is a feeling of helplessness and hopelessness in response to the inability to escape threat and the chronic state of anxiety. Psychological interventions intended to alter such a depressive state need to be framed in terms of affective, cognitive, and behavioral terms.

The interaction of anxiety and depression manifest as threats to self-esteem with associated feelings of hopelessness and helplessness. Diminished self-esteem comes from a loss of a sense of efficacy and confidence and/or the loss or absence of close supportive relationships. My application of the 38 principles and the specific interventions I will use with Victor, Brian, and Anne are based on increasing their self-awareness of the damage to their self-esteem, finding ways of their being in the world that can enhance that self-esteem, and, finally, how to bounce back from future threats to their self-esteem. All three are convinced that they are losers. How can I help them change that view of themselves and their current ways of being in the world that support that reattribution?

Victor—Depression

Victor is a 41-year-old Hispanic man who voluntarily presented for psychotherapy because of depressed mood for the past six months that meets criteria for a major depressive disorder. He has a life long history of dysphoria and his presentation also meets criteria for generalized anxiety disorder. Victor describes himself as always feeling weak and a failure but is recently experiencing more intense feelings of hopeless, helplessness and alienation from family, friends, and co-workers. He is deeply conflicted in his interpersonal relationships, seeking to assert himself and make changes in his life, but these wishes conflict with his fears of further alienating others by his actions. His loss of a sense of agency has resulted in his becoming more dependent and passive but, at the same time, more frustrated and irritable to those individuals from whom he seeks reassurance. He is convinced that he is permanently stuck, incapable of achieving the autonomy and sense of agency that will allow him to feel competent and confident in life and achieve the closeness he craves from others.

My initial formulation of the Victor's presentation is that is he facing a developmental hurdle in his life, and my goal is to facilitate his obtaining a cohesive sense of self that incorporates both his roots and wings. His roots are in his family life where he can experience a sense of secure attachment to his cultural community and family of origin, to his wife as they prepare to be empty nesters, and to his children as they leave home and he creates bonds with them as adults. These roots, though, are problematic. He has internalized a "demanding, critical, and emotionally unavailable father," a voice that is most likely related to Victor 's deeply ingrained belief that he is weak and unable to assert himself at work or at home. The work on his wings have to do with instilling a sense of hope in a future by reframing his conviction of being a failure, hopelessly stuck and powerless to make a difference at work and at home. This will entail validating a sense of how he been successful in creating a life that sustains his family. The developmental hurdle is how he can experience a groundedness in his past that differentiates his attachments to significant others from an inner critic. In other words, how can Victor identify with his roots to trust himself and his competence to face a new phase of life where the family he created changes with his children leaving home.

To engage Victor in psychotherapy I need to determine what he expects from treatment and how motivated he is to get help. I am going to assume that he is conflicted about being in my office, hopeful that he can get help, but cautious about the possibility of experiencing another failure. I have three tasks in the first session (probably more, but these are the ones that immediately come to mind). First, I want Victor to know that I am listening, and that even if I don't "get it," I am doing my best to understand his pain. I will be particularly sensitive to the fact that he is communicating to someone from the dominant culture who he thinks may be stereotyping him. Second, I want to establish myself as a credible professional who can be trusted to treat him and from whom he can accept influence. Third, I want to instill hope that he can get through a painful episode in his life, that the pain in his life has meaning, and that he can hope for a better future. A goal of treatment is to challenge that immutable belief that he is a weak failure. This will take the form of not only identifying and challenging internal "voices" at a cognitive level of specific beliefs about him being a failure but also putting these beliefs in the context of the narrative he has of his life, insight into the origins of those beliefs, and finding ways to rewrite that narrative. The more difficult piece will be identifying specific behaviors in specific situations that reinforce his belief that he is weak and exploring alternative behaviors that can alter his cyclic self-defeating pattern.

Prognostic Principles

THERAPIST: What impresses me about your life is how far you have come given where you started. You have provided for your family, sacrificing your own ambitions and even your connection to your roots and your own needs to be a provider, giving your wife and children a life. From what you tell me, you give a lot but don't feel that you are getting much back in return either at work or at home. Your life is a treadmill and in spite of your best efforts you can't get off it.

VICTOR: I feel trapped in this life. I don't feel that I have gotten anywhere. I just keep going and do what I have to do. Anything I try to do to make things better only ends up making things worse. I'm weak, and I'm a failure.
THERAPIST: You've been calling yourself that for a long time—a weak failure. We need to take a look at where that idea comes from. More importantly, we need to take a look at just what it is you are doing or not doing that makes you feel that way and come up with other options. Let's meet for a few sessions and see how things go.

Principle 1 specifies a class of risk factors, which indicate a mixed, but generally positive prognosis for Victor as a candidate for psychotherapy. Although he presents with a major depression that is mild to moderate in severity, he has no history of previous depressive episodes or treatment, although there is some concern about the chronicity of his depressed mood and anxiety since childhood and his suicidal ideation. His childhood role as a caretaker in a home with a domineering father, in addition to a family history of depression and anxiety are poor prognostic factors that could complicate treatment. Whereas his more advanced educational level and history of job stability indicates a willingness to persevere and demonstrate resilience in the face of challenge (both issues addressed in Principle 7), his experience of himself as a weak failure and his increasing social isolation raise concerns of increasing functional impairment if his depressions deepens. Importantly, he does not appear to suffer from a personality disorder (Principle 2).

The principles related to attachment (Principle 3), low socio-economic status (Principle 7), adverse childhood events (Principle 8), and negative self-attributions (Principle 9) speak to important cultural and developmental factors in Victor's presentation and are important in planning treatment. He is a second generation US citizen and the oldest of his siblings for whom he was a primary caretaker. This suggests that his role in his family of origin was as a translator for his parents who cannot speak English and an intermediary between the culture of his parents and the culture of a new country. His family relationships are complicated by a close nurturing relationship with his mother and a demanding, critical, and distant father. Developmentally, Victor has always lived with family with strong attachments. He went from being a caretaking son and brother to a caretaking husband and father, assuming adult responsibilities and expectations at an early age. He is presenting for treatment at a time when his children will be leaving home and there will be only his wife and him at home—empty nesters. Socially, Victor's needs for connectedness and affiliation are unmet. His work environment has turned into a repetition of his relationship with his father, facing demands from employers that he strives unsuccessfully to meet. His long hours make the hope of a gratifying social life another source of stress. His irritability and hostility have only led to others distancing him even more. Empathically communicating this to Victor as the narrative of his life early in treatment can facilitate the therapeutic alliance by communicating to him that his current pain makes sense given his history. This narrative needs to be communicated to Victor in a way that he understands how his anxiety and resulting sense helplessness are meaningful. This narrative needs to be presented in a way that he can increase his self-awareness of his anxious arousal and understand the cognitions and behaviors associated with these states in terms as his doing his best to manage these fears. I hope to convince Victor that solutions that may have worked for him in the past are not working and there are other options now.

Victor's now seeking treatment suggests that he wants to make changes in his life, consistent with the contemplation stage of change (Principle 6). In describing his depression, especially how this relates to his feeling a failure, he knows that he needs help but cannot envision how to change. How to explain his sense of failure and helplessness by articulating the narrative of his life and how he does not have to be determined by that narrative can facilitate his expectations (Principle 4) and motivation (Principle 5) for psychotherapy. If Victor expects quick results from treatment and these are not forthcoming, he may experience his contact with the therapist as yet another failure. By letting him know that psychotherapy is a collaborative effort, I would let him know that I am hopeful that we can work together to take another look at his life. This may be one way to get him to buy into psychotherapy. I would do my best to let him know that I want him to tell me how he feels things are going.

Treatment/Provider Moderating Principles

VICTOR: I just don't know what my problem is. I'm just messed up.
THERAPIST: From everything that you've told me, it sounds like you're depressed and may have been depressed for a long time.
VICTOR: So you're telling me that I'm depressed, that I'm crazy?
THERAPIST: Being depressed is not being crazy. How much do you know about depression and the ways we have to treat it?
VICTOR: Not much.
THERAPIST: I want to take some time and talk to you about depression, low self-esteem, and feelings of being a failure.

The moderating principles, especially the principle regarding the level of problem assimilation (Principle 10) provides a way of integrating stages of change (Principle 6), expectation (Principle 4), and motivation (Principle 5). These serve as a basis for actively engaging Victor in treatment, specifically by clarifying through psychoeducation what it means to be depressed and feel like a failure. I may summarize our initial interview with a "mini-lecture" on how individuals derive a sense of self-esteem though a sense of competence and connectedness. By focusing on his role as a provider for his family, he has attempted to be a success (something he feels has alluded him) but at the cost alienating himself from those close to him, geographically with his family of origin and emotionally from his wife and children. Therefore, positing one goal of therapy as enhancing his self-esteem thorough reconnecting with others in his life is one way of giving him a direction for therapy and a sense of hope in his life.

Although he does not appear to have a high level of resistance and may be receptive to more directive forms of psychotherapy (Principle 11), the initial phases of treatment should focus on establishing the therapeutic alliance and defining goals for treatment. From here we can collaboratively explore alternatives and what he thinks will work for him. We start with a nondirective, supportive, and empathic approach (Principle 12) that lets Victor know we understand his pain, that we can explain and give meaning to his pain, and collaborate to find ways of getting past that pain. This nondirective stance is balanced with a directive approach that provides a summary narrative of his life, a psychoeducational component, and ultimately to identify specific situations with his family and at work where he can respond differently.

THERAPIST: I think I have a good sense of how much you're hurting and how much you want to get help. It's important that you feel comfortable working with me and know that I am "getting it." Let's take a close look at how you feel disconnected from family and coworkers. Maybe the two of us can come up with some alternatives. Let's give this a try for a few sessions and see how things go.

In terms of therapist matching (Principle 13), it may be helpful if the therapist is familiar with the particular challenges of second-generation issues rather than assigning Victor a therapist based on specific demographics. Information regarding his preference for a therapist role and therapist type, as well as spiritually oriented psychotherapy (Principle 14), needs to be obtained and discussed in the initial session. I will ask when the last time Victor participated in a religious service. Does he feel that God has abandoned him?

THERAPIST: I like to think of people as needing to have roots and wings. They need to be grounded in family and a sense of community, but they also have needs to be independent and explore their talents and personal ambitions. How much do you feel you have lost your grounding? As the son of immigrants, you are grounded in two worlds, that of your parents and that of your children. That comes with a special set of problems, especially figuring out who you are. How much of your grounding in family and community came from religion? Is that something you feel you have lost?

The use of transference interpretations (Principle 15) needs to be done very carefully in any psychotherapy and would not be helpful in the initial sessions with Victor. A transference interpretation is "strong medicine." At its best, a transference interpretation is a meta-communication about how the client's interaction in the here and now with the therapist reflects patterns of behavior characteristic of maladaptive patterns in the client's interactions with significant others. Used early in treatment, such an interpretation has the danger of creating a dominant–submissive dynamic in the relationship that could alienate Victor. Later in treatment, though, a transference interpretation that could be effective if Victor, for example, feels that he is a failure in therapy the same way he is a failure in the rest of his life.

Consistent with Principle 16, a short-term therapy of approximately 20 sessions is indicated unless further evidence of pathology is uncovered. Given Victor's internalizing coping style (as related to Principles 17 and 18), the initial phases of therapy focuses on insight, particularly into how his pattern of dependence and passivity contribute to his compromised sense of agency and alienation from others. As treatment progresses and the therapeutic relationship deepens, we can address specific areas of behavior change related to increasing his self-esteem through enhancing his sense of closeness with others. Although Victor does not show severe functional impairment, Principle 19 is still relevant to his treatment as his social and medical needs can be addressed in the form of increased attention to self-care by balancing work–life issues.

Client Process Variables

While Victor appears willing to actively engage in psychotherapy without becoming overly resistant to change (Principles 21 and 22), I would not take this for granted. I will vigilantly monitor "blocking" as a form of resistance, that is, periods of silence and withdrawal where he is not verbalizing what he appears to be experiencing. I want Victor to move away from global attributions about his being a weak failure and encourage him to bring to our sessions specific situations where he feels like a weak failure, that is, moving from dispositional to situation-specific attributions. If he continues to discuss his life in global ways and resists reporting specific situations, I will interpret this as a poor prognostic sign for treatment.

Therapy Relationship Principles

Much of the preceding is geared toward creating an interpersonal environment where I see Victor responding to me as a credible and trustworthy figure who can help him, one with whom he can bond and collaborate (Principle 23). The enactment of Rogers's core conditions (Rogers, 1957; as captured by Principles 24, 25, and 26) are deeply embedded in my work with Victor, and as I mentioned earlier with regard to empathic communications, such enactment can foster a good alliance. Given his low self-esteem, Victor needs to perceive that his pain is empathically understood and respected by a professional whose speech and actions are congruent and who communicates a sense of competence and confidence. Victor needs to experience his therapist authentically communicating an understanding of his despair and who can instill a sense of hope. While I would strive to maintain a stance of positive regard, empathy, and authenticity, I would be sensitive to ways in which Victor may be testing me.

These tests may take the form of alliance ruptures (Principle 27) where Victor perceives me as culturally stereotyping him or assuming an authoritarian posture. I would also be sensitive to how my empathetic reflections are not accurate and how he responds to my misinterpretations as microaggressions.

THERAPIST: So what is it like to be the only Hispanic family on your block celebrating Cinco de Mayo?
(SILENCE)
THERAPIST: Something just happened. You became very quiet, and I felt you becoming distant.
VICTOR: It's just that we are different. You don't know what it is like to be me.
THERAPIST: Something I said triggered something. I think that it is important for us to take a look at what just happened. You're right, about the best that I can do is try to get it. But, Victor, when you say that no one gets it, I think you are not just talking about me but others that you feel can never understand, even your own family.

This exchange illustrates several principles. There is an alliance rupture (Principle 27), which the therapist identifies and communicates by means of self-disclosure ("I felt you become distant"; Principle 28). This form of self-disclosure is specific to my immediate experience of Victor rather that disclosing any personal information about my own history, which could risk deepening the rupture by placing the emphasis on me. This is an instance where a transference interpretation (Principle 15) may be useful by identifying how whatever was triggered in our interaction is something that happens in other areas of his life.

Therapist Intervention Principles

One way of conceptualizing psychotherapy interventions is organizing them as therapist actions that follow a client's lead or where the therapist leads the client. The former are nondirective interventions such as empathic restatements and reflections, and the latter are directive such as psychoeducation, psychodynamic interpretations, and suggestions for changing specific behaviors. From this perspective, the principle regarding therapist flexibility (Principle 33) can be understood in terms of knowing when to lead and when to follow. This interpretation of therapist flexibility moves beyond how one varies adherence to a particular protocol to a therapist's sensitivity and responsiveness to contextual factors that change moment to moment. The decision of when to lead and when to follow represents one of the most important decision points for a therapist and is usually discussed as an issue of timing. It is inevitable that a therapist will err in one direction or the other. The previous dialogue emphasizes fostering emotional experiencing (Principle 36) by focusing on the immediacy of the therapeutic encounter to identify how Victor can increase his self-understanding (Principle 35) of how he distances himself from others. The directive component here could be formulated as homework where I ask Victor to identify other instances where he experiences himself withdrawing from others and considering alternate responses.

The interplay of nondirective and directive approaches can be used to enhance self-awareness and to identify cognitive features of Victor's depressive lifestyle. The following dialogue is directed at reframing Victor's self-attributions as a failure and how to challenge his all-or-nothing view of himself.

VICTOR: It's like I said, I'm just a failure. Everything that I do just makes things worse.
THERAPIST: I'd really like to take a closer look at how you feel that you are failing. I hear you when you say that things are not working for you, but I want to understand just what is happening. Before I make any suggestions

about how you could do things differently, I want to understand what is happening.

VICTOR: I just get no respect. I walk into work and they laugh at me. I walk into my house and it's like I'm invisible.

THERAPIST: And you've gotten to the point that you've just given up even trying to change that. Maybe we can take another look at that. You keep these really long hours at work because you are anxious that something could go wrong if you are not there. Didn't you mention how you feel you have to micromanage everything at work? Then, you get home late from work and your family ignores you. They've already eaten dinner, the kids are off doing their thing and your wife is watching TV and ready to go to bed. So what do you think about that?

VICTOR: I think that you are suggesting that I get home at a reasonable hour. But what if something goes wrong at work and they need me?

THERAPIST: Yes, let's talk about the relationship between your "what ifs" and your anxiety about making changes in your life.

Victor starts with a very global statement of himself as a failure. The therapist responds by validating his sense of despair, but in contrast to the previous example where the emphasis was on identifying Victor's *experience,* the therapist responds by asking what Victor *means* in a way that communicates his desire to more empathically understand that experience of despair and how he has given up even trying to make changes in his life. Rather than just stop at that point, an interpretation is made regarding his behavior at work and how this affects his home life, core issues in his life (Principles 29 and 30). I want Victor to see how one part of his life affects other parts. Importantly, though, suggestions for changes are not directed at Victor's leaving work early as he suspects, which could make him more anxious. The focus is on increasing his self-awareness (Principle 35) by identifying the cognitive aspects of his anxiety, the "what ifs." When he has a better understanding of the association of his thinking and his anxiety, more behavioral changes (Principles 34 and 38) can be explored. The goal is to turn around the downward spiral of inadequacy and isolation and for Victor to risk changing behaviors to enhance self-efficacy and connectedness.

Consistent with Principle 29, I use different forms of psychodynamic interpretations. Of course, the goal is for all interpretations to be of high quality that focus on core interpersonal issues in each client's life (see Principle 30), but the timing and nature of those interpretations are dictated by specific circumstances. For instance, the goal of the responses in the previous dialogue is to let Victor know that I understand his resignation and despair and transform this into a sense of hope and empowerment about change in his life. Consequently, these responses reflect my effort to simultaneously foster four of the therapist intervention principles. By deepening his emotional experience (Principle 36) of his resignation, the goal would be to increase his self-understanding (Principle 35) of how he has abdicated his sense of efficacy in his life and to help him regain a sense of making adaptive interpersonal and behavioral changes (Principles 34 and 38). Concretely, as a way of indicating my understanding of Victor's pain, I may pose an interpretation that focuses on identifying his despair, alienation, and compromised agency by associating this to fears of his children leaving home. Such an interpretation would be presented in the spirit of fostering more self-understanding and allowing him to experience and express painful emotional feelings of fear and loss in future sessions. Consistent with the concept of flexibility previously emphasized, the use of these directive interventions (interpretations) would be accompanied, if and when needed, by nondirective interventions (restatements and reflections)—as captured by Principle 37. It should be noted that a number of other interventions aimed at conveying my understanding and facilitating Victor's self-understanding were previously described, such as my empathic communications, explanations (including mini psychoeducation lecture), and transference interpretations related to his life narrative, pain, and/or sense of failure.

The previous dialogue illustrates the cautious exploration of directive approaches aimed at interpersonal and behavioral changes (Principles 34 and 38) that test where Victor is in terms of the stages of change (Principle 6) and his level of problem assimilation (Principle 7). I would only consider directive approaches aimed at behavior and interpersonal changes when I have explored specific situations where Victor is willing to make them. The previous dialogue is based on my understanding of how Victor's anxiety is affecting his work and family life. Consistent with my previous discussion of Principles 17 and 18, his response indicates that a cognitive approach to deal with his anxiety is a precursor to his moving into action. When Victor understands how his catastrophic expectations create his anxiety about action, I may make suggestions about taking risks that could test those expectations. And, of course, the type of interventions that I would use to facilitate action might differ based on situations at work and/or at home. One possible scenario is to challenge Victor to risk leaving work at a reasonable hour to participate in a family activity and delegate responsibility to employees in his absence. After identifying his experience as anxiety, we can explore the cognitive correlates of this experience by identifying fears, the "what if," and getting him to challenge those beliefs. In terms of the stages of change, the preceding assume that he has gone through contemplation and preparation to move into action. Another possibility is to ask if he is willing to have his wife join us for one session, framing this not as an invitation for couple's work, although this may turn out to be a possibility, but as part of his evaluation.

It will be helpful to receive feedback in the form of psychotherapy outcome measures (Principle 31) that report changes in symptom severity and level of functioning. It will also be helpful to see if comments made to me during the session are consistent with responses to the outcome measure. The question of providing feedback (as highlighted by Principle 32) is more difficult since Victor may experience a lack of progress or deterioration as further evidence of his hopelessness and helplessness.

As the prognostic principles indicate, Victor is likely to have a positive treatment outcome. The absence of co-morbid problems allows treatment to focus on identifying the cognitive and behavioral correlates of his depressive affect, formulating his depression as injuries to his self-esteem, and using the principles to heal those injuries. Not all depressed clients present in such an uncomplicated manner. When a client presents with co-morbid, treatment needs to prioritize how other factors, such as substance abuse and personality disorder, requiring the therapist to consider how these complications affect the implementation of the treatment principles.

Brian—Depression and Substance Abuse

Brian is a 45-year-old single White male who voluntarily presented for psychotherapy for help with depression and alcohol consumption. He is currently experiencing a severe major depressive episode and has a history of at least three previous depressive episodes and a lifelong history of dysthymia. In addition, he admits to drinking an average of five beers a day, indicating an alcohol use disorder, and occasional marijuana use. His one experience in psychotherapy was 10 years ago that ended unsuccessfully after two sessions. He is hesitantly coming to treatment at the urging of friends and family.

Brian poses a different set of therapeutic challenge than Victor. The severity of Brian's drinking is a clear and urgent problem that needs to be addressed as a therapeutic priority. The treatment of depression is complicated when a client is actively abusing alcohol. Alcohol has a depressant effect when consumed; when clients attempt to abstain from using alcohol, they may become even more depressed. How to establish and maintain a therapeutic alliance given his history of resistance, externalizing style, his perception of himself as a victim, and reliance on alcohol as a form of self-medication is the challenge of the initial phase of treatment. As the prognostic principles will indicate, Brian has a great deal going against a good treatment outcome. In contrast to Victor, I experience a sense of urgency about his resistance to therapy and the high probability of his dropping out. What he does have going for him is that he kept his first appointment and he recognizes that he is drinking too much. This ambivalence gives me something to work with.

THERAPIST: From everything that you've told me, you have had a hard way to go.
BRIAN: Yeah, well, I do things my way.
THERAPIST: And you've taken some pretty serious punches along the way.
BRIAN: I can't help it if people don't get it, and I don't see the point of whining about it. I don't see how talking is supposed to help. Hasn't helped in the past.
THERAPIST: So, I've got to give you a lot of credit for even showing up here. That tells met you're really hurting and maybe willing to give this another try.
BRIAN: I don't know. I just feel like the hell with it all. What's the point? I've never been able to count on anyone. No different now.
THERAPIST: Like I said, you have taken some pretty serious punches in your life and are taking some pretty serious punches now. For starters, I'd like to get to know you better and talk about ways I could help. It's not like we can make things better in one session, so I'd like to meet for a few times and for you to let me know how things are going. You know if you feel that this is not working, we can discuss other options for your getting help.

Prognostic Principles

The prognostic principles indicate that Brian is a poor candidate for psychotherapy. His level of symptom severity and functional impairment (Principle 1), his history of insecure attachment (Principle 3), low socio-economic status (Principle 7), history of poor parenting (Principle 8), and negative self-attributions (Principle 9) all suggest that he is at risk for nonresponse and early dropout. As per the readiness for change stages, Brian is moving from precontemplation but is still resistant to moving into contemplation (Principle 6), suggesting an emerging ambivalence about getting help. Nevertheless, he has low expectations and motivations (Principles 4 and 5) for psychotherapy.

This is an important therapeutic moment since he has made and kept an appointment. Given his poor prognosis for continuing in psychotherapy, the primary goal is to make sure that he comes back for a second session. Even if he fails to return, I need to establish myself as a credible and trustworthy figure who Brian can seek out in the future. Just as Principle 4 addresses client expectations for therapy, therapists need to be realistic about their expectations for their clients in therapy. In contrast to Victor where our goal was to help him understand his roots and his wings, for Brian the most urgent goal is to get him to come to the second session and work with his ambivalence about how his drinking is not working for him.

Treatment/Provider Moderating Principles

Brian is increasingly aware that his life is in a downward spiral, but he is resistant to seeing how this is connected to his alcohol use, instead seeing himself as the victim of an uncaring world that he cannot control. Put in terms of problem assimilation (Principle 10), this indicates that Brian has an emerging, yet vague, awareness that his life is not working and that he needs help. In considering what kind of interventions can be used to address this ambivalence, I need to keep in mind Brian's refusal to take responsibility for his role in creating these problems and to see himself as a victim. Accordingly, I can expect a high level of resistance and reactance if I directly confront him on his use of alcohol or his self-destructive behavior. The previous dialogue emphasizes how Brian has "taken some pretty serious punches," illustrating the use of Principles 11 and 12 that state clients who are ambivalent and resistant to change benefit from a more nondirective and person-centered approach. This is similar to how I acknowledged Victor's pain by commenting how his life is a treadmill that he is trapped on. A significant difference between Victor and Brian is the latter's high level of reactance and resistance to accepting help. To increase self-understanding (Principle 35), nondirective and motivational approaches such as motivational interviewing are designed to reflect and heighten his awareness of his ambivalence with a view toward more specifically identifying his conflict and thereby moving into problem statement/clarification and contemplation (Principles 6 and 10). The therapist needs to represent an authority figure, but without being authoritarian so as not to activate Brian's resistance. Working with his ambivalence balances the dialectic of accepting his view as a victim of an oppressive and unsupportive world, while also leaning into his fragile desire to make changes in his life. One way of doing this is by heightening his awareness of his fear (see Principle 36 on emotional experiencing) that his life is out of control and in a downward spiral of alienating others and losing his job.

Brian's ambivalence and resistance will guide how and when (and even whether or not) I use interventions related to other moderating principles. I would address the principle of therapist and treatment matching (Principle 13) by paradoxically acknowledging (as a way of using Brian's resistance to motivate change) that I may not be the best therapist or even that therapy may not be the best option for Brian. My intention would be to let Brian know that he has choices in this treatment. I will ask him what he expects from me and what he thinks I expect from him. Some issues, however, would not be worth exploring. The absence of a spiritual/religious commitment suggests that he would not benefit from treatments that have a spiritual component (Principle 14)—and the simple act of raising this possibility might have a negative impact, especially if Brian thinks that it could be a lead to a 12-step program recommendation. Empirically, exploring the option of seeing a therapist with a history of substance abuse is not likely to be particularly helpful (Principle 20), and, clinically, it may be dangerous to do so, especially in the initial sessions, given that he is not in the contemplation stage (Principle 6) and may not even be willing at this point to admit that he has an alcohol problem.

Timing is a crucial factor in the appropriate and skillful implementation of the moderating principles. Brian's poor interpersonal functioning and symptom severity suggest long-term treatment (Principle 16), but it would be a mistake to even raise this as a possibility early in therapy given his likely resistance to such a course of treatment. Similarly, Brian's interpersonal difficulties suggest that he might not benefit from the frequent use of transference interpretations (Principle 15). Transference interpretations early in treatment are dangerous, and Brian will probably perceive them as condescending. Nevertheless, later in treatment if a stronger therapeutic alliance is established and there are ruptures in the relationship (Principle 27) either in the form of Brian's confronting or withdrawing from me, a transference interpretation could be very helpful. As the principle of flexibility (Principle 33) suggests, timing is everything.

Similarly, whereas his externalizing coping style suggests a more directive approach (Principles 17 and 18), this may be more helpful later in treatment when Brian has clearly identified that he needs help, that is, moving into contemplation stage (Principle 6). Then we could explore concrete options, even raising the option of working with a therapist with a history of substance abuse (Principle 13). At this early stage, a directive approach would likely only serve to make Brian more resistant (Principle 11).

The principle regarding clients with severe impairment and fewer social supports benefiting from therapists who address their social and medical needs (Principle 19) raises some interesting possibilities for establishing the therapeutic alliance (Principle 23). I would consider the following intervention as a way of showing my care for him.

THERAPIST: I'm concerned about your health and how well you have been taking care of yourself. When was the last time you saw your doctor for a checkup?

The intent here is to take the focus away from his psychological state and express to Brian that I am concerned not just about this emotional well-being but also his physical health to facilitate the emotional bond of the therapeutic alliance.

Client Process Variables

Taken together, the client process principles (Principles 21 and 22) indicate that clients who are more active and less resistant benefit more from psychotherapy; both suggest that Brian is a poor candidate for psychotherapy. Active engagement means getting Brian to return for more sessions. One way to do this is getting him interested in his internal life, for example, by empathetically focusing on his ambivalence in ways that will heighten his awareness for help but not activate his resistance. More specifically, I would be vigilant about power struggles where Brian perceives me as authoritarian and controlling. Alternatively, Brian may withdraw from me if he becomes anxious and vulnerable at my getting too close in using an empathetic approach. As previously discussed, I need to be vigilant about even the most minor of ruptures in the therapeutic alliance and to immediately address them in a nonthreatening manner (Principle 27).

BRIAN: So how are you supposed to help me. You think that you can make things better?

THERAPIST: I'm not going to make any promises about making things better. The one promise that I can make is that I will do my best to "get it." It's not like you're going to walk out of here with a prescription that's supposed to make things better, or that I'm going to tell you what you need to do. What I would like to propose is that we give this a chance. After three or four sessions, if you think that things are not working—no harm, no foul. Maybe you can work better with someone else. But after a few sessions, if you think we are getting someplace, we can talk about where we go from there. Like I said, I am going to do my best to understand where you are coming from. Maybe when I get to know you better we can get a better picture of where you're at and explore other paths for you to go down. It's all up to you.

Therapy Relationship Principles

Because of Brian's ambivalence about participating in therapy and his high reactance and resistance, attention to the therapy relationship principles are critical. Early on, I want to create an alliance (Principle 23) strong enough to have him return to a second session and then build on our bond so that he can sustain alliance ruptures and be willing to work on them (Principle 27). As the previous dialogue seeks to communicate, one way to establish and develop a good alliance is for me to be genuinely respectful, accepting, and empathic (Principles 24 and 25) to how he sees himself as a victim, externalizing blame to a hostile world that consistently frustrates him, and finding refuge in a bottle. My challenge is to empathetically communicate that understanding (Principle 26) without identifying Brian as a victim. An empathic validation of his fears and resentments would take the form of nondirective restatements and reflections of his deep sense of injury but countering this with how on some level he is aware that his use of alcohol as a coping method is not working. The challenge in working with his ambivalence is avoid him seeing me as yet another critic of his self-defeating behavior and drinking.

As with Victor, I would restrict self-disclosures (Principle 28) to statements about how I am responding to Brian in the here and now.

THERAPIST: So what do you think about how much beer you're drinking? What do you get out of it? How is that working for you?

BRIAN: Everyone is getting on my case about my drinking, but that is how I'm keeping it together. It's what keeps me going. You're not going to tell me to stop, are you?

THERAPIST: No, I'm not telling you to stop, but let's take a look at how well that beer is helping you to cope. How is that working for you?

BRIAN: Hey, everyone else may leave me, but I've still got that beer to look forward to. I've tried to cut down before, but then I really get bent out of shape.

THERAPIST: From what you've told me, things have never gotten this bad before. Maybe it's worth giving it another shot, and we can talk about how it's going. I'm hoping that we talk about some options that can help you get your life back on track.

Therapy Intervention Principles

As I mentioned earlier, the application of the therapy intervention principles needs to be guided by the balance of when to follow and when to lead, emphasizing the dialectic of accepting Brian's view of his current circumstances while simultaneously leaning into his desire for change, that is, acknowledging but not agreeing with his view of himself as a victim, while simultaneously leaning into his awareness that his life is not working and he needs to make some changes. Working with Brian's ambivalence involves heightening his awareness by carefully balancing nondirective (Principle 37) and directive interventions, including interpretations (Principles 29 and 30) as well as interpersonal and behavioral change approaches (Principles 34 and 38). The stages of change model (Principle 6) illustrates the difference in my approaches to Victor and Brian in these early phases of therapy. Victor enters therapy in the contemplation stage, acknowledging that he has problem and wants help. Brian enters therapy in the precontemplation phase very conflicted about asking for help. For Victor, the therapeutic alliance is a collaboration about how to get help. For Brian, the therapeutic alliance is based on getting him to see that he needs help.

Consistent with the fostering of adaptive interpersonal change (Principle 34), group activities would be very helpful, but suggestions about which type of group need to done carefully. He will most likely balk at the idea of a 12-step group but may be more open to reconnecting with his brothers or joining a sports group. A psychoeducational component needs to be worked in at some point early in treatment. Related to concrete behavioral changes (Principle 38), this could involve referring to specific documented guidelines for the evaluation of substance abuse and the interaction of alcohol and depression. Discussion of the relationship of exercise to depression could be beneficial. Given his family history and history of recurrent depression, I would also consider recommending a medication evaluation, clearly emphasizing that this is for him to get more information about treating depression and not to have anyone push something down his throat. An emphasis on change could also take a psychoeducational approach that explores treatment options, while strongly emphasizing that it is Brian's choice as to which path he takes, communicating support for his choices. Rather than jump into a discussion of a rehab program, it may be helpful to suggest that he try to reduce his drinking to two beers a night as he had in the past and see how that goes.

The principles regarding the frequency and accuracy of psychodynamic interpretations (Principles 29 and 30) require an understanding of the therapeutic benefit of such interpretations. The usefulness of interpretations is based on timing. The statement "Brian you came to see me because you are scared that your life is falling apart" is accurate but would not be helpful when we are focusing on heightening his ambivalence. The principle regarding flexibility and skillfully using interventions (Principle 33) is apropos. After we have established the therapy relationship (Principle 23) and empathically helped him to become clearly aware of his ambivalence about change (Principle 35, see also Principles 21 and 22), then we carefully foster Brian's deeper self-understanding of his fears through deepening his emotional experience (Principles 35 and 36). For example, in contrast to Victor where

I attempted to summarize the narrative of his life early in treatment as a way of communicating a context and meaning of his current suffering, I would wait until later in Brian's treatment to offer this type of interpretation. For example, I may suggest that he fears that he is reliving his father's life and that he is not condemned to carry on that family tradition. The goal of such interpretations is to provide insight into how Brian actively creates the circumstances that perpetuate his self-defeating behavior. Presented early in treatment, Brian could see this as blaming. The previous dialogue (related to Principle 28) represents an attempt to flexibly balance an empathetic, nondirective approach with a bolder move of clearly identifying the role of alcohol in Brian's life and emphasizing the role of fostering behavioral change. This could also lead to an opportunity for psychoeducation regarding substance abuse, depression, and their interaction.

Many of the intervention principles are more applicable in later stages of psychotherapy, when the therapeutic alliance is established and the goals of therapy are clearly stated. Consider the following exchange as an example of my implementation of Principle 38 (fostering behavioral change):

BRIAN: I am really struggling with cutting down. I told you I tried this before, and the same thing is happening. I cut down for a few days, and then I go back to drinking a six-pack.

THERAPIST: Thanks for being honest with me, Brian. I have to give you credit for working with this. When we discussed cutting down, I did not expect you to just change like that. The goal is progress, not perfection. You've been struggling with this for a long time. Let's talk about some specifics. Maybe one thing you could do is not keep all that beer in the house. Rather than buy a six-pack on the way home from work, just buy two bottles of beer. Also, let's look at some of the triggers for your drinking. I know you say that you drink as a way of dealing with stress, but a lot of your drinking is in the evening when you are alone with nothing to do. Let's talk about getting out of the house and finding things to do without the alcohol. While we are at it, I want to explain about how alcohol actually makes you depressed.

Providing supportive feedback through the use of self-report outcome measures (Principle 31), or as in the previous dialogue, acknowledging his successes and failures may be helpful (Principle 32) but could also discourage Brian if outcome measures do not indicate progress. Thus, to be attuned to his needs and personal characteristics, I would be selective in terms of what feedback about outcome and his performance to provide him and when.

As indicated in the previous dialogue, the principle regarding adaptive interpersonal changes (Principle 34) can be introduced early in treatment as a way of managing his isolation. The more important implementation of this principle will entail how his alcohol use affects his interpersonal relationships by making him more depressed and withdrawing from others and how it impairs his impulse control, leading to anger management problems. Later in therapy, when Brian has a better sense of the role of alcohol in his life, we can then deal with his self-defeating behaviors and how this compromises his sense of agency in the world and his relationships with others.

Victor and Brian present different therapeutic challenges. The prognostic factors indicate that Brian is more likely to have a poorer outcome, and the presence of a substance abuse disorder is a therapeutic priority that complicates the treatment of his depression. Relapse is a constant threat that looms over Brian's treatment and requires a vigilance on the part of the therapist. Since Brian is not ready to accept that he has a problem and ask for help, he will be far more reactive to accepting influence from the therapist. In contrast, Victor is not at risk for relapse, and the prognostic principles indicate that that he likely to have a good outcome. His history of family bonds and consistent employment indicate that he can form long-term attachments facilitating the formation of a therapeutic working alliance.

Anne—Depression and Personality Disorder

Anne is a 24-year-old single White female who presents for treatment of her long-standing feelings of depression. She is experiencing a major depressive episode and has a history of suicide attempts, inpatient psychiatric admissions, and outpatient psychotherapy. A diagnosis of borderline personality disorder is indicated by her frantic efforts to avoid feelings of abandonment, a pattern of unstable and intense relationships, impulsivity, self-destructive behavior (including self-mutilation), emotional dysregulation, and chronic feelings of emptiness. She is very ambivalent about entering therapy and establishing a relationship with her therapist. She is pessimistic about getting help and experiences strong feelings of hopelessness and helplessness about her ability to change, although she admits that she does need help.

Victor, Brian, and Anne are all ambivalent about entering therapy, and one of the ways that this ambivalence is expressed is how they test their therapists. For Victor, this may take the form of sensitivity to issues of ethnicity. Brian will be sensitive to power struggles and resist influence from the therapist.

Both Brian and Anne share a reactance and resistance to accepting help, but these manifest differently. Brian resists accepting that his life problems and depression are related to alcohol, and working with his ambivalence will involve his acknowledging how his life is not working and how alcohol contributes to that. Anne's ambivalence takes the form of a conflict between her intense desire for closeness and her fear that when someone gets too close they will see the terrible person that she is convinced she is. She is likely to challenge the therapist early in treatment, testing the boundaries of the therapeutic relationship; she desires the therapist to be a caring rescuer but simultaneously fears the therapist as a persecutory, rejecting figure. Anne's vacillation between desiring a rescuer and fearing a rejecting abuser is one way to distinguish her ambivalence from Victor and Brian. Anne's treatment needs to start with an understanding of the dialectic of accepting her fluctuating sense of self, her needs for attachment that are highly sexualized and result in feelings of engulfment, and her provocative behaviors that distance others and then engender fears of abandonment. The therapist needs to present as a stable figure who can set consistent and clear boundaries who can help Anne to contain the ferocious affective storms she experiences. Clearly, she is a candidate for a structured outpatient treatment program. The challenge will be in how to engage her in participating in this program. Treatment will start with individual psychotherapy.

My treatment of Anne assumes that her depression is based on her inability to understand and manage her internal life and that her self-esteem will be enhanced by a greater sense of competence in managing her emotional experience and how those experiences impact on her interpersonal relationships. To explain the experience of emotional dysregulation, I use the metaphor of someone living their lives in a climate subject to tornadoes or hurricanes. You don't know when a storm will hit, but you can be sure that eventually something will happen to precipitate feelings of internal chaos that lead to behaviors that create even more chaos. When Anne's storms hit, she becomes terrified and desperate to calm herself, but these efforts create their own chaos. It is necessary to provide Anne with an alternative perspective on her internal life and tools she can use to manage this. Facilitating self-awareness through the idea of mindfulness is one way to introduce the process of self-regulation. This approach communicates an acceptance that she lives in an emotionally stormy climate, while also providing hope that there are adaptive ways that she can cope with these storms. How I will deal such storms when they are directed at me and how the resulting alliance ruptures are repaired will be crucial aspects of the treatment. Engaging Anne in treatment means that I will inevitably bear the brunt of those storms.

Client Prognostic Principles

ANNE: OK, we've met twice already, and all I've done is answer questions about my background and what I want from therapy. You're the expert. Why don't you tell me how you are going to help me? I'm a mess; my life is a mess. What are you going to do to straighten me out?

THERAPIST: We need to be clear on something from the start. Therapy is a collaborative effort. There are things you need to do and things I need to do. It would help if I knew what kinds of things helped in the past.

ANNE: Well, when I was feeling really empty inside, my last therapist would give me a hug. That helped to take the edge off.

THERAPIST: There are things I need to do, and there are lines here that we need to discuss.

Anne's treatment will be complex. The prognostic principles (Principle 1) indicate that her impaired functioning will continue to create situations that perpetuate a chronic dysphoria and a sense of hopelessness and helplessness. Demographically, she has assets, such as her socio-economic status and education (Principle 7), but her patterns of insecure attachments (Principle 3), experiences of adversity as a child (Principle 8), and history of disappointment with previous therapists and low hopes for therapy (Principle 4) mean that the therapist, as with Brian, needs to be particularly attentive to signs of conflict about her engagement in therapy, as well as early dropout. As much as Anne is pessimistic about treatment, she knows that she is in trouble and desperately wants help. This despair and her sense of demoralization will provide a source of motivation for her to stay in treatment and work toward improving (Principle 5). Yet, in addition to her conflict about therapy, she may not be fully ready, as therapy begins, for the change she states she wants. Using the of stages of change (Principle 6), she states that she wants to move into action but has not done the work of preparation to clearly define what form action will take. In addition, the presence of a serious personality disorder presents challenges for the development of the therapeutic alliance, let alone treatment outcome (Principle 2).

The challenges of treating individuals with personality disorders (Principle 2) is captured in the previous exchange regarding expectations (Principle 4) and motivations (Principle 5) for therapy. Anne is placing responsibility on the therapist to "straighten me out," to rescue her with hugs. The prognostic principles address the challenges many clients have in creating and maintaining the therapeutic alliance, in identifying the goals of treatment, how the tasks of client and therapist are defined, and how to establish the boundary between the personal and professional. As with Brian, the tendency to externalize blame necessitates that the tasks of therapy be addressed early in treatment.

Formulations and treatment approaches of borderline personality disorder are diverse. Ideas such as an unstable sense of identity, emotional dysregulation, difficulty regulating self-esteem, splitting the self and others as idealized or devalued, boundary disturbances, and attachment disorders all have value in understanding and treating this serious problem. The approach that I have found most helpful is thinking of these individuals as experiencing high levels of anxiety and how this anxiety is managed by developing intensely close relationship with individuals who initially provide validation. Yet, because of deep-seated feelings of self-contempt about her "real self," Anne will engage in provocative behaviors that will likely result in others rejecting her, thereby confirming her negative self-image. The therapist needs to be vigilant to provocative-testing behaviors and be prepared to deal with ruptures in the therapeutic relationship. The highly sexualized nature of her relationships with men and her reluctance to talk about her relationship with her father suggests a desire for an idealized male figure she sees as distant and unattainable. The therapist needs to be prepared for a series of tests that challenge the ethical and professional boundaries of the therapeutic relationship.

Treatment/Provider Moderating Principles

THERAPIST: From what you have told me, the times that are most painful for you, and perhaps the times when you really need that hug, is when your feelings escalate to the point that you feel out of control. It's like you are in the middle of a storm with winds so strong that you get disoriented. One way we can start is for you to understand what is happening and that you always get through that storm.
ANNE: Yeah, that's what happens.
THERAPIST: I'd like to discuss some ideas with you about what could be happening when you feel like that and see if they fit for you. See if we can get a handle on what is going on when those storms hit and some ways that you can get through them.

Anne's severe functional impairment indicates the need for long-term intensive treatment (Principle 16). The challenge is how to frame the goals of treatment and what Anne can expect from me and me, from her. An important goal for Anne is to get her interested in understanding her internal life. As specified by the Assimilation of Problematic Experiences Scale (Principle 10), we need to agree on what the problem is. One way to do this is through psychoeducation and, as the previous dialogue illustrates, empathically articulating an understanding of her difficulties managing her internal life and how her emotional dysregulation defeats her efforts at gratifying relationships. Her ambivalence about treatment will likely manifest as resistance to directive approaches (Principles 11 and 22), and my explanation of her internal life needs to be carefully worded so as not to sound didactic and pedantic but as highly person-centered and congruent with Anne's experience (Principle 12) to facilitate her acceptance of her managing her emotional life as a treatment goal. I could then introduce a discussion of mindfulness, that is, increasing her awareness of her internal emotional life as an alternative to reflexively escalating when anxious. Her internalizing coping style (Principle 18) suggests an approach that emphasizes self-awareness and insight. Psychoeducation about the use of substances and how this is a poor attempt to manage her internal life is also important.

Early in treatment, I will be sensitive to Anne's history of tempestuous relationships with men, trying to determine if she would be more comfortable working with a woman (Principle 13). I would also evaluate Anne's religious/spiritual inclinations (Principle 14). I would explore how her social needs (Principle 19) could be supported by participating in group—for example, a yoga class, a 12-step program, or even a structured outpatient treatment program—carefully framing these as inquiries to test her openness to options rather than direct suggestions.

The use of transference interpretation (Principle 15) with Ann depends on where we are in the treatment process. In the early stages of treatment, an interpretation that focuses on Anne's reenactment in therapy of relationships with significant others would not be helpful. The role of a transference interpretation for Anne will be most helpful in the context of a rupture in the therapeutic relationship (Principle 27) that results in an episode of emotional dysregulation. When the "crunch" comes (and it will), this will be the opportunity to ask Ann if what is happening between the two of us is like what happens with others in her life. More than with Victor or Brian, Anne's heightened sensitivity to rejection makes the possibility of ruptures likely and increases the importance of processing these incidents as they emerge in therapy. The sensitive use of transference interpretations in this context can be very helpful in Anne's understanding how what is happening with her therapist reflects what happens with others.

Client Process Variables

Much of the previous discussion is grounded on the idea of how to engage Anne in treatment as an active participant (Principle 21), minimizing her resistance (Principle 22) by emphasizing how our treatment is going to be a collaborative effort. Anne will probably not present as an active participant in treatment. I can imagine how she will present with global statements about her life and resist identifying details. I attempt to facilitate this not by directly asking for more details, but by making statements of the form, "Help me understand better just what happened there?" By avoiding an overly didactic approach, my hope is that by getting Anne interested in understanding and managing her internal life, she will take an active and constructive stance in therapy.

Therapy Relationship Principles

ANNE: I called you five times last night! I was cutting myself and drank half a fifth of Jack. Where were you when I needed you? I really needed you to come over and help me. OK, so I know I was going through a storm, but it sure didn't feel like I was ever going to come out the other side. And when you did return my call, we just talked for five minutes and you said to come in today. I can't count on you. You let me down just like everyone else.
THERAPIST: What happened last night to set you off?
ANNE: I talked to my father, but that's not the point! Where were you?
THERAPIST: Anne, a couple of things. I see that you are still really worked up and angry at me. Remember that we talked about boundaries, things that I would do and things that I would not. That is part of the deal here. Also, when you go through these storms, there are usually triggers that set you off. Sounds like you went from zero to 100 after you talked to your father. I think that if we are going to get a sense of what sets these storms off, we need to take a close look at those triggers.

The therapeutic alliance (Principle 23) is usually formulated in terms of identifying goals, tasks for therapists and clients, and an emotional bond. Early in therapy, the challenge will be how to help Anne identify her tasks in treatment as an active participant without activating her resistance. Asking Anne to identify goals for treatment will only serve to frustrate her. Rather, the therapist needs very early on to communicate an understanding of Anne's intense fears through psychoeducation and identifying treatment options. Striving to maintain and foster a good alliance will be key for Anne to be engaged in, continue, and benefit from therapy. However, as previously stated, when talking about provocative testing behaviors (and as illustrated in the previous dialogue), alliance ruptures (Principle 27) are predictable with clients like Anne, and the therapy relationship principles need to be framed to anticipate and manage these episodes. Preparing for these episodes relies on facilitating therapist regard and affirmation (Principle 24) and empathy (Principle 26). The issue of therapist congruence (Principle 25) in the preparation and management of these episodes is more complex. For Victor and Brian, the therapist disclosing (Principle 28) of how their actions impact the therapist can provide an immediacy in the therapeutic interaction. This can be used as a learning moment to inform the clients how their actions impact others. For Anne, such a self-disclosure may only blur the boundaries of the therapeutic relationship, for example, running the danger of her perceiving me as focus of the interaction. Congruence in the context of Anne's therapy means my remaining clear and consistent what Anne can and cannot expect from me; trust will be built by consistency in my words and actions.

Therapist Intervention Principles

For Anne, the implementation of therapy intervention principles need to be understood as the interplay of the relationship and technique; that is, there are techniques to building therapeutic relationships, and the successful implementation of techniques is based on a working therapeutic alliance. The therapist needs to be flexible (Principle 33) to the effects of the quantity, quality, and kind of interpretations offered, skillfully framing those interventions in an empathic manner (Principle 37), sensitive to Anne's response to these interpretations (Principles 15, 29, and 30). Ideally for Anne, interpretations will be made in the context of deepening her emotional experience (Principle 36) in a mindful manner that provides a cognitive framework for understanding (Principle 35) and managing her internal experience in the context of a safe therapeutic relationship. Although true for all clients, for Ann it is particularly important that she not experience interpretations as objectifying and rejecting. The following dialogue illustrates how the principles that address deepening emotional experiences, ruptures in the alliance, and transference interpretations work together in the service of increasing self-awareness.

THERAPIST: Let's talk about what happened last night after you spoke to your father.

ANNE: It was all about him, about his boat, his country house, about how well my brother and sister are doing. Never once did he ask about me. I know my mother was on the other line, but she never said anything except hello and goodbye.
THERAPIST: Pay attention to how you are feeling right now as you remember that conversation.
ANNE: I'm pissed at them and I'm pissed at you for not being there when I needed you!
THERAPIST: What are those tears about?
ANNE: I'm hurt. This is when the cutting makes it better.
THERAPIST: How would you describe what you are hurt about?
ANNE: No one is there for me; no one cares about me. I'm alone and scared.
THERAPIST: If we think back on when you experience your emotional hurricanes and how they escalate, feeling rejected and abandoned is a theme that occurs again and again. It happens with your parents, with Peter, and even with me. Can you see that?

When and how to provide feedback (Principles 31 and 32) to Anne is challenging. For Anne, outcome instruments can be useful in documenting changes in the severity of her depressive symptoms or documenting fluctuations of these symptoms as a function of her emotional dysregulation. They can also be useful in documenting improvements in her interpersonal functioning, assuming that there are such changes. A more important use of feedback may occur in the following dialogue:

ANNE: I was doing so well and then I blew it. I was really looking forward to going out with this new guy I met. Then at the last minute he calls up and cancels. I just lost it. I was rejected, and the hurricane hit.
THERAPIST: Let's put this in perspective. The goal of what we are doing is not to eliminate those storms but to manage them when they occur. The goal is not elimination but decreasing their frequency, intensity, and duration. Let's take a look back on the last few months and see how you did that. The fact that you lost it does not prove that you are back at square one; it is evidence of how well you have been doing.

The last comment is particularly important in considering how to understand the principles. Although I have gone through the list of principles in a linear manner, they need to be seen as part of a more complex process. For example, the prognostic principle regarding expectations (Principle 4) for psychotherapy does not apply only to the initial phases but need to be considered throughout treatment, changing as different themes emerge and different goals are identified.

For Anne to further improve her ability to deal with stressful events such as the one described in the previous dialogue, she has to develop (by psychoeducation and self-awareness) a new perspective (Principle 35) about how her affective storms can lead to devastating effects on her life and how there are tools to adaptively cope with such experience. As I mentioned earlier, mindfulness can be helpful to foster processes of self-understanding and self-regulation. In line with both Principles 34 and 38, focusing on specific situations provides material for future sessions by identifying specific problematic situations and the triggers that start a pattern of escalation, followed by exploring alternate ways of dealing with these situations. The goal in working with the idea of mindfulness is that greater awareness of her internal life and different ways of coping with her emotional storms can lead to an increased sense of competence and confidence in managing her emotional dysregulation.

Response to the Cases

Completing the task of applying the principles to the treatment of Victor, Brian, and Anne was challenging. More challenging than articulating clinical formulations was how to make the principles actionable. I needed to find a way of mapping abstract and general principles onto my clinical judgment. My attempts to relate the principles to a specific clinical formulation remained very frustrating for me, despite the helpful feedback from the editors. The only way that I could satisfactorily complete the task was to imagine specific interactions with the three clients by "he said, she said" dialogues. As described earlier, after learning certain strategic principles of chess, there is the study of specific games that illustrate those principles. Those illustrations are valuable not just to illustrate successful games but, more important, what happens when you violate those rules. Similarly, the value of these principles becomes clear when a therapist ignores them.

I had to imagine what it would be like to sit with Brian, Victor, and Anne. For example, what form an empathic response would take for each of them in the initial sessions. For Victor, I would attempt to communicate my understanding of how his self-esteem has been shattered through a loss of a sense of efficacy in his work and alienation in his relationships. For Brian, I would start with a similar nondirective approach, but rather than focus on affect, I would start with leaning into how he sees himself as a defeated victim with a view toward identifying and emphasizing his desire to make changes in his life. The challenge with Anne is not so much to empathically communicate my understanding of her pain but to let her know that I can tolerate her pain and help her manage that pain through managing her internal life. In all three cases, I want to engage them in therapy by being nondirective and empathic, but this means very different things in terms of specific responses in the immediacy of therapeutic responsiveness.

Imagining those dialogues provided me the grounding to make the principles actionable. While the principles are very helpful in specifying the tasks of the initial phases of therapy such as identifying prognostic factors and how to establish the therapeutic alliance, they were less helpful in identifying the challenges of later stages of psychotherapy. Furthermore, the meaning of some of the principles are vague, and that ambiguity can lead to interpreting them in ways that may go beyond the research they are based on. For example, it is not clear how the principle that low outcome expectations (Principle 4) relates to poor outcome implies a treatment intervention of instilling hope.

Coherence of the Principles

I have always sought for a theory that would encompass the various schools of psychotherapy. Never identifying with any "tribe," I always leaned toward experiential, insight, and cognitively oriented perspectives. An integrative approach came very easily. The importance of the empirically derived principles is that they posit an evidence-based approach to different theoretical perspectives. Nevertheless, as listed, the principles are an example of shotgun empiricism that begs for a theoretically coherent organization. The challenge of our field is to find a way connecting the dots of the 38 principles without the need for referencing specific schools.

Finally, there are therapeutic principles not are not addressed. One example is the therapist's personal emotional reactions to a client and how the management of these reactions, especially negative ones, are important in the process and outcome of psychotherapy. Therapist reactions have traditionally been discussed in the psychoanalytic literature as countertransference and as detrimental to treatment. More recent discussions of therapist's personal responses both in the psychodynamic literature and in other schools of psychotherapy tend to view these as sources of clinical data that need to be managed (Wolf, Goldfried, & Muran, 2013). If a principle regarding a therapist's personal responses had been included in the list, I would have included it in my treatment approach. With Victor, I would have discussed how I identified with him as the eldest in a family of immigrants who served as a bridge between two cultures. More important, though, I would have discussed how my disclosing that information may have adversely impacted the therapeutic process by taking the focus away from Victor. With Brian, I would have discussed my inner frustration with his relapses while maintaining the outward posture of hope. With Anne, I would discuss the feeling of walking on egg shells anticipating her emotions directed at me.

In conclusion, the list of 38 principles represent an important step toward grounding the practice of psychotherapy in empirical principles based on a study of the research literature. One of the challenges in applying these principles to specific cases is the need to formulate how the 38 principles apply to the different ways that depressed individuals present. Ideally, the psychotherapy of the future will bridge the presentations of a Victor, Brian, and Anne by identifying how psychotherapeutic interventions specifically relate to different pathological processes and how those interventions and processes are grounded in the basic science of social and developmental psychology and neuroscience.

References

Rogers, C. R. (1957). The necessary and sufficient conditions of therapeutic personality change. *Journal of Consulting Psychology*, 21(2): 95–103.

Seligman, M. *Learned optimism*. New York, NY: Pocket Books, 1998.

Wolf, A. W., Goldfried, M. R., & Muran, C. M. (Eds.). (2013). *Transforming negative reactions to clients: From frustration to compassion*. Washington, DC: American Psychological Association.

6
Principles of Therapeutic Change in Treating Depression with an Integrative Application of the Cognitive Behavioral Analysis System of Psychotherapy

Dina Vivian

My Reaction to the List of Principles and Tasks That I Have to Accomplish

As a mentee of Marvin Goldfried, I "grew up" viewing psychological treatment through a "principles of therapeutic change" lens. However, in reviewing the empirically based list of principles provided by the editors (and those listed in Castonguay & Beutler, 2006), I realized that the process by which these principles guide my clinical work has become, in part, implicit and automatic. As will become evident in this chapter, I also find that many of the principles build on each other in treatment planning/delivery and are not as distinct within and across categories as the authors present them. On the contrary, they are highly interconnected and operate via a multifaceted, iterative, and dynamic process. Nevertheless, classifying them into unique, yet interrelated, categories is likely to provide a helpful heuristic for a systematic evaluation of how they affect treatment.

While compelling, the experience of reviewing the long list of principles and attempting to articulate how each principle may affect treatment for each of the three patients herein has brought to focus the complexity of, and challenges inherent in, delivering efficacious patient-centered treatment. In fact, due to the ideographic interplay of the mechanisms maintaining each patient's psychopathology, the task of identifying *which* principles are likely to play the most prominent role in each patient's treatment, *when* their role may be critical, and *adapting* treatment accordingly is arduous. Additionally, I suspect that because of the often unpredictable nature of in-session events, this process may remain, at times, elusively implicit. Nevertheless, I agreed to write this chapter in hopes that it would help me articulate how I apply the principles with the three patients, identify which principles most guide my work, and derive guidelines for how to translate this process into training.

Although I *think* clinically in terms of principles of change, my work is broadly framed within cognitive-behavioral therapy (CBT) approaches. Moreover, for the past two decades, it has been guided by the Cognitive-Behavioral Analysis System of Psychotherapy (CBASP), an integrative treatment based on contemporary learning theories that was specifically designed to address the entrenched interpersonal problems associated with chronic/complex depression (McCullough, 2000, 2006). Based on substantial research on chronic mood disorders, a main assumption in CBASP is that the impact of (malevolent) significant others plays a pivotal role in shaping depressive patients' maladaptive interpersonal need expectancies and dysfunctional self-perception. Relatedly, the ensuing lack of "perceived functionality," namely, the awareness of the role they play in affecting their own dysfunctional outcomes, is seen as maintaining low self-efficacy, external locus of control, and helplessness. The interplay of these factors, in addition to chronic negative affectivity and skills deficits, leads to a dysfunctional interpersonal approach characterized by disconnection from others and inability to recognize and/or benefit from positive regard. The associated paucity of positive connections with the interpersonal environment and/or social isolation fuels and maintains the mood problems.

As a result, the main goals for treatment include increasing patients' perceived functionality and fostering their (positive) connection with the environment and others. To this end, the situational analysis, a primary CBASP intervention, guides patients to (a) unpack their most distressing interpersonal and intrapersonal events in the here and now, (b) identify mismatches between actual outcomes and desired outcomes, and (c) become aware of the dysfunctional cognitive-behavioral patterns that preclude them from getting their needs met. In other words, cognitive-behavioral changes are always linked to their function (i.e., attaining a desired outcome). An additional therapeutic mainstay of CBASP, referred to as disciplined personal involvement (DPI), involves the planful and pinpointed use of the therapist–patient relationship as a vehicle of change. Specific DPI interventions, the interpersonal discrimination exercise (IDE) and the contingent personal responsivity (CPR), are designed to foster emotionally mediated change by increasing the patient's awareness of maladaptive transference patterns and therapy inhibiting behaviors, as well as by promoting in-session corrective interpersonal experiences to address the long-lasting impact of early adversity. Lastly, interventions from other CBT models, such as behavioral activation, behavioral rehearsal, and skills training (e.g., assertiveness, effective communication, stress management, emotion regulation/tolerance, sleep hygiene) can also be integrated into CBASP in a patient-centered and ideographic way to foster response.

Brief Case Formulation and a General Treatment Plan for the Three Patients

Victor: Case Formulation

Victor's depression results from the interactive effect of several long-standing situational antecedents, organismic variables, and the recent deterioration in his relationship with his wife, Leonora. Mechanisms include an anxiogenic cognitive style marked by low self-efficacy, poor perceived functionality, overdependence on others for recognition/affirmation, and hypersensitivity to criticism. Consequently, interpersonally, Victor tends to be dependent, avoidant, and, most recently, hostile. Concomitant skill deficits (unassertiveness, lack of self-affirmation, and poor anxiety management) compound the interactive negative effects of the previously stated factors.

In terms of the etiology (or origins of the mechanisms), adverse childhood experiences (i.e., his parents' physical and/or emotional unavailability, his father's hypercriticism, and the experience of growing up as a first-generation American in an immigrant/minority family) likely led to attachment anxiety and to acquired threat sensitivity. Relatedly, as his needs were subjugated to those of others (while growing up and as an emerging adult), Victor did not develop adequate self-affirming and self-nurturing skills, thus depending on others for these needs. The interplay of these factors most likely contributed to the onset of Victor's anxiety disorder. Furthermore, his maladaptive coping with long-standing life stressors (financial problems, job dissatisfaction, and social isolation) and his unrelenting self-deprecation placed him at risk for developing a co-morbid depressive disorder, which, I hypothesize, started at subclinical levels *before* his marital problems started. The ensuing increase in Victor's avoidance of his environment likely fueled Leonora's criticism, which, in turn, increased Victor's attachment anxiety with associated dysfunctional coping (avoidance and passive hostility). This negative dyadic cycle likely led to an erosion of intimacy and closeness in the marriage, which, in turn, may have increased Victor's negative view of self and low self-efficacy, further exacerbating his depressive symptomatology.

Victor: Treatment Plan

Victor's initial treatment plan includes a behavioral activation (BA) phase to increase the rate of pleasurable events in his daily life and activate his engagement in self-care. Subsequently, couple therapy is introduced to increase closeness in his marriage. Next, Victor's interpersonal functioning outside of the marriage is addressed with individual CBASP interventions to increase his interpersonal skills effectiveness and his positive connection with others, especially at work. If necessary, an additional component of treatment may include career counseling and problem-solving regarding the possibility of changing jobs. Lastly, although changes designed to improve Victor's depressive symptomatology are also likely to improve his anxiety problems, CBT protocols for generalized anxiety disorder (GAD) and agoraphobia can be administered, if necessary.

Brian: Case Formulation

Proximal antecedents to Brian's current depressive episode include the loss of his primary support system/romantic relationship and his alcohol abuse. Several interrelated mediators affect his current depression and co-morbid drinking problem, including maladaptive cognitions (i.e., emotional coping, preoperational thinking style, distrust of others, interpersonal "threat" sensitivity, and hostile attributions), emotion dysregulation problems (i.e., anger control-problems and poor tolerance of emotional distress), and maladaptive interpersonal patterns (i.e., reactance, avoidance, and hostility). As a result, Brian is socially isolated and unable to establish mutually satisfying relationships with intimate others. In fact, in his dating relationships Brian tends to be ego-centered and emotionally unavailable; furthermore, faced with adverse couple events (e.g., criticism), he becomes emotionally dysregulated and responds with anger/hostility and avoidance. His alcohol abuse disinhibits his anger control problems, further precluding him from establishing stable/mature and supportive intimate relationships. Lastly, his lack of perceived functionality and external locus of control bolster his perception that his environment is unsupportive and unyielding, augmenting his distrusts of others and his interpersonal avoidance.

In terms of etiology, Brian has a biological vulnerability for both chronic depression and alcohol dependence. Additionally, severe childhood adversity (i.e., his father's alcoholism and physical abuse and his mother's emotional unavailability) led him to perceive his environment as hurtful, unsupportive, unavailable, and unpredictable, with ensuing disruptions in his attachment needs and emotion regulation. These processes most likely played a detrimental role in his cognitive-affective development (e.g., leading him to fall back on a Piagetian preoperational thinking style when coping with stress) and impaired his acquisition of adaptive emotion regulation and stress management skills. Additionally, the early onset of dysthymia increased his risk for developing chronic depression, as it exposed him to an unremitting negative affectivity and mood lability, all of which further derailed and undermined his cognitive, emotional, and interpersonal development. As an emerging adult, Brian lost his father who was his primary attachment figure (albeit a negative one). This loss was a significant and traumatic event that triggered complex grief and a major depressive episode. Because of this stressor and the previously described vulnerabilities, Brian began using alcohol as an emotion-regulation strategy and to connect with others, which led to alcohol abuse over the next 25 years, with associated negative outcomes in his life. Subsequent episodes of depression continued to destabilize Brian's functioning across intra- and interpersonal domains.

Brian: Treatment Plan

At the beginning of and throughout treatment, ongoing assessment/management of Brian's risk for suicidality and implementation of containment strategies are needed. Relatedly, harm risk evaluation (related to his alcohol abuse) and harm reduction strategies are introduced early in treatment. In parallel, motivational interviewing (MI) modules are included to increase Brian's commitment to and engagement in treatment. Next, BA interventions are introduced to increase the rate of pleasurable events in Brian's day-to-day life. His maladaptive cognitions (e.g., preoperational thinking, external locus of control, lack of perceived functionality) and destructive interpersonal behaviors (e.g., disconnection from his environment, avoidance, and hostility) will also be targeted with CBASP interventions to increase his perceived functionality, internal locus of control, and connection with his environment. Behavioral skills training will address deficits in interpersonal effectiveness (e.g., communication and assertiveness skills) and reduce reliance on alcohol-based coping strategies. Lastly, emotion regulation/tolerance strategies will address his anger dyscontrol and poor stress management skills.

Anne: Case Formulation

Similar to Brian, Anne's current depressive episode was triggered by the loss of her romantic relationship with Peter, her primary/only social support system. Several interactive mediators maintain her current depression, including her dysfunctional cognitive style, which is marked by self-criticism/self-loathing, poor sense of self, lack of perceived functionality, low self-efficacy, preoperational thinking style, emotional/avoidant coping, and unremittent negative affectivity (emotional lability and emotion dysregulation problems related to her borderline personality disorder [BPD]). Skill deficits compound her problematic cognitive-affective functioning, including paucity of self-affirming skills and ineffective emotion-regulation skills. Anne's dysfunctional approach to her interpersonal environment, namely, her pattern of dependence and/or avoidance, maintains her social isolation and scarcity of positive events in her life.

In regards to etiology, Anne has a biological vulnerability for emotional dysregulation and depression. She also experienced childhood adversity (i.e., her parents' emotional unavailability, her mother's excessive control and poor modeling of emotional regulation, and her brother's abuse), which is likely to have led to several negative outcomes, including disruptions in her attachment experiences (with concomitant emotion regulation problems), acquisition of maladaptive interpersonal need expectancies (i.e., viewing her environment as emotionally unavailable and/or threatening), and a resulting schema of the self as vulnerable and unimportant/unlovable. The early onset of her emotion dysregulation problems is likely to have derailed Anne's cognitive-emotional development and to have fostered her interpersonally avoidant/dependent approach—all of which may have contributed to her BPD. In turn, the challenges of this debilitating disorder may have compounded her maladaptive coping (i.e., drugs, nonsuicidal self-injury [NSSI]).

Interpersonally, Anne's transitional attachment to deviant peers failed to provide her with corrective/healing interpersonal experiences or adaptive coping skills. Similarly, as an emerging adult, her involvement in a number of "intimacy avoidant" brief relationships with mismatched partners did not provide affirming or relationship-building experiences. On the contrary, they undermined her interpersonal maturation and compounded her negative view of the self. Anne's relationship with Peter was also not a healing experience, due to her limited resources and Peter's own inability to provide stable support. In fact, Anne's maladaptive coping with her abortion and Peter's lack of enduring support during that difficult time undermined the dyadic bond. The concurrent derailment in Anne's educational pursuits (her only area of competency) further compounded her distress. Peter's progressive emotional distancing is likely to have increased Anne's attachment anxiety and fueled her use of "hyperactivating strategies" (i.e., controlling, overdependence, enmeshment, intimacy-sabotaging affairs, suicide attempt) as a dysfunctional attempt to regain proximity and support (cf. Mikulincer & Shaver, 2005). The ensuing dysfunctional dyadic cycle of abandonment and reconnection compounded Anne's emotion regulation problems and led to the end of the relationship. This significant stressor further eroded Anne's connection with her environment and her ability to cope, thus precipitating her current depressive episode.

Anne: Treatment Plan

Similar to Brian's treatment, from the outset, Anne's treatment will target her risk behaviors (drug abuse, NSSI, and suicidality) via a thorough evaluation and ongoing risk assessment, management, and containment strategies. MI-based interventions will address treatment ambivalence and motivation. Next, BA—with particular emphasis on self-care—is implemented to increase the opportunity for Anne to experience pleasure in her daily life and to decrease her avoidance. A subsequent component of treatment will include emotion-regulation skills. Upon exhibiting initial success and skill acquisition, CBASP interventions are introduced to increase Anne's perceived functionality and sense of agency in her day-to-day activities and interpersonal environment. Skill deficits will be addressed through practice with mindfulness, emotion tolerance, and adaptive coping, along with other behavioral skills training modules (e.g., interpersonal communication and effectiveness). Throughout, procedures will be implemented to encourage Anne to progressively connect with her interpersonal environment via both exposure/response prevention strategies and CBASP interventions to decrease her interpersonal avoidance.

How I Am Implementing the Principles

Patient Prognostic Principles

Principles 1 and 16 (Baseline Impairment)
I see Principles 1 and 16 as being highly interrelated, as they are factors that both mediate and moderate change in treatment. More severe baseline impairment requires several treatment adaptations to maximize the probability of a successful outcome. I typically include (a) higher dosages of treatment in

the initial stages of therapy (e.g., two sessions/week for the first three to four months); (b) more foci of intervention; (c) greater use of the therapist–patient relationship as a vehicle of change; (d) greater attention to establishing and maintaining a strong therapeutic alliance to prevent premature termination; (e) more flexibility and sensitivity in treatment implementation; and (f) more ideographic implementation of treatment interventions. I also find that greater baseline impairment often requires treatment augmentation (e.g., medication, group modalities, involvement of collaterals/family) and long-term therapy (over one year).

Of the three patients, these considerations are especially important for Brian and Anne. Due to the chronicity of their mood problems, their pervasive/entrenched interpersonal difficulties, and their disconnection from their environments, they are likely to provide greater challenges in treatment than Victor will (e.g., in regards to establishing and maintaining a therapeutic alliance, readiness for change, commitment to treatment, and their response to treatment). In working with Brian and Anne, their risk status will affect treatment in significant ways, as described in their treatment plans. To maximize response and maintenance of gains, treatment will likely necessitate the integration of multiple pathways to change (e.g., cognitive-behavioral, emotionally focused, interpersonal/systemic), over and above skills training interventions and pinpointed use of the therapist–patient relationship. Furthermore, given the severity of Brian's baseline symptoms, his treatment should be augmented with medication, as a combination treatment will produce quicker and more pervasive changes than psychotherapy alone would. The same may be appropriate for Anne, but I would first attempt psychotherapy alone, because she may respond favorably to interventions aimed at behavioral activation and emotion regulation. For both Brian and Anne, I would also augment individual therapy with group therapy (e.g., 12-steps, dialectical behavior therapy [DBT] group skills training) to reinforce the process of change and increase opportunities for establishing social connections. Lastly, in treating Brian and Anne, I expect the treatment plan to change significantly over the course of treatment and to include additional foci of intervention and domains of function not readily predictable based on their initial intake information.

Principle 2 (Personality Disorder Co-Morbidity)
Due to the entrenched interpersonal problems and chronicity of mood lability associated with both depression and personality disorders (PDs), the co-morbidity of these two categories of psychopathology increases baseline impairment. Thus, the previous comments provided for Principles 1 and 16 apply here as well. Moreover, due to challenges to the therapeutic relationship, treatment adaptations related to Principle 2 also overlap with those included in

discussing other principles, such as all the therapy relationship and therapist intervention principles.

In terms of the three patients, I expect Anne's treatment to be significantly affected by her BPD. However, Brian also exhibits long-standing impairments, some of which are consistent with a co-morbid personality disorder (cluster B), namely, pervasive egocentrism, sense of entitlement, external locus of control, anger dysregulation problems, and long-standing interpersonal problems. Thus, both Anne and Brian's treatment plans include introduction of emotion-regulation skills, training in emotion tolerance, and stress management—all elements of DBT. I would also introduce interventions to increase their positive connection to their interpersonal environments (e.g., CBASP situational analysis) and interpersonal skills training. Furthermore, as I expect Anne and Brian's interpersonal problems to affect the therapeutic relationship, I would introduce process-related interventions early and throughout treatment to address their predicted difficulties in connecting with and trusting the therapist, as well as commitment to and engagement in treatment. As such, I would use CBASP interventions, such as the CPR and IDE, to maximize the planful use of the therapeutic relationship to promote corrective interpersonal experiences, to foster emotionally mediated interpersonal change in a safe milieu and to encourage healing of early interpersonal traumas/adversity.

Principle 3 (Attachment)
There are clear convergences concerning relationship issues highlighted by several principles, especially with regard to the planful use of the therapist–patient relationship and transference/countertransference processes associated with attachment anxiety. Thus, treatment adaptations based on Principle 3 overlap with those associated with other patient prognostic variables (e.g., Principles 8 and 9), as well as relationship (Principles 23–28) and intervention principles (Principles 29, 30, 35, and 36).

Due to their problematic histories with significant others, all three patients exhibit manifestations of attachment anxiety, with Brian and Anne exhibiting the most problematic patterns. In fact, they all share a pattern of similar maladaptive interpersonal expectancies (although to differing degrees of severity), including external locus of control, distrust of others, anxiety about intimacy, and low expectancy of having their needs met. Relatedly, their interpersonal styles exhibit a common underlying pattern of *avoidance* (Victor: dependence/avoidance; Brian: hostility/avoidance; and Anne: avoidance/dependence). Thus, attachment-related issues are likely to affect treatment for all three patients, both in terms of the content of treatment and the therapist–patient relationship.

In working to address their attachment anxiety, I would adopt interventions that foster awareness/acceptance of their respective learning histories regarding the impact of early attachment figures and significant others in shaping their interpersonal need expectancies. This would enable them to understand the nature of their attachment anxiety and the role that it plays in maintaining their past and current interpersonal problems and their dysfunctional approach to their environment and to intimacy. A main vehicle for change rests on providing patients with affirming and healing interpersonal experiences that capitalize on the planful use of the therapist–patient relationship, particularly in providing stable and predictable emotional availability, unconditional acceptance, positive regard, and enduring emotional support.

Principle 4 (Initial Expectations)
Due to the severity and chronicity of their psychological problems, Brian and Anne have lower expectations for benefiting from treatment than Victor does. Thus, it is important to explore the causes of their problematic expectations early in treatment. Specifically, I would encourage them to evaluate several factors that may affect their expectations, including their depressive symptomatology (e.g., anhedonia, hopelessness, fatigue), their approach to their interpersonal environment (e.g., distrust/avoidance), and the paucity of affirming interpersonal experiences in their lives. This intervention would enable me to normalize and validate their low or ambivalent expectations. I would also evaluate the role of prior negative treatment experiences or unsuccessful attempts to change, contrasting with new possibilities provided by the current treatment.

Overall, I see my task as one of increasing hope, motivation, and commitment to engage in treatment, especially for Brian and Anne. To increase hope, I would provide all three patients with evidenced-based information about treatment effectiveness (including combination treatment), while acknowledging limitations to change. I would underscore the fact that ideographically tailored interventions and a patient's engagement in treatment are the two most critical factors in ensuring positive response to treatment. Additionally, in addressing these issues with Brian and Anne, I would also talk to them about the prophylactic effect of continuation and maintenance phases of treatment to provide them with evidence-based and realistic expectations concerning treatment duration.

Principle 5 (Intrinsic [or Autonomous] Motivation)
Overall, in my experience, Principle 5 may (at times) require treatment adaptation at later stages of treatment. If early in treatment patients are not intrinsically motivated to engage, l would actually foster their extrinsic motivation to engage in treatment. Specifically, I want patients to be mindful of the contract they have with *me* in regards to attending sessions, even though they may be ambivalent about treatment, and I want them to know that it matters to me if

they show up or not. Most important, I want to make it clear to them that *we* are reciprocally connected and that everything they do affects me—I am a consequence for them that they cannot dismiss. As they start engaging in the process of change, the positive reinforcement they get from successful experiences in their daily life will increase their intrinsic motivation, a process that I would shape and reinforce throughout treatment.

Victor appears to be more intrinsically motivated to change than Brian and Anne are, as his depressive symptomatology is less severe and chronic. Moreover, he is significantly affected by the loss of his closeness with Leonora; thus, he may be eager to reconnect with her via couple work. He is also motivated to gain positive regard and affirmation from others; thus, he may be more ready for change and to engage in treatment than Brian and Anne are. Thus, I do not expect Victor's motivation for treatment to necessitate significant changes to the proposed treatment plan. In contrast, Brian's motivation for change is less intrinsically motivated, as he is seeking treatment at the insistence of friends and family (whose motives he misreads anyway) and for fear of losing his job (a negative reinforcement pattern). Further, Brian's external locus of control and lack of perceived functionality are likely to undermine his motivation to engage in treatment and inhibit the process of change. Similarly, Anne may also have difficulties engaging in treatment because she is isolated and disconnected from her environment and ambivalent about change.

To tilt the balance toward committing to treatment, as well as to increase outcome expectations (Principle 4), I would implement MI procedures (with all three patients, but especially with Brian and Anne) to focus on their ambivalence (anxiety, hopelessness) about treatment, to identify the costs for not changing, and to remove perceived barriers to change while conveying additional information about the potential value of changing. Throughout, I would make it clear that, ultimately, the choice rests with them, as I cannot take responsibility for the therapy work (a very important message for all three patients, especially for Brian). Thus, particularly with Brian and Anne, in addition to any change-based intervention, *key* aspects of therapy will include MI approaches, emphasizing their responsibility for change, building a strong alliance, and focusing on in-session process work to promote their engagement in and foster their response to treatment.

Principle 6 (Stage of Readiness)

With all three patients, the therapist's in-session process work and ability to address therapy-interfering behaviors (e.g., with CPR interventions) are of paramount importance in increasing their readiness to change. However, in contrast with Brian and Anne, Victor appears to be in a more advanced stage of readiness; thus, in my treatment with him I would expect to be able to proceed quickly with change-based interventions, such as addressing his marital discord. Brian and Anne will require the most effort (on the part of all involved) to "move" them to an active stage of readiness. As described earlier, MI strategies would be particularly appropriate to "tip the balance."

I also find that if I am successful in engaging pre-contemplative/contemplative patients in situational analyses concerning stressful interpersonal/personal events at *early* stages of treatment, the insight they gain from these experiences dramatically (and quickly) increases their perceived functionality, as well as their sense of agency. Typically, this experience moves them into a more active stage of change. In fact, when patients can define their daily stressful events in terms of actual outcomes (AOs) and desired outcomes (DOs) and can identify what role they played in *not* getting an AO versus DO match, they are likely to gain a sense of self-efficacy and "buy into" the treatment. Thus, I would guide all three patients to focus on the negative consequences of their maladaptive/avoidant behaviors vis-à-vis their desired outcomes. Victor, for example, may be able to "see" that when he is passively hostile or avoidant with his co-workers they distance themselves from him and he feels alienated rather than respected/affirmed. Brian may be able to identify that the consequences of his drinking negatively affect his work performance and are inconsistent with his intentions. Anne may be able to recognize that when she uses drugs or engages in NSSI, she feels ultimately more depressed instead of better able to cope with her emotional distress. Most important, through the situational analysis interventions, all three patients would come to identify thoughts and actions (and acquire skills) that increase self-efficacy and AO = DO matching. An increase in perceived functionality and self-efficacy may, in turn, increase readiness for change by clarifying awareness of needs and values; this process may also mobilize intrinsic motivation to pursue healthier outcomes in their daily interpersonal and intrapersonal events.

Additional interventions also increase readiness to change. For example, sharing initial assessment results and ongoing assessment throughout treatment increases patients' engagement in treatment and fosters a collaborative approach to treatment (a more through discussion of the use of feedback-informed treatment is included in Principles 31 and 32). Encouraging a patient to engage in self-care and pleasurable activities daily is also very effective in this regard, as is the introduction of relatively simple behavioral changes early in treatment (e.g., sleep hygiene) to foster hope and self-efficacy. This might be particularly relevant for patient with high level of impairment (see Principle 1).

Lastly, when patients are in early stages of change, they tend to *avoid* engaging in treatment, particularly when the focus is (or needs to be) on entrenched, long-standing, and self-destructive habits maintained by patterns of negative reinforcement and/or addiction, as is the case with Brian and Anne.

Thus, addressing treatment avoidance with interventions such as CPR may be pivotal in increasing readiness to change for both Brian and Anne.

Principle 7 (Socio-Economic Status and Employment)
This principle may affect treatment for these three patients, specifically in terms of financial resources to attend treatment (especially for Brian and Anne who will require more intense treatment initially and longer treatment over time). I would address obstacles to treatment with collaborative problem-solving solutions. To ensure that threats to or loss of employment (e.g., Brian) may not be a barrier to treatment, occupational functioning should be targeted early in treatment with all three patients.

Principle 8 (Adverse Childhood History)
I find Principle 8 to be closely related to Principle 3 (attachment anxiety), as early adversity tends to disrupt attachment processes. All three patients have a history of early adversity that, as articulated in their case formulations, is likely to have shaped their maladaptive interpersonal need expectancies and played a prominent role in their poor view of the self, as well as affected their interpersonal problems. I find that several foci of intervention are needed to foster healing of early traumas, including acquiring skills to provide the self with positive regard/nurturing and learning to perceive the interpersonal environment as safe and affirming. Thus, mindful of this principle, in my work with Victor, Brian, and Anne, I would place a heavy emphasis on the role of the therapist–patient relationship, as well as the application of flexible, ideographically based, integrated, and sensitively applied change-based interventions aimed at improving interpersonal functioning. As such, with all three patients I would foster an increase in interpersonal approach, acquisition of effective interpersonal skills and assertiveness, and ability to recognize and benefit from others' positive regard.

In terms of the therapist–patient relationship, the use of the IDE (illustrated next with Anne) is likely to be particularly helpful in addressing patients' maladaptive transference issues related to early adversity and healing of early trauma. In reviewing Anne's learning history with significant others, I would formulate the following top transference hypothesis (TH) regarding in-session events: "If I tell Dr. Vivian highly private information she will "hurt" me (i.e., be unavailable, invalidating, or controlling); therefore, I will avoid self-disclosures." Based on this TH, I would be vigilant for a pattern of in-session events wherein Anne may avoid, withdraw, and/or disconnect from me emotionally when I invite her to talk about a highly emotional/personal matter. The ensuing countertransference on my part may be as follows: "I cannot get close to Anne. . . . She is disconnected from me. . . . She does not trust me. . . . No matter what I do,

I am unable to provide her with support → She is not 'seeing' my concern/care. . . . I feel helpless." If this dyadic dysfunctional pattern emerged, I would address it directly with Anne in an attempt to understand and validate her anxiety and avoidance. I would also guide her to identify my genuine, affirmative, empathic, and validating response versus the expected negative one and, perhaps, to compare and contrast it with the expected maladaptive response associated with malevolent others (e.g., her mother or father). If necessary, I may also self-disclose my experience of powerlessness in trying to provide her with positive regard and my concern about its role in inhibiting change (CPR intervention). If Anne were able to engage in this type of communication, I would also guide her in a sensitive and reflective way to identify her desired outcome toward me; lastly, I would elicit her help in addressing our inability to connect positively (i.e., "What should we do about this Anne?"). I would use similar healing interventions based on the therapist–patient relationship with Brian and Victor.

Principle 9 (Negative Self-Attributions)
Of all three patients, Victor appears to have the most negative self-attributions, as he sees himself as a failure and he is chronically anxious about his interpersonal environment. Anne also engages in self-deprecating thoughts and sees herself as having failed in interpersonal and achievement domains, a process that potentiates her unrelenting emotional lability and maintains her anxious/avoidant approach to her environment. Similarly, Brian sees himself as unable to cope with his life stressors. However, he formulates external attributions for his problems; thus, he sees himself as a victim and tends to cope emotionally (anger dysregulation) and by externalizing behaviors (hostility) more readily than by engaging in self-criticism. Thus, I expect Principle 9 to play a more important role in Victor and Anne's treatments than in Brian's.

I provide next a clinical application of how this principle would inform my work with Victor, whose negative self-attributions are likely to emerge while doing situational analyses about negative interpersonal events. The CBASP approach to revising cognitions guides the patient to focus on three aspects of his or her "reads" about a situation: (a) inaccuracy (e.g., globally negative, not in the here and now), (b) irrelevance to the situation (e.g., unwarranted self-criticism, negative predictions about the future), and (c) irrelevance to (attaining) desired outcomes (e.g., "I can't do X because I am defective"). I expect Victor to offer "reads" about the self that fall into one or more of these categories. Many of these reads will interfere with his ability to get what he wants as they will elicit negative affectivity/arousal and consequent avoidance of, or hostility toward, his interpersonal environment. Through unpacking the elements of these unsuccessful interpersonal events (desired outcomes, reads, and behaviors),

I would guide Victor to identify the role that his negative self-attributions play in undermining his self-efficacy (i.e., he will acquire perceived functionality). Thus, for Victor, this principle underscores the importance of administering the situational analysis in both his couple and individual sessions to promote accurate and affirming self-attributions.

In terms of process work, Victor may perceive comments I make as criticisms, which may result in negative in-session behavior (e.g., withdrawal). On the lookout for such in-session events, I would address his maladaptive communication directly by clarifying reciprocal intent/impact and by using the IDE intervention as previously described. Victor's negative self-attributions may also lead him to engage in frequent self-deprecating comments in session (e.g., he may attribute his interpersonal dissatisfaction to his "defectiveness"). This process may inhibit change, as it would "pull" from me a friendly/dominant response to decrease his distress (e.g., trying to persuade him that he is *not* defective). This would place me in a "nurturing parent" role, which is a positive dynamic early in treatment to establish safety and increase a positive bond, but, if continued over time, it would maintain Victor's dependence on others for affirmation and emotional support rather than enable him to develop the skills to self-nurture. Should Victor fail to engage in actions reflecting growth in self-nurturance (e.g., by expressing self-acceptance and by taking a more assertive role in our dyadic communication), I would encourage him to "do the work" as much as possible, and I would shift to a moderately submissive/dominant role to avoid reinforcing his dependence on my "nurturing." The CPR procedure (exemplified in working with Brian with Principle 12) would allow me to address this type of potentially negative in-session dynamic to foster change and growth.

Treatment/Provider Moderating Principles

Principle 10 (Consistency with Level of Problem Assimilation)

I see the issue of problem assimilation as a prognostic variable closely related to patients' initial expectation to benefit from treatment (Principle 4), intrinsic vs. extrinsic motivation (Principle 5), and stage of change (Principle 6). In fact, these four principles appear to be related to the same construct: readiness to change/ability to engage in treatment. The three patients are on a continuum with regard to problem assimilation, with Victor and Brian at opposite ends. As Victor seems to have the greatest degree of problem assimilation, I expect that treatment implementation with him will be relatively straightforward. Conversely, due to Brian's and Anne's poor problem assimilation and low perceived functionality, I expect their treatment to present challenges, particularly early on. For example, in addition to the factors already discussed in the prognostic factors section, Brian and Anne present with immediate risk concerns (substance abuse and suicidality) that need to be addressed immediately, even though neither may be ready to engage in risk-containment contracts. To minimize reactance or lack of engagement, I would discuss my concerns with them for their well-being and ask their help in addressing my dilemma (i.e., my message would be: "I do not want to push you to change so early in treatment, especially when you are not entirely sure you want to do this, but I have to do, so what can we do?"). I would explain the potential consequences of their risk behaviors for their safety and for treatment delivery and ask them what they would like to do. In other words, I want to place the problem on their lap and give them responsibility for problem-solving. Ultimately though, I would let them know that, unless we collaboratively develop a safety plan (at least on a short-term basis) and they agree to follow it, it would be impossible for me to implement any component of their treatment.

Next, I illustrate how this principle may affect treatment with Brian. Once Brian is on board with the necessity of engaging in risk-containment strategies, I would use MI techniques to increase his commitment to change. Then, in a collaborative decision-making process, I would implement interventions designed to increase his ability to recognize the severity of one (or more) of his problem areas (e.g., his drinking problems, his poor work attendance) and his role in fostering these problems. To this end, I would use indirect/direct Socratic methods. For example, in addressing his problematic drinking pattern, I would encourage him to track daily the most stressful event leading to the drinking binges to enable him to identify the actual outcomes of his dysfunctional behavior (isolation, increase in depression, negative cognitions) and their function (avoidance). Relatedly, as he "buys into" the process, I would introduce in a very flexible way interventions based on the situational analysis to target multiple areas of distress (e.g., interpersonal distress at work, drinking, isolation) to increase Brian's awareness of the severity of his maladaptive behavior across domains and his lack of perceived functionality. Most important, treatment has to enable Brian to independently "connect the dots" regarding the role he plays in not getting what he wants and the high frequency with which that happens. If he can do that, together with the therapist, he will begin to concurrently identify what he can do to engage in more functional behaviors to be more effective in his daily life. I would use a parallel approach with Anne.

Principle 11 (Levels of Resistance and Levels of Treatment Directiveness)
I see resistance as the manifestation of multiple factors that inhibit commitment to and engagement in treatment/change (e.g., attachment anxiety, extrinsic

motivation, nonactive stage of change, poor problem assimilation, skill deficit, disconnection from the interpersonal environment, maladaptive interpersonal need expectancies). It can manifest through many common therapy-inhibiting behaviors, as well as poor attendance and lack of engagement in homework assignments. Resistance can also reflect a breach in the therapeutic alliance, in terms of the bond, agreement on methods, and/or agreement on goals for treatment. Thus, maintaining an optimal therapeutic alliance throughout treatment is an important goal with these three patients, especially with Brian and Anne, as they are likely to be most resistant.

Due to the reasons discussed earlier, I do not expect Victor to exhibit significant resistance in treatment. I would thus feel comfortable moving early on in his treatment to change-oriented approaches in both his couple and individual work. Nevertheless, due to his propensity to be other-oriented in seeking affirmation and validation, I would avoid being very directive in our work, as I would not want to encourage dependency. In contrast, I expect Brian to be more resistant, and as such, I would be prepared to do a lot of process work with him, particularly at early stages of treatment before introducing significant change-based interventions. For example, I find that the use of the CPR intervention is very useful with highly resistant patients who engage in therapy-inhibiting behaviors; thus, I would expect to use it with Brian early on (see clinical illustration in Principle 12). At later stages of treatment, addressing Brian's negative transference patterns toward me (e.g., hostility if he perceives my communication as invalidating or controlling) and inability to recognize/benefit from my positive regard, empathy, and genuine care will be important targets of process work to maintain and strengthen our alliance. When/if Brian can engage in this type of in-session close interpersonal work, I may also introduce IDE interventions to enable him to compare and contrast my affirming communication with the invalidating one he expected based on early adversity with his father.

Once Brian is willing and able to engage in change-based interventions, I would guide him to focus on what *he wants* versus what *he gets* in his daily life events and orchestrate in-session experiences to help him identify how he can *choose* and *control* actual outcomes in his daily life. To decrease resistance, I would present Brian with choices and work collaboratively with him. These approaches should decrease his reactance, particularly when he is directed to focus on what *he* versus *others* could do differently to attain a greater match between actual and desired outcomes. If successful, this is an indirect/direct change-based maneuver that will start to erode Brian's external locus of control and weaken his negative attributions about others.

I would proceed similarly with Anne by flexibly introducing process-based interventions to strengthen the alliance, as well as nondirective/directive methods for introducing behavior change (situational analyses, chain analyses, functional analyses) to increase perceived functionality and problem assimilation (see Principle 10) before introducing skills training. When Anne is "ready" to engage in more advanced change-based work, I would provide her with tools to better control her heightened emotionality and mood lability. If successful, her increased ability to cope with emotional distress is likely to decrease her resistance.

Principle 12 (Levels of Motivation and Therapist Level of Person-Centered versus Directiveness)
I find this principle to be closely related to several of the other principles already addressed, such as the prognostic principles (Principles 4, 5, and 6) and the treatment principle (Principle 11). Thus, the treatment adaptations already discussed for these previous principles also apply to Principle 12. All three patients show some ambivalence about change, particularly Brian. The use of the indirect/direct patient-centered approaches as discussed previously is optimal. Although the treatment plans I propose for the three patients include change-orientated procedures, I would be flexible in how and when skills training and change-based interventions are introduced. Across all patients, the ultimate goal in treatment is to connect them to the environment (including me) and increase their intentionality, self-efficacy, and willingness to have new corrective experiences, even though they are scared to do so. Thus, the therapist–patient relationship plays a prominent role in increasing change motivation.

Next, I illustrate how I may address ambivalence to change in my work with Brian in attempting to strengthen his motivation for change. For example, his avoidance of and ambivalence to engaging in therapy may manifest as a dominant/hostile communication, such as saying: "What you are asking me to do won't work for me. . . . I have already tried it. . . . I can't do it." In response, I would avoid engaging in power struggles or taking a dominant role. Instead, I would genuinely and empathically validate Brian's ambivalence about change or reluctance to engage in change behaviors, and I would try to identify and decrease obstacles to change (e.g., using MI strategies). If these approaches are ineffective and if he continues to exhibit treatment-inhibiting behaviors, I would rely on the CPR intervention to increase a collaborative approach and to create the opportunity for him to take responsibility for change. Specifically, I would self-disclose to him the impact that his communication has on me, and I would prompt him to tell me what *we* should do about it. For example, I may say "Brian, when you are telling me that X won't work for you, I feel as if I am running out of options, as if I am running up against a wall. . . . Not sure how to proceed from here; I feel somewhat helpless, what should we do about this?"

I may also add "Why do you think I am telling you this?" (This latter question would set the stage for me to let him know that his wellbeing matters to me.) In addition to the CPR intervention, the experience of conducting in-session successful situational analyses whereby Brian could independently demonstrate skill acquisition would directly show him that his distress diminishes when he identifies adaptive and effective strategies for attaining desired outcomes. This illustration acts as a negative reinforcement process that is likely to strengthen therapeutic change. As his locus of control begins shifting from external to internal and as he begins acquiring perceived functionality, his motivation for change may increase. At this point, more systematic change-based skills training procedures may be implemented (e.g., anger control, alcohol-specific coping, emotion regulation, emotion tolerance, and assertiveness).

Principle 13 (Match with Therapy Role, Therapist Demographics, or Treatment Type)

In working with the three patients, I believe that, of all the potential factors, the mismatch between therapist–patient demographics, particularly the socioeconomic status, may challenge the therapeutic alliance. For example, Victor, Brian, and Anne may perceive me to be financially comfortable, successful, and satisfied with my job, as well as having been privileged in attaining a higher educational level than they did; thus, they may assume that I cannot possibly understand and validate their struggles. If in-session events suggest the presence of such mismatch, I would address this issue directly, via reciprocal clarification of intent/impact, as well as strong genuine expression of empathy and validation on my part. In fact, all three patients face real-life challenges that are, in part, due to factors outside of their control, rendering their daily lives very stressful. They need to know that I fully understand and support them. If the problem persisted, I would engage in CPR interventions to strengthen the alliance and weaken therapy-interfering factors. Lastly, these patients' real-life hardships would be at the forefront in my mind, and I would make sure that changes targeted in treatment are realistic and within their reach. For example, even though it could be a good idea for Victor to get a better job, as a middle-aged man with a high school diploma, it may be an unrealistic goal.

Principle 14 (Accommodation with Patient's Preference for Religiously or Spiritually Oriented Treatment)

This principle is not likely to play a significant role in any of the three patients' treatment. However, religion played an important role in Victor's life, and it was also a source of social support for both him and Leonora. Therefore, I would explore the possibility for them to join their local parish to increase positive couple activities and to reconnect with their community.

Principle 15 (Level of Interpersonal Functioning and Proportion of Transference Interpretations)

Consistent with the CBASP approach, I formulate THs early in treatment to predict the occurrence of "hot" in-session events between the therapist and patient to promote positive interpersonal functioning and opportunities for corrective experiences and growth in the "here and now." The ensuing process work stemming from these therapist–patient events, such as the IDE, is designed to optimize the use of the therapist's disciplined personal involvement to promote change and healing of early traumas. As previously mentioned, the therapist becomes a "consequence" for the patient that he or she cannot avoid or ignore. These corrective, emotionally mediated, interpersonal experiences during sessions are designed to "break through" the patient's shield of disconnection and distrust to enable them to see the therapist for "who he or she is," namely, a positive and affirming individual who cares for them and who won't hurt them. It is expected that successful transference-based healing interventions promote change via counterconditioning and reinforcement mechanisms of learning. In sum, these transference-driven interventions enable the patient to "see" the therapist's positive regard, empathy, and affirmation; decrease the chance that they invalidate it; and foster the opportunity for them to benefit from it by beginning to trust others and internalize the therapist's positive regard.

As such, in my experience, process work related to the THs is optimal with most (if not all) patients, particularly those who present with complex and chronic depression and poor interpersonal functioning. So, in contrast to how this principle is formulated, I would use TH-based process work in line with the CBASP model (administered in a patient-centered, timely, and sensitive way to promote healing and foster hope) with all three patients, especially with Brian and Anne as their interpersonal functioning is poor and will affect their relationship with the therapist.

Principle 17 (Coping Style: Externalizing vs. Internalizing) and Principle 18 (Treatment Focus: Behavioral Change and Symptom Reduction vs. Fostering Insight and Self-Awareness)

I find these two principles useful in treatment, but only if applied *in context* and in a patient-centered and flexible way (as illustrated in the following discussion). Their usefulness is limited if they are viewed as absolute/dichotomous rules. Lastly, as they are negatively correlated, I will address them together in this section.

Brian exhibits the strongest externalizing coping style among the three patients, but he presents challenges to treatment with regard to readiness, motivation, and expectation for change (see Principles 4, 5, and 6); thus, his treatment has to strike a balance between behavioral changes and patient-centered, readiness-enhancing approaches (e.g., emphasizing the use of the therapeutic relationship). Additionally, his depression is chronic and related to early adversity (see Principle 8); therefore, insight about how his learning history affects his disconnection from his interpersonal environment and awareness of the role he plays in maintaining his own distress appear to be foundational changes (necessary) to increase in his perceived functionality and self-efficacy. Upon experiencing initial success in treatment, particularly in interpersonal functioning, and an increase in perceived functionality, he may be able to participate in the direct skills training components of treatment to address his problematic drinking, anger dyscontrol, and unassertiveness.

Anne exhibits both internalizing and externalizing coping styles, suggesting that, like in Brian's case (but maybe for different reasons), these two principles will only be helpful in guiding her treatment in a patient-centered and ideographic way. Use of the situational analysis, in parallel with MI interventions, may be optimal in this regard, as it is an indirect/direct approach to change and it effectively promotes engagement in treatment while concurrently providing opportunities for skills training and symptom reduction. Compared with Brian and Victor, though, I predict that Anne's mixed coping style will at times present additional challenges in session, as it will be unpredictable. Her internalizing style will pull for my dominant role, and her externalizing style will pull for my submissive role—a maladaptive pattern that is likely to happen with others in her life. I expect that this will require flexibility on my part and for remaining in the friendly, mixed dominant/submissive role. Thus, similar to Brian's, Anne's treatment requires a balanced, sensitively delivered, and patient-centered approach that includes an integration of relational work, fostering of perceived functionality and of awareness of her maladaptive interpersonal patterns, and skills training.

The importance of seeing Principles 17 and 18 in context and applying them in a patient-centered way is illustrated once again in considering Victor's coping style. In fact, although he has the most internalizing coping style of all three patients, compared with Brian and Anne he may respond well to treatment that fosters behavior change and symptom-reduction interventions (vs. insight and awareness), as he has the least baseline impairments, is in the most advanced stage of change, and is less severely depressed than they are. Therefore, while therapist–patient relational work, perceived functionality, and awareness of his maladaptive approach to his interpersonal environment are important elements of Victor's treatment, he is likely to respond well to an early introduction of behavioral skills training (e.g., self-affirmation/reinforcement, couple communication training, assertiveness training).

Principle 19 (Levels of Impairment and Social Supports and Attention to Social or Medical Needs)

This principle fundamentally shapes the treatments for all three patients, as they all have moderate to severe impairments in their interpersonal domain. Additionally, both Brian and Anne have an inadequate social support system. Therefore, the interpersonal focus of treatment inherent to CBASP that I am proposing and illustrating throughout this chapter is relevant for all three patients. Comments pertinent to this principle are found in earlier sections of the chapter and under Principle 34.

Principle 20 (Patient and Therapist Substance Problems [and Lack of Thereof])

Given the high rate of drop out and the difficulties inherent in the treatment of substance use/abuse, I believe that this principle is likely to inform treatment best when viewed in the context of what factors foster/strengthen alliance, increase the patient's commitment to change, and prevent premature termination in the treatment of these types of refractory problems. I do not think that the critical variable is the absence/presence of a substance abuse history on the part of the therapist. Rather, it is their the ability to experience attuned empathy toward the patient and ability to engage the patient in treatment, over and above implementing skillfully efficacious interventions that target the substance use/abuse. For example, in working with both Brian and Anne, to increase treatment success, I would strive to understand the complex mechanisms that maintain their substance abuse, validate their struggles, have realistic expectations regarding the difficulties inherent in their process of recovery, predict relapse, and be able to experience and communicate radical acceptance and total compassion.

Patient Process Variables

Principle 21 (Active Participation) and Principle 22 (Resistance)

In my experience, patients' participation in treatment is highly interrelated with other principles across categories, including Principle 1 (level of impairment), Principle 2 (personality disturbance), Principle 4 (initial expectations), Principle 5 (intrinsic motivation), Principle 6 (stage of change), Principle 10 (level of problem assimilation), Principle 11 (high levels of resistance), 1 Principle 2 (motivation for change), and Principle 22 (resistance). For example, when patients are in an active stage of change, they participate in treatment more readily and actively then when they are in a precontemplative or contemplative stage of change, and their engagement in therapy-inhibiting behaviors and resistance to treatment significantly decrease. More important, active participation and engagement in treatment manifests itself when the patient engages in new cognitive-behavioral changes outside the session as a result of the safety provided by the therapeutic relationship. Thus, as already discussed under previous principles, in addition to the timely and patient-centered implementation of skills training to foster behavioral and interpersonal changes, the alliance and process-level work play a major role in increasing patient's active participation in treatment and decreasing resistance to treatment.

Next, I will address Principles 21 and 22 concurrently by focusing on ways to decrease resistance, as I see this as vital to active participation in treatment. As discussed, I do expect Brian and Anne to show more resistance than Victor—although Victor will present some challenges in this regard as well. Across all three patients I would use the therapist–patient relationship as a tool for decreasing their resistance to treatment (and/or to me) by focusing on in-session events that reflect resistance. In addition, to connect the patient functionally to me, I would foster their acquisition of perceived functionality. This will provide them with the opportunity for asserting their needs in the here and now, including what they need from the treatment and me. I find that one of the most effective ways for attaining these goals is to address resistance behaviors with empathic attunement, namely, by discussing manifestations of resistance openly, collaboratively, and in a problem-solving way. Additionally, I find it pivotal for inducing change to create in-session opportunities to demonstrate to the patient that their negative expectancies toward me do not materialize and, subsequently to guide them to generalize this learning to others (i.e., "The therapist does not/will not hurt me"→ "Others do not/will not hurt me"). If successful, the focus on the therapist–patient relationship surrounding resistance events may provide a healing experience. In turn, this experience may increase the patient's trust in the therapist, so that he or she can participate in treatment more assertively and actively.

Therapy Relationship Principles

Principle 23 (Therapeutic Alliance) and Principle 27 (Alliance Rupture–Repair)

I believe that the issue of alliance, and quality thereof, emerges as a pivotal aspect of treatment in my work with all patients and cuts across most of the principles herein. Relatedly, repairing breaches of alliance (Principle 27) is essential for a high-quality alliance. Thus, I will address these principles concurrently.

I find that several therapist qualities/abilities, as well as in-session therapeutic maneuvers, are particularly important in promoting and maintaining a high-quality alliance. Most important is my ability to maintain a collaborative relationship with the patient at all times, in terms of treatment procedures, tasks related to change (e.g., homework), and treatment goals—the sine qua none of therapeutic work, especially with patients who present for treatment with severe impairments and chronicity of disorders. In terms of methods of intervention, I find that the flexible and patient-centered application of Socratic nondirective/directive methods (e.g., letting the patient set the pace for the session while guiding them to attain changes) when integrated with skills-based training is optimal.

In regard to therapist qualities, I think that the ability to tolerate patients' emotional distress (e.g., anxiety in Victor, anger in Brian, ambivalence in Anne) without "rescuing" them, deflecting their negative emotions, or indirectly punishing them for it is pivotal. Also important is the therapist's ability to address in a timely, sensitive, and nonjudgmental way the patients' treatment-inhibiting behaviors (e.g., using the CPR exercise). I also find that the in-session self-disclosure of vulnerable feelings (e.g., "I'm feeling closed off from you/hurt right now as you are disconnected from me"; "Why are you doing this?") promotes patients' empathic responses and increases their tendency to take responsibility for change. Any time a patient is walled off from me or is defensive and resists change, they are "blindfolding me and tying my hands behind my back, while desperately wanting help to relieve their distress—an impossible situation for me to resolve without the patients' help." (I have shared this metaphor countless times with patients and with very successful outcomes!) Relatedly, I find it useful to address in-session negative therapist–patient interactions by clarifying reciprocal intent/impact and using attuned empathy to validate the patient's distress. The previously stated therapist qualities, which I strive to maintain at all times, do require the willingness and ability to directly and closely engage emotionally with the patient—there is no room for remaining neutral—to produce change.

As demonstrated in many previous principles, explicitly or implicitly, I will expect alliance ruptures in my work with all of three patients due to their skills deficits and problematic interpersonal approaches. While I always initiate an alliance rapture-repair, I try to involve the patient into the repair effort to empower them and strengthen our bond. At all times, I am mindful that the patients are doing the best they can at any point in time, even when they are disconnecting from me or being hurtful. Thus, I strive to feel genuine empathy and radical acceptance toward them no matter what. Ultimately, if I cannot engage them in a constructive collaborative effort, I cannot help them, which is why alliance rupture–repair work is critical. I find that conducting in-session situational analyses concerning negative therapist–patient events to be most useful. In fact, this process creates the opportunity for me to validate the patient's struggles and to re-establish a collaborative alignment in the bond, treatment goals, and therapeutic methods. The CPR and IDE procedures are very useful, as is the opportunity to address alliance ruptures through in-session use of good listening and nondirective skills, such as summarizing, reflecting, empathic attunement, and validating.

For example, in working with Anne, in view of her mood lability and interpersonal impairments, I would predict a high likelihood of alliance ruptures, despite my best intentions and earnest attempts to maintain a positive alliance. She may, for example, come to a session emotionally dysregulated and cry throughout the session, unable to focus. Thus, upon validating her distress and responding in an affirmative way, I may have to introduce CPR approaches to help her focus productively. I might say: "Anne, whenever I ask you about anything at all, or try to help you focus on only one negative situation (so that we can learn from it), you cry. . . . You keep on crying, so I feel like I can't really say anything at all. . . . I do feel awful about your distress, but I am not sure what to do to help you." "How do you feel about what I am telling you? Why do you think I am telling you this? What do you want from me today?"

Similarly, if, in response to my attempts to guide Anne to focus on only one negative situation, she persistently talks about multiple negative situations (thus making it impossible for us to do in-session work), I might say: "Anne, I realize that so many stressful things happened to you this past week, and I can understand how upsetting this is for you, but I cannot deal with more than one situation at the time, and I am not sure how telling me about all these situations is helping 'you' or 'us' right now. In fact, the more you are telling me how everything is terrible, the more I feel helpless and hopeless. How do you feel about what I am telling you? Why do you think I am telling you this?" In response to my communication, she may say (as a depressed patient with BPD said to me recently): "Oh no, now I have to worry about you too? I thought we were here for me." As a preoperational child, Anne may not be able to experience much empathy for me; in fact, she is likely to be completely walled off from me while desperately seeking connection and intimacy. In response, I would say: "You do not have to worry about me, but you need to know that you are affecting me in a way that makes me feel confused, unable to decide how to best help you, and scrambling (unsuccessfully) to find a way to decrease your distress—in effect, you are ejecting me from the session. I don't know how to best reach you. Why are you doing this? What do you want to do about this or what do you need from me? Why do you think I am telling you this?" This type of communication would, hopefully, lead her to talk about her feelings and obstacles to engaging in change work and/or connecting with me, which would create the opportunity for me to empathically validate her difficulties and reconnect in a collaborative way. I would apply similar procedures with Brian and Victor.

Principle 24 (Therapist Regard and Affirmation), Principle 25 (Congruence), Principle 26 (Empathy), and Principle 28 (Supportive Self-Disclosures)

If we focus on the *bond* aspect of alliance, then quality of alliance and repair of alliance ruptures are inextricably connected with all remaining therapy relationship principles: therapist positive regard and affirmation (Principle 24), therapist congruence (Principle 25), therapist empathy (Principle 26), and therapist use of supportive self-disclosures (Principle 28). In the previous section (Principles 23 and 27), as well as when describing the implementation of several other principles (e.g., Principles 8, 11–13, and 20–22), I have already described examples of how these therapist–patient relationship factors affect treatment. Nevertheless, I will add a few comments.

Positive process work would not be possible without maintaining a strong bond with the patient at all times. As such, it is essential to directly, earnestly, and openly express unconditional positive regard, acceptance, care, and concern for the patient, even when the patient's behavior is maladaptive. Likewise, it is essential to communicate my unwavering belief that each patient has the potential to heal and change. To this end, it is useful to derive THs and to constructively manage transference and countertransference events and skillful use of interpersonal pulls in session.

In regards to therapist congruence, perhaps departing from the original definition of congruence proposed by Carl Rogers, I define this construct as an attitude of the therapist toward the patient whereby the therapist continuously strive to be (a) authentic, honest, present, and attuned to the patient; (b) comfortable in the session even when the impact of the patient's behavior is negative; and (c) able to *not* move away from the patient (or defend oneself) in response to the patient putting up a wall or engaging in hostile communications. In sum, with all three patients, I would rely on the most important pillars of therapist congruence, including the ability to work collaboratively, to express vulnerability, and to not take an authoritative role, all while continuously expressing care and positive regard.

As mentioned previously, I find the construct of empathic attunement to best encapsulate the foundation of alliance and to be the sine qua none of all other relationship principles embedded in alliance. In my opinion, the ability of the therapist to be in touch at all times with the patient's emotional experience, to accurately understand it, to process it emotionally as well as cognitively, and to share this understanding and experience with the patient is of paramount importance in affirming/supporting the patient and promoting change. Sometimes, it is challenging to genuinely experience unconditional positive regard toward, and acceptance of, the patient, especially when they are disconnected or hostile toward the therapist. When this is the case, I find the process of gathering information to derive a case formulation, including a thorough review of the origins of the maladaptive mechanisms that maintain the patient's problems, to be useful. Specifically, being able to see how maladaptive experiences with significant others, biological vulnerabilities, situational factors, and life stressors contribute to the patient's maladaptive approaches toward themselves and their environment provides a narrative (a model) that is logical and makes sense. Most important, inevitably, I feel true empathy for the "little child" who is unable to extricate themselves from the misery they are in.

Consistent with CBASP tenants, I believe that change will come about when the patient is able to connect in a reciprocally collaborative and affirming relationship with their interpersonal environment, starting with the therapist. Most important, when they are able to acquire perceived functionality vis-à-vis their interpersonal environment, they will acquire agency, self-efficacy, and control—changes that are likely to decrease depression. Thus, demonstrating to the patient the impact that they have on the therapist via the planful, disciplined use of self-disclosure is a primary change strategy in my work with depressed patients, as illustrated previously (e.g., see Principles 8, 11,12, 23, and 27). The most important role of self-disclosure is to connect the patient to the therapist and to increase the opportunity that they "see" and accept my positive regard, unconditional acceptance, affirmation, and genuine care. It is impossible for the therapist to effectively connect with the patient and promote healing interpersonal experiences if the patient is walled off from the therapist. Thus, therapist self-disclosures serve to dislodge the patient from their avoidance and isolation.

In the IDE, for example, the productive use of the therapist *objective countertransference* helps the patient learn to discriminate the supportive response of the therapist from the expected hurtful/negative one, as well as to separate the therapist from a malevolent significant other. The essence of using self-disclosure in communicating objective countertransference with the three patients herein may be captured by the following sentences: "I (DV) feel as though you want me to take care of you while you are not taking care of yourself, and that makes me sad because you are not caring for yourself" (with Victor); "I feel like you are keeping me at an arm's distance with your anger. I feel that you are not letting me show that I care about you and, in doing that, you are disconnected from me. I feel sad about that" (with Brian);"When you are pulling away from me and thinking that I am abandoning or criticizing you, I feel as if you are not trusting my stable and positive regard toward you and not seeing how much I value you. I feel discouraged by this" (with Anne).

Disclosure of having had similar experiences in life also helps alliance, as the therapist is joining with the patient. We all have had experiences of despair, hopelessness, and helplessness around which to join. I find it productive to share these experiences with the patients (and how we coped with them) in a sensitive and timely way to promote bonding, hope, and validation.

Therapist Intervention Variables

Principle 29 (General Psychodynamic Interpretations) and Principle 30 (Quality of Psychodynamic Interpretations)

Given the overlap between these two principles in my work, which departs somewhat from the use of interpretations stemming from psychodynamic theoretical models, I will address them concurrently. I will primarily describe my use of transference and countertransference within the CBASP framework.

As discussed throughout, the therapist–patient relationship is a primary vehicle for change (over and above skills training) in my work with all patients. Regarding the three patients, this is particularly true for Brian and Anne. Due to their adverse childhood experiences and ensuing maladaptive connection with the environment, I expect that they will repeat these maladaptive dynamics in their relationship with me. Specifically, I expect that they will "transfer" onto me the maladaptive expectancies they have toward others (e.g., regarding issues pertaining to intimacy, emotional needs, failure, and expression of negative affect). Their resultant dysfunctional behavior in session will elicit countertransference from me. I therefore find it important to derive THs early in treatment to better plan for constructive use of the therapeutic relationship. In line with the CBASP model, I collect historical information from patients about the perceived impact or "stamp" that significant others had on their lives to make them the persons they are today. This leads me to derive causal conclusions about their interpersonal needs expectancies. I then formulate THs concerning the top one or two interpersonal adversity or trauma domains likely to affect our therapeutic relationship, including (a) intimacy needs, (b) disclosure of highly emotive needs/private matters, (c) disclosure of mistakes/failures, and (d) expression of negative affect. As mentioned in previous sections of the chapter, these initial THs enable me to predict in-session transference-based "hot" events unique to each patient, increase my readiness to identify them and utilize them as opportunities to promote secure attachment, decrease therapy-inhibiting behaviors, decrease resistance, strengthen alliance, and promote healing—as discussed in earlier sections of this chapter (e.g., see Principles 3, 6, 8, 11, 15, 24, and 28).

Principle 31 (Feedback from Routinely Delivered Outcome Measures) and Principle 32 (Feedback from Routinely Delivered from Therapist)

The first of these principles (Principle 31) is very important in my work with all patients, and one that has received significant empirical support from the in literature in terms of enhancing treatment efficacy. As such, I use outcome assessment to measure change on a weekly basis in my clinical work by collecting patients' ratings on the treatment outcome package (TOP; Kraus, Seligman & Jordan, 2005). I also use pre–post dimensional and ongoing measurement of symptom severity to plan treatment, modify treatment, and involve patients in their process of change.

Using the weekly assessments, I review patients' functioning across domains and areas of symptomatology at the beginning of each session, which increases the breadth and depth of information I have for each patient in the here and now. I also find that these routine assessments provide a useful source of information for the therapist (like a "third eye"), particularly regarding areas of patients' functioning not directly targeted in treatment (e.g., sleep problems, suicidality, violence, psychosis, substance abuse). This information and response to treatment curves (or change profiles) across time and across domains enable me to monitor closely the patients' progress or lack thereof. They also provide me with very helpful warnings of premature or unexpected deterioration. Thus, I can modify the treatment to increase its effectiveness and prevent deterioration or early termination. As such, I find this information to be essential in informing treatment, as it is quantifiable and increases the methodic and systematic processes of intervention. In fact, I think that outcome-informed treatment is a powerful and an underutilized way to integrate science and practice in delivering treatment.

Sharing this information with patients is equally important. I typically review the TOP profile with each patient at the start of each session and invite the patient to collaboratively evaluate with me his or her progress. This provides the opportunity for orchestrating several treatment-enhancing maneuvers, such as mutual celebration of positive changes, trouble-shooting barriers to change, evaluating new situational events and stressors that may need to be incorporated in treatment, and/or modifying the treatment to better tailor it to the patient's needs. Routine outcome assessment also encourages the patient to become a participating member of the therapeutic dyad and to take responsibility for change. Sharing routine outcome in session also may pre-empt alliance ruptures, as it increases opportunities for in-session discussions concerning flexible changes to goals and methods.

In line with the second of these principles (Principle 32), it is also important to provide positive reinforcement to patients for their overall progress. For example, in my work with all three patients, especially Brian and

Anne, to encourage their active involvement in treatment and foster motivation and hope, I may "boost the signal" by letting them know how their progress is affecting me. For example, I may say: "Your depression seems to be really getting better, ever since you started doing X." "I feel so happy for you. . . . This is very important to me. . . . I feel like you are a hero." "How do you feel about what I am telling you?" "What do you think has helped you the most and why?" The reason I would want to augment the positive reinforcement given to Victor, Brian, and Anne by letting them know how their changes affect me is because, if they are still disconnected from me, they may not "see," appreciate, or trust that I am truly happy for them. I would therefore also ask: "Why do you think I am telling you this?" Similarly, in a nonjudgmental or punitive way, I would want to discuss the negative effect (e.g., concern, surprise, sadness, uncertainty, helplessness) that their lack of progress (or deterioration) has on me.

Principle 33 (Flexible Administration of Treatment)
As mentioned for the previous two principles, as well as several others before (e.g., Principles 1–3, 8, 10, 12, 17, 18), I apply treatment in patient-centered, flexible ways, guided by continuous outcome feedback. I see the case formulation component of treatment (and changes thereof based on the patient's response to treatment) as fundamental in guiding treatment delivery in ideographic and patient-tailored ways.

In treating depressive disorders, although I rely on a CBASP framework, I integrate elements of other treatments in line with the case formulation and to suit the evolving needs of the patient at all levels of treatment, particularly in regard to behavioral and interpersonal skills training. In Victor's treatment plan, for example, I have incorporated BA and couple therapy interventions (including CBT and acceptance procedures) to decrease his marital distress, increase dyadic acceptance, and provide communication training. Additionally, Victor's treatment includes assertiveness training, and, if necessary, CBT interventions for GAD and agoraphobia to address his anxiety disorders. Brian's treatment includes elements of MI, BA, and CBT approaches to harm reduction and strengthening coping skills for addressing his alcohol dependence, as well as behavioral and interpersonal skills training (assertiveness training, emotion regulation and tolerance, and mindfulness-based stress reduction practices). Similarly, Anne's treatment includes elements of MI, BA, mindfulness practices, emotion regulation, and distress tolerance modules of DBT and interpersonal skills training. Overall, the goal of CBASP treatment for chronic depression is to teach the patients a social problem-solving algorithm to increase their interpersonal effectiveness, perceived functionality, and self-efficacy. However, as described earlier, intrapersonal coping skills (e.g., anger control training, mindfulness practices, coping skills for alcohol reduction) are also targeted, as are therapist–patient in-session interactions to promote change.

The situational analysis method lends itself to flexible and patient-centered application. For example, as is common in severely/chronically depressed patients, Brian and Anne are socially alienated and isolated (see Principle 19). Thus, before being able to target interpersonal functioning and skills development, we need to foster approach to others. In this case, the situational analysis may focus on patients' intrapersonal events related to avoidance (e.g., avoidance of behavioral activities, interpersonal events, engagement in therapy work such as homework) as a first line of intervention. Changes in this regard, would then enable treatment to progress to increasing positive interpersonal connections.

Principle 34 (Fostering Adaptive Interpersonal) and Principle 38 (Behavioral Changes)

As discussed thus far, these two principles fundamentally shape my work with depressive complex/chronic disorders, and I have included numerous illustrations of applications of this principle throughout, including under Principle 33. Moreover, I find it hard to separate fostering interpersonal changes from behavioral changes, and thus I will concurrently address these two principles, as they apply to each of the three cases.

Victor's treatment includes couple therapy to strengthen this primary support system. His relationship with his co-workers is also an important goal for treatment to increase his satisfaction with his interpersonal functioning outside the marriage. Following a brief BA phase to increase the rate of pleasure, couple treatment will foster the following: (a) positive couple and family events; (b) spouses' acceptance of each other, (c) reciprocal validation and empathy; (d) recognition of the reciprocally negative cycle that maintains distress; (e) adaptive couple behavioral changes (e.g., for Victor, approach and involvement; for Leonora, acceptance and affirmation); and (f) use of positive communication skills. The administration of situational analysis procedure and social skills (e.g., assertiveness) training will enable Victor to gain a sense of control over and connection with his environment, self-efficacy, and an ability to engage in self-affirmation/self-soothing.

Although disconnected from others, Brian appears to have a few friends and relatives who care enough about him to urge him to seek treatment. Thus, I would guide him to reconnect with these people in his life, in addition to people at work, as an increase in his positive social interconnectedness is likely to decrease his hostile expectancies of his environment. The ultimate goal is to orchestrate opportunities for Brian to recognize that others genuinely care for him, disconfirming his negative expectations. Thus, I am adding to his treatment plan a *skills training/behavioral rehearsal* component, namely,

(a) alcohol-specific coping skills training (to acquire the abilities to engage in controlled drinking or abstinence); (b) social skills training (to approach others assertively and skillfully); and (c) elements of the mindfulness-based stress reduction protocol to decrease his anger dyscontrol and enhance his mood regulation skills. If necessary, elements of DBT, such as emotion-regulation skills and distress-tolerance skills, can also be implemented.

Anne is socially isolated, interpersonally avoidant, and does not have experiences of positive interpersonal connections growing up (with the exception of one friend). Hence, the early stages of her treatment will focus on building a strong alliance, fostering positive self-care changes (including BA strategies and emotion-regulation skills), and use of the therapist–patient relationship as a vehicle for increasing commitment to therapy and to begin building trust in others. Upon acquiring these foundations, in subsequent phases of treatment I would guide her to gradually establish positive connections with people in her life, such as co-workers and classmates, and to ameliorate her relationship with her mother. Later stages of treatment would aim to build new relationships to increase the breadth of her social support system. I would encourage Anne to begin approaching others via the situational analysis methodology to establish closeness with people already in her environment (e.g., at school and at work) and to begin forming new relationships, thus increasing connection with the environment and self-efficacy.

In addition to continuous practice with emotion-regulation skills, additional behavioral strategies may be included in her treatment, such as interpersonal skills/communication skills training (via direct instruction, modeling, behavior rehearsal, coaching, and response reinforcement) and elements of distress tolerance skills from DBT (e.g., crisis survival skills, reality acceptance skills, etc.) and/or from mindfulness approaches. Lastly, Anne would be encouraged to engage in attempts to connect with her environment (e.g., engage in activities that have social involvements) to increase her social support system and practice her new social approach skills.

Principle 35 (Fostering Self-Understanding)
As indicated throughout, one of my goals in working with the three patients is to teach them perceived functionality—the ultimate type of self-understanding that operates in the "here and now" and targets both the patient's awareness of their role in affecting maladaptive outcomes, as well as the effect they has on the interpersonal environment. Increases in perceive functionality are directly related to self-efficacy, intra- and interpersonal control, and decreases in depression. I have discussed or illustrated ways in which self-understanding and awareness are embedded in my interventions numerous times above (e.g., Principles 1–3, 6, 8–12, 15, 17, 18, 21, and 22). For instance, in my treatment

with Anne and Brian, increasing their awareness of the sequential relationships among their maladaptive coping strategies, increased affective arousal/distress, use of self-destructive (Brian: alcohol abuse) or self-harming behaviors (Anne: drugs, NSSI, and dysfunctional sexual experiences), and consequent negative outcomes (increased depression) is of paramount importance.

Principle 36 (Fostering Emotional Experiencing and/or Deepening)
Over the past three decades, I have come to believe that primary pathways to change (for patients with chronic mood problems and severe co-morbidities) are at the emotional, interpersonal, and skills levels of analysis in addition to purely cognitive or behavioral levels. Most severely depressed patients have long-standing psychological co-morbidities, and significant interpersonal and intrapersonal skills deficits. Thus, treatments that primarily address cognitive processes in sophisticated ways (e.g., thought disputation and restructuring) are out of reach for these patients or may increase rumination and avoidance of their environment. Approaches that de-emphasize emotional experiencing, fail to address entrenched, maladaptive, emotionally based problems that are core to complex depressive disorders (e.g., attachment anxiety, fear of intimacy). That is why I rely on an integrative application of the CBASP model in my approach to treating complex mood disorders, as it views emotional experiencing as a key pathway to change. In fact, as described at the outset, CBASP views depression as a mood disorder driven by conditioned fears of interpersonal encounters and maintained by a refractory pattern of interpersonal avoidances (McCullough, 2000). Thus, CBASP treatment techniques are designed to promote change in the patients' approach to their interpersonal environment through emotional experiencing/exposure pathways rather than cognitive restructuring and/or schema deactivation pathways. Emotional experiencing opportunities include in-session and outside-of-session exposure-based events as well as corrective counterconditioning interpersonal experiences (for a thorough discussion of exposure-based aspects of CBASP, see Neudeck, Wlater, & Schepf, 2012).

In addition to the affectively mediated aspects of CBASP (e.g., see Principles 1–3, 8, 9, and 15), I often use emotionally based experiential processes, such as the empty-chair and two-chair techniques from experiential models (Greenberg, Rice & Elliott, 1993), as well as cognitive-experiential intervention informed by Eric Berne's transactional analysis (TA) psychotherapy model (cf. Steiner, 1990). In implementing the latter, for example, I use visualizations (through drawings) of the metaphors provided by the TA model as a heuristic to foster the patients' understanding of the dysfunctional cognitive-emotional coping they use. Most important, borrowing TA language, I encourage them to use their nurturing parent "tape" or "script" (i.e., self-affirmation, self-efficacy, self-soothing), as well as their adult tape, rather than their critical/pig parent tape (i.e., self-criticism, self-deprecation) to address the emotional needs of their needy child tape (i.e., the scared, angry, sad child) and playful child tape. I use this TA technique in a cognitive-emotionally focused way to bolster patient motivation to use positive self-talk and affirmation, as well as to increase their self-nurturing and decrease their reliance on the therapist's nurturing parent tape. I expect that the use of this TA technique or the two-chair technique to effectively foster cognitive-emotional shifts and increase self-nurturing in all three patients. Lastly, in my work with Brian, if necessary I would use the empty-chair technique to help him accept and process his ambivalence about his father's death and the role his father had in his life.

Principle 37 (Nondirective Interventions)
This principle is very important in my work and its applications in treatment are reflected throughout this chapter, as it is interrelated to many of the other principles. Primarily, I believe that the use of the situational analysis (CBASP), MI interventions, and mindfulness-based interventions are effective nondirective/directive interventions with depressed patients, including the three example patients we've been discussing. Moreover, the disciplined use of the therapist–patient relationship as a timely, sensitive, and patient-centered vehicle for change maximizes and potentiates change with all of them.

Describe My Experience in Writing This Chapter

Writing this chapter was one of the most challenging, yet, gratifying projects I have embarked on recently. Although the task was as arduous as I suspected it would be, it enabled me to clarify and articulate in pinpointed ways how I "think" in my clinical work. Most important, it illustrated to me how I engage in multiple and concurrent treatment considerations in a dynamic way as I provide treatment based on the principles of therapeutic change. It also reminded me of the fact that the explicit process by which principles are applied may be more salient in early stages of a therapist's training than at later stages of clinical experience. In fact, a degree of automaticity and implicit use of principles *has* to become part of more advanced stages of training, as skillful interventions are applied in session in a timely, precise, and spontaneous way—all the while striving to integrate a strong alliance with an optimal process of change. Alternatively stated, a therapist does not have the time to think too much or withdraw from a patient to engage in a complex decision-making process, especially when confronted with a patient who is emotionally distraught and/or unable to engage in the process of change. Because the therapist has to act quickly and efficaciously, the internalization of this decision-making process may be important to ensuring success in treatment.

The list of principles provided by the editors is thorough and includes most (if not all) of the salient principles that guided my treatment planning across the three patients herein (and that guides my clinical work in general). However, consistent with my expectations, I used the principles in each category, mindful of their interrelatedness with one another. Thus, to some extent, the separation of the principles into 38 separate entities across five categories is artificial when it comes to clinical application. This is exemplified by the frequency with which I collapsed different principles within the same category and across categories (e.g., Principles 21 and 22 with Principles 1, 2, 4–6, and 10–12). It is also reflected by the links I provided to interventions that are pertinent to and reflected in various principles. Furthermore, as described throughout, I found that several clusters of principles were aspects of the same construct (e.g., readiness to change/ability to engage in treatment; alliance; resistance) rather than truly separate entities. I also found that some principles are redundant and repeated across sections (e.g., Principles 1 and 16).

While from a theoretical/research standpoint, the list of principles is compelling, in the reality of clinical work, the process is more global than granular. It is clear to me that these principles are not and cannot be applied in isolation; the interrelationships among the principles and how they play out within each patient's unique characteristics defines how prominently each principle is applied and how salient its role in treatment is. Put another way, the usefulness of the principles is defined by being able to evaluate each principle in relation to the other principles within each patient and within the *context* of each patient's reality; for example, I have illustrated this issue in discussing Principles 17 (externalizing coping style) and 18 (internalizing coping style), as well as Principles 21 (active participation) and 22 (less resistance).

In addition to the previously stated considerations, I found it hard to make predictions about interventions based on these principles with the three patients when presented with static information about them based on the initial assessment. In reality, I find that in early stages of treatment, the actual treatment plan maps out areas of change in a broad and often tentative way. As treatment progresses, the patients' response to treatment suggests what the next targeted areas should be and why. All of this is continuously guided by a dynamic case formulation that is then woven into the principles of change; thus, in "real" clinical work the principles-informed approach is easier, at times, than it was in discussing hypothetical treatment applications for the three patients.

On the other hand, at times, patients do present with unpredictable or unexpected situations, thus, creating challenges over and above those encountered herein.

In writing this chapter I also found that the *patient prognostic variables* category encompassed most of the principles that permeated treatment. In fact, the prognostic variables inform the therapist about what they can expect in the process of change and how they can be attuned to the needs and strengths of a particular patient. The process of integrating principles within and between clusters enabled me to realize how the prognostic principles should be viewed as the anchors for all subsequent principles. Similar considerations can be made as a result of my experience writing about the application of the therapist–patient variables/alliance category of principles (e.g., alliance-based and therapist–patient relationship variables are very interconnected and interwoven in all other principles).

Nevertheless, I found it useful to be reminded about both the interrelatedness of most principles of therapeutic change and, based on working with the three patients, to be able to suggest clusters while maintaining the distinct elements of the principles within each cluster. Interestingly, this process guided me in articulating how the nuanced elements of interrelated principles may guide interventions in overlapping, yet similarly nuanced, ways, in terms of what interventions to apply, when to apply them, and how to best use the therapist–patient relationship to promote change. In fact, reviewing the principles (albeit condensed in more discrete categories) before initiating and throughout treatment with each patient, and planning ways to address them, may be an excellent tool for designing treatments in more systematic ways and with an increased patient-centered approach.

Lastly, the process of writing this chapter has lead me to derive an initial (tentative) approach for translating the application of the principles into a heuristic to be used in supervision/training—an initiative that I am currently piloting with my supervisees. I found that once the principles are clustered in a more parsimonious and clinically informed way, they can be organized into a patient-specific table that can be populated by a trainee/supervisor at the outset of treatment to identify where the patient "falls" in terms of each cluster of principles. Initial (and subsequent) adaptations to the content of treatment, selection of interventions, planful ways to pre-empt challenges to the alliance, and pinpointed therapist–patient interventions to address patients' characteristics across each principle would follow. In fact, the presence of overlaps/clusters among the principles make the treatment plan more parsimonious, as interventions addressing one or more principles can be expected to be useful for other principles as well. This consideration is exemplified by the fact that in proposing principles-based interventions for the three patients herein, I often suggested very similar interventions across patients, even though each patient exhibited both common and unique dynamics. Lastly, if a patient does not evince a good response to treatment, various principles (or elements) within each cluster could be reviewed to modify treatment and guide use of the therapist–patient relationship.

In conclusion, the AO of writing this chapter has surpassed my DO. The process has been arduous, not only because the task was objectively difficult but also because my own expectations were high and my "reads" were not always helpful. Nevertheless, the journey was well worth it, as it strengthened and increased my perceived functionality in both my clinical work and supervision.

References

Castonguay, L. G & Beutler, L. E., (Eds.). (2006). *Principles of therapeutic change that work* (6th ed.). New York, NY: Oxford University Press

Greenberg, L. S., Rice, L. N., & Elliott, R. (1993). *Facilitating emotional change: The moment-by-moment process.* New York, NY: Guilford.

Kraus, D. R., Seligman, D. A., & Jordan, J. R. (2005). Validation of a behavioral health treatment outcome and assessment tool designed for naturalistic settings: The Treatment Outcome Package. *Journal of Clinical Psychology, 61*(3), 285–314.

McCullough, J. P., Jr. (2000). *Treatment for chronic depression: cognitive analysis system of psychotherapy (CBASP).* New York, NY: Guilford.

McCullough, J. P., Jr. (2006). *Treating chronic depression with disciplined personal involvement: Cognitive behavioral analysis system of psychotherapy (CBASP).* New York, NY: Springer.

Mikulincer, M., & Shaver, P. R. (2005). Attachment theory and emotions in close relationships: Exploring the attachment-related dynamics of emotional reactions to relational events. *Personal Relationships, 12,* 149–168.

Neudeck, P., Walter, H., & Schoepf, D. (2012). Exposure aspects of the Interpersonal discrimination exercise (IDE) and the situational analysis system of psychotherapy (CBASP). In P. Neudeck & H.-U. Wittchen (Eds.), *Exposure therapy: rethinking the model: Refining the method,* pp. 153–166. New York, NY: Springer.

Steiner, C. M. (1990). *Scripts people live* (2nd ed.). New York, NY: Grove.

7
Conceptual, Clinical, and Empirical Perspectives on Principles of Change for Depression

Benjamin Johnson, Dina Vivian, Abraham W. Wolf, Larry E. Beutler, Louis G. Castonguay, and Michael J. Constantino

The goal of this chapter, as well as the concluding chapter of the social anxiety section (Chapter 12), is to bring together different views about principles of change and future directions to better understand them. To do so, both chapters involve the collaboration of the three clinical authors who have respectively worked on each section of the book and the book editors to (a) delineate convergences and differences in the implementation of principles; (b) discuss the clinical importance of using principles in practice; (c) suggest possible combinations of principles perceived as redundant; (d) identify additional principles that could be the focus of future research; and (e) offer final thoughts about principles of change. Although the priority of these chapters is to give a predominant voice to the clinical authors in addressing these five issues, the editors have also offered comments and reactions to the clinicians' perspectives with the goal of fostering conversations and/or future collaboration about each of these important topics.

Convergences and Complementarities in the Implementing Principles of Change

Each therapist/author who contributed to the depression section of this book (Johnson, Vivian, and Wolf) read each of the two chapters in this section that were not written by them. They then wrote a relatively brief text regarding how each of these two chapters converge and/or diverge from their own in terms of how much emphasis they give to the 38 empirically based principles (see

Box 7.2), as well as how they generally implement them. Following these texts, which are presented next, the book editors have attempted to identify major themes of these convergences and divergences, as well as to link these themes with information revealed in profiles of interventions for the three authors presented in Chapter 3.

Dr. Johnson's Reflections

In this section, I will highlight convergences and differences in how much emphasis the three clinician-authors gave to the five clusters of principles in the three cases discussed. I will also note similarities and differences in the specific techniques the authors proposed to implement the principles.

Convergences and Complementarities among Authors

All three chapter authors used numerous principles from each of the five clusters. It doesn't seem to me that any author found an entire category unimportant. Indeed, this makes sense, as the clusters were derived from years of psychotherapy research.

Some principles received greater attention than others. All three authors explored the consequences of higher baseline impairment (Principle 1) and personality disorder (Principle 2) and how to manage these factors in the therapeutic relationship and with tailored interventions. We all discussed how we would moderate what we would do based on patient factors such as an externalizing style (Principle 17) or higher resistance (Principle 11). We described specific ways in which we would promote active participation in treatment (Principle 21) and try to avoid provoking client resistance (Principle 22). All authors were deeply interested in therapy relationship principles. We see the centrality of the therapeutic alliance to our work, we illustrate our attempts at deep empathy, and we can imagine using supportive self-disclosures. In all three chapters, there are numerous examples of therapeutic intervention principles. We describe fostering interpersonal and behavioral changes, self-understanding, and, at times, try specifically to deepen emotional experiencing in session.

The three therapist/authors paid less attention to some of the more specific principles—ones that are relevant in more narrow circumstances. For instance, less attention was given to the impact of socio-economic status and clinician substance abuse history. The three cases presented led us to focus more on other principles.

I would say that the techniques we proposed using to implement change with these patients had much more in common than not. First, we all proposed many, many techniques, moves, metaphors, skills, concepts, and phrases in these three rather lengthy chapters. We build rapport, explore patterns, suggest a reframe, and prompt new behavior in the session and outside of it. We deal with patient explanations for their problems and help them to develop more constructive ways of understanding their difficulties. We tend to the self-esteem and self-concept of patients, hoping our nurturing styles will promote them to relate better to themselves.

Were there any major differences in how the three authors suggested implementing the principles? I don't think so. On the other hand, it was clear that each treatment would be personalized and tailored and reflect a unique relationship between that clinician and that patient. Such is the beauty of psychotherapy, as a well-trained clinician forms a genuine relationship to promote the well-being of the patient. Each experience is unique, despite the common change principles at play.

Next I make a few additional and more specific comments on how my colleagues propose implementing change principles in the three cases of depression and how our approaches are both similar and different.

Dr. Johnson's Comments on Dr. Vivian's Chapter

Dr. Vivian, coming from the Cognitive-Behavioral Analysis System of Psychotherapy (CBASP) perspective, emphasizes using therapy relationship principles and therapist intervention principles. She proposes creating extremely close therapeutic alliances, filled with regard, affirmation, and congruence (Principles 24 and 25) and then giving direct feedback to patients about their interpersonal behaviors to promote self-understanding (Principle 35). To get such direct yet empathic feedback will likely foster emotional experiencing and deepening for the client (Principle 36). For example, Dr. Vivian discusses how she might bring Brian's attention to ways in which he keeps his distance from the clinician. There is significant overlap between my emphasis on therapy relationship principles and therapist intervention principles and Dr. Vivian's emphasis. Indeed, I am very focused on helping Victor, for instance, to feel heard, to be more aware of his underlying needs, and to change his interpersonal behavior, such as with co-workers and his wife.

The CBASP approach, as Dr. Vivian describes it, focuses on increasing patient's perceived functionality and "fostering their (positive) connection with the environment and others." A primary technique is the situational analysis. This is very parallel to my "rescripting" technique to embody the therapist intervention principles of fostering interpersonal and behavioral changes

(Principles 34 and 38) in which I help a patient identify new ways of responding to a predictable trigger.

Dr. Vivian describes her treatment plan for Victor. She focuses on behavioral activation, couple therapy, and interpersonal functioning outside of the marriage, as well as problem-solving regarding the possibility of changing jobs. Again, she describes working from the same clusters of principles as I do.

Regarding client prognostic principles, Dr. Vivian discusses how to treat patients (like Brian and Anne) with more baseline impairment. There is significant overlap between her approach and mine, such as the suggestion of bringing family members into the treatment of Brian.

Dr. Vivian discusses the strong connections between the prognostic principles and the therapy relationship and therapist intervention principles. For instance, clients with more baseline impairment may be less likely to benefit from treatment and yet also respond differentially to relationship styles and interventions. Her comments set the stage for future work examining different ways of organizing the change principles. There may be a benefit to grouping the principles across clusters or themes. Anxious, internalizing patients have a different prognostic profile and need different things from treatment than a lower functioning patient who has a more externalizing style. Her example of how to deal with attachment anxiety as a prognostic variable is helpful and informative. She suggests how all three patients manifest attachment anxiety and that skillful use of the therapeutic relationship can be used to address these attachment issues. I focused relatively less on the client prognostic principles, thinking that the other four principle clusters are more important because as a clinician I can do something about them. The more one sees the connection between the principle clusters, the more action-oriented the prognostic principles can be. Dr. Vivian writes, "I see my task as one of increasing hope, and motivation and commitment to engage in treatment, especially for Brian and Anne." This is a good, clear way of using the prognostic principles to influence treatment.

Dr. Johnson's Comments on Dr. Wolf's Chapter

Dr. Wolf begins by noting one key question—how to make the 38 principles actionable. As clinicians, the three of us share this bias toward identifying actionable concepts. He discusses the comparison between learning how to respond to your opponent in a game of chess and learning how to make therapeutic moves with a patient. In both, it pays to have broad principles in mind and yet be highly responsive to what the person in front of you is doing. I like this metaphor and find it useful and comparable to how I think about therapeutic work. He also emphasizes the importance of illustrating principles with specific language. I relate to this—I often want patients to show me the metaphorical videotapes of what they did and said.

Dr. Wolf's treatment approach to these three patients focuses on repairing their self-esteem and their core view of themselves as "losers." He believes the patients are suffering from a loss or absence of close, supportive relationships. This is consistent with the approaches in the other two chapters, which also emphasize more generally looking at dysfunctional interpersonal patterns and key expectations in relationships. Dr. Wolf discusses helping Victor to have a sense of self with healthy "roots and wings." This metaphor instantly catches my attention and feels right and useful clinically. I sense it would be highly memorable for the patient and may be instructive. It is an example of a technique that could relate to multiple change principles—such as Principle 36 (fostering emotional experiencing) and 21 (promoting active participation).

His chapter is similar to Dr. Vivian's and mine in that it suggests working on underlying beliefs (e.g., Victor's view that he is a "weak failure"), challenging internal voices, and helping patients rewrite old narratives and learn new behavior. I sense that there is much similarity between the principles we would have in mind and the nature of the discussions we would have with the patients.

"Your life is a treadmill and in spite of your best efforts you can't get off it." Dr. Wolf offers that memorable reflection in the form of a metaphor to Victor. This illustrates a fine chess move and an application of therapist empathy (Principle 26). I think this language highlights nice overlap between the three chapters in that we try to use evocative language to bring to life a change principle. Dr. Vivian illustrates powerfully direct things she would say to a patient when stuck that illustrate how she would use the therapeutic alliance to effect change. There is an art to bringing the change principles to life—an art based on language, emotion, and relationship.

Like Dr. Vivian, Dr. Wolf describes using prognostic principles to guide early moves in treatment. With Victor, he suggests communicating his understanding of Victor's life narrative to help validate that Victor's pain makes sense given his history. We can build hope in patients by communicating our understanding of their difficulties and explaining the good news—that patterns can be changed. Dr. Wolf also illustrates how he might foster self-understanding with patients (Principle 35) with a mini-lecture about how we derive a sense of self-esteem through feeling competent and connected to others. This approach is similar to the other two chapters, as selective psychoeducation plays a role in treatment and is one of many ways we help patients to understand themselves and their difficulties.

Consistent with Dr. Vivian's emphasis, Dr. Wolf acknowledges the importance of prognostic principles. Regarding Brian, he states that the "primary goal is to make sure that he comes back for a second session." The three authors all see moderating principles as important, as well—some patients levels of reactance and resistance require careful navigation by the therapist or risk-provoking defensiveness and power struggles.

Dr. Vivian's Reflections

Reading Drs. Johnson and Wolf's chapters has been a real treat. I admire the sharpness of my colleagues' thinking, the complexity of their conceptual and treatment models, the sophistication of their interventions, and the uniqueness of their patient-centered applications of intervention strategies and principles. Thus, I embark in the task of comparing and contrasting the three chapters with keen interest and eagerness. A systematic review of the three manuscripts gave evidence of a clear pattern; namely, despite some differences among the authors' theoretical models, case formulations, and related treatment applications, the similarities among the three authors (in terms of how they applied the principles of therapeutic change in their interventions across the three patients) vis-à-vis their differences are staggering. Next I will highlight parallels and uniqueness among the three chapters by organizing them according to case formulation and treatment planning, as well as application of the principles by principle category.

Case Formulation and Treatment Planning for the Three Patients
Similarities
There were many points of convergence in how Dr. Johnson, Dr. Wolf, and I conceptualized each of the patient's presenting problems. In Victor's case, for example, important factors maintaining his depression highlighted by each author included his maladaptive self-schema related to defectiveness and fragility, his loss of agency, and his dependence and passivity vis-à-vis others; consequently, interventions related to increase his self-awareness of the role he played in affecting his feelings were included in all treatment plans. Similarly, the importance of the early family history and early adversity was highlighted for all three patients. The importance of Brian's drinking problem in maintaining his depression was targeted by all authors in both their case formulations and treatment planning. Attachment anxiety and anxiety about closeness and intimacy were mentioned, particularly in Anne's case formulation and treatment. Expected challenges in establishing and maintaining the alliance were noted by everyone, particularly in approaching Brian's and Anne's treatments. Most important, in terms of point of intervention, the three of us evinced the

importance of fostering patients' awareness of the impact that their emotional and behavioral functioning have on their relationships.

Differences
Although all three authors emphasized the importance of targeting the three patients' interpersonal functioning, I believe I proposed treatments that targeted more directly interpersonal changes than Drs. Johnson and Wolf did. For example, I included couple therapy in Victor's treatment in early stages of treatment and as a substantial aspect of his treatment, as I believe his marital problems are proximal antecedents and mediators to his current depression. Especially compared to Dr. Johnson, I believe that I emphasized more the role that early adversity has in profoundly shaping all three patients interpersonal need expectancies and, relatedly, the role they played in affecting the three patients' maladaptive social interactions, including those with the therapist.

Lastly, in my view, both Brian and Anne presented with moderately high risk for suicidality and mood regular problems, issues which needed to be addressed early in treatment and monitored throughout, despite the challenges these two patients presented in regards to their readiness for change. My colleagues were less focused on these foci of treatment than I was.

Prognostic Principles
Similarities
The three authors were in agreement with predicting different prognostic outcomes for the three patients; all believed that Victor will be most likely to do well in treatment, as he presents with the most favorable prognostic features. Likewise, they predicted significant alliance issues, an uncertain outcome, and a longer and more challenging treatment course for Brian and Anne.

Differences
In terms of the principle related to attachment anxiety, I believe I saw it playing a prominent role across all three patients, whereas my colleagues did not emphasize it as much (e.g., for Victor and Brian). This is consistent with the pivotal role, as previously mentioned, that I ascribe to the three patients' early adversity.

Treatment/Provider Moderating Principles
Similarities
In discussing Victor, all three authors emphasized the importance of strengthening his poor sense of self and low self-efficacy by strengthening his connection with others and by targeting specific situations at work and in the family. Likewise, we all noted the importance of identifying in-session situations when Victor may feel controlled by the therapist, thus being mindful of the

need to address these negative in-session dynamics. With Brian, there was consensus, particularly between Dr. Wolf and me, that nondirective and person-centered approach, including use of motivational interviewing interventions was indicated. There was also consensus between Dr. Johnson and me about the need to address Brian's communication skills and conflict management skills and to strengthen his social support system. Harm reduction strategies were included by all to address Brian's disordered drinking. As far as Anne is concerned, her (expected) resistance to directive approaches, the need to increase her awareness of the role she plays in fostering her destructive behavior and emotional distress, and the need to build her social support system was underscored by all.

Differences

My colleagues advocated more caution than I did in using countertransference as a major vehicle for change across the three patients. Likewise, the use of transference interpretations, as illustrated by Dr. Wolf, differs from my use of transference hypotheses, which strives to get the patient to "connect the dots" versus highlighting patterns for the patient. Similarly, top–down psychoeducational/instructional approaches appeared to play more of a direct role in my colleagues' interventions than they did in my work with the three patients. For example, my introduction in treatment of behavioral rehearsal and skills training with the three patients emerges from the patients' recognition of their skills deficits (or inhibition) as a result of conducting the situational analysis procedure; in other words, the patient identifies the need to acquire the adaptive skills and the therapist provides the training.

Client Process Variables
Similarities

Consistently, across the three patients the therapists/authors discussed Principles 21 and 22 as overlapping principles (to some extent). For example, in treating Victor, there was consensus that it is important to make sure that he is actively engaged in treatment to pre-empt his resistance and passive participation. In working with both Victor and Brian, both Dr. Johnson and I pointed out the need to find a balance between change-based interventions (e.g., behavioral activation) and nondirective approaches (e.g., letting the patient set the agenda for the session). In treating Brian, both Dr. Wolf and I noted the importance of being vigilant for his propensity to see the therapist as a controlling authority, thus the need to pre-empt power struggles and resistance by focusing on the therapist–patient relationship and to address therapeutic ruptures, "even minute ones," as noted by Dr. Wolf. In treating Anne, all three authors underscored the importance of interventions aimed at promoting active engagement in treatment, collaborative participation, and decreasing her (likely) resistance (e.g., by not using didactic language).

Differences
No clear differences emerged herein.

Therapy Relationship Principles
Similarities
The consensus among the three authors about the therapy relationship principles was particularly strong. In Victor's treatment, Dr. Wolf and I were consistent in proposing Rogerian client-centered interventions and self-disclosing to the patient the therapist's in-session emotional experience to "increase immediacy in the therapeutic interaction" (Dr. Wolf) and to "promote closeness and change" (Dr. Vivian). I thoroughly appreciated Dr. Johnson's description of how he expresses positive regard toward his patients, flexibility, affirmation, congruence, and empathy; I adopt very similar approaches in my relationship with all my patients. In addressing Brian's needs, Dr. Wolf noted how "critically" important it was to attend to relationship principles by using genuine respect, acceptance, empathic communication and validation of his "fears and resentments." Dr. Johnson referred to Arnold Lazarus concept of "authentic chameleon" in promoting high-quality alliance—a reference that I completely espouse. Likewise, in treating Anne, all three authors advocated the use of high-quality alliance by showing her, using Dr. Johnson's words, "copious validation and compassionate understanding."

Differences
One of the differences between Dr. Wolf 's and my approach is his more cautious use of the therapist's self-disclosure to express congruence, particularly with Anne. Some minor differences that I noted between Dr. Johnson's approach and mine include Dr. Johnson giving patients more direct feedback (top–down) and suggestions for change (e.g., when Victor engages in the avoidance behaviors), as well as "sharing stories" with patients (e.g., with Brian) to join in but avoiding to talk about the emotional impact the patient has on the therapist (unless such impact is positive).

Therapist Intervention Principles
Similarities
Despite the theoretical differences among the three authors, there were by far more similarities in the therapist intervention principles category than differences. For example, in Victor's case, consistent with my approach, Dr. Wolf underscored the need to apply interventions flexibly and to foster

emotional experiencing by "focusing on the immediacy of the therapeutic encounter to identify how Victor can increase his self-understanding ... of how he distances himself from others." Moreover, all three therapists/authors included change-based interventions that foster acquisition of interpersonal effectiveness in Victor's everyday life. In parallel with my approach, Dr. Johnson emphasized the role of Victor's learning history (including the impact of his adverse childhood experiences with his father) in identifying the " "origins of his insecurities" and emphasizes the importance of unpacking difficult interpersonal situations to enable Victor to focus on his emotional experiences.

In treating Brian, all three authors stressed the importance of being mindful of his ambivalence, hence the need to balance nondirective and directive interventions to increase his perception of having a choice and agency in treatment. Furthermore, there was consensus about the importance of fostering Brian's understanding of the impact of his drinking problems, provide harm reduction interventions, and promote reconnection with significant others in his life. Overall, the need to deepen Brian's emotional experience and to provide him with interventions (e.g., Dr. Wolf: interpretations; Dr. Vivian: situational analysis; Dr. Johnson: cognitive-behavior therapy [CBT] strategies) to increase his awareness or insight about how "[he] actively creates the circumstances that perpetuate his self-defeating behavior" (as Dr. Wolf aptly puts it) is stressed repeatedly across the three chapters. Similarly, all authors, particularly Dr. Johnson and I, also advocate the importance of interpersonal skills training and the use of strategies (e.g., Dr. Johnson: CBT interventions, Dr. Vivian: CBT, mindfulness and distress tolerance) to decrease use of alcohol as a maladaptive coping strategy. Finally, both Dr. Johnson and I discuss the need to target Brian's "unfinished" businesses with his father via emotional processing interventions (e.g., I advocated the use of the empty-chair technique).

In working with Anne, the authors consistently emphasized the importance of therapist flexibility and sensitivity of her emotional lability and unpredictable interpersonal patterns, which will be reflected by challenging in-session events between the therapist and the patient. All three authors underscore the pivotal role that Anne's interpersonal problems, such as her dependence of others, her neediness, and her maladaptive need for external affirmation and approval plays in maintaining her mood and personality problems; thus, they all propose similar and unique interventions to foster her interpersonal functioning. Additionally, both Dr. Wolf and I include mindfulness interventions to foster Anne's emotion regulation and self-understanding; interestingly, Dr. Wolf proposed that such goals are attained by " by identifying specific problematic situations and the triggers that start a pattern of escalation, followed by exploring alternate ways of dealing with these situations," a strategy that is also at the core of the CBASP situational analysis (my work) and functional analysis

(Dr. Johnson). In parallel with my plan to use behavioral rehearsal to enhance communication skills and interpersonal effectiveness (e.g., assertiveness training), Dr. Johnson described the use of several behavioral and interpersonal change interventions.

Lastly, all three therapist/authors advocated the importance of using emotional experiencing techniques to deepen emotional experiences with all three patients to promote change and interpersonal healing. I was particularly intrigued by Dr. Johnson's use of the "timeline" exercise. Similarly, I proposed the use of emotional processing techniques, as those emerging from Greenberg et al.'s work (e.g., 1993), as well as from a CBT adaptation of the transactional analysis paradigm (Steiner, 1990).

Differences
The differences among the three therapist/authors in regards to this category of principles were relatively minor. In general, I thought that both Dr. Wolf and Dr. Johnson tended to provide top–down interpretations to patients to a greater extent than I did (e.g., by using psychoeducational interventions, and by "connecting the dots" for patients by describing to them their maladaptive patterns and their function). As indicated earlier, interventions aimed at interpersonal changes may have played a greater role in my treatment plans than in my colleagues' proposed treatments across the three patients. For example, I proposed couple therapy in Victor's treatment plan as a main strategy for change, whereas Dr. Wolf and Dr. Johnson did not include it. Likewise, in contrast with my use of outcome-driven feedback to patients as a powerful vehicle for increasing patients' participation in treatment and to foster a collaborative stance, Dr. Wolf and Dr. Johnson were urging caution in doing so to decrease the possibility of worsening patients' depression (hopelessness); similarly, in contrast with my suggestions, neither Dr. Wolf nor Dr. Johnson strongly advocated the use of systematic treatment outcome as a vehicle for promoting change. Lastly, the authors were not always in agreement regarding the goals for treatment; for example, in contrast with Dr. Wolf and me, Dr. Johnson did not include emotional regulation and emotional tolerance-building skills training in his treatment for Anne (and to some extent also for Brian).

In conclusion, the exercise of comparing and contrasting the writings of the three therapists/authors, highlights for me the important parallels among them in applying the principles of change, regardless of their theoretical orientation and unique intervention techniques. Thus, despite any caution we may have expressed in how the principles should be regarded (e.g., the comments provided by Dr. Wolf and myself), this experience demonstrates powerfully, as Dr. Johnson states, the usefulness and heuristic value of these principles and their important role in bridging differences in theoretical orientations and applied interventions.

Dr. Wolf's Reflections

I was relieved and gratified to read Drs. Johnson and Vivian's case formulations and treatment plans for Victor, Brian, and Anne. Even though our training backgrounds are different—Drs. Johnson and Vivian as cognitive-behavioral and mine as humanistic-experiential-psychodynamic—our agreement on the importance of most of the 38 principles indicate how our work as practicing psychotherapists minimize theoretical differences when faced with how we respond to individuals in pain. Our chapters reflect how we each emphasize the five clusters and how the principles are implemented with specific techniques and interventions. Nevertheless, I diverge from Drs. Johnson and Vivian, specifically, in the use of behavioral techniques. I will start by identifying areas of agreement and then discuss how we diverge.

Convergence

Dr. Johnson, Dr. Vivian, and I are in agreement on the importance of the principles, and our chapters illustrate how our psychotherapeutic practices are consistent with these principles. We all provide clinical illustrations of how we translate abstract research based principles to specific situational and contextual responses to the individual sitting in front of us—how, in other words, we make the principles actionable. Dr. Vivian's references to situational analysis, Dr. Johnson's emphasis on contextualizing problems, and my use of dialogue all illustrate how the results of systematic reviews and meta-analysis are made clinically actionable. Given the differences in our training, I was surprised to see how consistent we are in our case formulations and treatment plans, which all emphasize the role of increasing self-efficacy and autonomy, as well as nurturing supportive and gratifying interpersonal relationships; we interpreted and implemented the principles in the service of achieving these goals. How we make the principles actionable illustrates how, in practice, we are all integrative. Finally, we are in agreement in our understanding of depression as an experiential state that is characterized not solely by despair, hopelessness, and helplessness but also by anxiety, more specifically, avoiding specific behaviors. This is not a statement of the diagnostic co-morbidity of depression of anxiety but the experiential relatedness of despair and the fear of trying something new.

Dr. Johnson, Dr. Vivian, and I agree that how the principles are applied vary as a function of the psychotherapist's phase of professional development. My metaphor comparing the 38 principles to basic chess strategies is echoed by Dr. Vivian when she discusses how the explicit application of the principles is more salient in the early stages of a therapist's training than in later stages. Similarly, Dr. Johnson states that there are large differences in how he, as an experienced clinician, implements the principles than how graduate students implement them. Even though we learn these principles in a descriptive manner, experience is how we learn them in a procedural manner.

The primacy of the prognostic factors is evident for all of us when we describe how Victor is a better candidate for psychotherapy than Brian or Anne. Dr. Johnson discussed the prognostic principles as a guide to develop realistic hopefulness while Dr. Vivian emphasizes how they serve as an anchor for all subsequent principles. Many of the prognostic principles use the phrasing "may benefit less from psychotherapy," suggesting that they are moderating factors and could be interpreted as contraindications for psychotherapy. In applying these principles, Dr. Johnson, Dr. Vivian, and I understood their importance in terms of grading our expectations and as challenges in treatment planning but not as contraindications for psychotherapy. These principles were presumably developed on the basis of outcome research rather than process research that illustrate how they are therapy interfering factors. My low rating for several of these principles, which are presented in the following discussion, reflects this interpretation as contraindications for psychotherapy rather than factors that moderate treatment planning.

When Dr. Vivian discusses the interrelatedness of the 38 principles and the artificiality of separating them into different categories, she makes explicit a point addressed implicitly by Dr. Johnson and me. What made the writing of these cases so arduous was how a specific intervention that illustrates one principle also serves as an illustration of several other principles! The construct of the therapeutic alliance is inherent to the six principles under the therapy relationship principles, but how the 10 therapy intervention principles are applied also has direct and indirect effects on the therapeutic alliance. The construct of the therapeutic alliance represents a higher order factor containing relationship and intervention principles. The principles are illustrative of a nomothetic research approach that requires the operational definition of a specific variable; however, while those variables are conceptually distinct in terms of their operational definitions, they are not distinct from other variables in practice. For example, the role of therapist congruence (Principle 25) and self-disclosure (Principle 28) in repairing alliance ruptures (Principle 27).

Dr. Johnson, Dr. Vivian, and I also routinely reference principles so obvious that they do not appear on the list. I once spoke with a surgeon about evidence-based practices. He responded by asking, "Is there any research on the need for oxygen during surgery? How would you design a randomized control trial for that?" Similarly, there are things we do in the practice of psychotherapy that are taken for granted. All three of us describe the role of psychoeducation in our treatment plans, but, apparently, there is no research on the role of psychoeducation that warrants inclusion in the list of principles. While psychoeducation is not specifically identified as a distinct principle, Dr. Johnson, Dr. Vivian, and I all describe how we educate our clients about the nature of depression, the rationale for our treatment plans, and reasons for the use of specific intervention.

Divergence
While there are minor differences in how the three of us interpret and implement the therapist/provider moderating principles, client process variables, and therapy relationship principles, our chapters differ regarding the implementation of the therapy intervention principles related to behavior change.

As cognitive-behavioral therapists, Drs. Johnson and Vivian both emphasize the use of interventions that focus on behavior change. Both describe the importance of teaching social skills, interpersonal skills effectiveness, stress management, assertiveness training, behavioral skills training, and so forth. In comparison, my focus emphasizes the cognitive and affective aspects of the client's experience. I diverge from Drs. Johnson and Vivian in minimizing the behavioral. This is most clear in how we describe our treatment of Anne where I focus on her awareness and management of her internal life to the exclusion of specific interpersonal skills training. This reflects both a bias in how I see my role as a psychotherapist and a lack of training in the implementation of specific behavioral techniques. Different schools of psychotherapy can be organized along a continuum of those that emphasize increasing awareness and those emphasizing behavioral change. My training defined the role of psychotherapy as increasing a client's awareness of their internal and interpersonal worlds to facilitate a greater sense of agency and responsibility for their actions. In contrast, I see an emphasis on behavior change as a form of coaching. Even if I were to receive training and supervision in interpersonal skills training or behavioral activation, I would need to find ways to integrate this into my treatment-as-usual practice. In my practice, I would refer Anne to a structured program that does skills training. A therapeutic approach that emphasizes skills training for behavior change is very powerful. Furthermore, clients who successfully change behaviors do experience an increase in self-esteem and a strengthening of the therapeutic alliance. In contrast to specific behavioral interventions, I routinely rely on cognitive interventions. I do not provide my clients with a list of cognitive distortions or homework to track these distortions. Rather, as when I suggest alternatives to Victor about leaving his job early and he responds with "What if something goes wrong?" I will then discuss how "what ifs" lead to anxiety and avoidance with the goal of increasing his awareness of the relationship of how certain thoughts affect feelings.

While not specifically a point of divergence from Drs. Johnson and Vivian, I am uncomfortable with how the principles regarding transference interpretations (Principle 15) and psychodynamic interpretations (Principles 29 and 30) are presented by the editors and how they are interpreted by cognitive-behavioral therapists. I agree with Dr. Vivian regarding the importance of developing transference hypotheses early in treatment and the careful use of these hypotheses through disciplined personal involvement as used in CBASP. Similarly, Dr. Johnson acknowledges the dangers of using transference interpretations with vulnerable clients. Furthermore, all three of us have accommodated to the definition of a psychodynamic interpretation as "the central interpersonal themes for each patient," rather than how the goal of psychodynamic interpretations is to make the unconscious conscious. My discomfort has to do with how Principles 15, 29, and 30 relate to a body of research that deal with technical problems that are specific to psychoanalytic and psychodynamic practitioners and, as such, may not apply to practitioners trained in the techniques of other orientations. There are psychoanalysts who believe that interpretations are the sole mechanisms of change and that transference interpretations are the most powerful form of interpretation. Principles 15, 29, and 30 are primarily directed toward psychoanalytic practitioners who rigidly adhere to certain techniques in the same way that Principle 33 regarding flexible adherence to treatment approaches is drawn from research regarding the use of manualized treatments. While these principles are grounded in the empirical work of diverse psychotherapeutic orientations, there appears to be a higher order construct they relate to regarding the use and timing of interventions, whether interpretations or manualized treatments, with a specific client.

What is noteworthy in this exercise is how three psychotherapists from different perspectives have made 38 research-based abstract principles come alive in the understanding and treatment of Victor, Brian, and Anne in ways that are remarkably similar. The listing of the 38 principles represents the distillation of a huge body of psychotherapy research—a remarkable achievement. I hope that the identification of congruence and divergence in how Drs. Johnson and Vivian and I discuss the implementation of the 38 principles will serve as the basis for identifying a set of higher order principles that will result in a more cohesive theory of psychotherapy.

Editors' Comments

What stands out prominently from the previous reflections is the agreement among the three authors regarding the high level of convergence in their implementation of principles of change. In Dr. Vivian's eyes, the similarities are "staggering" relative to existing differences between these expert therapists, which, in the words of Dr. Wolf, shows that theoretical divergences are minimized when therapists describe how they work in their day-to-day practice. Similarities were identified in case formulations and treatment plans, such as an attention to early adversity, as well a focus on intrapersonal (self-efficacy, autonomy) and interpersonal (gratifying and supportive relationships) goals. More prominently, convergences were noted by all authors at the level of each of the five clusters of principles—and especially for treatment/provider moderating, client process, and therapeutic relationship variables. Commonalities in techniques that are used to concretely implement some of the shared principles have also been highlighted, especially by Dr. Johnson. Furthermore, one author, Dr. Vivian, pointed to the balance between nondirective and directive interventions used by all authors in the case of Brian.

Each therapist also identified principles and types of interventions that are more or less important in their practice as compared to either one or both of their colleagues. This is the case, for example, with Dr. Wolf's acknowledgment that despite their therapeutic value, many behavioral change techniques are not part of the way he conducts therapy. For Dr. Vivian, her clinical work differentiates itself, among other ways, by her greater focus on direct interpersonal changes, early childhood events, and attachment issues, as well as her systematic use of outcome measures to monitor and promote change. In contrast with Drs. Johnson and Wolf, Dr. Vivian also appears to focus more on risk assessment and management as prominent foci of intervention throughout treatment—particularly for Brian and Anne.

Dr. Johnson, for his part, recognized giving less attention to prognostics principles than his colleagues. He also stated that reading their work led him to appreciate how a careful attention to clients' characteristics, such as the level of hope and motivation, can significantly influence the way that other principles are implemented. This, needless to say, is only one instance of an author providing a specific example of how the chapters of their colleagues offered them with insights about how to conduct therapy, such as the use of feedback and specific techniques to foster emotional deepening, the fostering of hope via empathy, and the skillful work with the therapeutic relationship to resolve alliance breaches and facilitate change.

The authors also highlighted many principles can be implemented in a contrasting manner, including how differently transference interpretation and feedback can be delivered and how different techniques can be used to facilitate self-understanding, to communicate self-disclosure, as well as to promote adaptive interpersonal and behavioral changes. They also pointed differences that appear to be magnified for one particular case, such as the use of self-disclosure with Anne.

Perhaps not surprisingly, differences noted by the authors in terms of the reliance on some principles and the way to implement them parallel several particularities that emerged from their respective profile of interventions described in Chapter 3. Among them are Dr. Johnson's focus on behavioral changes, including as a way to foster insight; Dr. Vivian's integration of exploratory (to increase self-understanding) and behavioral (with an emphasis on assessing the consequences of client's behaviors) interventions; and Dr. Wolf's view of himself as evocative rather than directive therapist.

Clinical Importance of Principles in Practice

When the clinical authors had completed their respective chapter, they were asked to rate the helpfulness of each of the 38 empirically based principles on 10-point scale, with 10 being most helpful and 1 being least helpful. These ratings (which are presented in Box 7.1) are briefly summarized here, within the order of the five categories in which the principles were clustered. They are also complemented with notes provided by the clinical authors in terms of perceived helpfulness (or statements made in their chapter) of particular principles, as well as accuracy, that is, addressing the possibility that some principles may not be clinically valid or may not work under certain circumstances.

Based on the helpfulness ratings, it appears that most of the nine prognostic principles are perceived as clinically relevant, with seven of them averaging a score above 6, and three of these seven averaging a score of 8 or above: baseline impairment (Principle 1), secure attachment (Principle 3), and stage of readiness (Principle 6). Interestingly, one of the authors, Dr. Wolf, reported lower scores than his colleague on two principles: the inhibiting effect of personality disorder co-morbidity (Principle 2) and adverse childhood events (Principle 8). As noted in his comments in this chapter, this low rating does not reflect, in his mind, a lack of clinical importance of these client's characteristics; rather, they reflect his disagreement with the view that these principles are comparable to the others among the list of 38 principles. Specifically, he does not view them as contraindications for therapy and suspects that they are indicative of particular types of therapy intervention (i.e., they are moderators of *specific*, or *comparative*, therapy effects).

Box 7.1 Rating of Helpfulness of Empirically Based Principles

Depression Section
Client Prognostic Principles

1. Clients with higher levels of baseline impairment may benefit less from psychotherapy than clients with lower levels of impairment.
   Dr. Johnson: 8; Dr. Vivian: 10; Dr. Wolf: 10
   Mean: 9.33
2. Clients whose primary presenting problems are complicated by a co-morbid secondary personality disorder diagnosis may benefit less from psychotherapy than clients without a co-morbid personality disorder diagnosis.
   Dr. Johnson: 8; Dr. Vivian: 10; Dr. Wolf: 5
   Mean: 7.67
3. Clients with more secure attachment may benefit more from psychotherapy than clients with less secure attachment (i.e., more attachment anxiety).
   Dr. Johnson: 7; Dr. Vivian: 10; Dr. Wolf: 7
   Mean: 8
4. Clients with higher initial expectations for benefitting from psychotherapy may benefit more from it than clients with lower initial outcome expectations.
   Dr. Johnson: 6; Dr. Vivian: 10; Dr. Wolf: 7
   Mean: 7.67
5. Clients who are more intrinsically (or autonomously) motivated to engage in psychotherapy may benefit more from it than clients who are less intrinsically (or autonomously) motivated.
   Dr. Johnson: 7; Dr. Vivian: 9; Dr. Wolf: 7
   Mean: 7.67
6. Clients in advanced stages of change readiness (i.e., they are actively preparing for or currently taking action toward healthy behavior) may benefit more from psychotherapy than clients at lower stages of change readiness.
   Dr. Johnson: 7; Dr. Vivian: 10; Dr. Wolf: 10
   Mean: 9
7. Clients with low socio-economic status and employment problems may benefit less from psychotherapy than clients with higher socioeconomic status and no employment problems.
   Dr. Johnson: 6; Dr. Vivian: 5; Dr. Wolf: 3
   Mean: 4.67

8. Clients who have experienced adverse childhood events may benefit less from psychotherapy than clients who did not experience adverse childhood events.
   Dr. Johnson: 6; Dr. Vivian: 10; Dr. Wolf: 3
   Mean: 6.33
9. Anxious clients with more negative self-attributions may benefit less from psychotherapy than clients with fewer negative self-attributions.
   Dr. Johnson: 5; Dr. Vivian: 6; Dr. Wolf: 3
   Mean: 4.67

Treatment/Provider Moderating Principles

10. Clients whose therapist uses interventions consistent with the client's level of problem assimilation may benefit more from psychotherapy than patients whose interventions are not consistent with their assimilation level.
    Dr. Johnson: 6; Dr. Vivian: 8; Dr. Wolf: 7
    Mean: 7
11. Clients with higher levels of resistance may benefit more from psychotherapy that is more nondirective compared to clients with lower levels of resistance who may benefit more from psychotherapy that is more directive.
    Dr. Johnson: 8; Dr. Vivian: 10; Dr. Wolf: 7
    Mean: 8.33
12. Clients with lower motivation for, or higher ambivalence about, change may benefit more from psychotherapy when their therapist is responsive and person-centered versus more directive and change-oriented.
    Dr. Johnson: 9; Dr. Vivian: 10; Dr. Wolf: 10
    Mean: 9.67
13. Clients who are matched to their preferred therapy role, therapist demographics, or treatment type may benefit more from psychotherapy than clients unmatched on these preferences.
    Dr. Johnson: 3; Dr. Vivian: 5; Dr. Wolf: 3
    Mean: 3.67
14. Clients whose preference for religiously or spiritually-oriented psychotherapy is accommodated may benefit more from treatment than clients whose preference is unmet.
    Dr. Johnson: 1; Dr. Vivian: 3; Dr. Wolf: 5
    Mean: 3

15. Clients who present with poorer interpersonal functioning are likely to benefit less from psychotherapy when their therapist uses a higher versus lower proportion of transference interpretations.
    Dr. Johnson: 7; Dr. Vivian: 2; Dr. Wolf: 7
    Mean: 5.33
16. Clients higher in baseline impairment may benefit more from psychotherapy that is longer-term and/or more intensive compared to clients lower in baseline impairment who may benefit equally well from psychotherapy that is long- or short-term and/or more or less intensive.
    Dr. Johnson: 8; Dr. Vivian: 10; Dr. Wolf: 10
    Mean: 9.33
17. Clients with externalizing coping styles may benefit more from psychotherapy that is more focused on behavior change and symptom reduction than fostering insight and self-awareness.
    Dr. Johnson: 8; Dr. Vivian: 5; Dr. Wolf: 5
    Mean: 6
18. Clients with internalizing coping styles may benefit more from psychotherapy that is more focused on fostering insight and self-awareness than behavior change and symptom reduction.
    Dr. Johnson: 8; Dr. Vivian: 5; Dr. Wolf: 5
    Mean: 6
19. Clients with moderate to severe impairment and/or fewer social supports will benefit more from psychotherapy when their therapist helps them address their social or medical needs.
    Dr. Johnson: 7; Dr. Vivian: 10; Dr. Wolf: 7
    Mean: 8
20. Clients with substance use problems may be equally likely to benefit from psychotherapy delivered by a therapist with or without his or her own history of substance use problems.
    Dr. Johnson: 6; Dr. Vivian: 3; Dr. Wolf: 3
    Mean: 4

Client Process Variables

21. Clients who more actively participate in the treatment process may benefit more from psychotherapy than clients who less actively participate.
    Dr. Johnson: 9; Dr. Vivian: 10; Dr. Wolf: 10
    Mean: 9.67

22. Clients who are more resistant to the therapist or therapy may benefit less from psychotherapy than clients who are less resistant.
Dr. Johnson: 9; Dr. Vivian: 10; Dr. Wolf: 10
Mean: 9.67

Therapy Relationship Principles

23. Clients experiencing a higher quality therapeutic alliance in group psychotherapy (group cohesion) or individual psychotherapy (bonding/collaboration) may benefit more than clients experiencing a lower quality alliance.
Dr. Johnson: 10; Dr. Vivian: 10; Dr. Wolf: 10
Mean: 10
24. Clients experiencing more therapist regard and affirmation may benefit more from psychotherapy than clients experiencing less therapist regard and affirmation.
Dr. Johnson: 10; Dr. Vivian: 10; Dr. Wolf: 10
Mean: 10
25. Clients experiencing more therapist congruence may benefit more from psychotherapy than clients experiencing less therapist congruence.
Dr. Johnson: 10; Dr. Vivian: 10; Dr. Wolf: 7
Mean: 9
26. Clients experiencing more therapist empathy may benefit more from psychotherapy than clients experiencing less therapist empathy.
Dr. Johnson: 9; Dr. Vivian: 10; Dr. Wolf: 10
Mean: 9.67
27. Clients who experience alliance rupture–repair episodes and/or who work with therapists trained to repair alliance ruptures may benefit more from psychotherapy than clients who experience no or unrepaired ruptures and/or work with therapists not trained specifically on rupture–repair interventions.
Dr. Johnson: 6; Dr. Vivian: 10; Dr. Wolf: 10
Mean: 8.67
28. Clients whose therapist uses more supportive self-disclosures may benefit more from psychotherapy than clients whose therapist uses less supportive self-disclosures (or does not disclose at all).
Dr. Johnson: 9; Dr. Vivian: 10; Dr. Wolf: 7
Mean: 8.67

Therapist Intervention Principles

29. Clients whose therapist uses a higher proportion of general psychodynamic interpretations may benefit more from psychotherapy than clients whose therapist uses a lower proportion of general psychodynamic interpretations.
Dr. Johnson: 6; Dr. Vivian: 10; Dr. Wolf: 7
Mean: 7.67

30. Clients whose therapist uses higher quality psychodynamic interpretations may benefit more from psychotherapy than clients whose therapist uses lower quality psychodynamic interpretations (see glossary for definition of quality of psychodynamic interpretation).
Dr. Johnson: 4; Dr. Vivian: 10; Dr. Wolf: 10
Mean: 8

31. Clients whose therapist receives feedback based on a routinely delivered outcome measure may benefit more from psychotherapy than clients whose therapist does not receive feedback.
Dr. Johnson: 5; Dr. Vivian: 10; Dr. Wolf: 3
Mean: 6

32. Clients who receive feedback from their therapist on their performance in treatment may benefit more from psychotherapy than clients who do not receive feedback.
Dr. Johnson: 8; Dr. Vivian: 10; Dr. Wolf: 10
Mean: 9.33

33. Clients may benefit more from psychotherapy when their therapist is more versus less flexible in their administration of, or adherence to, a given treatment approach.
Dr. Johnson: 10; Dr. Vivian: 10; Dr. Wolf: 10
Mean: 10

34. Clients whose therapist selectively/responsively fosters more adaptive interpersonal changes may benefit more broadly from psychotherapy than those whose therapist fosters fewer adaptive interpersonal changes.
Dr. Johnson: 10; Dr. Vivian: 10; Dr. Wolf: 10
Mean: 10

35. Clients whose therapist selectively/responsively fosters more self-understanding may benefit more broadly from psychotherapy than clients whose therapist fosters less self-understanding.
Dr. Johnson: 9; Dr. Vivian: 10; Dr. Wolf: 10
Mean: 9.67

36. Clients whose therapist selectively/responsively fosters more emotional experiencing and/or deepening may benefit more broadly from psychotherapy than clients whose therapist fosters less emotional experiencing and/or deepening.
Dr. Johnson: 9; Dr. Vivian: 10; Dr. Wolf: 10
Mean: 9.67
37. Clients whose therapist selectively/responsively uses nondirective interventions skillfully may benefit more from psychotherapy than clients whose therapist uses nondirective interventions unskillfully.
Dr. Johnson: 10; Dr. Vivian: 10; Dr. Wolf: 10
Mean: 10
38. Clients whose therapist selectively/responsively fosters more behavior changes may benefit more broadly from psychotherapy than clients whose therapist fosters fewer behavior changes.
Dr. Johnson: 10; Dr. Vivian: 10; Dr. Wolf: 5
Mean: 8.33

Note. Ratings of helpfulness is based on a 10-point scale with 10 being most helpful and 1 being least helpful.

Notably, two prognostic principles were scored relatively low (both averaging 4.67). For the first of these principles (Principle 7, which suggests the inhibiting effect both of socio-economic status and employment problems), the rating indicates that the therapists feel they can be attuned to client needs, somewhat irrespective of their social and financial conditions. Dr. Johnson indeed notes he is comfortable doing problem-solving work with people to help them make progress on financial and employment-related issues. He believes that these issues are important and could interfere with therapy but are not necessarily a huge barrier to doing good work with the patient. Dr. Vivian points out that while employment problems do not hinder treatment, they have to be taken into account—as unemployment may create obstacles for therapeutic change. This is very much in line with Dr. Wolf's perspective. Similar to his low ratings on the principles related to inhibiting effect of personality disorder co-morbidity and adverse childhood events, Dr. Wolf does not view employment and financial related issues as contraindications to therapy, but he believes that treatment needs to be tailored to mitigate the effects of these factors.

Principle 9 (which notes the impediments introduced by negative self-attributions) also averaged a relatively low rating. In part, this may reflect a lack of saliency. All three therapists/authors have noted that attributions are central/intrinsic to depression. For Dr. Vivian, they are strong cognitive mediators of poor interpersonal functioning and depression across all three patients. But because of their prominence, they may not provide very salient, informative, or discriminative information related to case formulation and treatment plan. Dr. Johnson concedes that clients with extreme negative self-attributions (highly self-critical, shame-filled patients) are going to be more challenging, but he also believes that therapy can still benefit them. Similarly, Dr. Wolf believes that negative self-attributions are intrinsic to depression, but he also argues that the content of these attributions are important to treatment formulation. It is not enough to know that clients believe they are "losers"; *why* they think they are "losers" needs to be understood and addressed.

Of the 11 moderating principles, 7 received an average score of 6 and above, with 4 of them averaging a score of 8 or higher. High ratings were given to the positive role of matching treatment with resistance level (Principle 11), selectively using a person-centered intervention depending on patient motivation level (Principle 12), and varying support and treatment intensity that fit with patients' impairment levels (Principles 16 and 19).

Two of the four moderating principles that average less than a rating of 6 refer to client preferences, in terms of therapy role, therapist demographics, or treatment type (Principle 13) and religiously or spiritually oriented psychotherapy (Principle 14). This reflects that therapists feel that they can engage client and/or be attuned to their clinical needs, irrespective of clients views and values. With regard to Principle 14, for example, Dr. Johnson is curious about the studies on this topic and how they are conducted and framed, as he believes that he can generally do good work with patients coming from different religious traditions and help them make behavioral changes in line with their values (despite not conducting religiously oriented therapy). It must be noted that the lack of relevance of religious/spiritual views may also be related to the location of the therapists practice. Dr. Vivian states that where she lives in the New York metropolitan area, most patients do not seek religiously oriented treatment, but that this may be different in other geographical locations. Similarly, in Dr. Wolf's experience, he finds that most clients do not seek out religiously oriented treatment. Nevertheless, as with other cultural values, a client's religious orientation needs to be assessed and part of the treatment formulation. In line with this, Dr. Johnson cautions that it would be difficult to form a good relationship with a client if the client is determined to see a religiously oriented therapist and is angered that this wish has not been accommodated.

The therapists sense that they can be attuned and responsive to their clients' needs in a variety of clinical situations is also signaled by the perceived relative irrelevance of the therapist's history of substance use (lack of thereof in the present cases) when treating clients with substance use problems (Principle 20). A relatively low average score was also recorded for Principle 15 (i.e., clients who present with poorer interpersonal functioning are likely to benefit less from psychotherapy when their therapist uses a higher vs. lower proportion of *transference* interpretations). This, however, may have less to do with a question of helpfulness and more with a question of validity, at least for one therapist. Dr. Vivian gave a low score (2, in contrast with 7 for both Drs. Johnson and Dr. Wolf) to this principle because she makes frequent use of transference work with all of her clients. In fact, inconsistent with the way that this principle is formulated, she reports focusing more on transference (within a CBASP framework) with clients who have poorer level of interpersonal functioning. This reflects that the treatment model she espouses (CBASP) was specifically designed to address the entrenched interpersonal problems of chronically depressed persons and their lack of perceived functionality, with, among other interventions, the planful use of the therapist–patient relationship and the therapist's disciplined personal involvement as a powerful vehicle for change.

Similarly, Dr. Vivian has questioned the validity of Principles 17 and 18, at least in their current form. Principle 17 states that clients with externalizing coping styles may benefit more from psychotherapy that is more focused on behavior change and symptom reduction than fostering insight and self-awareness, and Principle 18 asserts that clients with internalizing coping styles may benefit more from psychotherapy that is more focused on fostering insight and self-awareness than behavior change and symptom reduction. In her view, she observes that these distinct principles may have inappropriately presented coping styles as categorical in nature when they may actually be more accurately described as patterns among continuous expressions. Thus, she argues that most, if not all, clients make use of both externalizing and internalizing coping strategies. In addition, the matching of specific types of interventions identified in these two principles, in her view, is not straightforward and needs to take into account client's characteristics (prognostic variables) other than coping styles. As she illustrates in her chapter, even a client with a strong externalizing tendency is likely to require insight-oriented interventions based on a diversity of issues, such as readiness for change and the experience of childhood adverse events. Underlying her view is the notion that in clinical practice these principles, albeit important, cannot be viewed in a static and monothetic way, but they become useful when applied in an ideographic and patient-centered way.

All of the principles that were contained in the clusters identified as *client process variables* and *therapeutic relationship* were rated as being highly helpful (each with a mean score >8). In fact, the two client process principles (Principles 21 [active participation] and 22 [resistance]), as well as two of the six relationship principles (Principles 23 [therapeutic alliance] and 24 [therapist regard/affirmation]) were rated as 10 by the three therapists. Interestingly, the principle of alliance rupture–repair (Principle 27) was rated lower by Dr. Johnson (with a score of 6) compared to his colleagues (who both gave a 10 for this principle). He did so because, in his view, the principle focuses too narrowly on training and on specific interventions. He would have given a rating of 10 for the same principle if it had been reformulated to reflect more broadly on therapists ability to prevent, notice, and resolve alliance ruptures skillfully.

Most of the nine principles that focused on *therapist interventions* were given high scores, all but one averaging 8 or above, and three had a mean of 10: Principles 33 (flexibility), 34 (fostering interpersonal change), and 37 (the use of nondirective interventions). The provision of feedback based on a routine outcome measure was rated 6 on average, but this reflects a discrepancy of opinion, rather than a shared perception about the clinical usefulness of this principles. While Dr. Vivian rated it as very important (10), Drs. Johnson and Dr. Wolf gave it a score of 5 and 3, respectively. Dr. Johnson sees merit in this principle, but he is also concerned that patients might feel dehumanized by psychometrically derived assessment, that such assessment may not reflect their concerns or their goals, or that the motivation for the use of routine outcome measurement is primarily bureaucratic. Dr. Wolf values the use of outcome measures in theory; in clinical practice, however, he has not found these instruments sufficiently discriminating in terms of initial level of symptom/functioning severity or change over time. Patients are impatient with repeated administration of these instruments when they make the same responses. This is most likely a function of the lack of sensitivity of items to the specifics of a patient's presenting problems and the lack of relevance of many items to presenting problems.

Rating discrepancies also emerged for two other principles related to interventions: Principles 30 (use of high quality of psychodynamic interpretations) and 38 (fostering of behavior change), with the former found to be only minimally helpful (with a rating of 4) by Dr. Johnson, and the later rated only as 5 by Dr. Wolf. These differential ratings reflect, at least in part, distinct therapeutic focus emphasized in the primary theoretical orientation of these therapists—that is, cognitive-behavioral for Dr. Johnson and psychodynamic for Dr. Wolf. It should be mentioned, however, that while Dr. Wolf rated Principle 30 very highly (score of 10), he also argues that cautiousness should guide the use of psychodynamic interpretations, including transference interpretations. Even if a psychodynamic interpretation is accurate in identifying "the central interpersonal themes for each patient," he believes that this does not take into account contextual factors, such as the timing in presenting these interpretations or the style in which they are presented. This is especially true, in his opinion, with transference interpretations, which can have the effect of creating ruptures in therapeutic alliance if presented in a manner that the patient experiences as condescending.

Editors' Comments

From the perspective of researchers, it is both exciting and reassuring to note that most of the empirical based principles that were presented to the clinical authors were perceived as being clinically helpful. This convergence between diverse sources of knowledge increases, in our view, the level of confidence that one may have toward the validity and usefulness of a wide range of therapeutic factors.

However, it is also important to recognize discrepancies between clinical perspectives and empirical findings with respect to a number of principles. Some of these discrepancies may be due to the absence of helpful clinical heuristics in particular principles. From comments made with regard to Principles 7 and 9, for instance, it may be difficult to find therapy interventions that moderate the influence of socio-economic status and negative self-attributions; if this is the case, removal of such principles might be considered in future revisions of the list of principles of change.

Of course, clinical and research discrepancies may also reflect that some principles fail to capture the complexity of the process of change (what to use, when, how, by whom, and for whom), but they may also reflect a reliance of theoretical assumptions that may, at times, be too broad and/or not optimal to fit client's personal needs and characteristics. For example, as Dr. Wolf noted, approaches in psychotherapy vary on a continuum in terms of emphasizing awareness at one pole and behavior change at the other pole. Principles 17 and 18, however, rest on solid evidence that therapists may need to change what they are doing with regard to such emphasis, as a function of a patient coping style. This raises important questions: If it is likely to be more beneficial to use a behavior change procedure for a particular client, should an insight-oriented therapist refrain from providing it because it is contrary to one's training? Alternatively, should one use a behavior change technique when there is reliable empirical evidence suggesting that it might not be an optimal intervention to facilitate the improvement of a specific type of clients? These questions, which are emerging in the present context of a collaborative relationship between researchers and clinicians, underscore the need for dialogues about the role of theoretical principles and empirical findings in guiding clinical practice.

Also, with regard to Principles 17 and 18, most research on fitting interventions to coping style do align with Dr. Vivian's view regarding the continuous nature of coping styles and patient use of multiple styles. However, research assumes that one style tends to be dominant (Beutler, Edwards, Kimpara, & Miller, in press). Accordingly, most measurement in this body of research utilizes a measurement comprised of a ratio among two or more coping style scores as an index of their relative strength (Beutler, Clarkin, & Bongar, 2000), and Beutler et al. (2000) assert that a significant body of literature supports the use of a staged process, in which symptom/behavior change is the recommended first step among all patients and insight/awareness interventions are recommended to follow among internalizing patients.

Possible Combinations of Separate Principles

Throughout their respective chapters, the three clinical authors have illustrated that none of the principles of change can be implemented independently. They have indeed provided various examples of how most, if not all, principles are used in context and combination with others. They have also, more or less explicitly, pointed out that many principles overlap with one another. Dr. Wolf comments that many of the factors relate to higher constructs, such as the rigid use of manualized treatments of interpretations. Relatedly, Dr. Vivian suggested that some of the principles that show particularly strong degrees of overlapping may be combined into "principle constructs," each having two or more highly interrelated elements. Examples of such potential constructs or combinations are:

Readiness to Change and Ability to Engage in Treatment

Principle 4 (clients with higher initial expectations for benefiting from psychotherapy may benefit more from it than clients with lower initial outcome expectation), Principle 5 (clients who are more intrinsically [or autonomously] motivated to engage in psychotherapy may benefit more from it than clients who are less intrinsically [or autonomously] motivated),

Principle 6 (clients in advanced stages of change readiness [i.e., they are actively preparing for or currently taking action toward healthy behavior] may benefit more from psychotherapy than clients at lower stages of change readiness), and Principle 10 (clients whose therapist uses interventions consistent with the client's level of problem assimilation may benefit more from psychotherapy than patients whose interventions are not consistent with their assimilation level).

Internalizing/Externalizing Coping Styles

Principle 17 (clients with externalizing coping styles may benefit more from psychotherapy that is more focused on behavior change and symptom reduction than fostering insight and self- awareness) and Principle 18 (clients with internalizing coping styles may benefit more from psychotherapy that is more focused on fostering insight and self- awareness than behavior change and symptom reduction).

Involvement during Treatment

Principle 21 (clients who more actively participate in the treatment process may benefit more from psychotherapy than clients who less actively participate) and Principle 22 (clients who are more resistant to the therapist or therapy may benefit less from psychotherapy than clients who are less resistant).

Therapeutic Bond

Principles 24 (clients experiencing more therapist regard and affirmation may benefit more from psychotherapy than clients experiencing less therapist regard and affirmation), Principle 25 (clients experiencing more therapist congruence may benefit more from psychotherapy than clients experiencing less therapist congruence), and Principle 26 (clients experiencing more therapist empathy may benefit more from psychotherapy than clients experiencing less therapist empathy).

Transference Interpretations

Principle 29 (clients whose therapist uses a higher proportion of general psychodynamic interpretations may benefit more from psychotherapy than clients whose therapist uses a lower proportion of general psychodynamic interpretations) and Principle 30 (clients whose therapist uses higher quality psychodynamic interpretations may benefit more from psychotherapy than clients whose therapist uses lower quality psychodynamic interpretations)

Obtaining/Sharing Feedback

Principle 31 (clients whose therapist receives feedback based on a routinely delivered outcome measure may benefit more from psychotherapy than clients whose therapist does not receive feedback) and Principle 32 (clients who receive feedback from their therapist on their performance in treatment may benefit more from psychotherapy than clients who do not receive feedback).

Interventions for Clients with High Severity of Impairment

Principle 2 (clients whose primary presenting problems are complicated by a co-morbid secondary personality disorder diagnosis may benefit less from psychotherapy than clients without a co-morbid personality disorder diagnosis), Principle 15 (clients who present with poorer interpersonal functioning are likely to benefit less from psychotherapy when their therapist uses a higher versus lower proportion of transference interpretations), Principle 19 (clients with moderate to severe impairment and/or fewer social supports will benefit more from psychotherapy when their therapist helps them address their social or medical needs), Principle 34 (clients whose therapist selectively/responsively fosters more adaptive interpersonal changes may benefit more broadly from psychotherapy than those whose therapist fosters fewer adaptive interpersonal changes) and Principle 38 (clients whose therapist selectively/responsively fosters more behavior changes may benefit more broadly from psychotherapy than clients whose therapist fosters fewer behavior changes). Despite recognizing the overlaps among many principles, Dr. Vivian believes that keeping them as distinct elements within discrete constructs is helpful as it may provide the clinician with suggestions for how to increase the breadth and depth of patient-centered therapeutic interventions and/or modifications to the therapist–patient relationship to increase response to treatment—particularly when a patient does not seem to respond to the initial treatment plan. Adopting a nuanced approach to this issue (upon collecting information across clinicians) may be very helpful, in her view, in deriving a parsimonious list of principles based on the integration of science and practice. Irrespective of whether such list would involve a large number of discrete variables or a smaller number of more global constructs, she maintains that the implementation of principles should also be viewed in a patient-centered context—adapted to the needs and resources of each individual, rather than in a nomothetic way. Furthermore, she believes that therapy should be conceptualized within a principle-based context. Namely, the particular combination of principles playing a prominent role in each patient's treatment may, in and of itself, play a moderating and/or mediating role in treatment.

Editors' Comments

Dr. Vivian draws meaningful connections between several principles, within and across the five clusters that has been used in this book to organize them. With the exception of her combination of Principles 17 and 18 (for reasons stated in our previous comments), we found these connections to be conceptually appealing. We can also see how reducing the number of principles by aggregating several of them in a theoretically cohesive manner can be advantageous in efforts to disseminating them in teaching, training, or supervising contexts. Short lists of principles of change, such as Goldfried's (1980), have been viewed by many (including the three of us) has very apt heuristics to capture core processes of therapeutic change. At this same time, we are in full accord with Dr. Vivian that maintaining the 38 principles as distinct elements (within each construct) can be very helpful clinically. Doing so broadens the focus of therapists' assessment and interventions—allowing them to be attuned to wide range of client's needs, as well as to increase their repertoire of appropriate therapeutic responses.

From a research perspective, we would also like to point out that conceptual overlap and dependence that seem apparent in the definitions of some principles is not the same as empirical overlap and confluence. In our effort, we strived for some degree of empirical purity by having independent raters review the existing literature on concepts that have been determined to be reliable and valid. In the end, we believe that it is important to recognize the difference between conceptually and empirically derived constructs, as well as their respective merits, usefulness, and limitations.

Future Research Directions about Principles

Two strategies were used for encouraging clinicians to generate possible directions for future research on principles of change. First, once they completed their respective chapter, they were asked if they could identify principles or strategies of intervention that guide their treatment but that were not covered in the list of 38 empirically based principles that they were provided with. At a later stage, they were also asked to rate the helpfulness (using the same previously mentioned 10-point scale, with 10 being most helpful and 1 being least helpful) of nine principles that were not previously presented to them because the review of the literature described in Chapter 2 indicated a lack of sufficient empirical support. The rationale for this second step was to assess whether the authors felt that these deleted principles show enough clinical potential to deserve more empirical attention.

Clinically Based Principles

We first present principles that were initially generated by each of the clinical authors and then formulate collaboratively (or co-constructed) with the editors.

Dr. Johnson's Suggestions

- Clients whose therapist is highly engaged during therapy may benefit more from psychotherapy than clients whose therapist is less engaged.
- Clients who experience their therapist as fully and deeply understanding them will benefit more from psychotherapy than clients who experience being less fully and deeply understood by their therapist.

Dr. Vivian's Suggestions

- Clients with medical co-morbidity will benefit more from psychotherapy when therapist helps them address their medical needs. [Note: *This principle is addressing, as a separate focus, the medical needs highlighted in Principle 19 of the list of empirically based principles provided to the clinical authors. This implies that such medical needs would be deleted from Principle 19, if both principles were to be included in a revised list.*]
- Older clients will benefit more from psychotherapy when their therapist adapts treatment to address their social and/or medical needs.

- Clients who are experiencing stress related to minority status will benefit more from psychotherapy when their minority status fundamentally informs treatment.
- Clients with autism spectrum disorder co-morbidity and significant mood regulation problems will benefit more from psychotherapy that is more focused on behavior change and symptom reduction than fostering insight and self-awareness.
- Clients with stronger intellectual proficiency, greater cognitive flexibility, and good verbal skills will benefit more from psychotherapy than patients with less strong intellectual proficiency, rigidity/dogmatic thinking, and poor verbal skills.
- Clients who present with a very ruminative/obsessive cognitive style and perfectionistic tendencies will respond less favorably from psychotherapy that targets primarily CBT cognitive interventions (e.g., cognitive restructuring) compared with other interventions (e.g., behavioral changes and emotionally based interventions).
- Clients whose therapist focuses more on factors that buffer against adverse outcomes/impairments associated with psychopathology will benefit more from psychotherapy than clients whose therapist focuses less on these factors.
- Clients whose therapist uses a planful and systematic approach to addressing their countertransference as a vehicle or change will benefit more from therapy than clients whose therapist does not do so.

Dr. Wolf's Suggestions
Very similar to Dr. Vivian's last principle, Dr. Wolf made the following suggestion:

- Clients whose therapist more successfully manages and utilizes countertransference reactions will benefit more from psychotherapy than clients whose therapist less successfully manages and utilizes such countertransference reactions.

Principles Deleted from Empirically Based List

Box 7.2 presents each therapist helpfulness scores and mean for nine principles that were not deemed, based on the literature review conducted for this book, to be empirically based. Three of these were not scored above 6 by any of the three therapists (Deleted Principle 4: "If patients and therapists come from the

Box 7.2 Rating of Helpfulness of Principles Deleted Based on Lack of Sufficient Evidence

Depression Section

1. The benefits of therapy may be enhanced if the therapist is able to tolerate his or her own negative feelings regarding the patient and the treatment process.
   Dr. Johnson: 2; Dr. Vivian: 10; Dr. Wolf: 10
   Mean: 7.33
2. The therapist is likely to be more effective if he or she is patient.
   Dr. Johnson: 3; Dr. Vivian: 10; Dr. Wolf: 10
   Mean: 7.67
3. If psychotherapists are open, informed, and tolerant of various religious views, treatment effects are likely to be enhanced.
   Dr. Johnson: 2; Dr. Vivian: 5; Dr. Wolf: 10
   Mean: 5.67
4. If patients and therapists come from the same or similar racial/ethnic backgrounds, dropout rates are positively affected and improvement is enhanced.
   Dr. Johnson: 5; Dr. Vivian: 2; Dr. Wolf: 3
   Mean: 3.33
5. Patients representing underserved ethnic or racial groups achieve fewer benefits from conventional psychotherapy than Anglo-American groups.
   Dr. Johnson: 4; Dr. Vivian: 7; Dr. Wolf: 1
   Mean: 4
6. Positive change is likely if the therapist provides a structured treatment and remains focused in the application of his/her interventions.
   Dr. Johnson: 6; Dr. Vivian: 3; Dr. Wolf: 5
   Mean: 4.67
7. Therapists working with a specific disorder may increase their effectiveness if they receive specialized training with this population.
   Dr. Johnson: 7; Dr. Vivian: 10; Dr. Wolf: 7
   Mean: 8
8. The positive impact of therapy is likely to be increased if the therapist is comfortable with long-term, emotionally intense relationships.
   Dr. Johnson: 6; Dr. Vivian: 10; Dr. Wolf: 7
   Mean: 7.67

> 9. Younger clients may benefit more from psychotherapy than older clients.
> Dr. Johnson: 4; Dr. Vivian: 5; Dr. Wolf: 1
> Mean: 3.33
>
> *Note.* Ratings of helpfulness is based on a 10-point scale with 10 being most helpful and 1 being least helpful.

same or similar racial/ethnic backgrounds, dropout rates are positively affected and improvement is enhanced"; Deleted Principle 6: "Positive change is likely if the therapist provides a structured treatment and remains focused in the application of his or her interventions"; and Deleted Principle 9: "Younger clients may benefit more from psychotherapy than older clients"), suggesting that more research on these factors might not be viewed as particularly relevant—at least for some practitioners.

In contrast, two principles were rated 6 or above by the three therapists (Deleted Principle 7: "Therapists working with a specific disorder may increase their effectiveness if they receive specialized training with this population"; and Deleted Principle 8: "The positive impact of therapy is likely to be increased if the therapist is comfortable with long-term, emotionally intense relationships"). The other four deleted principles, interestingly, show discrepancies among the therapists' ratings. In contrast with Dr. Johnson, Drs. Vivian and Wolf rated very highly Deleted Principle 1 ("The benefits of therapy may be enhanced if the therapist is able to tolerate his or her own negative feelings regarding the patient and the treatment process"). This principle is related to the concept of countertransference, which, as previously described, both Drs. Vivian and Wolf identified as a construct guiding their practice but yet absent from the list of 38 principles provided to them. Drs. Vivian and Wolf also gave a much higher score than Dr. Johnson to Deleted Principle 2 ("The therapist is likely to be more effective if he or she is patient"). Dr. Vivian further rated Deleted Principle 5 more highly than her colleagues. This principle ("Patients representing underserved ethnic or racial groups achieve fewer benefits from conventional psychotherapy than Anglo-American groups") shares a focus on minority status with one principle that she generated from her own clinical observation (see previous discussion). Finally, Deleted Principle 3 ("If psychotherapists are open, informed, and tolerant of various religious views, treatment effects are likely to be enhanced") was perceived as more helpful by Dr. Wolf than by Drs. Johnson and Vivian.

Editors' Comments

From a researcher's perspective, the previous information highlights an interesting target of investigation. It may indeed be indicated for future research to provide attention to six of the nine deleted principles to clarify the lack of consistency between the current state of research and the views of some therapists and/or between the perspective of various clinicians. The combination of these principles and those previously generated by the therapists provides a wide range of topic and, hopefully, a basis of researcher–practitioner partnership to guide clinically relevant studies.

Final Thoughts

As a closing step for this chapter, therapists/authors were invited to offer final thoughts about principles of change and how they are implemented in clinical routine. This was presented as an opportunity to express ideas that they did not raise (or sufficiently emphasized) in their respective chapter, as well as to discuss implications of principles of change with regard to training and the therapist effects (the research findings showing that some therapists are more effective than others). It was also design to provide space for the therapists/authors, if they chose to do so, to react to the comments that the editors provided in the previous sections of this concluding chapter—as well as for the editors to briefly engage in a final exchange about principles of change.

Dr. Johnson's Closing Remarks

I find the 38 principles organized into five clusters incredibly helpful and reassuring. It feels like there is solid ground underneath my feet. I can push off in directions with patients knowing they are guiding me. I might not know where the intervention will precisely lead, but I can feel good knowing I am using a proven change principle. In one moment, I may be promoting self-understanding, and in another, I am building better self-management (and thus fostering behavioral changes).

As a way to facilitate the integration of these principles in clinical practice, I will offer suggestions about how to refer to them, as well as how to organize them. I will end my comments by drawing some implications of these change principles with regard to training and our understanding of therapist effects.

Fostering the Integration of Principles in Clinical Practice

First, I believe it may be helpful to refer to the change principles using shorthand terms that can promote a clinician's ability to remember the concept. For instance, I refer to Principle 24 as "regard and affirmation," which can capture the essence of the fully-stated principle. This may also make it easier to train and supervise treatment involving these principles.

Second, there may be alternative ways of organizing these 38 principles, as Dr. Vivian discusses. For some purposes, it may be useful to organize them based on patient type (such as patients with personality disorders). Alternatively, it may be useful to note which principles are relevant to all patients (perhaps Principle 23, regarding the helpfulness of the therapeutic alliance), which ones are relevant to specific subgroups (e.g., low socio-economic status patients), and which ones are relevant in specific situations (e.g., alliance ruptures). We do not want the number of principles to be overwhelming. At the same time, the headings of the current clusters do not suggest direct ways of intervening, as they are quite general (e.g., "client process variables"). Perhaps in a book designed to teach beginning therapists, these principles could be organized in more of an action-oriented scheme. For example, a heading might be, "Foster Interpersonal Changes" or "Use Skillful Nondirective Interventions."

Implications of the Principles for Training

Because psychotherapists in the real world are often called upon to see a full caseload of patients—often 30 or more per week for a full-time clinician—they need to find ways of practicing that are effective at that volume. I believe that strategies for "caseload management" are tremendously neglected in most training programs. I believe that when clinicians' practice stems from evidence-based principles, they are better able to provide effective treatment to the many different patients they see. In this context, focusing on patterns and principles of change is helpful and more feasible than using 20 different treatment manuals with their caseload. For instance, "avoidance" is well understood to be central process connected to many mental health problems. Depressed patients avoid going out much as anxious patients may want to avoid being alone. By training students to become alert to patterns of avoidance in their patients, they will be able to understand many dysfunctional cycles. Similarly, by training psychotherapists in the importance of helping people confront avoided situations gradually—as in exposure therapy—they can help many patients build confidence and overcome obstacles. For some people, this may mean approaching their spouse about a difficult topic, and for others, it may mean going on an elevator repeatedly.

One way to facilitate the training of these principles, for both novice and experienced therapists, is make their implementation (when and how) more explicit. In the three chapters of this section on depression, such implementation is described in rather implicit ways—where the clinician would not necessarily know, in the moment, that they were using a particular principle. However, there are times when I find myself quite consciously aware of a change principle; and I intervene in a straightforward way because of it. For instance, because I am aware of the importance of alliance ruptures, I express to patients early on that I am not a "mind-reader" and I ask them to please try to tell me if at any point it seems like I am not fully getting what they are trying to express. As another example, I might try to promote emotional experiencing by quite consciously proposing an experiential exercise. Perhaps treatment can be made easier to train and more straightforward to apply if more connections between principles and particular techniques are developed.

How the Principles May Relate to "Therapist Effects"
I suspect that some clinicians end up employing more of the change principles than others. This may be a combination of nature and nurture—some people are likely wired to connect more quickly and deeply with people than others, for instance. What if we could somehow run a regression and control for all of the 38 change principles? How much of the variance do we think these principles would account for? I think a gigantic amount. "Super-shrinks" likely read prognostic variables well, adjust their stance and style accordingly, and find ways to actively engage patients in the treatment process. They avoid relationship problems but manage them well when they show up. They facilitate interpersonal and behavioral change in many different ways. Future research may be able to study how many of the change principles therapists employ and connect that to their own sense of efficacy and patient reports of outcome.

I think there is another benefit of focusing on change principles. Since they are more at the level of "the big picture," I suspect they will orient students to take a more holistic view of the patient's life and functioning. Indeed, I want my students to continually reflect on how the patient is feeling and functioning in all the different roles they play in their lives. I want them to help patients connect to their values, find deeper meaning in their pursuits, and to thrive.

Dr. Vivian's Closing Remarks

As final thoughts, I would like to take a bird's eye perspective to offer some general comments about the principles of change and their implementation. I would also like to discuss implications of these principles for training and underscore their importance for understanding the therapist's role in affecting the patients' response to treatment.

In parallel with Dr. Wolf's view, I think that it is important to recognize that there are difficulties and challenges in identifying how, when, and with which patients these principles can be applied. We both argue that they need to be seen in "context," namely, within the unique reality that each patient presents at each point in time during treatment. In other words, these principles come to life primarily when they are applied in an ideographic and patient-centered way versus in a nomothetic and rule-oriented way. All three authors noted as well the interrelatedness among clusters of principles. I would further argue that, to some extent, many of these principles are not only highly interconnected but also operate via a multifaceted, iterative, and dynamic process that at times may remain elusively implicit—particularly for a highly experienced therapist. Relatedly, Dr. Wolf, Dr. Johnson, and I believe that a therapist stage of training may also affect the application of principles in terms of how automatic and implicit this process can be.

Echoing some of my reactions, Dr. Wolf believes that although the principles were "very helpful in specifying the tasks of the initial phases of therapy . . . , they were less helpful in identifying the challenges of later stages of psychotherapy." Dr. Wolf also pointed out the fact that, as the case formulation changes dynamically across treatment, the application of the principles may change. Similarly, I would like to add that, as the course of treatment is marked by a dynamic process of change, the importance of most of the principles is likely to shift accordingly and continuously; thus, it is difficult to predict in early stage of treatment the role that some principles may play in later stages of treatment. Further, I agree with Dr. Wolf's conclusion that, although empirically based and helpful in bridging the gap among different theoretical models, these principles of therapeutic change are, using his elegant form, "an example of a shotgun empiricism that begs for a theoretically coherent organization." Lastly, I suggest that a consensus-driven and clinically relevant taxonomy of higher order constructs of principles (which may include highly intercorrelated principle elements) may provide a more useful approach than a long list of principles, particularly for training and dissemination in the clinical community.

In regards to *training*, in reflecting back, my own personal experience did not include a structured introduction to a long list of evidence-based principles of therapeutic change as those presented herein, despite "growing-up" under Dr. Marvin Goldfield's tutelage. Rather, upon discussing the empirical literature about similarities and differences among theoretical and applied approaches to treatment, a few key emerging principles or "strategies" of change that were similar across theoretical approaches were discussed in supervision, and they were viewed in terms of how they informed/modified treatment applications in integrative ways. In fact, clinical supervision was the primary pathway to learn how to apply ideographically and in a patient-centered way basic principles of therapeutic change. The ensuing assimilation, internalization, generalization, and extension of the principles of change to multiple categories and elements of principles (as those listed herein) occurred over time and with the accumulated experience of treating hundreds of patients, as well as supervising countless trainees across the years. I believe that is why the principles seemed so implicit and automatic to me when I began reflecting on how they affect my work when I embarked in the task of writing my chapter.

However, I think that it would be very important to identify effective training and dissemination approaches to increase early acquisition and maximize integration of the principles of therapeutic change in graduate and postgraduate curriculum and practicum. The complex, dynamic, patient-centered, and interrelated nature of the principles provides a challenge for training, and a full assimilation and application of the principles may be only attainable with accumulated clinical experience over time. Nevertheless, I think it is worthwhile to design and evaluate training pathways to maximize learning of the principles via a structured approach that encompasses curriculum and practicum.

To this extent, as I indicated in my chapter, I am currently piloting a method to incorporate in a systematic way principles training in clinical supervision with graduate trainees. Overall, I guide my supervisees to evaluate systematically the role of each principle presented herein in planning each patient's treatment (and re-evaluate it throughout) in an ideographic and patient-centered way. I began this process by inviting all my supervisees to read the intake information concerning the three patients herein, Victor, Brian, and Anne, and I asked them to populate a blank table that lists all the principles grouped by their respective five categories in terms of how they would plan and modify treatment proactively with each patient and in view of each principle. (The process was congruent with how I approached writing my chapter, and all the supervisees found it quite instructive and helpful.) Subsequently, I asked them to apply the same approach with their patient at the start of treatment (after they derive a case formulation) and at different times in treatment. Although this process seems to be particularly useful in early stages of treatment, it seems to be also very helpful at other points in treatment as well, especially when supervisees are confronted with challenges such as resistance, alliance breaches, lack of patient response to treatment, and/or patient deterioration.

However, while quite useful, the list of 38 principles is daunting and most supervisees feel overwhelmed, as they are trying to concurrently identify mechanisms of change, create and maintain optimal alliance, and apply competently treatment interventions. Thus, I am hoping that the outcome of the collective effort herein will provide us with parsimonious and clinically relevant clusters of evidence-based and relevant principles across categories, as this would make the process of teaching how to approach treatment informed by the principles of change more effective for therapists, particularly novices. Relatedly, training would be further enhanced if the main ways (common and unique) in which the principles were implemented by the six authors herein (in their treatment of the six patients) were to be listed in a summary form for each principle within each superordinate cluster/category. This would provide novice trainees with information on how experienced clinicians apply these principles in ideographic ways with their clients to maximize change. Including this information in a table that trainees can populate for each of their patients may simplify treatment planning and modification thereof.

Lastly, approaching treatment in terms of the principles of change underscores the importance of the *therapist effects* in treatment. I believe I have illustrated throughout my chapter the importance for the therapist to be mindful of all the client's prognostic variables, treatment/provider moderating factors, patient process variables, therapy relationship principles, and intervention variables to provide effective, timely, sensitively delivered, patient-centered, and ideographically tailored treatment. While I have emphasized some categories of principles over others in my work (e.g., prognostic principles, therapy relationship principles, and intervention variables), I ultimately believe that all of these principles (in one way or another) provide a heuristic for guiding and maximizing change in treatment, particularly if approached in a context-driven and ideographic way. A therapist that can intervene guided by these principles is likely to establish a strong and trusting relationship with his/her/their patients, a relationship that will increase motivation, collaborative participation in the process of change, hope, and emotional healing in the patients. Consequently, a flexible approach to skills acquisition, along with increased agency and enhanced self-efficacy will enable patients to cope more adaptively with their psychological distress and respond to treatment in a transformative way.

Dr. Wolf's Closing Remarks

The editors have done a remarkable job distilling an enormous body of psychotherapy research into 38 principles. The challenge is how to make these abstract principles actionable, not just at the level of a treatment plan but also as guides to responsiveness in the immediacy of the therapeutic encounter. From this ground-level perspective, the principles are far more interrelated than the five categories suggest. The distinction between the therapeutic alliance and interventions is blurred; behavioral interventions can serve to enhance the alliance while a positive alliance serves in implementing behavioral interventions. For example, the confluence of principles can be viewed as part of a higher order factor that applies to repairing ruptured alliances (Principle 27) through the action of therapist congruence (Principle 25) and self-disclosure (Principle 28). To make the principles actionable, we need to understand contextual factors of a specific encounter. Another problem is how the wording of some prognostic principles. Specifically, the words "may benefit less from psychotherapy" pose the danger of their being interpreted as contraindications for psychotherapy rather than indications of treatment challenges, thereby using the principles as a way of rejecting individuals who could potentially benefit from treatment.

The issue of therapist effects is important both at the level of therapist stage of professional development, with its implications for psychotherapist training, and individual differences among therapists. Graduate students may take a very literal interpretation of the principles while more advanced practitioners will be more nuanced in their interpretation, even to the point of violating them depending on context. Indeed, too literal an interpretation may lead to just the problems described in the principles, namely, inflexible use of manualized treatments and psychodynamic interpretations, including transference interpretations. Dreyfus and Dreyfus (1986) propose a model of skill acquisition that details specific stages from novices who implement principles regardless of the situational in contrast to higher stages of development where practitioners who are increasingly aware of contextual factors as they gain more experience. Furthermore, therapists vary in terms of how they manage and utilize their own personal reactions, especially their negative reactions to their clients (Wolf, Goldfried, & Muran, 2017). Even experienced therapists who function at a high level are vulnerable to acting on their frustrations with certain types of clients or even in situations where they have a positive alliance with a client. As previously indicated, the research on countertransference/therapist-interfering behaviors needs to be included as a principle in the list of 38.

Editors' Closing Remarks

The same way that the three therapists/authors saw a lot of similarities across their respective chapters, we find abundant convergence and complementarity between their final remarks and our way of thinking about change principles. We agree with Drs. Vivian and Wolf that these are interrelated constructs and that their effective implementation depends on the particular needs of individual clients and different phases of treatment. Like Dr. Johnson, one of us

(Beutler, 2002) has argued that as components of evidence-based practice, the principles are likely to be more flexible to use and more cost-effective to learn than voluminous piles of distinct treatment manuals (a point also made in Chapter 12 by Dr. Weinberg). Furthermore, we share Dr. Johnson's excitement about future studies assessing the precise amount of outcome variance explained by these principles (both in isolation, for which a fair amount of research exists, and in complex interactions, for which much less research exists). Expanding on this point, we are eager to see studies comparing the predictive validity of common principles of change, interventions associated with particular orientation, and their interaction. However, even this point undersells the complexity of psychotherapy, as it may be as, or likely even more, important *who* delivers the interventions than simply comparing what is delivered or addressed (Constantino, Boswell, Coyne, Kraus, & Castonguay, 2017).

Not surprisingly, we agree with Dr. Johnson and Vivian that the practice of effective therapists is likely to be characterized by the skillful and contextually responsive use of the principles that are included in the five clusters retained in this book. We also believe that both of them make helpful recommendations for organizing these principles in various ways including, as we previously mentioned, for training purposes. We are particularly impressed by the protocol that Dr. Vivian has developed and began to pilot with her supervisees. We cannot emphasize enough how we would love to be part of such training! We think that her suggestion to construct a table featuring how each therapist involved in this project implements all 38 principles is an optimal way to draw the connections between principles and techniques that Dr. Johnson has promoted. In our view, it is a creative and effective way to disseminate the collaborative product of knowledge that we intended our book to generate. Interestingly, such display of a rich repertoire interventions linked to the same principles and tailored to a variety of clinical needs and situations is very much consistent with the "context-responsive" model of integration that some of us have developed (Constantino, Boswell, Bernecker, & Castonguay, 2013).

We also believe that supervisors should take seriously Dr. Wolf's warning that in contrast with experienced practitioners, therapists in training may show more rigidity in the implementation of principles; this is consistent with some of findings obtained in one of our training clinics (McAleavey, Castonguay, & Xiao, 2014). We also agree with his view that more experienced therapists are not without vulnerability and that the ability to manage countertransference should be considered in future revisions of the list of principles. We find particularly insightful his comment that therapist's negative reactions can occur even in the context of high alliance. As yet another sign of convergence and complementarity, one our laboratories has been investigating countertransference and alliance in clinical routine (Castonguay et al., 2018).

We are also in total agreement with Dr. Wolf's suggestion that the prognostic principles should not dictate whether or not one should employ psychotherapy as a treatment. Hidden within them are doubtlessly unrecognized moderators that, if known, could guide therapists in how to modify treatment in the face of these prognostic qualities. At least one of us (LEB) has expressed doubts about including prognostic variables in the list of efficacious principles at all until their implications for treatment modification can be better articulated.

And, finally, it bears repeating that discussing intervention and principle types is largely fruitless without considering the persons receiving them or implementing them. Just like we would all expect that different patients would respond to different types of strategies, it follows that different therapists will have different facility in providing psychotherapy principles or interventions. We suspect that as the research evolves, the principles that we have uncovered will become more nuanced, inherently representing complex links that exist between patient, provider, trait, state, and intervention (e.g., see research on the alliance that parses the construct's state, trait, and therapist influences on clinical outcomes; Coyne, Constantino, Westra, & Antony, 2019; Zilcha-Mano, 2017).

References

Beutler, L. E. (2002). It isn't the size, but the fit. *Clinical Psychology: Science and Practice, 9*, 434–438.

Beutler, L. E., Clarkin, J., & Bongar, B. (2000). *Guidelines for the systematic treatment of the depressed patient.* New York, NY: Oxford University Press.

Beutler, L. E., Edwards, C. J, Kimpara, S., & Miller, K. (in press). Coping style. To appear In J. C. Norcross & B. E. Wampold (Eds.), *Psychotherapy relationships that work* (3rd ed.), Volume 2. New York: Oxford University Press.

Castonguay, L. G., Xiao, H., Youn, S. J., Perdersen, T., Falkenstrom, F., Hayes, J. A., & Locke, B. D. (2018). *Working alliance and counter-transference: A preliminary study in day-to-day clinical routine.* Paper presented at the North American Society of Psychotherapy Research, Snowbird, UT (September).

Constantino, M. J., Boswell, J. F., Bernecker, S. L., & Castonguay, L. G. (2013). Context-responsive integration as a framework for unified psychotherapy and clinical science: Conceptual and empirical considerations. *Journal of Unified Psychotherapy and Clinical Science, 2*, 1–20.

Constantino, M. J., Boswell, J. F., Coyne, A. E., Kraus, D. R., & Castonguay, L. G. (2017). Who works for whom and why? Integrating therapist effects analysis into psychotherapy outcome and process research. In L. G. Castonguay & C. E. Hill (Eds.), *Why are some therapists are better than others? Understanding therapist effects* (pp. 55–68). Washington, DC: American Psychological Association. doi:10.1037/0000034-004

Coyne, A. E., Constantino, M. J., Westra, H. A., Antony, M. M. (2019). Interpersonal change as a mediator of the within- and between-patient alliance-outcome association in two treatments for generalized anxiety disorder. *Journal of Consulting and Clinical Psychology*. Advance online publication. http://dx.doi.org/10.1037/ccp0000394

Dreyfus, H. L., & Dreyfus, S. E. (1986). *Mind over machine: The power of human intuition and expertise in the era of the computer.* New York, NY: Free Press.

Goldfried, M. R. (1980). Toward the delineation of therapeutic change principles. *American Psychologist, 35,* 991–999.

Greenberg, L. S., Rice, L. N., & Elliott, R. (1993). *Facilitating emotional change: The moment-by-moment process.* New York, NY: Guilford.

McAleavey, A. A., Castonguay, L. G., & Xiao, H. (2014). Therapist orientation, supervision match, and therapeutic interventions: Implication for session quality in a psychotherapy training practice research network. *Counseling and Psychotherapy Research, 14,* 192–200.

Steiner, C. M. (1990). *Scripts people live* (2nd ed.). New York, NY: Grove Press.

Wolf, A. W., Goldfried, M. R., & Muran, J. C. (2017). Therapist negative reactions: How to transform toxic experiences. In L. G. Castonguay & C. E. Hill (Eds.), *How and why are some therapists better than others? Understanding therapist effects* (pp. 175–192). Washington, DC: American Psychological Association.

Zilcha-Mano, S. (2017). Is the alliance really therapeutic? Revisiting this question in light of recent methodological advances. *American Psychologist, 72,* 311–325. doi:10.1037/a0040435

PART III
ANXIETY DISORDERS

8
Anxiety Disorders Cases

Louis G. Castonguay, Michael J. Constantino, and Larry E. Beutler

Presented in this chapter are three cases of social anxiety disorder that were provided to three clinical authors who wrote the next chapters of this section: Eva D. Papiasvili (Chapter 9), Catherine S. Spayd (Chapter 10), and Igor Weinberg (Chapter 11). These therapists refer to the clinical cases when describing how they implement the empirically based principles of change delineated in Chapter 2.

With the exception of the primary diagnosis, the three cases are very similar to those described in the first chapter of the depression section: Whereas the first (Phillip) is presented with neither a co-morbidity of substance abuse nor personality disorder, the other two are depicted as having one of these co-morbid conditions, that is, alcohol abuse (Robert) and borderline personality disorder (Marie). We created these cases from on our own knowledge and clinical experience, as well as from psychopathology research (Teachman, Goldfried, & Clerkin, 2013). As for the depression cases, they were built to provide material relevant to the 38 principles of change retained for the book (see Chapter 3 of this volume for more details). Appendix 8.1 presents the list of these principles, with the addition of notes relevant to the social anxiety cases.

As previously described (again, see Chapter 3 of this volume for more details), profiles of therapist behaviors and interventions were derived from the Therapy Process Rating Scale (TPRS; Kimpara, Regner, Usami, & Beutler, 2015) to guide the assignment of cases between the depression and anxiety disorders sections. The same profiles are also used in the concluding chapter of these two sections to shed light on the convergences and divergences between clinical authors in their implementation of principles of change. The profile of the three authors working with the social anxiety disorder cases are presented Appendix 8.2.

Anxiety Disorder Cases

Case 1: Phillip (Social Anxiety Disorder without Substance Abuse or Personality Disorder Co-morbidity)

Phillip is a 41-year-old Hispanic man who has been experiencing severe social anxiety since his teenage years. He reports feeling nervous and uncomfortable when he is around most other people. Work is particularly anxiety-provoking for Phillip, especially when participating in group meetings or interacting individually with others (colleagues, supervisors, or supervisees). In most, if not all, social situations, Phillip is afraid that people are evaluating him negatively and with judgment of how he is acting and who he is. And during interactions, Phillip looks for signs that support his expectation of negative evaluation. He also focuses on his own behaviors (like stumbling over his words) and physiological reactions (such as blushing and sweating) that confirm, in his eyes, that he is performing awkwardly. Except with his family members and a few close friends, Phillip tends to avoid most interpersonal situations. When avoidance is not possible, such as at work, he is forced to tolerate significant anxiety until he feels it is possible to escape. Phillip is aware that his fears and anxieties are unwarranted, as he knows that he is respected at work and that he can, when he has to, converse with people he has either never met or barely knows. In addition to his social anxiety, Phillip meets criteria for depression and agoraphobia. He is, however, most distressed by his social anxiety disorder, which has been his longest-standing problem.

Phillip has been married for 20 years to Christina, a Hispanic woman two years his junior, with whom he has been best friends since he was 15 years old. They have two children, a girl aged 21 and a boy aged 18. Phillip and Christina share many values, including the importance of family relationships, hard work, their children's education, and their religious faith (Roman Catholic). Their relationship has been very close and intense. While the first several years of their marriage were harmonious, over the past four years they have argued frequently and have grown more distant from each other, both emotionally and sexually. The main topics of discord are about what Christina perceived as Phillip's lack of engagement in carrying out his responsibilities regarding home and children, as well as Phillip's perception of Christina's lack of support and validation. Financial difficulties and the couple's social isolation have also contributed to marital distress. While both Phillip and Christina are working (full-time and half-time, respectively), they are living in an expensive part of the United States, many miles away from each other's parents and siblings.

Like Christina, Phillip was born in the United States following his parents' immigration into the States from Central America. He described conflicted feelings about his youth. He respects the fact that both of his parents had to work long hours at nongratifying jobs to survive in a country where, for many years, they did not speak the prevalent language. He remembers fondly the nurturing ways his mother would relate to him when he was young. Phillip reports that his mother was very caring and attentive toward her children, to the point of being overly concerned and protective about their venturing outside of the house activities. He is also grateful for the inspiration he got from both of his parents to work hard and to be personally disciplined (especially in choosing "the right" friends and avoiding risky situations involving sex, drugs, alcohol, and gang-related activities). At the same time, he regrets the fact that, as a child, he had to spend many hours alone and many more hours caretaking his three younger siblings while his parents were working. With painful emotions, he also remembers how demanding, critical, and emotionally unavailable his father was during Phillip's youth.

After completing high school, Phillip when straight to work. He began community college when he was 20 years old, but he had to drop out after a year when he learned that Christina was pregnant. He returned to work to take on the increasing responsibilities required of being a parent. Phillip is now manager of a small business, which imposes long hours, six days a week. Although his advancement in the company has led to some modest salary increases, they have always lived on the edge financially. His job also comes with constant stress between the demands from his employers and the expectations of the workers (and former peers) that he now supervises. Phillip feels that he has little control or power over the pressures that he faces at work. He also finds that the organizational and managerial challenges that he has to address on a daily basis are neither stimulating nor gratifying. He feels stuck in a static and unsatisfying occupation that he cannot leave because of the revenue it provides (although it is not nearly sufficient for him and his family to be financially comfortable).

Phillip had a strong connection with his siblings as a child. Although he was not as close with them as he was with Christina, he had male friends in and outside of schools. He was involved in many sports as a teenager and maintained regular contact with a few male friends until the birth of his son. For the last several years, he has not made time to pursue sports or other hobbies nor to enjoy the company of friends. Thus, now and even before he became depressed one or two years ago, Phillip has not been involved in any activities that bring him pleasure and personal satisfaction. His agoraphobia has also imposed restriction to the couple's social life.

Phillip also reports a number of issues that have had an impact on his interpersonal relationships, both at work and at home. He reports that in several social situations, over many years, he has been acting angrily toward other people. Especially since becoming depressed, he has found himself easily and increasingly irritated, and he has noted that his frustration and hostility has made both Christina and his co-workers annoyed and frustrated with him. Their negative feelings and criticism toward him, as well as their occasional avoidance of him, have been quite hurtful (especially considering that Phillip has always felt the desire to be close to others). In fact, Christina has told him several times that she wishes he was less needy of her reassurance and that he was more assertive and less submissive at work. Phillip recognizes that he has always been insecure, which has made him frequently rely on advice from others. He also admits that his tendency to seek guidance and reassurance from others, as well as his expectation of being negatively evaluated, have limited his ability to develop and exercise leadership at work. When dealing with stressful situations, he frequently feels that he does not have what it takes to control or handle them successfully; and when these situations get solved, he tends to attribute the positive outcomes to other people' skills. Christina complains that he lets others, both bosses and supervisees, control him. Phillip agrees that he is uncomfortable when others rely on him for support, seek his opinion, and expect him to take initiative and control over situations at work or at home.

Indeed, his tendency to let others control him, if not dominate him, is a major cause of painful ruminations for Phillip and arguments with his wife. He has always showed a tendency to blame himself for problems and failures and, for years, Phillip has been stuck in a constant and uncontrollable cycle of wishing to assert himself, anticipating embarrassing failures prior to social events, and then focusing on signs (even ambiguous ones) of anxiety, unskilled behaviors, and negative evaluation of others during these events. Because he is so anxious, self-focused, and apprehensive of negative evaluation during social interactions, others are sometimes cold, distant, dismissive, or critical of him—thereby providing confirmation to his worst fears. After the events, he frequently finds himself focusing on what he thinks he did badly and the negative consequences that this could have, which not only triggers memories of past failures but also increases his anxiety about future social events. He is convinced that these traits reflect an immutable weakness of his personality, which he uses to explain to himself why he has not been able to be successful personally and professionally. He is also convinced that he will not able to change this core aspect of who he is and that it will always preclude him from achieving meaningful accomplishments and gaining genuine affection and respect from others.

Case 2: Robert (Social Anxiety Disorder and Substance Abuse)

Robert is a 45-year-old White man who is hesitantly seeking help for his social anxiety and alcohol problems after repeated urging of friends and family. Robert completed high school and has been working in the construction business for the last 28 years. He has been apprehensive and afraid of interactions of with others for as long as he can remember. He saw a therapist in his 30s to help him be more comfortable during social events, but he terminated after two sessions without benefit. About a year before his current consultation, he began experiencing more intense and distressing social fears, leading him to avoid public situations (including eating, drinking, going to parties) and to withdraw from others as much as possible. He reports being constantly worried and hypervigilant of any possible signs of being judged negatively (as a boring and stupid person) or rejected because of his extreme anxiety. He describes that he frequently feels paralyzed with fears in social events, not knowing what to say or how to ask questions, staring at the other person, being stuck in rigid body postures, and experiencing embarrassing and painful physical sensations (stomach discomfort, sweating and blushing profusely, muscle tension). He also reports that when he is not in social situations, he frequently anticipates how painful future ones will be, thinks about how to avoid them, and ruminates with shame and humiliation about how intimidated and unlikeable he had been in previous interactions. As his social fears and isolation intensified, Robert began experiencing depressive symptoms, including dysphoria, anhedonia, insomnia, weight gain, and fatigue. Most concerning to those close to him, Robert has talked about killing himself on numerous occasions in the last few months.

Robert's alcohol problems have also been a serious concern. He began drinking with peers as a teenager but progressively began to drink alone. Although a primary motivation for his drinking was to reduce his social fears, it has contributed to social isolation from early on. (Although he still has friends from high school and work, he sees them rather infrequently.) Robert has been drinking nightly since the age of 21, and while he used to restrain himself to two beers during most of his 20s, he gradually increased his consumption and now drinks an average of five per evening. He also smokes marijuana but only occasionally. He admits that his drinking has led him to engage in dangerous behaviors, such as driving while impaired on several occasions. Robert has tried several times to reduce his alcohol consumption, but he has been unsuccessful in part because he feels strongly that alcohol helps him relax and tolerate his stress. He also felt anxious and physically uncomfortable when attempting to drink less.

Robert's substance use has numerous negative consequences. In addition to the increased social isolation, his ability to show up on time to work and to meet the physical demands of his job have suffered (this was true even before his chronic depression became severe). His boss has complained to him several times about his work performance and recently warned him that he might be fired. His drinking also has had an impact on his romantic relationships. While his social fears have made it difficult for him to date, he has had a few girlfriends in his life. However, his last girlfriend, like the one before her, told him that his alcohol problems and his unwillingness to address them, were the main reasons for her terminating their two-year relationship. She complained that his drinking made him lethargic, irritable, and difficult to get along with. She also complained of his low level of sexual drive or ability, as well as his lack of interest in activities, social or otherwise, outside of his apartment. Although Robert claimed that he never physically abused the current or previous girlfriends, he acknowledged that another reason for their separation was that she became afraid of his violent temper when he was heavily intoxicated.

Robert recognizes that he drinks too much, but he claims that most of his problems at work and with his former girlfriends were not his fault. Likewise, he attributes his work problems to his boss being stressed out all the time and thus being too demanding. He also complains that his boss has different standards and favors some other employees over him—including some who drink at least as much as he does. He also says that his former girlfriend had never been happy about what he was doing for her or their relationship and was always looking for a fight. Furthermore, he states that his boss and former girlfriend are/were both critical and controlling of him, making him feel upset and angry. He feels that neither of them can/could trust and accept him as he is, give him the space and the right to make his own decision, do what he wants to do and how he wants to do it, and be who he wants to be. He also believes that over the last few years the unrealistic demands from his boss and the constant critics of his former girlfriend are the main reasons for his increased and excessive alcohol use. Nevertheless, he recognizes that her leaving him, as well as his threat of losing his job, are two stressful events that have contributed to his current and most serious depression episode. He also admits that his anger, distrust of others, and poor impulse control will make it difficult for him to find, let alone keep, another girlfriend and job. He is, however, not convinced that therapy will be helpful for his problems.

Robert also feels alone more than at any time in his life. He maintains that he has never been good at meeting new people. He also feels that it would be difficult for him to find a new job—especially a job that, like the one he has had for many years, does not involved interaction with many people. He describes himself as having poor "people skills." He does not participate in community activities (social and/or athletic) and does not belong to a church (his parents were Protestant, but religion was not emphasized at home, and he neither paid attention to nor rejected the Christian faith). Highly demoralized, he feels stuck in his current life, without prospect for major changes or positive things, personally and professionally; not surprisingly, he describes his life as unfulfilling and lacking in meaning.

In terms of family history, Robert reports that he had a difficult upbringing. His father was frequently unemployed and drank heavily. His father also had a violent temper and was both verbally and physically abusive with him and his two brothers. His father passed away when Robert was 20, and he never really talked about his conflicted feelings. These feelings consist both of profound sadness and, equally, intense resentment for the loss of his father. Robert describes his mother has being a very anxious person. She was not only stressed out about her husband's occupational failures but also afraid of him. Robert recalls that she rarely got out (she did not have a job outside of the house) and that she was extremely shy and nervous around others. He describes her as being cold and rejecting. Although he remembers having always been anxious and withdrawn as a child, he has no memories of her comforting him, encouraging him to make friends, or helping him deal with being frequently teased as a shy kid. Robert felt distant from both parents during his childhood and adolescence and seldom sees or talks to his mother even to this day. He fought a lot with his brothers when they were young, but he also feels that they ultimately developed a strong bond, especially around doing and watching sports. Like with his friends from high school, Robert has not had regular contact with his brothers. He feels that it is mostly they who have failed to maintain their connections. Although he feels grateful that both of them have reached out to him in difficult times, especially recently, he also has wished that they would contact him at times other than when they feel that he is depressed.

Case 3: Marie (Social Anxiety Disorder and Personality Disorder)

Marie is 24-year-old White woman who is seeking treatment for her social anxiety. She reports being extremely anxious around people since she was 13 years old. She also describes herself as being socially awkward, rarely knowing what to say during a conversation and behaving in ways that she thinks others find weird and crazy—such as having difficulty maintaining eye contact, blushing and trembling, speaking with a very soft voice, and stumbling over her words.

Out of anticipatory anxiety, she has long avoided many social situations, and when she interacts with others, she tends not to reveal much about herself for fear of being judged negatively and rejected. For the last six months, Marie has also been struggling with strong feelings of sadness and self-loading. These depressive feelings are primarily related to the end of a romantic relationship with a man of her age, Marc, with whom she is still deeply in love. They were together for three years by her report, but the last two were characterized by a cycle of break-ups and make-ups. She had a number of brief affairs with other young men during the last two years that she was with Marc, but none of them created for her the same wishes for closeness and intimacy as she has been longing for with Marc. Before meeting Marc, she had experienced a few sexual relationships with men that she had found exciting (a musician, ski instructor, drug dealer), but she never considered them "a boyfriend." Neither does she have many close relationships with women, with the exception of a friend from high school with whom she has had infrequent contact. At the time of intake, Marie was taking two classes at the university and was working part time in a public library—where most of her time was spent alone. She was also living at her parents' house.

Marie has never felt that she fits in with peers. Being introverted, and because of her social fears, she spends a lot of time reading novels, listening to music, and doing outdoors activities on her own. Yet she has rarely felt at peace or happy to be alone. While always feeling a yearning to be with others, she has viewed herself as not being strong, interesting, and socially skilled enough to develop and maintain close relationships. The only time she did not feel socially isolated was when she was part of a small group of high school students who had counterculture social and political values and consumed hard drugs together (including heroin).

Extremely smart, Marie did well in school until college. Having been an avid reader of classic literature, she majored in both English and philosophy. Although she excelled in her first year, getting recognition from several of her teachers for the creativity and insightfulness of her writing, she started having difficulty completing and passing her courses in her second year. These increasing difficulties followed an abortion she had early in the fall semester. She admits that this event may also have had an impact on her relationship with Marc: she became dependent on him, but at the same time she was fearful of closeness and reluctant to engage in sexual intimacy. After several months, Marc began to be less engaged in the relationship, which made Marie cling to him even more. She progressively withdrew from others, as most of her social contacts at that time were with Marc's friends. Her academic difficulties became exacerbated, in part because of her difficulty concentrating but also because of her avoidance of anxiety-provoking issues (class presentations, exams, deadlines) and her preoccupation with possible ways to cope with them (e.g., contacting advising resources). She never quite followed through with these plans, however. Attempts to separate, always initiated by Marc, triggered depressive episodes and suicidal gestures. A serious suicide attempt led to a brief psychiatric hospitalization. Even when she and Marc re-established their relationship, Marie remained constantly insecure, emotional unstable (especially vacillating between periods sadness, anger, and anxiety), jealous of any time he spent with others, and periodically engaged in self-harm (cutting). She also occasionally resumed her consumption of hard drugs, which she had stopped after meeting Marc.

The relationship with Marc ended, according to Marie, when she spent the summer alone at her parents' country house, during which time she had an affair. Although they both agreed that the separation was inevitable, almost immediately afterward she became depressed. Her social fears and sense of isolation also seriously intensified, which, after six months, led her to seek psychotherapy.

During the intake, which took two sessions, Marie revealed persistent patterns of fluctuation in both her self-confidence and her sense of having a direction in her life. She also reported being frequently impulsive and "irresponsible." She remembered several moments of excitement and motivation in her life, including periods when she became very focused on one or another potential career choices. Ultimately, all of these interests and moments of motivation rapidly extinguished into a general state of disinterest, boredom, frustration, depression, anxiety, and self-doubt. She complained about not having a clear sense of what she wants or who she is. She also reported that her self-esteem and life choices were frequently based on others' opinions or her expectations of such opinions. Yet, despite her being drawn to others, most of Marie's relationships have been emotionally draining and disappointing. She explained that because of her social fears and negative expectations, it takes time to let others close to her but that once she feels attached, friends usually stop being interested in being around her. She believes that what she views as her being a real friend, others view as her as being too needy, dependent, and even clingy, which not only has made her frequently and extremely angry at others but also resentful of her own tendency to let her hopes build up and her fears to lessen, thus opening the door to another cycle of disappointment. People have been hard to trust throughout her life, and personal relationships always seem to turn sour and painful. This was certainly the case with Marc, whom she described at different times during the intake sessions with a mixture of opposing emotions. She describes him, even now, as being a most gentle, loving, romantic, and inspiring man but also a selfish, manipulative, shallow, and untrustworthy man.

Marie was reluctant to confide information about her parents and her childhood. She described her mother as having been socially anxious, not very warm, and overcontrolling. She was particularly vague about her relationship with her father, presenting him glowingly in terms of his personality (hard-working, highly intelligent, no-nonsense), but also noting his frequent absences from home—either for his job or for selfishly taking time alone to build and enjoy the country house. Marie has not had a close connection with her siblings. She described her older brother as distant, dismissive, and extremely mean (verbally and physically). She also acknowledged having been envious and jealous of her younger sister, whom she described as always being happy, bubbly, carefree, and popular among her peers and adults. Although she recognized having felt alone and as having been treated as an outcast, attempts to clarify her history or to explore remaining feelings and thoughts toward her childhood and family were met with resistance.

During the intake sessions, Marie also seemed conflicted about entering therapy. Although she appreciated the therapist's desire to listen, she communicated subtle annoyance at some of the therapist's questions about her goals for therapy and evinced noticeable frustration at some of therapist's questions when suggesting topics to be explored during therapy. Marie seemed to have low expectations about treatment, feeling that no one is likely to be able to change her life for the better. Yet, she admitted to needing therapy, not only because of her distress level but also because of how unfulfilling, meaningless, lonely, and hopeless her life has become following the end of her relationship with Marc and her academic drifting. She described having dwelled in thought for at least six months on what she views as lifelong failures in relationships and in school and especially her frustration at being stuck in patterns of rumination, regret, and sadness about what she could have done better in all areas of her life.

References

Kimpara, S., Regner, E., Usami, S., & Beutler, L. E. (2015, August). *Systematic Treatment Selection (STS): How to monitor therapists' interventions and cross-cultural differences between north America and Argentina*. Annual Meeting of the American Psychological Association, Toronto.

Teachman, B. A., Goldfried, M. R., & Clerkin, E. M. (2013). Panic disorder and phobias. In L. G. Castonguay & T. F. Oltmanns (Eds.), *Psychopathology: From science to clinical practice* (pp. 88–142). New York, NY: Guilford.

Appendix 8.1

List of Principles of Change with Notations for Authors Working on Social Anxiety Cases

Client Prognostic Principles

1. Clients with higher levels of baseline impairment may benefit less from psychotherapy than clients with lower levels of impairment.

   As outlined in the following discussion, all three cases show impairment in terms of depressive symptoms, co-morbidity, global functioning, and interpersonal functioning. In general, Case 2 (with substance use problems) has higher level of impairment and distress, followed by Case 3 (with personality disorder) and Case 1. Although varying in terms of intensity, some features of impairment are shared either by two or the three of them. Other clinical features, however, are specific to one of the three cases.

Social Anxiety

- Severity of social anxiety symptoms: severe (Case 2); moderate (Case 3); mild (Case 1)
- Early onset (Cases 2 and 3)
- Risk of suicide (Cases 2 and 3)
- Genetic factors/family history (Cases 2 and 3)
- Chronicity (especially Case 2)
- Not fully recover from previous treatment (Case 2)

Co-Morbidity

- Alcohol use disorder (Case 2), depression (Cases 1–3), agoraphobia (Case 1)

Global Functioning

- Quality of life (Cases 1–3)
- Stressful events and inadequate or lack of coping skills to deal with them:
  - Occupational failure/difficulties (Cases 1–3); social difficulties (humiliation, rejection, loss, social exclusion (Cases 1–3)

- Reduced work performance (Cases 1–3)
- Behavioral avoidance (Cases 2 and 3)

Interpersonal Functioning

- Lack of support (Case 1–3)
- Isolation/loneliness—personal and professional (Cases 1–3)
- Romantic dissatisfaction/discord/difficulties (Cases 1–3)
- Anger and annoying to others (Cases 1–3)
- Social skill deficit (Cases 2 and 3)
- Loss of parent (Case 2)
- Seeking reassurance (Cases 1 and 3)
- Seeking confirmation (Case 1)

2. Clients whose primary presenting problems are complicated by a co-morbid secondary personality disorder diagnosis may benefit less from psychotherapy than clients without a co-morbid personality disorder diagnosis.
    - Case 3

3. Clients with more secure attachment may benefit more from psychotherapy than clients with less secure attachment (i.e., more attachment anxiety).
    - Parental problems potentially related to attachment insecurity are present in all three cases.

4. Clients with higher initial expectations for benefitting from psychotherapy may benefit more from it than clients with lower initial outcome expectations.
    - Low or mixed expectations about therapy (Cases 2 and 3)

5. Clients who are more intrinsically (or autonomously) motivated to engage in psychotherapy may benefit more from it than clients who are less intrinsically (or autonomously) motivated.
    - Low motivation about therapy (Case 2)

6. Clients in advanced stages of change readiness (i.e., they are actively preparing for or currently taking action toward healthy behavior) may benefit more from psychotherapy than clients at lower stages of change readiness.
    - The three cases show different levels of readiness for change, with Case 1 being the most advanced and Case 2 the least.

7. Clients with low socio-economic status and employment problems may benefit less from psychotherapy than clients with higher socio-economic status and no employment problems.
    - Socio-economic status: low-mid (Case 2); mid (Cases 1 and 3)
    - Education: high school (Case 2); some college (Cases 1 and 3)

8. Clients who have experienced adverse childhood events may benefit less from psychotherapy than clients who did not experience adverse childhood events.
   - Inadequate parenting: neglect (inattention, withdraw, emotional unresponsiveness, lack of reinforcement; Cases 1–3); abuse (verbal/physical; Cases 2 and 3)
9. Anxious clients with more negative self-attributions may benefit less from psychotherapy than clients with fewer negative self-attributions.
   - Case 1

Treatment/Provider Moderating Principles

10. Clients whose therapist uses interventions consistent with the client's level of problem assimilation may benefit more from psychotherapy than patients whose interventions are not consistent with their assimilation level.
    - Case 1 may show signs of higher level of problem assimilation than Cases 2 and 3.
11. Clients with higher levels of resistance may benefit more from psychotherapy that is more nondirective compared to clients with lower levels of resistance who may benefit more from psychotherapy that is more directive.
    - Resistance/reactance: low (Case 1); high (Case 2); mixed (Case 3)
12. Clients with lower motivation for, or higher ambivalence about, change may benefit more from psychotherapy when their therapist is responsive and person-centered versus more directive and change-oriented.
    - Cases 2 and 3
13. Clients who are matched to their preferred therapy role, therapist demographics, or treatment type may benefit more from psychotherapy than clients unmatched on these preferences.
    - This could be relevant to all 3 cases.
14. Clients whose preference for religiously or spiritually oriented psychotherapy is accommodated may benefit more from treatment than clients whose preference is unmet.
    - Strong Catholic faith (Case 1); no commitment to Protestant faith (Case 2)
15. Clients who present with poorer interpersonal functioning are likely to benefit less from psychotherapy when their therapist uses a higher versus lower proportion of *transference* interpretations.
    - Cases 2 and 3
16. Clients higher in baseline impairment may benefit more from psychotherapy that is longer-term and/or more intensive compared to clients lower in baseline impairment who may benefit equally well from psychotherapy that is long- or short-term and/or more or less intensive.
    - Cases 2 and 3

17. Clients with externalizing coping styles may benefit more from psychotherapy that is more focused on behavior change and symptom reduction than fostering insight and self-awareness.
    - Externalizer (Case 2); mixed externalizer and internalizer (Case 3)
18. Clients with internalizing coping styles may benefit more from psychotherapy that is more focused on fostering insight and self-awareness than behavior change and symptom reduction.
    - Internalizer (Case 1); mixed externalizer and internalizer (Case 3)
19. Clients with moderate to severe impairment and/or fewer social supports will benefit more from psychotherapy when their therapist helps them address their social or medical needs.
    - Cases 2 and 3
20. Clients with substance use problems may be equally likely to benefit from psychotherapy delivered by a therapist with or without his or her own history of substance use problems.
    - Case 2

Client Process Variables

21. Clients who more actively participate in the treatment process may benefit more from psychotherapy than clients who less actively participate.
    - Potential difficulty of engagement in therapy (Cases 2 and 3)
22. Clients who are more resistant to the therapist or therapy may benefit less from psychotherapy than clients who are less resistant.
    - Resistance/reactance: low (Case 1); high (Case 2); mixed (Case 3)

Therapy Relationship Principles

23. Clients experiencing a higher quality therapeutic alliance in group psychotherapy (group cohesion) or individual psychotherapy (bonding/collaboration) may benefit more than clients experiencing a lower quality alliance.
24. Clients experiencing more therapist regard and affirmation may benefit more from psychotherapy than clients experiencing less therapist regard and affirmation.
25. Clients experiencing more therapist congruence may benefit more from psychotherapy than clients experiencing less therapist congruence.
26. Clients experiencing more therapist empathy may benefit more from psychotherapy than clients experiencing less therapist empathy.
27. Clients who experience alliance rupture–repair episodes and/or who work with therapists trained to repair alliance ruptures may benefit more from psychotherapy than clients who experience no or unrepaired ruptures and/or work with therapists not trained specifically on rupture–repair interventions.

28. Clients whose therapist uses more supportive self-disclosures may benefit more from psychotherapy than clients whose therapist uses less supportive self-disclosures (or does not disclose at all).

Therapist Intervention Principles

29. Clients whose therapist uses a higher proportion of general psychodynamic interpretations may benefit more from psychotherapy than clients whose therapist uses a lower proportion of general psychodynamic interpretations.
30. Clients whose therapist uses higher quality psychodynamic interpretations may benefit more from psychotherapy than clients whose therapist uses lower quality psychodynamic interpretations.
31. Clients whose therapist receives feedback based on a routinely delivered outcome measure may benefit more from psychotherapy than clients whose therapist does not receive feedback.
32. Clients who receive feedback from their therapist on their performance in treatment may benefit more from psychotherapy than clients who do not receive feedback.
33. Clients may benefit more from psychotherapy when their therapist is more versus less flexible in their administration of, or adherence to, a given treatment approach.
34. Clients whose therapist selectively/responsively fosters more adaptive interpersonal changes may benefit more broadly from psychotherapy than those whose therapist fosters fewer adaptive interpersonal changes.
35. Clients whose therapist selectively/responsively fosters more self-understanding may benefit more broadly from psychotherapy than clients whose therapist fosters less self-understanding.
36. Clients whose therapist selectively/responsively fosters more emotional experiencing and/or deepening may benefit more broadly from psychotherapy than clients whose therapist fosters less emotional experiencing and/or deepening.
37. Clients whose therapist selectively/responsively uses nondirective interventions skillfully may benefit more from psychotherapy than clients whose therapist uses nondirective interventions unskillfully.
38. Clients whose therapist selectively/responsively fosters more behavior changes may benefit more broadly from psychotherapy than clients whose therapist fosters fewer behavior changes.

Appendix 8.2

Therapists' TPRS Profile

Following is a brief description of each therapist in terms of their TPRS profile and how they are likely to behave in psychotherapy.

Eva D. Papiasvili

Dr. Papiasvili is confident in her skills. She also has strong theoretical beliefs regarding her formulations of patient's problems. At the level of technical application, she shows flexibility particularly in managing patients emotional experiences. She seems quite able to adapt the way that she approaches strong and often uncomfortable feelings. True to her convictions, she is among the most strongly focused on insight as the main mechanism for instigating change and generally seems skeptical of direct behavior change.

Catherine S. Spayd

Dr. Spayd has a relatively strong conviction of her abilities, but she also values her ability to adapt and adjust. She, like the others in this cohort, tends toward being nondirective or low directive. She prefers an evocative approach that encourages the patient to search for his or her own meaning. She is likely to be quite low key, being both low directive and by not relying on procedures that induce patient arousal. She lets things unfold slowly rather than trying to identify points of anxiety that can be increased and followed to what she considers productive material. Dr. Spayd is inclined to let the patient search slowly and methodically for answers within her or his self. Interestingly, however, her efforts are not particularly directed to achieving insight. Instead, she values direct behavior change and seeks to help the patient seek and find ways to engage the world and her problems differently.

Igor Weinberg

Dr. Weinberg also rates his skill level highly. He also rates the importance of raising patient arousal very highly and seems to see affect arousal as a very central part of the therapeutic process. Finally, he rates the role both of direct behavior change and insight very highly. Achieving such a balance is likely to be difficult, and when he must choose between the two, he favors insight and awareness over direct behavior change.

9
Principles of Therapeutic Change

A Psychoanalyst's Perspective

Eva D. Papiasvili

Faced with the prospect of participating in this project, I was aware of two chief concerns: (a) the long-standing dilemma between the unique (clinical phenomenology) and the universal (theory and research), and (b) the "translatability" between the conceptual universes of different clinical (and theoretical) orientations. In my first phone conversation with the editors/authors of the book, I addressed my initial concerns about "translation" among different conceptual universes by stating, "I am not sure that you are aware that I am a psychoanalyst." The reply was reassuring, as one of the authors chuckled, "We won't hold it against you." And we all were able to laugh.

Of course, the tension between individualized "clinical art" with a particular client and the research, looking for common generalizable characteristics on the other, is not applicable only to psychoanalysis. It may be just more acutely felt by us psychoanalysts, as our thinking about change takes into consideration metapsychological constructs of unconscious processes, which are, by definition, not directly observable. And yet, communicative bridges among those involved in clinical process, those who construct various theories, and researchers who test processes and constructions are vitally needed. Otherwise, the theory and research risk losing relevance for the rich clinical work, and vice versa.

To begin with, I experienced myself sitting on "both sides of the fence." In 1976–1977, in the course of my own clinical research study on effectiveness of humanistic/dynamic therapeutic systems in Europe (Papiasvili & Papiasvili 1983), evaluating symptomatic improvement, along with change in behavior and attitudes and gaining of insight, I became familiar with the pitfalls of research methodology, aptly described by Bergin and Garfield (1971) and Meltzoff and Kornreich (1970). Since then, some of these pitfalls have begun to be attenuated by empirical advances such as the use of meta-analyses. Converting findings from many studies worldwide into a common metric of effect sizes, a number of these meta-analyses have suggested mostly comparable outcome among different therapeutic approaches (Schedler, 2010). Over the years, research has also linked treatment outcome to a broad variety of process variables, like quality of therapeutic relationship, affective expression, and identification of recurrent themes and patterns. For the most part, however, these advances have not predominantly featured anecdotal contributions of clinicians. The effort of the current editors to give voice to both the researchers and clinicians, encompassing both the *common* principles and their *unique* application is rather unique in and of itself, and the editors ought to be commended for instigating such an pioneering endeavor.

My further concern about translatability between different conceptual universes, arrived at by different methodologies, arose from my experience as one of the chairs of the Inter-Regional Encyclopedic Dictionary of Psychoanalysis (IRED). It has been challenging enough to translate among various schools of psychoanalysis, finding commonalities, as well as unique rich regional diversity, in the evolution and clinical application of the psychoanalytic concepts. Even within dynamic thinking and practice alone, the differences in the assigned meaning and clinical utility of the same conceptual base are remarkable. In this context, from the point of view of a dynamically thinking yet methodologically aware clinician, I felt we were facing a daunting, but uncommonly worthy task. As I was reading through the principles and the presented individual cases of Phillip, Robert, and Marie, I found myself getting engrossed and captivated by them. I was still experiencing the tension, especially as I was switching between the individual cases and the principles, but now I was intrigued and curious: Where will I take it? Where will it take me? I was expectant, as I would be in my office when behind the door a new patient enters the waiting room.

Principles: General Overview

It has been my experience that while for research and theory purposes it is extremely valuable to formulate abstract generalizable principles, in an "alive" clinical work, there is a complex, unique configuration of interactively connected principles applicable to each patient–therapist dyad, rather than any principle being implemented on its own merit or in isolation.

Psychoanalytical therapy, as I practice it (Papiasvili, 2016), is generally a broad-based inquiry into all aspects of the patient's life, including the past, the present, and the anticipated future. The quintessential method is free association (anything that comes to mind), involving sometimes seemingly unrelated material whose previously unknown internal connections are to be explored. At its best, it is a collaborative creative endeavor, where the patient and the analyst work together, in admittedly different functions, to learn from everything and anything that transpires in the room between them and in the patient's mind, to increase the patient's affective insight into themselves. In the language of the principles we are working with in this book, it might correspond to the combination of emotional experiencing (Principle 35) and self-understanding (Principle 36). Given this broad-based approach, it has been my experience that the manifest level of observable behavior, attitudes, and overt statements ("I am fine") pertaining to such attitudes may not be congruent with (to the point of sometimes being quite contrary to) the underlying, often unconscious experience. An example would be Robert walking in and stating "Hi . . . I don't think I need this . . . therapy, or whatever . . ." In my mind, Robert just found himself (once again) in a situation where he is lost and does not expect his needs to be met, which is prognostically (Principle 1) complicated, expressive of low initial expectation (Principle 4), low initial readiness (Principle 6), and manifesting low motivation and high ambivalence (Principle 12), together with potentially high resistance (Principle 11). But at the same time, in a paradoxical way of negation, he just brought up the issue of his needs (and losses). Hearing him this way, I might try to engage him nondirectively (Principle 11): "I understand. And yet, sometimes one takes a chance at this . . . after one already made an effort to get himself here. We might as well make use of the time. What do you think?" "Mhmmm," Robert might say, "It's not like I am rushing somewhere else . . ." Therefore, the application of principles, in my mind, will always include not only the complexity of their mutual relatedness but also listening/being attuned to both the manifest and underlying (latent) levels of each principle of therapeutic change, as they unfold over the course of assessment and treatment.

In terms of the prognostic principles, for instance, the prognosis will depend not only on the patients' characteristics (Principles 1–3, 5, 6, 8, and 9), but also very much on the possibility to establish (and subsequently maintain) a viable working/therapeutic alliance (Principle 23), right from the start. To me, the therapeutic relationship consists of two large categories: the part that is rooted in reality (therapeutic/working alliance; Principle 23) and the part rooted in previous interpersonal/attachment experiences (Principles 1, 3, and 8) and consequent fantasy of this relational experience (transference, resistance; Principles 11 and 15)—a fantasy that translates into the patient's expectations (Principles 12 and 22). Keeping in mind the duality of the nature of the therapeutic relationship is crucial from the beginning. I constantly monitor these two levels during all subsequent phases of treatment, namely, how the fantasy level interferes with the working alliance and objectives of the treatment. The inevitable ruptures of working alliance (Principle 27) are the most dramatic manifestation of such interference, but there are more subtle markers as well, as will be exemplified with each individual case.

The specific illustrations pertaining to each case and the related specific, intertwined principles will be provided with each client. To explicate the full extent of such an approach, I followed Phillip more closely, and consequently, his section is the longest. On the other hand, the case of Robert and Marie contains more comparisons with the other two, at what I would anticipate to be critical moments of the therapeutic work.

Phillip

Case Formulation and General Treatment Plan

As to the presenting problem, Phillip stresses the most subjectively distressing issue of social anxiety, pervading and intruding into all of his daily activities. I would tend to see his social anxiety, and adjacent depression and agoraphobia, as related to the overall personality organization. Specifically, I would conceptualize these symptoms, developmentally and dynamically, as being underlaid by multilayered conflicts around aggressive versus affiliative needs. When his self-protective attempts at passive submission to the authority and rumination (as well as other self-attacking measures that result in psychic pain, sense of weakness, and psychosomatic symptoms) are not enough to contain the conflict and maintain a sense of safety, Phillip's anxiety threatens to erupt. Subjectively feeling acute anxiety, lack of safety, or being "cornered," Phillip then may try to avoid social interactions altogether (flight into agoraphobia, avoidance, social withdrawal). When he cannot avoid social interaction at that point, he may become argumentative, erupt in angry outbursts with subsequent self-reproach and self-recrimination.

In a very general way, Phillip re-enacts his parents immigration experience every time he enters a social interaction within a group. Responding to his father hypercriticism, Phillip might feel ashamed and guilty over his developmentally appropriate assertive and competitive strivings toward both parents. (From the intake report, it seems like there was no room in his early home for safe expression of any aggressive strivings towards his parents or siblings, which would eventually develop into a socially appropriate self-assertion.) Today, he anticipates such hypercritical attitudes from other social contacts, especially when advancing above his peers' at work. Yet, there is also strength; Phillip's resilience is evident in his involvement in team sports during school years. Such an involvement may have temporarily mitigated the conflict of aggression versus affiliation. Being a valued member of a team may have provided a safe arena for his aggressive strivings and affiliative needs (e.g., he was aggressive on behalf of his team). But the "permission" to exercise his masculine assertion and physical prowess was apparently short-lived. He may have experienced himself being "punished" for asserting himself and getting gratification through the intimate sexual connection with Christina: He learned that Christina was pregnant, which required drastic change of major life plans. This occurred just as he was apparently starting to assert himself on both fronts—as a man in a sexual relationship and as a student at a community college, potentially aspiring "higher" than his father. The college needed to be interrupted (a fitting punishment for aspiring to enjoy his life to a fuller measure than perhaps both suffering hard-working parents and for enjoying himself perhaps a bit too much sexually).

I would note for myself the choice of the words for his parents' jobs as "nongratifying." In this context, he, too, is not to have a gratifying job, identifying with the parents' experience. In fact, the safest attitude to take is not to feel gratified in his life altogether, and his depression, anhedonia, rumination, psychic pain, sense of "core weakness," agoraphobia and ever-present anxiety could be viewed as a motivated attempt toward (a compromise formation) of nongratification.

In this context, Phillip allows himself to be financially, professionally, and socially successful, but he must not enjoy it—it must feel painfully uncomfortable, turning into a burden. He feels inept and worthy of harsh judgement. Moreover, he is to perpetuate this internally imposed prison as a safety measure against further growth, claiming he is immutable, that he cannot change, that he is "stuck." His financial advancement is apparently acknowledged only in terms of "living on the edge" of what he can afford, turning the gains into a burden—a curse (e.g., living in an expensive neighborhood, without friends, etc.).

Overall, the avoidance of anxiety-provoking situations (phobias, acute anxiety states) presents an unsuccessful attempt at actively fleeing from situations where he might need to assert himself actively, "as a man." Even when "forced" to participate, he is silent (mentally absent) or responds angrily (in behavior or in attitude), driving people (protectively/self-punitively) away. Behind his overt passive-submissive and internally protective detached position that is so irritating to his wife may be hidden an active attempt at maintaining stubborn control of the environment to his detriment. Withdrawing and isolating himself socially, Phillip strives to prevent anticipated pain incurred through interpersonal interactions. However, at the same time, while retreating into his agoraphobic withdrawal, he restricts his and Christina's social life, isolating both of them from potentially supportive networks of friends—which, in turn, incurs Christina's resentment and criticism. Subsequently Phillip resorts to further withdrawal and self-recrimination.

My treatment plan, allowing, of course, for the unpredictable, would be to monitor how this core pattern unfolds in the therapeutic setting. I would focus on it and explore it throughout. Schematically simplified, I would expect the following sequence to emerge: Phillip gets involved; he experiences needs for closeness, which he fears, owing to frustrating early experiences. Under the agreeable surface, he grows progressively more anxious, frustrated, and angry and will tend to withdraw to prevent an altercation. Preventing an imaginary "fight," Phillip inserts "flight" into his symptoms, and once again, he experiences defeat. To change the pattern, Phillip needs to bring this sequence (to transfer it, as referred to in Principle 15) into the treatment. Yet, if not closely monitored, the very sequence threatens potentially the treatment's success. In the language of the principles we are working with, Phillip's tendency to withdraw is likely to present at first subtle roadblocks to establishing and maintaining *therapeutic alliance* (Principle 23), leading to ruptures (Principle 27), fueled by underlying ambivalence (Principle 11), and growing into transference-resistance (Principles 11 and 15). I would expect that once we explore and interpret this immutable pattern in the here and now, emotionally alive yet safe therapeutic context, as well as link it to Phillip's past experiences and his current life, we can bring about the change of Phillip's self-concept and concept of himself in the world.

Implementation of Principles of Change

While the initial case formulation may contain certain core dynamic pattern, the initial approach, to some degree maintained throughout, is the one of the broad inquiry. This not only allows one to gain an understanding of Phillip's past, his current difficulties, and the link between them, but it also leads to an increase of self-understanding (Principle 35) and emotional experiencing (Principle 36). Such therapeutic processes might, early in treatment, foster adaptive interpersonal and behavioral change (Principles 34 and 38).

Specifically, in terms of client prognostic principles, I would tend to be mindful of the potential early sources of impediment to the favorable prognosis (complex co-morbidity; Principles 1 and 2) of Phillip's anxiety–depression–agoraphobia. I would tactfully inquire about his present experiences pertaining to impediments to global functioning (Principle 1), especially in areas of social difficulties, work satisfaction, interpersonal functioning difficulties, including romantic intimate area (Principle 1). We might make initial link between his self-reported underlying anger and irritability, which draws others away from him and fosters his suffering in isolation and loneliness (Principle 1). I might encourage Phillip to see how feeling lonely is a repeated experience since childhood and how it in turn may increase his neediness, which he fears may drive others away. I would respectfully inquire about potential difficulties in his early history of attachment (Principle 3) and the presence of adverse childhood events (Principle 8), which may contribute to the persistence of negative self-attributions and complicate initial expectations (Principle 4) of the effectiveness of therapy. I might remark that it would be understandable that all his life experiences might be connected to the extent he sees himself as able to change (readiness vs. resistance to change; Principle 6). Further, I would inquire about his report of a lack of support (Principle 1—within the larger category of interpersonal functioning). For instance, I might inquire about how it came about that Phillip and Christina chose to not live close to their parents and siblings. Depending on what I hear, I might say that sometimes, regardless of who moves away from whom, it feels as if the others are not there for the person. This might be a meaningful way to initiate an inquiry into dynamic emotional issues possibly having to do with the history of somewhat problematic attachment (Principle 3) and parenting (Principle 8). The overall objective would be to foster a sense that both of us are "getting to know him" and how his suffering came about. Increased self-understanding (Principle 35) and emotional experiencing (Principle 36) might be emerging through this process.

According to the data provided, I would tend to see Phillip's baseline impairment (Principle 1) as mild to moderate, with an onset of acute social anxiety clinically significant symptomatology in adolescence. However, subclinical subjective distress are likely to be linked to important issue of the past, like his childhood dysthymia, history of loneliness, parental emotional unavailability, and being an "auxiliary parent" to his younger siblings with restriction of peer activities. This overall view of Phillip would inform my tone in speaking with him: sensitive to his fragility, due to long-term suffering depleting his sense of strength, yet respectful of his resilience and ability to self-reflect. I would take it as a sign of inner resources and ability to function under stress that we do not hear about any impediments to his cognitive/academic functioning through the school years. This would be one area to which I would attend to track also the possible areas of (ego) strength: frustration tolerance, conflict-free sphere, and resilience early in life. Acknowledging his strength might provide an important emotional scaffold while delving into his problem areas. In this regard, I see it as important that the inquiry would be balanced: Phillip is a whole person. He has both strengths and problems. (Even though at the time of starting therapy, Phillip likely experiences himself as only weak and having only problems.) I might comment that if the parents entrusted him with the babysitting his younger siblings, they must have viewed him as rather competent and responsible youngster, no matter what otherwise their (father's) criticism about him may have been. In this vein, I would tend to inquire about his early school experiences and his early experiences with the birth of his siblings. Was the birth of children perceived as a burden? As a joy? What happened when Phillip was sick? Who was the person he would seek help from? Was the help he received commensurable with his needs? Was he valued in his role of a caregiver/babysitter of his siblings? Also, I would tend to inquire about his earliest memories, possibly before the birth of younger siblings, going back to the time of his being the only child.

Throughout such initial inquiry around help-seeking, help-receiving, and help-providing experiences and potential inadequate parenting (Principle 8), I would watch for any initial expectations from therapy and from me (Principle 3). Specifically I would be listening for Phillip's expectations of me as capable of empathy (Principle 26). Simultaneously, I would watch for initial ambivalent transferences turning prospectively into transference resistance (Principles 11, 12, and 15) where I would be perceived as being burdened by the patient or see him as incompetent, insufficient, or inept (likely criticism he incurred early). I would wonder aloud about specifics of his mother's nurturance, specifics of his own interpretation of "dangers" his mother wanted to protect him from, and the specifics of his father's emotional unavailability. The exploration of potentially problematic anxious attachment (Principle 3) to the primary caregiver (traumatized émigré mother, who may have unwittingly/unconsciously transmitted messages of isolation and loneliness, needing her son to provide her with the feeling of love, belonging, and self-worth) might follow. Such a complicated *anxious attachment* (Principle 3) would form a shaky ground on which further development rested (Principles 8 and 9). This might be transferred into his ambivalent expectations from therapy and me (Principle 4) as his therapist. In addressing his early feelings of loneliness, it might be possible to link them etiologically to those of his mother's, and with some recovered strength, he might start to discern his father's hypercriticism as reflective of his father's disappointment and criticism of himself. In line with the treatment objectives, this might provide an emotional scaffold for the exploration of himself as having a restricted choice of fight or flight when facing people, his needs from them, and their needs from him. Here, he starts seeing himself as a separate person from others with his own feelings and sense of self, while his father may have had his own frustrations with himself.

In addition, I might strive to address Phillip's own painful memories of loneliness in connection with missing out on the pleasure of being with his peers: Did he wish he could spend more time with friends? What would have been the experiences he felt he missed? The objective of such recovery of wishes and desires, frustrated and denied because of external circumstances and not because he was unworthy (Principle 9), would be to recover, accept, and credit his natural wishes for pleasure and gratification, as well as promoting the process of separation; that is, others' frustration was expressed to him and he attributed it to himself (Principle 9) as being a cause of it. I might say: "One thing is to perceive (and be frustrated by) one's mother's anxiety and one's father's self-disappointment as theirs; another thing is to interpret it and attribute it to one's self as being a cause of their anxiety and frustration" (Principle 9). At the same time, this is another example of implementing therapeutic relationship principles of building self-understanding (Principle 35) and effecting emotional experiencing (Principle 36).

Viewing his negative self-attributions (Principle 9) as potentially constituting major *resistance* (Principle 11) to the effectiveness of his therapy, I would tend to address them from multiple angles early in the treatment and throughout, consistent with his level of *readiness to change* (Principle 6) and what, in a particular context, would make sense to him. I would strive to draw affirmatively on his strength (Principle 24) as part of his resource for addressing his problems, making use of his own self-reflective insightful (Principle 18) comments in the intake about not paying too much attention to anything positive about himself. A type of early interpretation leading to insight (Principle 10) would be employed because of his internalizing capacity (Principle 18).

It is my experience that reflecting back to the patient his own comments (Principle 37) draws them into more active participation (Principle 21), which is crucial for change. In Phillips's case, this has an added importance, counteracting his self-reported passive, cautious, and withdrawn attitude. I might convey to him that he seems to see himself, and to anticipate that others (present company included), will see him in the same critical way that his father saw him, who was usually disappointed in him. Additionally, I would strive to convey that his father's hypercriticism of him may have been an expression of his frustration and disappointment in himself, his own unrewarding job, etc. Specific wording would depend on where we were at the moment of our interaction. For instance, if Phillip were making a case as to why he is immutable and why he should not expect himself to change, with all his inherent weaknesses, I might say: "You seem to be using the same words describing yourself, as when your father used to snap at you, when he arrived home all tired from his unrewarding work. . . . And you anticipate me thinking about you in those unflattering terms even before I open my mouth." Dynamically, I would see addressing this characterological *transference/resistance* (Principle 11) as a vital early transference interpretation (Principles 15 and 30) to mitigate the stringent self-judgmental agency, which, if not attended to, could depress and weaken his (and our) effectiveness in therapy. Here, Phillip's initial expectation (Principle 4) is addressed by bolstering intrinsic motivation (Principle 5) and countering core self-attribution (Principle 9) as unable to change ("immutable"). thus fostering the overall readiness to change (Principle 6). The vignette also illustrates the interaction between client prognostic principles (Principles 4–6 and 9), treatment/provider moderating principles (Principles 10, 11, 15, and 18), client process variables (Principle 21), and therapist intervention principles (Principle 30).

The intertwining of the treatment provider moderating principles (Principles 10–20) with client process variables (Principles 21 and 22) is crucial for any therapeutic progress in Phillip's case as in any other case. It would also be important in planning the overall strategy of intervention (Principles 29–38). In this context, also Phillip's low level of initial overt resistances (Principles 11 and 22) and ambivalence (Principle 12), his intrinsic motivation (Principle 5), and his capacity for self-observation and insight (Principle 10) is especially relevant. Phillip observes and describes his habitual response patterns in various situations, even appreciating that some of his perceptions of himself and expectations from others are not always based on what is rationally warranted. I would estimate his initial level of understanding of his own problems is in the realm of level 2, as specified in the Assimilation of Problematic Experiences Scale (APES), which, with continuous active participation (Principle 21), would be progressively increasing. It is my impression that the verbal understanding via interpretation, as related to connections regarding interpersonal and internal conflicts in an intensive in depth analytical therapy might be a method of choice.

Prospectively, this approach would strengthen his self-awareness, master, build up, and mobilize his own psychic resources. He would be invited to say what is on his mind and to join me in looking at his problems and underlying emotional and relationship-related dynamics. He would be enlisted as a partner in the therapeutic process; for instance, every interpretative comment of mine would be accompanied by a variation of: "How would this sit with you . . . ," fostering his active involvement (Principle 21) and continuous therapeutic alliance (Principle 23). In Phillip's case, this might translate into my offering encouragement along the lines of "let us look at it together," even in cases of his asking for advice, as a way of seeking support and affirmation (Principle 24). The dependency needs behind his asking for advice would be explored rather than gratified. This would be presented as a way of crediting his capacity and developing ability for self-understanding. There is an underlying acknowledgment of his inherent (ego) strength/inner resources, as well as strengthening his self-esteem and sense of competence (Principles 24, 30, and 35) via joint exploration, joint interpretation, and insight (Principle 30). The gradual internalization of such a joint exploratory attitude would foster increasing levels of problem assimilation (Principle 10). This would not be approached only from the cognitive point of view, but his emotional experience of, and affective involvement in, such an exploration would be also an object of refection (Principle 36). I could imagine Phillip engaging in work on a deeper level and bringing in dreams, uncovering previously repressed memories and utilizing free-associative method, in an atmosphere of more intensive analytic therapy, of two to three sessions weekly, if not more.

The level of intrinsic motivation (Principle 5), his resistances (Principle 11) and perceived threats/rewards of further exploration would be monitored throughout. It would be expected to vacillate, depending on a particular transferential context. Especially with upcoming holidays, vacations, weekends, and all events bringing up the issues of separation and separateness. The markers would include silences, lateness, increased self-criticism, feelings of irritability and annoyance, and a sense of helplessness. These would be all explored with a sense of curious inquiry about the dynamic meaning, empathy, and acceptance. The specific demographics of therapist–patient similarities/differences (Principles 7 and 13) would be addressed in a similar manner as to their dynamic meaning. I would be especially sensitive to his indirect allusions to difficult experiences of children of immigrants, feeling isolated, speaking different languages at home and at school, and his potential indirect allusions to my ethnic and religious background, etc. I envision a possible scenario where the winter holidays are approaching and Phillip ambivalently wondering if I celebrate and what I do during the holidays:

PHILLIP: Holidays make me feel weird. I don't have family around. . . . Other people maybe celebrate something else . . .
THERAPIST: Other people?
PHILLIP: Yeah, like people I know . . .
THERAPIST: Any particular person you know?
PHILLIP: Oh, just, you know . . . like people in this part of town. . . . I mean . . . like there is the Christmas tree in the lobby, and then the Hanukkah candles . . . well . . .
THERAPIST: So you are wondering about all of this . . . what the heck do these strange people in this strange part of town do?
PHILLIP: Yeah (relief) . . .
THERAPIST: So one of those strange people is your therapist . . . what might she do with her strange holidays in this strange building in this strange part of town?
PHILLIP: Yeah (laughing).

And then we explore Phillip's feeling like a stranger in a strange place since forever, with the consequence of having the moderating principle of demographics mismatch (Principle 13) becoming therapeutically dynamically intermingled with emotional experiencing (Principle 36) and self-understanding (Principle 35) to Phillip's advantage.

Other moderating principles, those of externalizing versus internalizing copying styles (Principles 17 and 18), correspond in a psychoanalytic conceptual repertoire to developmentally early versus developmentally more evolved psychic structure. These principles have implications as to the development-specific prevalent defensive operations (reliance on more primitive projective-identificatory mechanisms vs. more advanced repression, internalization, intellectualization, and displacement) in and out of therapy. In Phillip's case, a prevalent internalizing coping style (Principles 5 and 18) is coupled with self-acknowledged vulnerabilities stemming from possible problems from anxious attachment (Principle 3) and problems around the separation. When under stress, he may regress to more primitive means of relating to himself and others, resorting to externalization/projection (Principle 17), somatization, and enactments as means of communicating his distress. The periodic failure of symbolization (utilizing speech as a communication tool) would be anticipated and interpretively (Principles 29 and 30) linked with early experiences of a potentially traumatic nature (Principles 3 and 8). While interpreting, I would also express genuine appreciation (Principles 25) for his struggle to communicate something very important that we have yet to understand.

During such periods, the focus would be on his affective experience in the here-and-now context. I might lend/offer my own thoughts about his internal state for him to consider. This would be a special case of tailored self-disclosure (Principle 28) and a way to construct bridges to see if he could use them to recreate a missing link. Throughout, his active participation (Principle 21) on an affective level (Principle 36) would be monitored, acknowledged and encouraged: "Would this make sense to you . . ." If Phillip were to say, "That doesn't make any sense . . . ," I might inquire if he could think of something making more sense and acknowledge his valuable feedback in saying no. The specific dynamic interpretations (Principles 29 and 30) would always be tailored to Phillip's emotional state, developmental level, defenses being employed, and his prevailing means of communication.

To me, the therapy relationship principles are the most crucial ones around which all of the other principles revolve. The working alliance (Principle 23), which provides a basic sense of safety and trust within the context of a collaborative effort, is essential for any therapeutic progress. The experience of therapeutic regard and affirmation (Principle 24) and congruence (Principle 25) has unconscious, archaic, and transferential underpinnings. The feelings, thoughts, and experiences that were not acceptable to his parents will likely color his experience of both regard and congruence. Interpretation of such transferentially colored perception of regard and congruence may increase Phillip's experience of feeling empathized with (Principle 26) accepted (Principle 24).

With Phillip, empathy would contribute to the deepening of the therapeutic process, and empathic ruptures would be explored from transferential and developmentally reconstructive perspectives. The experience of rupture of empathy and alliance (Principle 27) would be inevitable during the course of intensive therapy with someone like Phillip and would potentially lead to accessing deeper layers of unconsciously buried (potentially posttraumatically dissociated or repressed) early traumatic experiences of abandonment and intrusion. In Phillip's case, it is hypothesized that the (not avoided) rupture itself would be already a signal of readiness to revisit originally unacceptable parts of his experiences and readiness for the reparative reintegration and restoration of continuity and a sense of mastery, competence, and recovery of trust and safety in the world and relationships.

A potential sign of such a rupture would be his previously mentioned regression into earlier modes of responding. For instance, he may be projecting his frustrated enraged parts of himself, which were once his father's projection of his self-disappointment onto Phillip. If frustrated by his own need of me, before or after my absence due to vacation or holiday, he might interpret my absence (a trigger for rupture) as a confirmation of me not caring about him and resort to his self-criticism as not being enough of an interesting or good patient, not making enough progress, etc. He might be either quiet and sulk, or he might dare to lash out and then profusely apologize. If he verbalizes his angry feelings, I would acknowledge them as a brave and constructive way of experiencing something and openly communicating it. If he were to silently sulk, I might inquire that "maybe there are some troubling feelings about something here that he feels would be impolite to communicate." In any case, I would encourage him to "say the unsayable," to the extent that he can allow himself.

A hypothetical situation might look something like:

THERAPIST You figure, I would judge you . . . or I would try to prove you wrong in some clever way . . .
PHILLIP: Everything is fine, I just don't feel like talking . . .
THERAPIST Nothing on your mind . . .
PHILLIP: Yeah. Why should always something have to be on my mind? (hint of irritation)
THERAPIST Indeed . . . could be a bit annoying . . . if something's gotta be on your mind, just because I say so.
PHILLIP: Yeah. I don't need this shit . . . to always say everything and not have any privacy . . .

THERAPIST Especially when I go on a private vacation . . . return . . . and on a cue demand that you do as I say . . . really annoying

PHILLIP: That's what I think, too . . . wouldn't you?

THERAPIST I would . . .

PHILLIP: You would? (relief)

THERAPIST Of course . . . like, who does this person think they are? They just show up, and I should drop everything and do what they say?

This would be a time for both of us possibly to make an eye contact and chuckle. We could then explore where and when, besides here and now, he may have felt that way and where it would have been unacceptable for him to realize and communicate his feelings.

Another relationship principle, self-disclosure (Principle 28), remains a controversial subject in an analytic therapy. I have found it helpful to share my thoughts and associative processes, linked to the patient's material, when it presents a bridge to their own choices and alternatives, freedom of their associative and fantasy process. It ultimately depends on what I would evaluate to be the value of such disclosure for the patient. The basic principle here would be that it needs to be useful to the patient (as in previous examples) and needs not to come at the price of narrowing down the patient's own space (and time) for exploration of their own process.

Also, self-disclosure need not be given on demand. I consider it one of the basic instructions at the beginning to let patients know that during the therapeutic work all sorts of questions may come to their mind, which we will treat those questions to their best advantage as anything else that they bring up, with outmost respect and curiosity. There may be some questions that I choose to answer unequivocally (e.g., my qualifications), which relates very directly to the establishment of trust as a condition of working alliance (Principle 23). There may be other questions, which we may get curious about and want to know more where it is coming from, given our objective. A hypothetical example of such a questioning situation may be as follows.

PHILLIP: Where do therapists like you go on a vacation?

THERAPIST: Supposing I go on a vacation to . . . you fill in the blank, what would that mean to you? Or supposing I go to some other place. What would that mean . . . and what might be the feelings you might have about it?

After such a rich exploration of where the question is coming from, Phillip may not care where I actually go at all. Of course, there is not one standard way (Principle 33) to deal with any issue, including questions and self-disclosure. There might be times when I might consider it therapeutic to let Phillip know that I would answer his question, if after exploration of where the question is coming from, he still wants the answer. But, I would stress, "You are not obliged to really want the answer." In this way, I would be letting him know that I am aware of his underlying conflict: "Who is this therapy for, anyway?" I could imagine a scenario, when Phillip is not interested in getting an answer and exploring his "selfishness" ("Who cares where you go?"). I can also imagine him being disappointed that I do not go to some magical place that he never heard of. Both alternatives would be further explored.

In other words, questions about me or anything else always would be addressed. I would respond to each question, though I may not directly answer it. Addressing questions that seek advice, like, "What should I do?" on Phillip's part (which I might anticipate) would be therapeutically dealt with analogically as previously discussed, as symptomatic of dynamic issues around regression, dependency, and passivity. My general approach here would be to acknowledge Phillip's capacity to benefit from inquiry and insight into his inner life and see what the best way would be to proceed with anything he brings up to further that capacity.

In regard to therapist intervention principles, in my experience, psychodynamic interpretation (Principles 29 and 30) needs to be individually tailored and close to the clinical material rather than theoretical and detached. With Phillip, the interpretation would be a rolling process in which we would both participate. Optimally, it would link the here-and-now with the there-and-now and, finally, also the there-and-then. The ongoing feedback loops (Principle 32), in conjunction with the interpretative process (Principles 29 and 30), would be an integral part of the therapeutic process, fluidly expanding on what was previously known, experienced, linked together, and integrated. In analytic therapy, the issue of feedback in its multiple individualized facets is an important component of the process of change. However, while there is a recognition of general criteria of mental health in terms of interpersonal and professional functioning, feedback is not based on standardized quantifiable metrics. Feedback in conjunction with interpretation might differ according to the stage of the therapeutic process. For instance, in the middle stages of the process, when understanding of some basic links between his historical and present experiences are established, the feedback loop may take the following hypothetical shape. After several sessions, when we explore Phillip's feeling of being afraid of speaking up in the presence of others, I may watch how this may be reflected in his behavior in the treatment and prioritize this aspect of his behavior over others. Supposing he excuses himself in the course of the session to go to the washroom and get a drink of water. Rather than reflecting other potential aspects of such a behavior, I may say something like, "I do not want to spook you too much, but it sounds like you are starting to make room for your needs rather than waiting for a permission. Just here, now, you asserted yourself, rather than waiting quietly, feeling ignored, and suffer through that." He may minimize his progress and say, "It's just a drink of water" to which I might say, "Gotta start somewhere. Maybe it's the drink you did not ask for long time ago . . ." And then we may explore his early feeling that to ask for anything his suffering overworked and self-sacrificing mother would be selfish and he would be a burden.

Some of the intervention principles can find venues of implementation via the process of "reverie," which I imagine would take place the highly dynamic interpretative process of Phillip's therapy. Reverie takes place in the therapist-patient dyad when the deeper connection between two unconsciouses communicate with each other in what may look like a rolling dream-like process. This might signal Phillip's emersion in the process, his increased sense of safety, self-acceptance, and capacity for spontaneity. Reverie here designates a co-production of free-associative process where both participants expand on each other's free associations, filling in the gaps, condensing different times and spaces, using shorthand. The therapist goes customarily a step further beyond where the patient stops. In practice, the principles of fostering of the change of behavior and attitudes, deepening of self-understanding, and emotional experiencing, (Principles 34, 35, 36, and 38) by selective acknowledgement of his achievements in these areas would be embedded within such an unfolding of the overall reverie free-associative interpretive process (Principles 30 and 37).

Specifically, to illustrate reverie, I offer the following hypothetical. Phillip, who has a characterological tendency to sensitively register his failings rather than his progress, might bring in something like, "After the last meeting here, I thought I already could assert myself, but once again, I failed like a coward . . ." When he pauses, I might repeat his last word: "a coward . . ." Phillip would extend further: "Cannot say a word . . ." I would continue: "Afraid . . ." Phillip extends further: "Paralyzed . . ." I might extend: "Like being small and telling off this big person . . ." Phillip would go still further: "Scary . . ." I might fill in: "Someone gets hurt . . ." At this point Phillip may spell out his next association: "Feeling like that with Dad." This might be followed by Phillip's recalling a dream, where he held his mother's hand, told his father off, and then ran away, looking back only to see that both his mother and father disappeared. The associations would go further to his need for closeness with his mother and father, his anger at his father, telling him off (i.e., "killing him off"), fear of retaliation, guilt, running away, and losing both his parents. Extending the associative chain could lead both of us to make an interpretive connection to multiple meanings behind asserting oneself: "To assert oneself would be like 'killing someone off,' leaving them, losing them forever." Phillip might tear up, get angry, and express his love for his father. The displacement of his frustrated needs for affection from his parents at the time when he was a helpless little child onto those with whom he wants to be close in his present life (wife, bosses, co-workers) and imagined retaliation and losses would come to light. The difference between him as a helpless child and his current status as a resourceful adult would be gradually worked through, with alternative nuanced ways how to assert himself with each of the people concerned would follow.

Robert

Case Formulation and General Treatment Plan

Severely impaired in all aspects of his baseline functioning (Principle 1), Robert's manifest presenting problem is an intensification of long-standing social anxiety, with co-morbid alcohol use and episodic depression. All of these problems have been recently exacerbated to the point of urgency, when the friends and family were apparently alarmed and urged him to get help. From a dynamic perspective, this would be viewed as a regression to a preadult level of functioning, possibly triggered by the impediments to progress and actual losses incurred. However, even previously, Robert impresses me as someone whose development was traumatically and posttraumatically stunted and who never reached the full internal independence and agency that is characteristic of adulthood.

Robert resorts to social withdrawal, drinking, self-injurious/self-defeating behavior (being late for work and driving while intoxicated), and occasional violence as a means of managing his overwhelming anxiety, pain of unmourned losses, depression, and affective states in general. Such impulse-driven actions, lacking thoughts of consequences, along with habitually externalizing his problems ("Others are not fair") indicate to me his self-perception of a helpless child in the hands of all-powerful uncaring adults. Like a child of limited resources (no social skills), no thought of consequence and impact of his behavior on others, he interprets others' attitudes towards him as "They do not want me; they do not like me as I am." This perpetuates (identifies with) his early experience of parental neglect and abuse in two ways: in the way of how he treats himself and in the way of how he treats others. It seems that since graduating high school he tried to "play adult"—even show up for work, stay with a girlfriend for two years—but to no avail: Once again, he is not wanted: The boss threatens to show him the door, and the girlfriend leaves him anyway. In his adult years, Robert, thus, perpetually finds ways to retraumatize himself.

Clinically significant symptomatology and behavior revolved around his responses to multiple losses: His everyday drinking use started after his father passed away, and the current exacerbation of his multiple anxiety-depressive symptomatology, including self-defeating and potentially life-threatening behaviors, followed the loss of his two-year romantic relationship and the threat of losing his job. Loss is the experience on which Robert, who habitually externalizes and projects his problems onto the environment and others (Principle 17), can self-reflect (Principles 35 and 36). Surprisingly eloquently (for someone who insists on being/acting "stupid"), he describes conflicted feelings around his father's passing, which he, as per his self-observation, never had a chance to talk about. Similarly, he seems to be able to reflect on complex feelings toward his brothers, with whom he fought and bonded and whom he misses.

My treatment plan, overall consistent with that of Phillip, would be to monitor how these core patterns unfold in the therapeutic setting. The focus here would be on Robert's unwittingly bringing about retraumatizations and losses, as well as his potential misinterpretations of even nontraumatic events without a threat of loss as trauma and loss. In this vein, mindful of Robert's proclivity to action and his tenuous hold on reality when emotionally overwhelmed, I would monitor the early threats to *working alliance* (Principle 23) and would be prepared to clarify how he may (mis)interpret and experience the meaning of my interventions throughout. Aware of his background of multiple traumas, utterly lacking in parental support and guidance, I might frequently check in with him: How does he feel (Principles 26 and 36) we are doing? I might observe aloud that certain feelings may be hard to put into words or "talking about trauma/loss may sometimes feel like it is happening all over again, no matter how long ago it happened," etc. Watching his withdrawn expression, I might inquire: "I wonder if you heard what I said as a criticism/rejection?" or preface my comment by "This is not a criticism, but have you noticed . . . ?" I would refrain from commenting on his behavior without making link to some feeling; for example, commenting on his drinking and driving, I might say, "You must have been so upset about something when you 'had to have a beer.' I wonder what upset you?" Frequent clarification of potential misperceptions and making causal links between feelings and behavior might provide emotional scaffolding, which was probably missing during his childhood. The next step would be to explore alternative (not self-defeating) ways to process, calibrate, and constructively address and express his feelings.

I would hypothesize that this modified dynamic/analytical exploratory approach would yield the following sequence: Robert's previous traumas, lack of support, and multiple unmourned losses will emerge in the treatment via tendencies to enact them; he will misperceive my comments/gestures/facial expressions as rejecting; he will close up and tend to flee from therapy; I will reflect to him what may be going on in his experience; we will make a link between his experience and actions; we will make links of this kind as they occur with various people in his current life; and we will make similar links to his past experiences with people in his past. In the language of the principles we are working with, Robert's tendency to enact roadblocks to establishing and maintaining a viable therapeutic alliance (Principle 23), leading to ruptures (Principle 27) and growing fast into transference resistance (Principles 11 and 15). I would expect that once we name and explore his emotional experience and interpret verbally, the links between traumas, retraumatizations, what was lacking, and what was lost, as exemplified in the here-and-now safe therapeutic context, Robert's sense of agency and his concept of himself in the world can change. In line with Principle 20, I believe that such treatment processes (and their potential benefits) are not contingent upon his therapist history (or lack of thereof) of substance use problems.

Implementation of Principles of Change

As with Phillip, so now with Robert, the initial approach would be promoting the exploration of his past and his current difficulties, as well as the link between them, all of which is aimed at increasing of self-understanding (Principle 35) and emotional experiencing (Principle 36). Such therapeutic processes might, early in treatment, foster adaptive interpersonal and behavioral change (Principles 34 and 38). In addition, considering Robert's level of problem assimilation, resistance, and motivation (Principles 10–12), a modified approach of carefully monitoring his tendency to "enact" rather than reflect verbally on his emotional experience would be implemented throughout, in the here-and-now context; for example, "You looked at the door, maybe wanting to get out of here, because there was some feeling you had about what I just said. Supposing you look into yourself and try to say what it might be." If Robert says: "What? I wasn't listening . . .", I might say, "Okay, one may not want to listen if they feel that one might not hear anything interesting anyway, or one might feel bored, annoyed, or perhaps rejected and sad . . ." "All of it?" Robert might say, to which I might volunteer: "All of it, or just some of it . . . or maybe something entirely different". If he says, "So many feelings!" I might sum it up: "Yeah, could get kind of overwhelming . . ." "That's it!" Robert might sigh with relief, "I feel overwhelmed!" "There you go!" I might reflect, echoing his triumph of realizing how he feels. I would expect we might look at each other with understanding that something important just happened here, and I might take a chance at making a further link: "And perhaps, sometimes, when you feel overwhelmed, you feel like getting away." This might outline our work for the next several months.

Specifically, in terms of client prognostic principles, I would tend to be mindful of the potential early sources of impediment to the favorable prognosis (complex co-morbidity (Principles 1, and 2) of alcohol use disorder, depression, and impulsive self-defeating behaviors. I would tactfully inquire about his present experiences pertaining to impediments to global functioning (Principle 1), especially in areas of social difficulties, work satisfaction, interpersonal functioning difficulties, including the romantic/intimate area (Principle 1). The intent would be to lay the groundwork for linking his self-defeating (impulsive and habitual) behaviors and his unhappiness in various areas of his life.

In view of the numerous impediments and apparent *low motivation* (Principle 5), while inquiring about his growing up, some of my first interventions would be to acknowledge his own (disclaimed, externalized) motivation and his ability to reflect on his conflicted feelings about the loss of his father. I might say something like: "Reading the intake, I noted that one of the things you mentioned you never had a chance to talk about was the passing/loss of your father. Might it be that you are giving yourself a chance to talk about it now . . . and maybe talk about some other things you never had a chance to talk about?" Similarly, he is capable of describing his complex feelings about relationships with his brothers, which I would consider a psychological life-saver. I might say, "For someone who insists that he does not have tools to interact, 'freezes,' and can dismiss himself as 'stupid,' you seem to demonstrate quite an aptitude for complex thinking and feelings when it comes to a very important relationship with your brothers." In such and other ways, I would convey to him that his ability to express his complex feelings toward his father and his back-and-forth fighting/bonding relationship with his brothers are signs of his (hidden, for most part, from others and himself) strength and potential for growth.

On one hand, all prognostic principles (Principles 1–9) indicate that Robert's chances at an adaptive change through therapy are minimal. Namely, his symptoms are severe, on the edge of independent functioning, with early onset and chronic risk of suicide. He also has potential genetic factors on both sides of the family of origin, and he has failed to benefit from previous psychotherapy, which he terminated after two sessions. In addition, there is a stated co-morbidity (Principle 1) of alcohol use and unstated *co-morbidity* (Principle 2) of possibly personality disorder of mixed type with borderline, narcissistic, dependent, and schizoid-paranoid features. His global functioning (Principle 1) is deteriorating in all of its categories (i.e., quality of life, work performance, behavioral avoidance, coping skills, interpersonal functioning, personal and professional isolation, and failure to mourn the death of a parent). Furthermore, there is an early and recent history of possible attachment problems (Principle 3), unrealistic (underneath probably excessive, overtly protectively nonexistent) expectations that therapy could make any difference (Principle 4), and he is not intrinsically motivated (Principle 5) and is in the lowest precontemplative stages of change readiness (Principle 6). His mounting employment problems (Principle 7), history of adverse childhood events, with features of both neglect and abuse (Principle 8), and presence of negative self-attributions (Principle 9) complete the picture of Robert's doubtful chances at being able to benefit from therapy.

On the other hand, the crisis also presents a potential opportunity to mobilize, grow, and finally address what has never been addressed before. This is what I might present to him, consistent with such moderating principles (Principles 10–20), as his low level of problem assimilation (Principle 10), his high level of resistance (Principle 11), and his low motivation (Principle 11): If he succeeded to alarm himself that if he does nothing he may lose his job and that his prospects at finding another one and another girlfriend are dismal and if he succeeded to alarm people who care about him, that is a sign of his strength. "That is a 'good fear,'" I might say, "a signal inside of you—a beginning of giving yourself a chance to change. If you are alarmed, there is a recognition that you want to change the course, even if you are not cognizant of feeling hopeful."

Going forward, I would pay very close attention to the therapy relationship principles (Principles 23–28). I would share/disclose (Principle 28) my thinking with him that even if it is all those other people who urge him to be here and work on himself and even if he feels he could care less, something inside of him made him answer the phone or an email to let these people know that he was not doing well. If we know anything about him, we know he is smart enough to predict how they were going to react: urge him to seek help. But he and I know he has been through a lot (affirmation [Principle 24] and empathy [Principle 26]) and that he is experiencing potentially life-threatening problems, which will take many more than two sessions to get better. I might say something like: "In my experience of having worked with many people, people can change, if they truly work on themselves. It may get at times very difficult. One may get discouraged, as there are no guarantees for what and how one will change. But what is guaranteed is that, without therapy, nothing will change." Then I would pause and let him respond and say anything that is on his mind, as he was (hopefully) listening. I would expect him to say something like: "Hmm, I don't know . . ." Then I might say: "This sounds like a good start. Not knowing might be first step towards finding out." He might try to make it into "pulling teeth": "Finding out what?" If he does that, I would not immediately interpret the resistance in any heavy-handed way but also would not jump to gratify his question, making it "what my therapist wants me to talk about." I might say something like: "It is, of course, up to you, but if you want my input . . ." Then I would wait. Supposedly he might say something noncommittal, unclear, vague, like "Yeah, maybe . . ." I might remind him of his own words: "There are many things we might talk about. There is nothing unimportant here, as long as it concerns you and it comes to your mind. You can talk about how you feel here, talking to a stranger, how you felt about your previous therapy and therapist, or something that you had a feeling about this morning before you got here, or this week, or something you stated you never had a chance to talk about before, like your conflicted feelings about your father passing. . . . There are so many things to talk about, all up to you . . . I am here, listening . . ." If he is silent, I might wait about two minutes and only then address the silence: "Hard to choose from all these things coming to your mind at once?" If the silence persist, it becomes the object of inquiry itself.

Such clinical approach illustrates the intertwining of the moderating, client process, therapy relationship, and therapeutic interventions principles. It aims at fostering working alliance (Principle 23), active participation (Principle 21), and dealing with structural/characterological resistances (Principles 11 and 22) directly and indirectly (Principle 37) while simultaneously fostering self-understanding, emotional experiencing, and adaptive interpersonal and behavioral changes (Principles 34–36 and 38). I would take my clues from the history, especially Robert being an abused and neglected child who experienced bonding and attachment mostly with his brothers, through engaging in aggressive back-and-forth dialogue/combat and both direct (playing sports) and indirect (watching sports) physicality. Mindful of such experiences, I would inquire about and attentively listen for specific details of Robert's relationship with his brothers, for example, what sports they watched, how each of them responded, what teams they rooted for, and how was it when they engaged in playing sports with each other. I might also wonder aloud if there was any "coaching" involved, that is, if any of the older brothers took on an informal role of a coach or if, by any chance, his father would at times join them. Recovering Robert's subjective experience of relative safety and enjoyment would be important factor, providing emotional scaffolding in face of his current depression and "giving up" attitude.

My invitation would be to such 'back and forth,' with me as a "coach" or a "brother in arms." This invitation would not be explicitly spelled out but would be indirectly fostered (Principle 37) by my overall approach, especially when in need to set limits to his potential self-defeating acting out (drinking, social withdrawal, lateness for work, lateness for therapy sessions). Such limit-setting might potentially include a modification to otherwise overall nondirective approach (Principle 37), a therapeutic contract, delineating his responsibilities of a member of the viable therapy team, variably worded, depending on where in the process we are. One example, stressing "team participation" might be: "For therapy to be effective, both members of the therapy team are to arrive to sessions regularly and sober." If needed, this might be followed by "If Robert decides to drink, he stays away from cars" and "If Robert cannot stop drinking beyond two beers, he goes to AA meetings or enlists another similar help/medication, etc. and stops drinking all together." If needed, I would make a referral to a medical specialist to oversee Robert's temporary medication regime and his withdrawal from alcohol (Principle 19). We would address the dynamic and historical references for such a contract.

I might envision a back-and-forth dialogue as follows.

THERAPIST: I wonder, what would happen if one shows up for baseball practice late and intoxicated . . .
ROBERT: Depends if you are a star or just warming a bench. . . . If you are a star, you would be hurting the team. . . . Coach would probably have you sit out the next game. . . . If you are just warming the bench, it really does not matter . . .
THERAPIST: Hmmm . . . sounds like "just warming the bench" is safer . . .
ROBERT: Maybe. . . . Never thought of it that way . . .
THERAPIST: At work, all kinds of places . . .
ROBERT: Yeah . . . maybe . . . everywhere . . .
THERAPIST: Everywhere would include here, too . . .

I would hypothesize we might make an eye contact and exchange a knowing smile. The interpretative dialogue (Principle 30) might continue:

ROBERT: Isn't it too late . . . to change this? I am doing it everywhere . . .
THERAPIST Not if you show up on time . . . heading for the field rather than for the bench . . .

Exploration of Robert's fears of getting seriously involved in anything might follow.

I would conceptualize in my mind the historical background of the relationship with his brothers as the grounds for working alliance (Principle 23) as well as the potential positive aspect of transference, providing the emotional scaffolding needed to withstand the inherent frustrations of the intensive and prolonged therapeutic work (Principle 16) envisioned in his case. This would be an indirect reference to his relationship with his brothers, which seemed to have been, at least as reported, the rare example of his model of positive interpersonal experience he could count on. The pitfall here would be that, in his adult years, they "only contact him when he is depressed," which I read not only as a complaint of a "baby brother," for whom the older brothers fill the needed father role but also as a curious paradoxical multilayered overdetermined statement: On one hand, he must first get in trouble and be depressed for them to notice, contact him, and possibly become alarmed but on the other hand it as a coded statement of some other times when he is not in trouble and not depressed. I might share with him this example as illustrative of his secondary gains derived from his problems, in a way of drawing more direct psychodynamic interpretative connections (Principle 30), like "If you lose your job/if you hurt yourself driving intoxicated, great! At least they will contact you!" or/and fashioned as more indirect, yet individually tailored interpretation and intervention (Principles 30 and 37 combined): "What has the guy to do for someone to take an interest in him—is driving intoxicated or not leaving one's room enough?" This might be followed by a softer statement: "How much does one have to hurt for anyone to care?" This would not only be addressing the masochistic/self-defeating dynamic but also (gradually more and more) his dependent longings, which were apparently met with a distant cold "nonmotherly" mothering.

This, in turn, might get us on the subject of his feelings for his mother and (understandable) ambivalence about, and distrust surrounding, closeness to women (possibly even more than toward men). These unmet needs are likely behind his drinking (feeding himself, consoling himself) and, at least in part, behind his social withdrawal and erratic anger eruptions, which scared and put off his ex-girlfriend. These frustrated dependency and primary attachment needs (to be taken care of and soothed) may be behind what is impossible to regulate and contain, as no one modeled for him such a containment and regulation. This would be up to therapy and the therapeutic relationship to experience to symbolize, express, and process/understand verbally (Principles 35 and 36), with an envisioned cycle of rupture–repair (Principle 27) repeated many times.

I would hypothesize that in his case, where there may not have been a model for verbal expression (never talked about it with father, does not talk much to mother), much of the work would have to create a template on how to talk about feelings, in a way similar to taking first steps when he was a toddler or how he learned to play sports with his brothers. I would be attuned to his difficulty in naming his feelings and describing his experiences, encouraging him at every step; I might say, "You see, it is hard, but you are doing it . . ." My attitude would be based on empathy (Principle 26) rooted in deeper understanding and insight (Principles 29 and 30) into how his past of a lonely, abused, and neglected child, who, at times, ambivalently identified with those who neglected and abused him and internalized their problems as his. However understandable, his holding onto them in this way causes his current problems with people and self-advancement at work. Only gradually would this be interpreted (Principle 30); for example, "The next best thing to be with your father was to be like him . . ." or, after a prolonged silence, "It is your prerogative to shut me out . . . I wonder where you are . . . in your cold room and staying there alone . . . distant from everyone else behind the door . . . cold, distant . . . no one to touch . . . no one to take care of you . . . and you are waiting . . . and you want a drink, at least something to get rid of that pain of loneliness and cold . . . why should you trust me, a stranger . . ."

Throughout, the interpretations (Principles 29 and 30) would be given on a trial basis, in a flexible manner (Principle 33) as in "Would this make sense to you?" or in a free associative, rolling way, and his response—verbal and nonverbal—would be closely monitored and tactfully fed back to him (Principles 32, 35, and 36); for example, "When I said such and such, you smiled, before you said 'no.' . . . Maybe you are getting a kick out of it, maybe you let me just say all those silly things about how you might feel, but you know better . . . but, let her try, let her make a fool of herself . . . and now you smiled again . . ." I could envision Robert, responding, "Okay, okay, it is funny when you are trying to tell me how I feel . . ." Then, I might continue: "Hey, maybe when you get enough kick out of me missing the mark, you can tell us how you really feel and what you really think . . ."

I would not delude myself that therapeutic work with someone like Robert would be easy, but if he were to give us a chance, it might be worth it. I would find a way to consistently, directly and indirectly (Principle 37), communicate this to him in response to his discouragement, at any time throughout, taking my clues from him as to when and how he would be ready to receive it, trust it (Principle 6), internalize it (Principle 18), and make it his own (Principle 5). If Robert stayed in long-term intensive therapy (Principle 16), I would anticipate the progression toward a high degree of change readiness (Principle 6), intrinsic motivation (Principle 5), increased level of problem assimilation (Principle 10), and the unlocking of his own creativity in fashioning a flexible career and interpersonal adjustment, including satisfying viable intimate relationships. He would not necessarily live without ever subjectively experiencing anxiety or mild dysthymia, but these experiences would not constrain him, and he would have internal tools to deal with them; for example, "This is a reminder how far I have come. Wow!" or "This is what at one time scared me so that I could not tell people what I thought and felt . . ."

Comparisons between Robert and Phillip

Whereas both Phillip and Robert cite opinions of other people about them, there is a difference in how these are utilized: Phillip focuses mostly on his own perceptions of himself and his experiences (and fantasies) of others' opinions of him. Robert not only complains about others' problematic views of him but also uses those who care about him as alarming him enough to justify bringing himself to therapy. From the start, Phillip presents as a more mature adult, functioning on a higher level than Robert in both the work context and personal life.

Phillip is intrinsically motivated (Principle 5) for therapy (as in other pursuits of his life), although he registers doubts if he can change in the direction he desires. Robert is much more extrinsically motivated and clearly more ambivalent (Principle 12) about therapy, with low initial expectations (Principle 4). Although both of them experienced problematic parenting (Principles 3 and 8), Robert was outright physically abused/beaten. Phillip recalls his mother's nurturance; there is no such recall on Robert's part. The line between reality and fantasy, and connection between one's action and its consequences, is more blurred for Robert, who has trouble owning his problems and tends to externalize (Principle 17) them. However much Phillip suffers subjectively, his overall functioning both professionally and personally is much higher than that of Robert's.

According to virtually all prognostic factors (Principles 1–9), Phillip's impairment, however subjectively troubling and limiting, still allows room for favorable prognosis for an exploration/insight-oriented therapy (Principle 29 and 30), where he would be an active partner (Principle 21), utilizing transference interpretations (Principle 15) as a vehicle for fuller understanding of the overall context of his problems, throughout development and in his current life. Robert, with his moderate to severe impediments in both work and relational context, would benefit from individually tailored analytic-dynamic therapy with modifications (Principles 10, 12, and 15) of the therapeutic approach, with increased focus on specific parameters, like limit-setting in terms of substance use behavior (Principle 17) and increased attention to the establishment and maintenance of working/therapeutic alliance (Principle 23,), ruptures of which would require interpretation in the here-and-now (transferential) context (Principle 27) before there-and-now (extratransference interpretations) and there-and-then (genetic interpretations) historical reconstructions. This modified dynamic approach might need to also involve more active interpretive approach (Principle 30) in terms of Robert's early resistances (Principle 22), including possible tendency to regress and act out against his interests overall and against his involvement in therapy (Principle 21). In addition, there might be a need for referrals to medical specialists (Principle 19) and sensitive ongoing monitoring of how hard the ongoing work may be for Robert and the consequent need to recognize and affirm (Principle 24) and flexibly (Principle 32) provide needed frequent feedback of results of such an effort on his part.

Both treatments would be intensive, but Phillip's would be more traditional psychoanalysis from the start for three to four times a week, while Robert's would start at two times a week and gradually build toward three to four times a week predicated on stopping his alcohol self-abuse. Due to the seriousness of Robert's problems, his treatment would take longer time (Principle 16). Overall, the analytical approach for both Phillip and Robert could be described in language of principles as consisting of a succession of nondirective interventions (Principle 37), as the analytical therapy is essentially nondirective. The previous modifications of this approach, as pertaining to Robert, would be employed to preserve a viable frame for our work and prevent early relapses detrimental to ongoing working alliance and consequent withdrawal from therapy. But even here, the interpretation of underlying struggles and exposition of consequences of his choices would be a preferred method over giving directives.

Marie

Case Formulation and General Treatment Plan

A number of issues raised as part of Marie's prolonged intake procedure alert me to a possibly serious problems with issues of self-identity. These include her noted reluctance to speak about her parents and childhood, as well as the onset of reportedly multiple "extreme" social anxiety symptomatology during early adolescence, with previous long-standing history of social unease, feelings of "not fitting," and not being equipped to form friendly relations with peers. Her later periodic acute depressive episodes with several suicidal attempts and self-harming behaviors in response to an abortion and a stormy relationship and repeated break-ups with her boyfriend, together with reported fluctuating self-esteem, might be indicative of an underlying sense of self-constancy, including body image and integrity, and affect dysregulation. When faced with actual or perceived and imagined or anticipated losses, she seems susceptible to regress into a state of incomplete separation between self and others, with vacillating idealization and devaluation of both. Splitting into incompatible "all good" and "all bad" may be an attempt to contain overwhelming emotions and flooding of contradictory impulses, in response to a deep-seated experience of total rejection. Overall, the pattern of fluctuation between excitement and boredom; enthusiasm about involvement with people and activities, followed by disappointment; and distancing and isolation indicates to me a lack of a sense of continuity of self and others, a possible repetition of her early experiences with unreliable caretaking environment (Principle 8).

Temporarily, these serious problems, were managed not only in part by sublimation using her considerable intellectual ability and creative potential but also by finding a small-group identity and experimenting with hard drugs. Paradoxically, her suicidal attempts and acute states of anxiety and depression could possibly be viewed as primitive cries for help, to be noticed and saved, while consciously rather doubtful that she can be helped at all. Her difficulty in trusting people, isolation (Principle 1), and belief that she is "crazy," not understandable to herself and to others, may stem from a deep-seated experiences of a basic lack of trust and support from her parents and siblings (Principle 8).

With abortion as a trigger, the problems reached acute clinically significant picture of social anxiety, depression, and personality disorder. She regressed to the point where she could not continue to function effectively in two main areas that provided her with a precarious sense of identity and belonging—as a student and as part of a (however problematic) couple. Marie's contradictory feelings toward her boyfriend intensified beyond the previously manageable level. She responded by distancing herself from him, while clinging to him. He then responded in his usual fashion by yet another break-up, to which she responded with a serious suicidal attempt. I would contend that Marie experienced the abortion as an aborting of herself—death to her own vitality. In this deeply regressed state, triggered by a recent trauma of the abortion, Marie (re) experienced her traumatic childhood (Principle 8) of neglect and abuse, with early history of seriously problematic attachment (Principle 3). In this context, cutting herself presents a most primitive way of sensing/painfully confirming that she lives.

As there was apparently no one in the family with whom she felt close or by whom she felt supported, Marie feels like an outcast in and outside of her family. In comparison to Robert, who knows that he was physically abused but who knows also that he was in the same boat as his brothers were and could bond with them, Marie's maltreatment was suffered in silence, alone and with self-condemnation.

Her prolonged intake interview also gives me a glimpse at what might be Marie's self-identification as being "crazy," while uncommonly creative and talented: Marie is an enigma to herself. She does not have access to her own fragmentation and splintering of self and others' continuity when flooded with overwhelming feelings and is at a loss to see herself and others coherently. Her reluctance to talk about her parents and history, her annoyance about the questions about the goals of therapy, and her concern that no one is going to be able to change her life for the better shows a more significant underlying personality disorder (Principle 2) and more confusion than that of Robert's. Both repeated (likely traumatic) experiences of abandonment (Principle 3) by both parents (overly anxious, cold, and overcontrolling mother; an idealized self-involved father; and then retraumatization and possible reenactment in the context of the relationship with the boyfriend), however horrible, may be superimposed upon some even more serious compromise of her baseline physical integrity. I would be wondering to myself if there was an early abuse (combination of physical boundary violation and subsequent abandonment) or maltreatment of some kind, which had to be kept silent. A mildest form of the same could be a traumatizing physical illness, her own or some else's in the family, handled in a inattentive anxious manner by adult caretakers. A child could have misinterpreted it as expression of dooming parental rejection and hate. My treatment plan would be to monitor how the repeated pattern of initial distrust, possible enthusiastic involvement, stirring up of strong feelings of idealization, followed by devaluation, feelings of bitter disappointment and betrayal, and consequent tendency to withdraw unfolds in the therapeutic setting. I would focus on it and explore it its various permutations throughout. Like in cases of Phillip and Robert, Marie needs to bring this sequence (transference [Principle 15]) into the treatment. Yet, the very sequence threatens potentially the treatment's success, if not closely monitored. In the language of the principles, the pattern, starting with distrust and ending with confirmation that she was right not to trust and to withdraw, presents a substantial roadblock to establishing and maintaining therapeutic alliance (Principle 23), leading to ruptures (Principle 27), fueled by underlying ambivalence (Principle 11), growing into transference resistance (Principles 11 and 15). Mindful of Marie's strengths of intellect and creativity as well as her tendency to regress to magical thinking of being saved or condemned, splitting and disconnecting when overwhelmed, I would seek ways to meet her increased need for my firm, but nonintrusive, emotionally available, predictable, and reliable presence (Principles 10, 11, 12, 16, and 17). Examples of such responsiveness to her needs will be further specified in the following discussion. I hypothesize that once we explore and interpret this pattern in the here-and-now setting, which Marie may gradually begin to experience as reliable and safe, the past traumatic experiences can be located back into the past and will not be so readily permeating her current life.

Implementation of Principles of Change

As in the previous two cases, the initial approach, and to some degree maintained throughout, is one of broad inquiry. With regard to Marie's case, this would also include going in detail over her experience with the intake interview, where it was difficult for her to talk about some aspects of her growing up and prospective goals for herself. The objective would be to instill a sense of transparency and trust that we know things together. Additionally, mindful of her traumatic early background, specifics of which we might not know for some time, I would institute an added flexibility (Principle 33) as a safety measure: I would explicitly state that she has a right to a "stop signal," when she "does not want to talk about something for now." The objective here would be to give her sense of control over her boundaries. Under such conditions, the broad-based inquiry and her current and past life experiences can lead to increase of self-understanding (Principle 35) and emotional experiencing (Principle 36). Respect for her boundaries, increased self-understanding, and emotional experiencing might, in turn, begin to foster incremental adaptive interpersonal and behavioral change (Principles 34 and 38).

While going over the intake interview, I might share with her my impression of her strength: her gifts of intellect and creativity and also her youth. In response to her possible distrust, I might remark that "nothing is written in stone when one is 24." Focusing on the establishment of a viable working alliance (Principle 23) and surmising from the intake interview that she did not have an easy time talking about her childhood and her goals here in therapy, I might tell her, in one of the first sessions: "You have a lot of strength on your side, but you have suffered throughout your young life immeasurably. A lot of it in silence. You had wishes, aspirations, and goals, but you got disappointed and hurt too many times. You may feel that to have a goal is for you to get disappointed. Now you bravely want to change it. But you can't imagine what change can happen and how it would come about. Not a bad start. Acknowledgement that one does not know is the first step toward learning something. Let us take time and just listen first what is on your mind. . . . We don't have to have specific goals right now. Or you may think of a goal and later change your mind . . ."

In terms of *prognosis* (Principle 1), while anxiety symptoms may be in a moderate range (although she retains capability to take classes part-time and maintain part-time employment), the picture is complicated by evident risk of self-injurious behavior and suicide (Principle 1). Possible familial genetic factors, co-morbidity with acute depressive episodes and personality disorder of a bordeline-narcissitic range (Principle 2), as well as recent decrease of global functioning (Principle 1) in school and interpersonal personal areas present further complications. In addition, a problematic attachment history (Principle

3), mixed expectations from therapy at best (Principle 4), and her proneness to regression spell difficulty in maintaining her intrinsic motivation (Principles 5 and 12) and impede her ability to establish and maintain a viable working alliance (Principle 23). Consequently, the prognosis may be rather guarded, and the fluctuations in self-esteem and an easily shattered sense of self-continuity and self-cohesion may need to be closely watched, for premature "abortive" fleeing from therapy.

Because it is most likely to contribute to the fragility of working alliance (Principle 23) and its easy rupture (Principle 27), I would be attuned to any signs of reluctance to confide any follow-up information on anything about herself directly. This has already been noted during the intake interview, in which she had difficulty in sharing information about herself for fear that the other person would judge her negatively (Principles 9 and 17). The previously mentioned extra safety measure would represent just a beginning to address the issues of trust, safety, and fragility of a working alliance. I would be continuously attuned to the fluctuation of trust and possible underlying paranoia (i.e., externalization [Principle 17]). In contrast to Robert, who seems to be more coherently blunt about his mistrust, Marie may feel actually more painfully ambivalent, feeling ashamed and "crazy" (Principles 12 and 9). To attempt to address the fragile basic trust in our working together (Principle 23), I would pay exquisite attention to the nuances of client process variables (Principles 21 and 22) and plan the strategy of interventions (Principles 29–38) accordingly, watching any vacillation of her level of active participation (Principle 21), resistance (Principle 22) and the "temperature" of all therapy relationship factors (Principles 23–28). In view of a possible traumatic attachment history (Principle 3) underlying a fragile working alliance (Principle 23), I would expect regular reoccurrences of alliance raptures (Principle 27) around such themes as intrusion, abandonment, control, and judgement. They may not be communicated directly but rather indirectly by vagueness and silence. In such cases, I might make follow-up interventions as, for example, "Our work includes knowing and learning together about your experiences, your thoughts and feelings, memories, just as they come to your mind. The pace is up to you [Principles 35 and 36]. If there is something you do not want to go into it further, do let me know. I will, of course, respect it." I might add an interpretation (Principle 29) of the meaning behind the resistance (Principle 11): "As you told us before, it is hard to talk about yourself when you anticipate the other person might misunderstand and judge you..."

Now, of course, I consider the reluctance to speak without censoring in her case, if not in all cases, as multiply determined. But I would start with feeding back to her (Principles 10 and 32), her own self-reflection and/or interpretation. It could be an example of an off-target, less than direct transference interpretation (Principle 25 and 15), one guided by a genuine affirmation of her own interpretative competence (Principles 24 and 25), crediting her active participation (Principle 21), and attuned to her fragile sense of self (Principles 28 and 33). It is also an example of the intertwining treatment moderating principles (Principles 10–12, 15, 17, and 18), client process principles (Principles 21 and 22), therapy relationship principles (Principles 24–26 and 28), and therapist intervention principles (Principles 29, 30, 33, 35, and 37). This might be then utilized progressively in a more direct way on many further occasions when she finds it difficult to continue any line of inquiry or associations. First, engaging her beliefs and thoughts, I might say, "Maybe one of the reasons why you fell silent is that you find it difficult to believe I would not judge you . . . ," and later, engaging her emotions, I might state, "Maybe you are afraid I would judge you . . . should you, God forbid, tell me what's on your mind now . . ."

A word about my use of humor/sarcasm in this case may be in order: The "God forbid" is my shorthand communication to Marie that I am aware this is a struggle/conflict for her. Use of humor playfully engages the absolute forbidding (self) judgmental agency. The gradual progression throughout from less direct/off-target to more direct transference interpretation would reflect my respect for her pace, her fragility, and, at the same time, her progress (Principles 10 and 24–26).

The objective here would be a gradual containing of her anxieties and depressive feelings, building and fortifying internal structure and continuity of self, mobilizing her resilience and creativity. In language of the principles, this process would involve progressive internalization of her motivation (Principles 5 and 18) together with progression toward higher stages of change readiness (Principles 5 and 6), which, in turn, increases active involvement (Principle 21) in deepening and intensification of therapy (Principle 16). Admittedly, intermittent experiences of rupture–repair (Principle 27), as a necessary component of such a process, might lead to her growing sense of interpersonal competence. This flexible approach (Principle 33) includes emotional scaffolding of continuous feedback (Principle 32), empathically (Principle 26) acknowledging her efforts toward progressive changes in and out of therapy (Principle 34). This, in turn, furthers emotional involvement (Principle 36) and self-understanding (Principle 35), which promotes internal coherence and bridges previous gaps, especially those that are typical of traumatic dissociation, giving Marie the impression of herself as "crazy." Consistent with such an approach, I would be also inviting her to explore the times when she did feel motivated and excited about her career choices, even for a short period of time. The objective of such an inquiry would be to explore together what happened (internally) after her past experiences of inspiration and excitement. My hypothesis would be that there was a threat felt behind such an excitement and inspiration, which may be associatively connected with the repressed or dissociated trauma. I would expect transference resistance (Principles 11, 15, and 22) to reappear at such junctures, but, gradually, these could be explored and understood (Principles 35 and 36) with the help of material unfolding in the middle phases of treatment, with fortified working alliance (Principle 23), active engagement (Principle 21), progressive internalization (Principle 18), and self-understanding (Principle 35).

I can envision the scenario where Marie, intensifying the frequency of sessions to at least two to three times a week (Principle 16), brings in dreams of exciting content, which is followed by a catastrophe. Even if not remembered specifically (as early traumas may not be in autobiographical memory), the link between the excitement and danger could be interpreted as pertaining to the dream imagery, with the ensuing effect at reconnecting to her core vitality and sense of aliveness. I would expect during such work the suicidal ideation to subside, her creativity and intellectual passions to be restored, and her sense of self-respect, self-regard, and continuity of self-identity and self-esteem to increase. Similarly, as with Robert, Marie may never be conflict-free or anxiety- and depression-free. But there would be new internal resources to which she would have access and a capacity for sublimation and interpersonal refueling, which she would derive pleasure from, balancing out the displeasure, disappointments, and frustrations (Principles 34 and 38).

Comparisons between Marie, Robert, and Phillip

In terms of basic support system (Principle 1), Marie has experienced less of it apparently than both Robert and Phillip. Whereas all of them experienced problematic attachment (Principle 3) and adverse childhood events having to do with problematic parenting (Principle 8), Phillip remembers his mother's nurturance; Robert at least had his brothers, with whom he could wrestle, fight, compete and play; but Marie seems not to have had any such support, bonding, and sense of belonging with/from anyone in her family of origin. She perceived herself and may have been treated by her family as an outsider, an experience that carried over into her adolescence and many other relationships. Their initial expectations from therapy (Principle 4) differ—whereas Phillip may have doubts if his core personality can change, he seems to have clear vision of what changes he would target: meaningful accomplishments at work and genuinely affectionate and mutually respectful relationships. Both Robert and Marie are much more vague in what they would like to change, which could relate to their low level (level 0–2) of initial problem assimilation (Principle 10), greater ambivalence (Principle 12), and tendency to externalize (Principle 17) their problems. Robert, who seems to at least own his "poor impulse control," "distrust of others," and "violent temper," is doubtful if therapy can help with these rather serious issues. But Marie feels that "no one is likely to change her life for the better," which is still a more passive stance, driven by fantasy of a magical rescue at the hands of an omnipotent therapist-rescuer, who will either be able/want to rescue her or not. Although both Robert and Marie struggle more profoundly than Phillip with impulse control, regulation of affect and finding meaning in their existence, which is manifested in their self-injurious actions and co-morbidity of a personality disorder diagnosis (diagnosed in the case of Marie; undiagnosed in the case of Robert, but underlying his alcohol use), Robert "thinks and talks of suicide" and Marie has to be hospitalized for an acute suicidal episode. Robert has people to talk to, who get worried about him and to whom he reluctantly listens. Marie does not. Those are just some essential client prognostic factors (Principle 1), which, together with some characteristics of problems assimilation levels (Principle 10) that would lead me to implement different modes of treatment (Principle 33) within the dynamic-analytic model for each client.

Phillip's problems can be viewed in terms of underlying, rather coherent conflicts. His self-account is coherently verbally presented, reporting eloquently on a range of internal and interpersonal experiences, with affect being for the most part congruent with the content of his self-report. His statement of "inner immutability" can be viewed as his conflict around change: He wishes to change but is fearful that he may not be able to, unless we look underneath his troubling symptoms and patterns of behavior and attitudes into what is not yet known and not visible—the underlying problems of his personality, character, and temperament. Consistent with the underlying conflicts, we learn about Phillip's achievements and strength (he almost says so much) from his failures; for example, he has difficulties managing his managerial responsibilities: He knows he is considered trustworthy and is respected but has a problem holding onto it. He was elevated into the managerial position over all other co-workers, but he experiences problems occupying that position, etc. The treatment method of choice would be individually tailored (as it always needs be) exploratory insight-oriented dynamic (analytic) therapy. In the context of favorable prognosis, in the language of therapeutic principles, such a method would lead to the level 7 of APES (Principle 10)—mastery and integration.

In Robert's case, where prognosis is more guarded due to numerous previously discussed factors, the approach would be modified. I would envision being more interactively involved in addressing his initial externalization style, lack of motivation (fears of disappointment and yet another failure behind it), low problem assimilation, and initial characterological resistances, drawing on his strength and his internal choices to use others (adaptively) to further his goals. At times, this might include setting limits and drawing contracts. As previously stated, such a therapeutic contract could take various forms, specifically tailored for where the process would be at the time. For example, it might state: "For therapy to not be jeopardized, Mr. Robert X is to arrive to sessions regularly and sober"; "If Mr. Robert X decides to drink, he stays away from cars"; and "If Mr. Robert X cannot stop drinking beyond two beers, he goes to AA meetings or enlists another similar help/medication, etc. and stops drinking all together." Once he does that, he is credited with his accomplishments (Principle 32). This would, of course, be accompanied by me encouraging him to express/reflect on verbally any frustration with such a contract, and with me, who suggested such a frustrating measure on the first place. Developmentally, we would be constructing a sense of firm presence of someone who cares about him not wasting his time, once he decided to do therapy, taking him seriously, and respecting his resolve. If he fails, we would start again, start a new contract. I would be there, as long as he does not give up. This would be clearly spelled out to him. His fears of failure would be empathically interpreted (Principles 23–28). He would be encouraged to name his feelings, even if it is very hard (Principles 21 and 22). I might offer the sample of range and nuances but would take care as to not suggest how he might feel. If Robert would be able to make a commitment to therapy and work intensively and long-term (Principle 16), I would envision him being able to achieve a level of mastery over his problems, which would bring him to the level of finding more fulfillment in work and relationships.

In Marie's case, prognosis is also more guarded, due to numerous factors as previously mentioned. On a surface looking/sounding more together than Robert, underneath, Marie may need full acknowledgement of how, besides being very gifted and talented, she is also battling severe problems. Appreciating the depth of her despair, hopelessness, and loneliness, I would be communicating to her gently, but unequivocally, that I am there for and with her, no matter how long it takes. The intent would be to allow for her to take time and space to start trusting that it is possible to hope that something different than what she has experienced until now is possible and to prepare her for a long-term therapeutic involvement (Principle 16). I would draw on her strength (intellectual gift, creativity, youth), while acknowledging her fears of all the unknown and un-understandable about herself.

I would acknowledge her bravery (Principles 10 and 37) in face of not knowing what to expect, selectively reinforcing the unknown to become known (Principle 35), rather than focusing directly on the dimension of the negative expectations and attributions (Principles 4 and 9) with their protective function to fill the void. It would be very important to stress opening and discovering

(Principle 37), rather than having to know and foreclosing. In this context, even the ambivalence (Principle 12) and resistance (Principle 11) would have a positive valence, as long as we are learning something about her; for example, "learning about feeling, thinking and experiencing anything is always a gain, because it is YOUR feeling. . . . YOU are entitled to all of YOUR feelings . . ."

In comparison to Robert, who was afraid of the other person not being there (loss of his father, not having a chance to talk about his feeling, his brothers not contacting him unless he was in trouble), Marie is afraid of herself not being fully there (loss of her mental faculties, loss of her self, loss of her creativity, parts of her body, etc.). Whereas with Robert it was important that the other person in the room (me—the therapist) is firmly reliably there, with Marie what needs to be established is that Marie is fully, firmly, and continuously there. I would reflect/comment affirmatively (Principle 24) on anything that comes out of her ("When you say this, you sound very clear;" "When you say this and sound doubtful, you must have some good reasons for your doubts. . . . Let's try to find out what they might be . . ."). My presence, in case of Marie, would be important so as to reflect the reality of her presence. This might be Marie's chance at learning that even if there is another person in the room, Marie does not have to disappear (in reference to the roots behind it: overcontrolling mother and "absent" father). Only then, Marie could start registering my empathy (Principle 26) and my support (Principles 23 and 25). Only then, therapy becomes *her* therapy. With the long-term (Principle 16) commitment on both of our parts, I would envision that Marie could experience herself, step by step, more whole and more internally separate. She could gradually benefit more and more from insight-oriented dynamic work (Principles 29 and 30), in the end mastering her problems, getting actively involved in her career plans and follow through, and becoming capable of close, affectionate, friendly, and romantically satisfying relationships.

Conclusion

Although at first the task to reflect on my clinical conceptualizations of Phillip, Robert, and Marie, and to match the relevant empirically derived principles without resorting to psychoanalytic jargon, was a challenge. In the process of it, I enjoyed the discovery of internal links between the "language of the principles" and the "language of my clinical work." Moreover, as the work proceeded, I found what I initially feared as constricting and reductive to be actually expansive and creative, increasing the range of my clinical voice in many directions. Paradoxically, this could be casted as a case of "something being found/added/

enriched in translation, not lost." In the end, I realize that one thing comes unmistakably through—the clinician's commitment to the creative, individually attuned work with a unique individual person who always presents a unique configuration of problems and strengths to be respected in any language and any translation.

References

Bergin, A. E., & Garfield, E. S. (1971). *Handbook of psychotherapy and behavior change.* New York, NY: Wiley.

Meltzoff, J., & Kornreich, M. (1970). *Research in psychotherapy.* New York, NY: Atherton.

Papiasvili, E., & Papiasvili, A. (1983) Residential therapeutic community for neurotics. *International Journal of Group Psychotherapy, 33,* 387–395.

Papiasvili, E. (2016). Translational aspects of interpretation today: A developmental and dynamic view. *Psychoanalytic Inquiry, 36,* 88–101.

Shedler, J. (2010). The efficacy of psychodynamic psychotherapy. *American Psychologist, 65,* 98–109.

10
A Cognitive-Behaviorist's Report from the Trenches

Catherine S. Spayd

Although honored to be asked to contribute to this book, I also admit to initially feeling somewhat overwhelmed with the task of applying or dismissing each of 38 principles to each of three psychotherapy case studies. However, after careful consideration, I realized that in any actual session I am likely contemplating, individualizing, and then implementing or rejecting many more than 38 "pieces" of service delivery. To my best recall, in my graduate school training and as an early career psychologist, my consideration of such interventions was often quite explicit. But at this later point in my career, I'm sure that I make a good percentage of these clinical decisions with little or no conscious awareness; for better or worse, I am on clinical "automatic pilot" much of the time. Upon initial review of this book's principles of change, all of the client prognostic principles and most of the client process, therapy relationship, and therapy intervention principles seem to be stating obvious and intuitive truths that almost any clinician would assume. Conversely, a number of the moderating principles seem counterintuitive. Thus, a formalized review of the principles is a way for me to assess my initial impressions, review my overall approach to therapy, and perhaps again make my clinical practice more conscious.[1]

Case Formulations and Treatment Plans

Our first client, Phillip, experiences painful social anxiety that limits his occupational and interpersonal functioning. In reviewing his history, a likely

---

[1] It may be interesting for the reader to know that (as an experiment for myself), other than a first cursory review of the book's identified principles of therapeutic change, I did not refer to these principles again until after writing my treatment plans for the three cases.

hypothesis is that his mother's overprotectiveness, combined with his father's critical behaviors during his childhood, were the initial causes of his social anxiety. Over time, however, anxiety typically begets more anxiety by becoming a learned response in which self-cognitions (distorted by initial anxious thinking) combine with avoidance to create even stronger anxiety, which then takes on a life of its own independent of its initial cause. In Phillip's case, this phenomenon is manifest first in his anxious searching of others' reactions for confirmation of his self-perceived social gaffes. Because of his negative expectations in this regard, he then attributes others' critical reactions as reaffirmations of his poor self-image. His resultant heightened anxiety is then physically manifest by such overt symptoms as stumbling speech and blushing, providing some credence to others' negative evaluations. Finally, he attempts to avoid future interactions of this type, thereby completing the anxiety cycle.

Such avoidance, which Phillip implements in spades, is a quite typical response to anxiety. But by avoiding social interactions, Phillip does not give himself the opportunity to practice more realistic cognitions and social skills during such encounters and thereby experience the social success he longs for, which would mitigate his anxiety. His avoidance thus both reinforces his anxiety and leads to problems interacting with co-workers (e.g., passivity with his subordinates and superiors), problems with his wife (e.g., agoraphobia that limits their social life), and problems in pursuing leisure activities (e.g., going out with friends). Complicating Phillip's case is his more recent depression, which has likely developed in response to problems caused by his anxious approach to life, including his poor self-concept due to perceived social ineptitude, his lack of enjoyable recreational activity, and rejection from his wife due to her annoyance with his habit of seeking excessive reassurance.

I believe that Phillip would respond best to an approach initially focused on improving his "buy-in" to the idea that he *can* change both his thoughts and his behaviors and thus who he perceives himself to be. In other words, he needs help understanding that his anxious self does not have to be a permanent state; rather, it can be changed with conscious effort and practice. Then, I would help him evaluate, challenge, and change his distorted negative cognitions, not only identifying their underpinnings in his mother's overprotectiveness and his father's criticisms but also helping him to understand that, as an adult, he can choose to think differently. We would use real-life examples of perceived negative reactions that he encounters between sessions (and, perhaps, within sessions, with me). I would explicitly educate him about the anxiety cycle that he has inadvertently created and how he may contribute to others' mild negative evaluations of his anxious behaviors, while again emphasizing the hopeful notion that he can change such behaviors. Similarly, I would educate him about his understandable, yet unhelpful use of avoidance behaviors, which only serve to reinforce his anxiety symptoms. Prominent behavioral strategies that I would use include (a) assertiveness training, first via role play in sessions and then via graduated homework assignments with work associates and his wife; (b) teaching him several relaxation strategies, such as deep breathing, deliberate prayer, guided imagery, and progressive muscle relaxation, to implement in anxious situations; and (c) gradually increasing his enjoyable leisure activities, first with his trusted wife and then with some old friends.

Robert, our second client, suffers from social anxiety, alcohol abuse, and more recent depression. His alcoholic and verbally and physically abusive father and his anxious, passive, and ineffectual mother initially influenced his childhood development of social anxiety. His mother directly modeled anxiety, and neither parent provided Robert with emotional support or training on successfully negotiating his environment and developing effective interpersonal skills. Consequently, he does not accept personal responsibility for his behaviors or the negative consequences of his actions. His anxiety primarily manifests as severe social isolation and excessive negative ruminations about the interactions he does experience, focusing on his perceived social failures. Unfortunately, Robert's situation is complicated by his excessive alcohol intake, initially used as a way to manage his social anxiety, but now a self-perpetuating addictive response. This alcohol abuse has led to work and interpersonal difficulties, although Robert denies this connection. His recent depression appears to have developed in response to both his social isolation and, likely, this excessive alcohol use.

I believe that successful treatment with Robert would depend on first developing a positive therapeutic alliance, especially in light of his previous premature treatment termination and current resistance to treatment. My operational definition of a positive alliance with Robert is one in which he feels that I understand him and have unconditional positive regard for him and that he can trust me to do no intentional harm. My initial approach would be not only to empathize with his rough life events and recent distress but also to emphasize his control over his treatment attendance, course, and outcome (and, thus, implicitly, his life course). This strategy is designed both to engage him in treatment and to begin, subtly at first, challenging his tendency to blame others for his behaviors. Once trust is established, I would more overtly explain to him that the good news is also the bad news: His life situation will very likely not change (the bad news) until *he* makes significant efforts to change, but this change is within his and only his control (the good news)—no one else can negate his good efforts.

If this approach is successful, I would move forward in a manner similar to Phillip's treatment, focusing first on social anxiety symptom reduction via cognitive reframing of negative thoughts about peers' perceptions of him (e.g., challenging his mind-reading beliefs), then relaxation skill-building, and then gradual behavioral changes to increase social interaction. Given Robert's limited support system, I would encourage him to first reach out to his brothers (rather than waiting for them to reach out to him) in an effort to engage them in initially low-threat behaviors that they previously enjoyed together, such as watching televised football. Then, I would help him to deliberately evaluate the success of such socialization efforts before attempting such interactions with other peers. (Note that with Robert, our treatment focus on improved socialization is more deliberate and conscious than with Phillip, who is assumed to be more socially skilled and thus less in need of such deliberate coaching on successful peer interactions.)

After success in social anxiety symptom reduction, I would suggest that Robert identify the cost–benefit ratio of his current alcohol use. In particular, I would help him identify alcohol's negative impact on his depression, sleep, weight gain, and reduced social inhibition leading to negative interpersonal interactions (e.g., with his prior girlfriends). I would then encourage Robert to identify his own reasonable amount of alcohol intake, again emphasizing his personal responsibility, by suggesting that he conduct carefully self-monitored "experiments" to assess the impact of more or less alcohol intake.

Our third case, Marie, is a young woman with social anxiety complicated by a personality disorder that includes avoidant, dependent, and borderline traits. Based on the limited family information that she provided, her upbringing with a nonnurturing mother and an emotionally absent father was the likely origin of her personality disorder, while her avoidant and dependent characteristics, combined with her mother's modeling of social anxiety, were apparent contributors to her development of social anxiety symptoms. As previously noted, social anxiety becomes self-perpetuating when the individual, like Marie, focuses excessively on perceived and/or actual negative social responses of others, responses that are exacerbated in her case by her clingy, insecure interpersonal reactions and erratic mood states and behaviors.

As with Robert, but in contrast with Phillip, and especially in consideration of her personality traits, my treatment plan with Marie would initially focus on developing a strong therapeutic relationship, after clarifying her current abstinence from substances. This relationship-building work would be a necessary first step with Marie, and my focus would be on unconditional positive support within clearly defined therapeutic boundaries. I would educate her regarding the benefits and challenges of being in therapy and explicitly discuss using our therapy relationship as a model to explore and improve how she interacts with others. I would anticipate "bumps" in our relationship as inevitable and perhaps even painful. However, I would suggest to her that these bumps would not be disastrous but rather could be viewed as fodder for the therapeutic mill. Then, I would attempt to help Marie clarify her values about what a healthy friendship or romantic relationship looks like, to be used as a template in evaluating her past, and especially her current and future, relationships. Only then would we move toward similar cognitive-behavioral approaches as I've described for Phillip and Robert, to address her social anxiety.

Implementation of Principles of Change

Using these case formulations and treatment plans as a backdrop, I now explore how this volume's identified principles of therapeutic change do, or do not, apply to my conceptualization of Phillip, Robert, and Marie's psychotherapy. Being a pragmatist, I've chosen a straightforward approach of starting at Principle 1 and moving through to Principle 38, although where the principles seem to overlap, I address them out of numerical order. The first prognostic principle states that clients with higher baseline levels of psychological impairment may derive less benefit from treatment. Whereas all three of our cases exhibit some impairment in functioning, Phillip appears the relatively least impaired, as exemplified by his history of climbing the career ladder and continued employment in a management position, his long-term marriage, his lack of psychopathology complications such as substance use or suicidal risk, and his relatively mild social anxiety symptoms. Not surprisingly, therefore, my treatment plan for Phillip is also the simplest and most straightforward—of the three clients, he will be able to begin work on his social anxiety symptoms most quickly. In my experience, initial quick treatment success on the client's identified referral issue is a reinforcing event, facilitating his or her positive motivation for continued efforts and, thus, typically a more beneficial treatment outcome.

Robert, conversely, appears to be the most impaired client of our three cases, with chronic substance abuse threatening his employment status, no positive long-term or current intimate relationships, recent suicidal ideation and other depressive symptoms, unresolved conflict regarding his abusive father, and the relatively most severe and chronic symptoms of social anxiety. My biggest concern regarding Robert's treatment is that he remains in it. Treatment is obviously not beneficial if it is not happening, but Robert's history of premature psychotherapy termination, combined with his chronic difficulty accepting responsibility for his own behaviors and, thus, negative life outcomes, suggest that he is at risk for early dropout. Therefore, although this first therapeutic change principle does seem to apply, it also serves to emphasize the importance of my initial proposed treatment focus—to ally with Robert, attempt to gain his trust, and build an positive therapeutic alliance. For example, I might say early on in treatment "You know, Robert, I hear from your voice how upsetting it must have been for you to hear your boss's comments about your job being at risk and to have your girlfriend choose to leave the relationship, especially when both occurred within a short time frame. And I'm right there with you—no one would feel good about those life changes. What I'm hoping, though, is that through our work together, you'll be able to identify some new ways to cope with these life disappointments and others that will inevitably come up. It's possible that therapy might also help you learn to approach future such events in a different manner, to increase the odds of a better outcome for you. But, this goal will take some work, which means you showing up for sessions and both of us working hard within them. Your job history tells me that you can do that—you're no stranger to hard work. And if you feel that I've stepped on your toes, for example, by saying something you don't agree with or feel angry about, I'd like you to please tell me about it right away so we can talk about it and resolve the issue—the last thing I want to do is to hurt you, even unintentionally."

Marie is moderately impaired. Her personality disorder, with concomitant past suicidal behavior and therefore ongoing suicidal risk, certainly complicates her therapeutic picture. However, her degree of impairment is somewhat mitigated by her attributes of youth (thus relative lower frequency of reinforcement of dysfunctional socially anxious behaviors), intellect, and some degree of self-motivation for treatment. Her pattern of erratic relationships is likely the biggest challenge in that it predicts difficulty establishing and maintaining trust with me, the therapist, a necessary ingredient if we are to employ my treatment plan of using the therapy relationship as a template for modifying her interpersonal functioning. For example, if I anticipate Marie's hot (e.g., "You're the only one who understands me") and then cold (e.g., "I knew you wouldn't see my side of things") reactions to me and comment on such contradictions without overreaction or conveying personal injury, I can demonstrate to her unconditional positive acceptance, thereby fostering her trust (i.e., she can act out and I do not reject her). Such anticipation of her unstable interpersonal responses toward me is facilitated by an awareness of this client prognostic principle of change, as well as the second principle of change, which predicts less therapy benefit when a client has co-morbid personality disorder.

Note that my treatment plans for the three clients also exemplify several other therapeutic principles, including Principle 16, which states that clients with higher baseline impairment may benefit from longer and/or more intensive psychotherapy, whereas clients with lesser impairment may benefit equally from shorter and less intensive treatment. My described treatment for Philip will likely be shorter and fairly straightforward, while Robert and Marie's therapies will necessarily be longer and more intensive, due to their specific challenges and the corresponding additional therapy steps as previously described. Similarly, Principle 23 states that clients experiencing a higher quality therapeutic alliance may benefit more from psychotherapy, and the previous discussions of Robert and Marie's treatments emphasize adherence to this principle.

The client prognostic principle stating that clients with less secure attachment may benefit less from therapy (Principle 3) seems particularly relevant to our cases, which share the presenting issue of social anxiety, a common outcome of insecure attachment. The origins of attachment insecurity, also called attachment anxiety, were present in all three of the clients' childhoods. Although Phillip is described as having developed secure attachment with his mother, his father and both of Robert and Marie's parents were described as nonnurturing and emotionally, if not physically, absent. These latter parents were also emotionally and sometimes physically abusive. Given this prognostic principle, one might postulate that the diagnosis of social anxiety disorder inherently puts a client at higher risk for poor treatment outcome compared to other psychological diagnoses.

However, in my experience, socially anxious clients can be effectively treated, in part by an awareness of, and mitigation of, insecure attachment. Establishing a positive therapeutic relationship, as I emphasized especially in Robert's and Marie's treatment plans, is a deliberate effort to overcome these clients' lack of childhood nurturance by providing them, in adulthood, with the Rogerian treatment variables of trust, empathy, unconditional positive regard, as well as warm and genuine acceptance (Principles 24–26). For example, Marie, in discussing her frustrations with friends who eventually push her away, might comment "It's always the same—no one really cares about me in the end." In response, I might state, "I understand that it feels like no one is there for you. But I can tell you, Marie, that *I'm* here, and I care about you." (Alternately, I could respond "What about in our relationship, Marie? Do you think I care about you?" Although this second approach has more potential to be a "teaching moment" by helping Marie learn to identify and then challenge "all or nothing" thought processes, I would likely choose the first option, which I believe in its simplicity has more power to communicate my unconditional positive regard.) Principle 26 states that clients experiencing more empathy may benefit more from therapy. Using this principle, I might respond to Robert's descriptions of his paralysis in social situations by stating, "It sounds like it would be exhausting to try to watch and interact with all those people when you feel they are judging you. I am so sorry you have that experience in what is supposed to be a fun setting." Additionally, note that Principle 8 suggests that clients with a history of adverse childhood events may benefit less from psychotherapy compared to clients with no adverse childhood history. To me, considering our three social anxiety cases, this principle and its mitigation are redundant with the secure attachment principle just discussed.

Prognostic Principle 4 is that clients with higher initial expectations for benefiting from psychotherapy may, in fact, benefit more from it. Although this statement appears obvious, it is a truism to which the clinician is wise to attend, particularly in initial treatment sessions. One of my standard intake questions is to ask what a client expects to gain from therapy, which helps identify both his or her specific treatment goals, as well as what level of hope he or she holds for benefiting from therapy at all. Thus, one of my general, initial treatment objectives is to reinforce a client's positive expectations for, or gently challenge his or her pessimism about, therapy gains. To remain empathic, I might first acknowledge and process a client's low expectations for treatment success (e.g. "It sounds like you're not at all sure that psychotherapy will be helpful for you. That seems like it would have made it tough for you to come today. Can you tell me more about that?") Then, based on the client's response, and after reassuring him or her that I understand these concerns, I would attempt to instill reasonable hope for treatment benefit. For example, I typically cite statistics about overall rates of psychotherapy success, emphasizing the simple truth that staying in treatment, despite it evoking distressing feelings at times, will enhance the odds of its success. I might also ask the client to give therapy a fair chance before giving up on it, which I often define as completing three sessions, and suggest that we make a plan to re-evaluate his or her progress at that time. Similarly, as noted in my treatment plan for Phillip, who believes that his social anxiety is an unchangeable component of his core being, one of my first strategies would be to challenge this belief by noting that psychotherapy is all about change, but within a supportive environment.

Robert will likely be more of a challenge in this regard, in that he entered treatment only after the repeated urgings of others. Additionally, his past premature treatment termination and lack of success in attempts to curtail his alcohol use likely reinforce his low expectation of behavior change and, thus, treatment success. But I believe that the biggest contributor to Robert's low expectations about the benefits of psychotherapy is his external locus of control for his life experiences; that is, if others are always to blame for what goes wrong in his life, how can individual psychotherapy, focused on him, improve his life? My treatment plan for Robert therefore includes a push toward gently challenging this world view, by suggesting that not only (a) he *does* have primary (though never complete) control over his life outcomes, but also (b) this is a preferable place to be, because it gives *him* the power to manage his own life, rather than leaving this control to others. Psychotherapy would thus be presented to Robert as a conduit to learning how to take and manage this self-control, using his experimental outcomes in the areas of social interactions and alcohol intake as evidence of his personal (and thus therapy's) success.

Note that client prognostic Principle 5 appears to overlap with Principle 4 in Robert's case. Principle 5 states that clients who are more intrinsically motivated to engage in psychotherapy will derive greater benefit from it. I see the application of this principle as a rewording of the concept just discussed, the importance of moving Robert toward more of an internal locus of control versus his current external locus. Another way to operationalize this idea would be to clarify to Robert that, although family and friends encouraged his entry into treatment, it was ultimately his choice to accept their suggestions, and it is certainly his choice to remain.

Although Marie independently sought treatment, and did acknowledge "needing psychotherapy," she also exhibited ambivalence about entering treatment and expressed low expectations for treatment success. These opposing views of treatment are likely symptomatic of her borderline personality traits, and I believe that her ambivalence would need to be addressed, albeit in a respectful and supportive manner, within the treatment approach I've previously outlined. Specifically, establishing a strong, positive therapeutic alliance (Principle 23) would be key. Strategies in establishing such a positive alliance might include simply listening to Marie's life story without criticism or judgment, validating her experiences of emotional pain as legitimate and not taking personally, and thus overreacting to, her anticipated criticisms of me.

Note that client process principle stating that clients with more resistance to therapy or the therapist may benefit less from psychotherapy (Principle 22) seems to me to be both obvious and generally redundant with Principle 5. That is, I see therapy motivation and resistance to the idea of therapy as opposing client responses to the same concept. Thus, my same treatment conceptualizations for Principle 5 would apply. However, a client might be motivated for therapy but resistant to specific interventions or approaches or simply to a particular therapist. Principle 13, discussed in the following text, addresses this issue by stating it's opposite—that clients who are matched to their preferred therapy role, therapist demographics, or treatment type may benefit more from psychotherapy.

Prognostic Principle 6 states that clients in more advanced stages of change readiness may achieve more psychotherapeutic benefit. The five consecutive stages of change summarized by Norcross, Krebs, and Pochaska (2011) include precontemplation, contemplation, preparation, action, and maintenance.

Assuming that Phillip self-referred to treatment, it would appear that he is in the preparation stage; that is, he has attempted in the past (though in his mind unsuccessfully) to challenge his social anxiety by pushing himself to talk to strangers, and he has taken the positive step of entering treatment. These behavioral efforts could effectively be framed to Phillip as initial therapeutic progress, another strategy to counter his belief that he cannot change.

Robert's attitude, however, appears to hover between precontemplation and contemplation. He appears fully unaware of, perhaps even in denial of, some of his issues, such as the difficulties created by his alcohol use and accepting personal responsibility for his actions. As a therapist, my awareness of his *lack* of awareness is key to carefully introducing these concepts in a supportive manner but only after a good alliance has been established. Conversely, Robert is more aware of his social anxiety symptoms and their negative influence on his life; this awareness is the apparent impetus for Robert contemplating behavior change, by allowing himself to be "talked into" another psychotherapy attempt. This relatively greater change readiness is my reasoning behind focusing treatment techniques first upon his social anxiety symptoms—his self-identified referral problem. He is relatively more ready for change in this area, and, as noted previously, initial treatment success in reducing social anxiety will both keep Robert in treatment and hopefully move him ahead one readiness stage in addressing his other difficulties.

Marie appears to be in the readiness stage of preparation in that she also self-referred for treatment. However, her ambivalence, previously identified as characteristic of her personality disorder, could alternately (and perhaps less judgmentally) be viewed as her intermittently falling back into a stage of contemplation. Explicitly recognizing this shift might promote effective therapeutic exploration of her level of commitment to behavior change, despite the effort required (e.g., "You know, Marie, you've taken the huge and positive step of entering treatment, and have told me more than once that you felt for a while you really needed to be in therapy. But we've also discussed that it will be difficult to do the *work* of therapy, like confronting challenging issues and moving forward with making changes in your life. It seems to me that maybe we're at that point now. When I asked you to come up with some ways you might approach Cindy about how disappointed you were when she didn't call yesterday like she promised, you told me you 'can't think of a single way' to do that. Do you think your mental block on responding to Cindy might be an example of you finding it hard to put your plans for change into action?").

Therapeutic change Principle 7 states that clients with low socio-economic status (SES) and employment problems may benefit less from psychotherapy. Despite therapists' (including my own) general proclivity for YAVIS (young, attractive, verbal, intelligent, and successful) clients, in my experience, greater verbal skills, education, and/or intelligence do not directly predict better therapeutic outcome. Rather, if I deliberately attempt to match my vocabulary and the complexity of my statements to a client's and watch him or her carefully for nonverbal signs of incomprehension and then adjust my delivery accordingly, I do not find SES to be a primary determinant of effective treatment. Similarly, I try to remain aware of a client's familiarity with psychological concepts, check for understanding, and explain unfamiliar information in user-friendly terms, when necessary. For example, with Robert, likely the least sophisticated client, I would work to de-emphasize the discrepancy in our educational levels by talking to him in common vernacular. Similarly, I would automatically describe treatment concepts to him in concrete, behavioral terms, rather than using psychological lingo that might increase my credibility with another client, like Marie.

Overall, however, in my experience prognostic Principle 7 is true more often in a pragmatic versus a therapeutic sense. Drawing on Maslow's (1943) hierarchy of needs, if a client has a stable income and, thus, adequate housing and nutrition, he or she is more able to focus on higher-order needs, such as improvement in relationships and self-awareness. Similarly, higher SES and stable employment suggest more likely availability of health insurance with which to pay for psychotherapy. Through this lens, I see this principle as a nonissue for Phillip and Marie. But my initial treatment goal with Robert (keeping him *in* treatment) would clearly be compromised if he were to lose his job, as he is in danger of doing. Indeed, it may be therapeutically effective to anticipate this potential scenario with Robert. For example, I might question, were he to lose his job, if such a sequence of events would be a result of his own behavioral choices or an external confirmation of his belief that "the world is out to get you."[2]

Principle 9 suggests that anxious clients with more negative self-attributions may benefit less from psychotherapy. My work with anxious clients does not support this research finding. Certainly, the majority of clients seeking treatment have some degree of negative self-attribution, especially those with anxiety, so we are most likely comparing relative degrees of such negative thinking. But negative self-talk, including self-attribution, is a fairly concrete therapy construct, readily understood by most clients after the concept is presented to them. Thus, I have observed it to be something relatively easy for them to change, thereby successfully reducing anxiety, but only once they learn to identify this overlearned and often-elusive negative thinking. Further, I believe that the more severe the negative self-attributions are, the more easily they can be

---

[2]I have found that anticipating future hypothetical events is less threatening and thus can elicit better insight with clients than reviewing real-life events postmortem.

identified by the client, once he or she knows to monitor for them. (I would liken this to the concept of a caricature drawing that deliberately exaggerates certain physical traits to make them more obvious to the viewer.) My sense is thus that clients with *very* negative self-attributions may benefit *more* from therapy, compared to those with relatively less severe negative self-cognitions, which may be more difficult to for them to "catch" in their ongoing thinking.

As previously discussed, Phillip demonstrates negative self-attributions when he blames himself for perceived life failures and when he expects others to be (in his mind deservingly) critical of him. Assuming his successful buy-in to the initial therapeutic concept of his ability to change his thinking, I am confident that a straightforward cognitive therapy approach would help him to identify, evaluate, challenge, and then modify distorted negative self-attributions. But, the more severe the distortion, the easier it would be for him to complete the first step of identifying such negative thinking. For example, if Phillip were to review in his mind an interaction with an employee in which he stumbled over his words and concluded "Wow, I'm the stupidest man alive," this thought should be easier for him to "catch" as a possible distortion with negative impact than if he thought "She probably thinks less of me now." Further support to my challenge to Principle 9 comes from Robert, with his tendency to blame others for his negative life events rather than accepting personal responsibility for his behavioral choices. He thus represents the antithesis of more negative self-attribution—that is, he possesses negative *other*-attribution. As previously discussed, in part because of this world view, he also presents a relatively greater therapeutic challenge.

The next set of principles involves treatment and treatment provider characteristics. Principle 10 states that when a psychotherapist uses interventions consistent with a client's level of problem assimilation, more therapy benefit is likely. Stiles (2002) defines problem assimilation as a developmental sequence from low to high integration of problem experiences into a dominant sense of self. In my mind, this principle overlaps significantly with the earlier client prognostic Principles 1 and particularly Principle 6, though viewed through the lens of intervention strategy versus client characteristic. That is, a client's level of problem assimilation would appear to strongly correlate with his or her levels of psychological impairment and readiness for change. So, it is unsurprising that Phillip would place further along this developmental sequence than either Marie or especially Robert. That is, Phillip appears to have awareness about his social anxiety, yet in the moment of a social encounter, it stills feels overwhelming to him. This awareness places him at Stiles's (2002) level of problem statement/clarification. I might therefore begin work with Phillip by helping him develop a clear and succinct self-statement to counter his overlearned social anxiety response, as a quick mental reference he can use when encountering challenging social situations in his daily life (e.g., "I know what this is—I'm reacting with anxiety because I expect to be judged negatively by others. But I really can't read their minds—I don't know how they view me, and the best thing I can do now is to speak calmly and confidently, assuming nothing about their beliefs.")

As previously noted, attention to this issue suggests more multilayered treatment approaches for Marie and Robert; the goal of my initial greater focus on establishing trust with these two clients is to facilitate their gradually increasing awareness of, then the dismantling of, resistances in identifying, owning, attending to, and understanding their problem experiences. For example, with Robert, we would likely need to start with working through Stiles's (2002) level of active avoidance, an earlier stage than I would begin with the other two clients. I might suggest that Robert conduct the experiment of putting himself into a situation where he will likely encounter some low level of social anxiety (e.g., a phone call to his brother) but armed with his newly acquired anxiety management resources. I would give him the explicit instruction of observing his own emotional and cognitive responses throughout the interaction to better clarify the precipitants of his anxiety. For example, what was he anticipating would happen before he made the call? What thoughts ran through his mind during the call? What did his brother say prior to any anxious thoughts he experienced? To increase the likelihood of Robert's taking this step away from avoidance and toward awareness, I would first attempt to shore up his trust in me and the therapy process (e.g., "I know it might seem like I'm asking a lot of you, but I believe you can do this—you've made it clear that you want to beat this anxiety by showing up here for sessions each week. And remember, we are not sending you into battle unarmed—you now know how to manage your anxiety by deep breathing, and we have the escape plan in place, of you saying you need to hang up to get ready for work").

Principle 11 suggests that clients with higher levels of resistance may benefit more from psychotherapy that is less directive, and vice-versa. I believe that I intuitively, if not consciously, apply this principle, especially in cases of overtly expressed resistance like Robert's. In fact, this principle is the very reasoning behind my emphasizing to Robert early on, in both words and therapeutic interventions, that *he* is in control of his psychotherapy treatment. For example, if he states, "Therapy won't do me any good," I could allow that statement, taken together with his multiple other examples of resistance, to bait me into an argument about the benefits of psychotherapy, perhaps citing supportive research or my own success rate. A different and likely more effective response to his resistive statement would be "Maybe you're right. I guess we'll have to wait and see." The previously discussed "good news/bad news" concept is another example of a nondirective treatment approach (Principle 37) that I believe would be most successful with Robert. And even the behavior therapy-based experiments that

I suggest he complete regarding his drinking (more direct intervention in line with Principle 38) would be couched in nondirective terms (e.g., "*You* decide the significance and applicability of the experiment's results").

Marie represents our mid-level resistance client—she both wants therapy and is ambivalent about it (e.g., exhibiting annoyance and frustration with the therapist's early interventions). Considering this principle, I similarly think a mid-level degree of directiveness would be most effective for her. For example, my proposed early intervention of outlining therapy boundaries to Marie would be fairly directive, but my later strategy, of encouraging her to clarify her own values surrounding healthy romantic relationships, is more nondirective.

Phillip, conversely, has a low level of resistance and thus will likely respond well to a more directive approach (e.g., the provision of homework assignments). However, I would be remiss in not pointing out that, unfettered, Phillip's anticipated receptivity to a directive approach may well perpetuate, versus diminish, his difficulties. Due to his tendency to seek out reassurance and advice of others, Phillip has not had much life experience in asserting himself and thus being reinforced by such self-initiated successes. Indeed, his passive tendencies have created problems in his marriage, with his wife wishing he were more assertive and less reassurance- and advice-seeking.

I once had a very passive (and very socially anxious) long-term client who would often begin sessions with "Doc, here's the problem [then described in detail the problem of the day].... What should I do?" Of course, I would not provide "the answer" but instead encouraged him to identify what *he* thought might be possible solutions, which we would then consider one by one. And, after all that processing, he would then ask, "But what should I *do*?" Over time, he came to learn that I never did tell him what to do, to the point that it became our inside therapy joke (e.g., "Doc, there's a new job listed at work—just tell me if I should take it."). Gradually, he began to enter sessions with possible problem solutions and to demonstrate more willingness to self-determine a course of action.[3] Similarly, my hope is that Phillip would demonstrate the ability to learn more self-directed thinking and action if I grant him autonomy and I am not *too* directive.

Principle 12 states that clients with higher levels of ambivalence about change may benefit more from a psychotherapeutic approach that is responsive and person-centered, rather than directive and change-oriented. This first half of this statement appears to me to be redundant with Principle 11, but the second

---

[3]To this end, I make a point of (gently) correcting clients who refer to our work as "counseling." I note that, unlike, say, an attorney who gives "counsel," I do not, because there is no good outcome: If my advice is effective, the client learns not how to solve his or her problems but instead to come back to me for more advice. And if I give ineffective counsel, he or she may just lose faith in me.

half seems to be contrasting Rogerian versus behavioral therapy approaches.[4] My treatment plans for Robert and Marie, who both demonstrate lower motivation and more ambivalence about change than does Phillip, do indeed initially focus more on a person-centered approach and then later incorporate behavior change techniques after an alliance has been established. Specifically, in Marie's case I would focus particularly on our relationship and provide unconditional positive regard, whereas with Robert I would work especially hard to present myself as both genuine and genuinely concerned about him. Note that these approaches are also consistent with therapy relationship Principle 24, which states that clients experiencing more therapist regard and affirmation may benefit more from therapy, and Principle 25, which notes that clients experiencing more therapist congruence (i.e., therapist authenticity) may benefit more from psychotherapy. Additionally, Principle 37 applies here, stating what seems to be self-evident: If a therapist selectively and responsively uses nondirective interventions in a skillful manner, the client will likely benefit more from treatment.

Principle 13 suggests that clients who are matched to their preferred therapy role, therapist demographics, or treatment type may benefit more from psychotherapy. The presented case scenarios do not specify Phillip, Robert, and Marie's preferences in these regards. However, given his described interpersonal behaviors, an educated guess would be that Phillip would exhibit a passive role and, thus, prefer a directive therapist. As noted in my discussion of Principle 11, this would likely be a good therapy match for him, as long as the therapist recognizes and addresses the danger that a purely directive approach may perpetuate his passivity.

Given my experiences with male clients who seem similar to Robert (I'm guessing that he holds a more traditional masculine world view), I assume that he would feel relatively less threatened by a female therapist to avoid the perceived shame of exposing his feelings to another man. I believe this match would be therapeutic for him, as he would likely more readily discuss emotions and, over time, consider accepting personal responsibility for his life choices, with a woman. But I also think Robert would prefer a very nondirective therapist; that is, someone who would not disconfirm his perspective of blaming his negative life outcomes on others. Of course, I do not believe that this match would be in his best interest. Whereas my treatment plan with him does include empathizing with his emotional distress and current undesirable life circumstances (being alone, threatened job security), I would be careful initially

---

[4]I do take exception to the implied suggestion that being person-centered is the opposite of being change-oriented. In my view, all psychotherapy should be both person-centered *and* change-oriented—why would someone seek treatment if they didn't want to change?

to not inadvertently endorse his other-blaming world view by any nondirective statements.

Later, after our trusting relationship is established, I would more directly, albeit kindly, challenge such blame. For example, I might say, "You know, Robert, I'm going to go out on a limb here and say something you may not like. And, if you don't like it, please let me know, OK?" (Wait for his affirmative response.) "Well, it sometimes seems to me as if you would prefer I just join in with you in blaming the world at large, or people in your life in particular, for your problems. But even though my agreement might feel good to you, I really don't see how that's going to help improve your situation. That is, I don't see how we have any control over other people, do we? Just ourselves. What do you think about how you and I see things differently in this regard?"

Marie's ambivalence to treatment makes it difficult to guess what her treatment preferences might be. Her avoidant, dependent, and borderline personality traits suggest that she may see me, the therapist, in differing lights on different days. Similarly, her role in treatment will also likely change from session to session, from dependent (wanting a savior) to covertly or even overtly defiant (wanting a sparring partner.) I therefore think that matching these therapist and treatment variables is less important in Marie's therapy than consistently and genuinely treating her with patience, empathy, and unconditional positive regard (illustrating again the importance of Principles 24–26), despite her anticipated variability in behavioral and interpersonal responses.

Principle 14 states that clients whose preference for religiously or spiritually oriented psychotherapy is accommodated may benefit more from treatment. I am not a spiritually oriented therapist and thus refer such initial inquiries elsewhere, so have little input on this topic. However, I would note that part of establishing a good therapeutic rapport is to be respectful of clients' values, including their discussions of religious beliefs. And after a client initiates discussion of his or her faith, I consider it fair game as a therapeutic resource. Given Phillip's strong Catholic identity, for example, I might ask him if he prays and, if so, suggest prayer as a relaxation tool to incorporate in his antianxiety toolbox. Conversely, I would not likely initiate a discussion of religious beliefs in either Robert's or Marie's treatment but would readily process their broaching of this topic.

Principle 15 states that clients who present with poorer interpersonal functioning may benefit more from therapy if the therapist uses a lower proportion of transference interpretations. Note first that, as a primarily cognitive-behaviorist, I use such interpretations sparingly, if at all. However, to couch it in my language, I may offer a social reality check to a client regarding my observation of how he or she communicates with me based on (possibly erroneous) assumptions about me. Although by definition all three of our socially anxious case examples have some degree of difficulty with social interactions, until recently Phillip has enjoyed fairly positive interpersonal relationships with his wife, some friends, and, presumably, his children. Consistent with this principle, I might effectively use my permutation of transference interpretations with Phillip. For example, if he voices an assumption of my negative perception of him, we could explore this belief as a possible distorted cognition, working to identify concrete evidence for or against it.

Robert, however, has had more difficulty in the area of interpersonal functioning (no close friendships or romantic relationships), and it is true that I would likely shy away from offering commentary on our relationship to him, especially early in treatment. My gut feeling is that he would dismiss such interpretations as "psycho-mumbo-jumbo," resulting in hampering, versus helping, to build our alliance. However, I can easily imagine Robert at some point blaming me (or, in a more veiled comment, "this psychotherapy" in general) for his perceived lack of therapy progress. In such an instance, he may benefit from carefully worded feedback on how this dynamic reflects his thinking in general. I've found that introducing such an interpretation with a mildly humorous/self-deprecating approach sometimes works well: "Not to sound too much like a psychologist, but do you think that perhaps your accusation about me sounds a little like when you blame your boss for your problems at work? Or your girlfriend for the break-up?"

Conversely, my planned treatment approach with Marie is inconsistent with Principle 15, in that explicit discussion of our therapeutic relationship is anticipated to be a central component of our work *because* she demonstrates poor interpersonal functioning. Her borderline personality traits predict that she will likely develop alternately positive and negative transferences toward me over time. Openly discussing such transferential reactions would be a vehicle to teach Marie more effective management of these reactions that cause her such pain in other relationships. This concept is also supported by Principle 27, which states that clients who experience alliance rupture–repair episodes may benefit more from psychotherapy. Indeed, in her initial treatment formulation, I predicted to Marie that we may well experience difficulties in our relationship, but that these bumps could be overcome; more important, she could learn from this process more effective ways to deal with tensions in other relationships. I believe that effective behavioral change in overcoming Marie's social anxiety will only occur after this work is done—otherwise, we would just be trying to build a solid house on a shaky foundation.

For example, I might say, "Marie, we've talked before about my reactions to you being a way for you to learn how other people in your life might feel about you. I've also told you and I hope that I've demonstrated that I care about you. With that in mind, I think it's important to tell you that I'm feeling frustrated with your recent behavior—and I'm guessing you might feel the same about me. You say you are interested in my perspectives and that you want to change. But last session when I suggested that Mark may have reacted negatively to your overdependence on him, seeing you as too clingy, it felt to me like you shut me down, when you quickly changed the subject. Then, you canceled your next two scheduled sessions. And today, when I attempted to bring up the topic again, I noticed your voice tone shift from pleasant to annoyed. Can you see why I might be frustrated by these behaviors? . . . And, can you share with me how you are feeling about my frustration? . . . And, what should we do about this?"

Principle 17 suggests that clients with externalizing coping styles (e.g., impulsivity, social gregariousness, emotional lability, external blame for problems) may benefit more from psychotherapy that is more focused on behavior change and symptom reduction, rather than treatment focused on fostering insight and self-awareness. Again, elements of this principle are congruent with my earlier discussions of Robert, who certainly meets at least some of the criteria of being an externalizer, including his impulsivity, aggressive tendencies (especially when intoxicated), and external blame. Most clients are motivated to enter psychotherapy to reduce symptoms, and they assume, at least on a subconscious level, that it will occur by some behavioral change. Given Robert's questionable treatment motivation, I would try to engage him in the treatment process as soon as possible by teaching him effective behaviors to reduce his anxious symptoms. This concrete approach, and a general avoidance of insight-oriented discussions, would also serve to minimize his assumed negative bias about psychologically laden concepts.

Conversely, Principle 18 states that clients with internalizing coping styles (e.g., indecisiveness, introspection, and overcontrol) may benefit more from psychotherapy focused on fostering insight and self-awareness versus behavioral change and symptom reduction. Phillip appears to be a classic internalizer, with his described indecision about work and marital issues and his ruminations about perceived social gaffes and others' views of him. However, my treatment plan for Phillip does not follow this principle: It is focused less on fostering insight and self-awareness (though does so, to some degree, by teaching him to evaluate distorted self-cognitions) and more on symptom reduction via cognitive and behavioral change. My clinical sense is that if our focus was instead more on *thinking* (increasing self-awareness) and less on *doing*, we would only be reinforcing his unhelpful tendencies to ruminate and avoid effective behavioral change.

Marie exhibits a mixture of externalizing and internalizing traits. She is certainly impulsive in her relationships and emotionally labile, but she is also indecisive (about interests, career goals, and therapy) and introspective. Consistent with Principles 17 and 18, my therapeutic approach with Marie involves elements of both insight-oriented therapy (e.g., exploring her internal reactions to toward our anticipated relationship tensions) and behavioral change (e.g., role plays of prosocial skills). As this discussion of all three of the cases illustrates, I see behavioral change as a primary therapeutic focus and goal for all of my clients, as supported by the final treatment-based Principle 38, which notes that when a therapist selectively and responsively fosters more behavioral change, clients will benefit more broadly.

Principle 19 states that clients with greater impairment and fewer social supports will benefit more from psychotherapy when it addresses their social or medical needs. This "medical needs" reference caught me off guard—again using Maslow's (1943) framework, it seems self-evident that if a client has unmet medical issues negatively impacting his or her physical health, they need to be addressed first and foremost. Certainly, if I identify or suspect a client has unaddressed health issues, I strongly encourage him or her to have them examined. For example, Robert's long-term alcohol abuse may have caused or contributed to as yet unidentified physical health concerns, and I would likely encourage him to get regular physicals—and to be honest in sharing his level of alcohol use with his physician. I also agree with the importance of shoring up clients' social support systems when they are underdeveloped; over time, I hope that these individuals will become my replacement! Indeed, my treatment plans for all three clients include this focus. Phillip already has a relatively better support system than the others, although the quality of these relationships has declined in recent years due to his social anxiety with partial agoraphobia and his depressive withdrawal. Our job with Phillip thus entails revitalizing these relationships, via assertiveness training and social interaction challenges.

Robert, conversely, has a very limited support system, apparently consisting at this point solely of somewhat distant relationships with his two brothers. In my mind, developing and maintaining more meaningful, two-way connections with his brothers, as well as other supportive friendships and eventually a healthy romantic partnership, are thus important therapy goals. Elements of Robert's treatment plan are designed to assist his gradual development of such positive relationships, including reframing distorted negative thoughts of peers' perceptions and graduated challenges for increased social interaction while employing subtle in vivo skills, such as deep breathing, to manage his social anxiety.

Marie's current support system apparently consists only of her parents. Even then, although they provide practical support via housing, her limited comments about them suggest that they may not be emotionally supportive. She has struggled to establish healthy friendships and romantic partnerships, but despite "yearning to be with others," she currently finds herself alone, with no romantic connections and in an isolated job at the library while taking college classes part-time (thus limiting her identity as a student). Of the three cases, Marie's treatment plan focuses the most on building healthy relationships, first using our therapy relationship as a model, then creating internal templates for healthy friendships and romantic interactions, and later using role plays to both practice and evaluate her emotional responses to healthy interpersonal communications.

The final moderating principle (Principle 20) suggests that clients with problematic substance use are equally likely to benefit from a psychotherapist with or without his or her own history of substance abuse. Being fortunate to have never experienced problematic substance use, my personal frame of reference is that of a therapist without such issues. Honestly, I sometimes question if this lack of experience puts me at a disadvantage with clients like Robert. I hope, though, that in working with him over time I would learn his behavioral patterns and thus might detect inconsistencies in them that indicate changes in his alcohol use. But, reversing the old adage of "You can't bullshit a bullshitter," I do sometimes wonder if I accurately discern when a substance-abusing client is leading me astray about his or her use. This point provides another justification for placing the responsibility on the client to self-monitor and manage his or her own substance use. I might openly state to Robert that I have no way to know if he is being truthful with me about his alcohol intake, but that it doesn't really matter. He is the one who will ultimately decide his most healthy usage, but I hope he will do so with his eyes open, being honest with himself about his use and its impact on his life. Despite these efforts, if his treatment progress stalls in this area, I may well refer him, at least for this issue, to a therapist specializing in substance abuse.

Principle 21 deals with client process and states that clients who more actively participate in the process of treatment benefit more. Active participation includes such behaviors as showing up reliably for sessions and completing homework assignments between them. I often remind clients that our one hour of work per week will *not* change their lives; for effective gain, they need to incorporate insights discovered and techniques learned in session into their daily lives. Clearly this principle overlaps with our earlier discussion of a client's motivation for treatment, but it focuses on the practical implementation of his or her desire for change, which may legitimately be thwarted by everyday responsibilities or may be subconsciously sabotaged by a client's vague excuses.

Phillip is described as working long hours and also having family responsibilities. I would attempt to be respectful of this busy schedule, discussing openly with him how to reasonably make time for therapy assignments within it. For example, the first relaxation technique I typically teach clients is deep breathing, and I explicitly inform them how quick it is to practice and implement. I might suggest as Phillip's first homework assignment practicing this technique for about two minutes per day, while he is lying in bed at night before going to sleep. I might also ask him to estimate how many minutes he spends per day in ruminative worry about his social anxiety, suggesting he times these thought episodes if he doesn't know. Then, I would challenge him to spend the same or less time daily practicing cognitive reframing techniques learned in session.

Although he has more free time, Robert is anticipated to be more resistant to actively participating both within and between sessions due to his limited motivation for therapy. If I judged him to be receptive at the moment, I might gently suggest that such lack of active participation may have contributed to his earlier therapy's failure. Examples of indications that Robert might be receptive to such an intervention would include his commenting on "not wanting therapy to be a waste of time" or his stating, "I don't get how seeing you an hour a week is going to change my life." As with Phillip, I would educate him about the value of incorporating treatment strategies into his daily life. But given my overall theme with Robert of having him assume responsibility for his treatment, I might ask him to propose how many minutes per day he is willing to engage in practicing skills outside of sessions and then work with him to tailor homework assignments to fit this schedule—if he proposes even two minutes, I have the first task of deep breathing practice ready and waiting. Especially in cases such as Robert, with his notable treatment resistance, it is essential to follow up in the next session on how the homework assignment went. This check-in will allow us to either explore and hopefully resolve barriers to even attempting the assignment (as is so often the case) or to tweak the assignment if he attempted, but had difficulty completing, it. But, just as important, checking in will demonstrate to Robert my respect for the time he spent outside of session, serving to reinforce his future homework efforts.[5]

Marie's demonstrated ambivalence about treatment and her general indecisiveness suggest that she may also have difficulty actively participating in treatment. Further, she will likely (and accurately) see our therapy work on relationships, including our own, as threatening and difficult, which predicts she may attempt to deflect focus from this topic. I believe that actively engaging Marie in treatment, including helping her to stick with difficult topics during sessions and apply concepts learned between them, is paramount to her

---

[5]For reasons I can't fully clarify (but which often include a client jumping into some new treatment topic as soon as he or she walks in the door) and even while I recognize its importance, I often have trouble remembering to check on clients' homework experiences. To help remind me to do so, I added a standard "homework" line in my self-designed fill-in-the-blank psychotherapy transaction note, which I review immediately prior to a client's next session. Additionally, I put a sticky-note stating "Check on homework!" on the outside of the client's folder, which sits next to me during sessions.

treatment success. But maintaining her active engagement will require a delicate balance of reassurance, unconditional positive regard, and expressed and/or implied confidence on my part that we are headed in the right direction (i.e., working toward her long-term treatment goals of decreased social anxiety and rewarding relationships).

Principle 28 focuses on the therapeutic relationship. It states that when therapists use more supportive self-disclosures, clients may benefit more from psychotherapy than when they use fewer or no such disclosures. Let me say first in this regard that I am one of the least self-disclosing therapists that I know, particularly as related to information about my personal life and my activities outside of work. (As discussed throughout this chapter, I differentially view limited self-disclosures of my emotional reactions to the client as the distinct—and sometimes very effective—circumstance of a social reality check.) For whatever reasons, the discussions in graduate school of therapeutic self-disclosure as potentially damaging to the work of therapy have stuck with me more than many other topics. And, after many years of work as a therapist in a small town (where clients inevitably end up knowing each other and comparing notes about their therapist—sometimes in the waiting room!), this tendency has been reinforced. I cannot guarantee that what I share with one client will not be heard (possibly misstated or out of context) by another. Having clarified this bias, I do believe that disclosing limited personal information can be helpful in *some* situations.

For example, I might share with Robert that I sometimes use deep-breathing exercises at night when I have difficulty falling asleep, as a way to normalize this technique. However, I would be unlikely to disclose any personal information with Marie, though her borderline traits suggest that she may well pull for it. My explanations for this lack of disclosure, which I would review in some detail with Marie when she quite possibly challenges my reticence in this area, include (a) I think our therapy efforts will be best focused on her; (b) I don't wish to lead her in any particular direction by my life choices—we need to help her establish her own life direction; and (c) as a private person and to respect the privacy of others in my personal life, my preference is to keep my personal and professional lives separate. Of course, given our therapy's focus on relationship development, I would need to check with Marie about how she feels when I rebuff such questions about my personal life (however nicely)—an excellent opportunity for possible alliance rupture and repair (Principle 27).

Finally, we move on to consider principles of therapeutic change that focus on specific treatment interventions. Principle 29 states that when psychotherapists use a higher proportion of general psychodynamic interpretations (those that are not transference interpretations), clients may benefit more from therapy. Again, having a primarily cognitive-behaviorist orientation, I do not often consciously think about offering psychodynamic interpretations but likely do so at times, translated into my cognitive language. For example, when I discuss with Phillip the likely origins of his distorted negative cognitions as being his mother's overprotectiveness and his father's criticisms of him, this is an interpretation. And I do believe it would be helpful to provide him this feedback; I have found that clients seem to have an intrinsic need to understand the causes of their behaviors. (This belief seems very consistent with Principle 35, which notes that if a therapist selectively and responsively fosters more self-understanding, the client will benefit more broadly from therapy.) But as I would further remind Phillip, his childhood causes are no longer present in his adult life (or if they are, as an adult he can choose to dismiss them), freeing him to change his current behaviors.

As previously discussed, in my ongoing efforts to ally with Robert, I would be more cautious offering any form of interpretation, suspecting his resistance to hearing such "psycho-mumbo-jumbo." However, even with Robert, occasional interpretive comments would likely creep in, as exemplified by my pointing out to him his behavioral commitment to therapy (i.e., although family and friends encouraged his entry into treatment, he is choosing to remain in it). On the other hand, given her emotional lability and contradictory behaviors, I see Marie's therapy as ripe for interpretations, though I would be cautious in offering too many too close together, so as not to overwhelm her. Examples of general interpretive comments that could be beneficial for Marie include suggesting that (a) her exaggerated beliefs regarding others' negative reactions are reflective of her own poor self-esteem, and (b) her erratic on–off again relationships may be caused *by*, rather than be the cause *of*, her own chronic emotional roller-coaster ride.

Principle 30 states that clients may benefit more from treatment when therapists use higher quality psychodynamic interpretations—that is, interpretations that are accurate and focus on each client's central interpersonal themes. I have learned to listen to a client's story carefully to float an accurate interpretation. That is, although I may think I have a brilliant interpretation, I typically tend to hold back for a while, looking for confirmatory evidence in additional client statements, before presenting it. This approach seems particularly important in Robert's case, supporting my efforts to be genuine and present myself as authentically interested in him and his individual worldview.

Despite such efforts, in my own clinical experience some of my interpretations are of lesser quality than others. But such therapeutic misses are not disastrous—they can be corrected. Relatively less resistant clients, such as Phillip and Marie, will typically tell me if my interpretations are inaccurate or off-base—either directly or via nonverbal communications such as a blank stare (Phillip) or more passive-aggressively sighing and/or eye-rolling (Marie). I would then use this feedback to check in with them, eliciting their differing interpretations or themes of importance and altering my treatment course accordingly. (Such an approach also has the side benefit for our anxious clients of my modeling of how to handle inevitable interpersonal errors without undue anxiety.)

The next two principles are complementary: Principle 31 supports the tenet that clients whose therapists receive feedback on a routinely delivered outcome measure may benefit more from psychotherapy than those whose therapists doesn't receive such feedback, while Principle 32 indicates that clients who themselves receive feedback about their therapy performance may have better treatment outcomes. Having had the good fortune to previously participate in a practice–research network study that explored these very issues, I have personal experience with these concepts (Castonguay et al., 2010). Based on that experience, I will first note that it is difficult to solicit structured feedback from clients, a challenge mitigated somewhat if the outcome measure is matter-of-factly introduced at the start of treatment, presented as a normal part of therapy, and its completion is not requested too often—maybe once every two to three months. Even then, it takes time from treatment for clients to complete the measure.

As a balance to these concerns, my experience is consistent with Principle 32—clients do seem to appreciate and benefit from efforts to determine their responses to treatment. In addition to sharing with them my subjective impressions of their progress, or lack thereof, another mechanism to accomplish this feedback is by the repeated use over time of objective tests such as self-report measures of depression or anxiety or formalized treatment outcome assessments. Considering our cases, I could see Phillip responding well to such objective feedback regarding his lessening severity and/or frequency of social anxiety symptoms over time, which could also be used as a way to challenge his initial belief that he cannot change. Similarly, learning that his anxiety symptoms have improved may reinforce Robert's treatment efforts; I could also use this documented success to emphasize his successful personal control over his life outcomes (e.g., "Great job, Robert—look at how your anxiety score has started to come down over the past three months! That is due to *your* efforts.") And with Marie, who expressed low expectations for treatment success at the start of treatment, I might suggest using objective measurement of her progress as a way to either support or refute these expectations.

In addition to providing feedback about treatment progress to Phillip, Robert, and Marie, the results of such measurement tools would simultaneously provide me feedback regarding the efficacy of my therapy strategies; if little or no positive behavioral or emotional change is identified, I may need to re-evaluate my treatment plan(s). Alternately, I might interpret a demonstrated lack of change, or even deterioration, in functioning as being due to client variables (e.g., "Unfortunately, Marie, your social anxiety scores actually went up over the past two months, after initially going down in the initial round of test results. Can you point to any significant differences in your life during the past two months that may have increased this anxiety? Do you think that your sudden decision to end the friendship with Megan last month might have impacted the change?" and, if so, "What can we learn from your situation with Megan to help you negotiate future relationships with an outcome of less anxiety?")

Principle 33 states that a client may benefit more from therapy when his or her therapist is more flexible in adherence to a given treatment approach. My clinical experience does back this claim—effective psychotherapy follows the client's needs, not a textbook. Although I have referred to myself in this chapter as *primarily* a cognitive-behaviorist, we have seen that Phillip's treatment plan, for example, also includes an early focus on increasing his self-awareness regarding his anxious self not being a permanent state of being, certainly a humanistic perspective. Similarly, Robert's proposed therapy includes a strong emphasis on developing his sense of his free will, another humanistic concept, while his treatment is simultaneously couched in a person-centered treatment approach emphasizing genuineness and empathy. And, finally, with our exploration of the therapy relationship, including her transference (and likely my countertransference) reactions, Marie's treatment plan clearly includes more of a psychodynamic bent but also incorporates the humanistic component of increasing her self-awareness of her own values regarding healthy interpersonal relationships.[6]

Another perspective on this principle of change is to understand that therapy will likely be more effective if the therapist avoids being rigid in promoting an intervention or pushing an agenda to which the client is unreceptive. I will often repeat an interpretation or suggested course of action that a client has not initially responded to, especially if I believe it will be particularly helpful. Sometimes we need to hear an idea more than once before it takes hold in our minds. But there also comes a point when we need to back off, heeding the client's overt or covert resistance to accepting an intervention. If we do not, we risk alienating the client by demonstrating our inability to listen carefully or to accept his or her view of the issue. There may also be important, new

---

[6] I have been asked by this volume's editors to elucidate my decision-making on when I would adhere to a treatment approach and/or theoretical orientation versus under which circumstances I would choose to be more flexible and change my therapeutic approach. After much deliberation on providing a reply to this request, I realize that I simply don't have clear rules in my head about when I make this switch—for me, it's one of those times in life (and therapy) when you can't put a concept into words, but "you know it when you see it." I will say that I believe I've gotten better over the years at intuitively (or experientially?) knowing when the switch will be beneficial to the therapeutic work.

therapeutic information to be learned from the client's resistance. For example, I might repeatedly suggest to Robert the social experiment of the phone call to his brother, as detailed previously. And even though he might agree each time to make that call, when I check in each subsequent session, I might learn he has not completed it, offering various excuses. If I back away from that assignment and instead explore with him what such a telephone call means to him, he might share that his father once berated him mercilessly when, as a child, he called home from camp because he was homesick.

Another therapist intervention principle (Principle 34) suggests that when a therapist selectively and responsively fosters more adaptive interpersonal change, the client may benefit more broadly from treatment. Clearly, my treatment plans for the case examples support this principle. As I am fond of saying to my clients, unless you are a hermit living on a deserted island, you do not live in an isolated vacuum; rather, your life satisfaction and meaning is greatly dependent upon positive human interactions. Therefore, assuming the client doesn't have them, or enough of them, I see healthy interpersonal relationships as a central goal in most therapies, a broader perspective than most clients' initial referral focus of symptom reduction. Phillip, for example, has enjoyed positive interpersonal relationships in the past, but these relationships, especially his marriage, are now eroding. So, while his initial referral problem is reduction of social anxiety symptoms, clearly a major benefit to achieving this goal will be his more relaxed, thus improved, interpersonal functioning. But, in a reciprocal process, improving his interpersonal relationships will likely also foster his further symptom reduction. That is, shoring up his relationship with his wife, then gradually renewing some friendships, will provide him both social support (Principle 19) and real-life participants for practicing combined relaxation and prosocial skills (e.g., deep breathing plus assertiveness) learned in therapy. Needless to say, the use of such relaxation and assertiveness training strategies, in addition to encouraging his gradually increase in leisure activities with others, not only reflect the implementation of Principle 34, but also of Principle 38 (fostering behavioral changes).

Robert's treatment also includes elements that simultaneously combine adaptive interpersonal and behavioral changes; in his case, these changes first involve (via relaxation skill building and social skills training) establishing relationships that are more meaningful than his current work acquaintances and emotionally distant connections with his brothers. Whereas his initial presentation again focused more on symptom reduction, there are signs of this client's dissatisfaction with his lack of close relationships—Robert acknowledged that his anger and distrust make it unlikely he will find another girlfriend, and he wished his brothers would initiate contact more often. Our treatment plan thus includes his gradual behavioral change of increasing social interaction, first manifest by reaching out to his brothers to initiate low-threat social activity (see implementation of Principle 10 for more details). Another important component of this strategy is for Robert (initially, with my guidance) to then deliberately evaluate the success or challenges he experiences in other such efforts, with a goal of developing healthier interpersonal skills. Similarly, the alcohol intake experiments I described earlier in the case formulation and treatment plan section include evaluating the quality of his interactions with others—as well as fluctuations in his depression, sleep, and weight—while using more or less alcohol.

Due to her personality disorder traits that, by definition, lead to problems in this area, Marie's proposed therapy includes an even more direct focus on improving her interpersonal functioning. As previously discussed, one therapeutic strategy I would anticipate is the processing of our relationship "bumps" and then later using this work as a model for easing or avoiding tensions in other relationships. Similarly, helping Marie early on to clarify her values about what a healthy friendship or romantic relationship looks like would then be used as a template in improving her current and future interpersonal functioning (e.g., "Marie, you've told me before that an important value for you in a friendship is honesty. If that's so, how do you think that your decision to keep information from Lisa is going to impact that friendship?").

As with Philip and Robert, I would also rely on cognitive-behavioral interventions to foster Marie's interpersonal and behavioral change (Principles 34 and 38). I would likely first use in-session role plays to practice prosocial techniques and explore her emotional responses to such efforts. Additional likely areas of focus would be on (a) the development of, and then consistent work toward, a career goal, to provide Marie an increased sense of life meaning and satisfaction, and (b) working toward individuating from her parents, including moving out of their home and away from their presumed long-standing and nonsupportive, if not negative, influences on her.

As I previously mentioned, Principle 35 regarding self-understanding is consistent with my observation that clients need to make sense of the causes of their problems. I believe that psychoeducation and interpretation can be helpful because they provide a rationale, hopefully a credible one, to explain what may have led to and what may maintain client difficulties. As illustrated in each of the three cases' treatment plans, however, I aim to foster new self-understanding by increasing client awareness of negative thoughts, faulty information processing, and maladaptive schema and then by challenging these cognitions—such as Philip's belief that social anxiety is an unchangeable core aspect of who he is, as well as his negative self-attributions, Robert's patterns of mind reading and his external locus of control, and Marie's exaggerated beliefs about others' reaction to her.

Treatment-focused Principle 36 notes that if a therapist selectively and responsively fosters more emotional experiencing and/or deepening, the client will benefit more broadly from therapy. I see this principle as applicable for some clients, but not others. For example, I question if Phillip would benefit from experiencing more emotional distress than he already does. It would appear that his current levels of anxiety and depression have already been effective in motivating him for treatment and can be referred to, if necessary, to continue motivating him to make difficult but necessary behavioral changes to his socially anxious cognitions and behaviors. Similarly, Marie overemotes already, and I do not believe she would benefit from emotional deepening. Conversely, I see her treatment being more focused on emotional regulation in response to the perceived slights of others and working toward calm consistency in emotional experience versus her current lability.

However, I do see benefits of applying this principle to Robert's case. In particular, I might educate him about his (externalized) anger being a secondary emotion that serves a protective purpose of limiting his experience of underlying (internalized) primary emotions of depression and anxiety. His anger thus not only serves to cover/limit his emotional pain but also contributes to blaming others for his issues and can practically get him into trouble when acted out, as may well occur when mixed with alcohol. As a way of beginning to acknowledge these more painful emotions, I would then ask him to estimate what proportion of his anger he thinks is due to underlying depression versus anxiety. The primary goal of this emotional deepening in Robert's case would be to motivate his adherence to treatment in general, as well as to specific cognitive-behavioral change strategies suggested. A secondary benefit would be to facilitate his acceptance of more personal responsibility for his emotions, thus his behaviors. However, Robert's generalized treatment resistance will make employing this technique tricky, risking damage to our therapeutic alliance. I would thus likely begin such discussions only well after a positive therapeutic relationship is established and, even then, in response to Robert introducing the specific topic of his anger.

Final Reflections

My final task is to look back on my review of the 38 principles of therapeutic change, revisiting my initial assumptions that all of the client prognostic principles and most of the client process, therapy relationship, and therapy intervention principles seemed to be stating obvious and intuitive truths, whereas a number of the treatment/provider moderating principles appeared counterintuitive. Taking myself off autopilot and more carefully considering these principles by applying them to Phillip, Robert, and Marie's treatments, I have discovered that whereas some of my initial assumptions held true for these clients, others did not. Specifically, contrary to my initial prediction, I ended up disagreeing with four of the nine client prognostic variables (Principles 3 and 7–9). Also, in opposition with my initial assumptions, I only disagreed with two treatment/provider principles and then only when applied to some clients (Principle 15 with Marie; Principle 18 with Phillip). As initially predicted, I did agree, and helpfully applied, both client process principles and all but one of the therapy relationship principles, Principle 28 (dismissed due to my general, but not absolute, avoidance of self-disclosures in treatment). Finally, as initially assumed in considering the therapist intervention principles of change, I also only disagreed with one, Principle 29, again due to my general lack of use of psychodynamic interpretations with clients. However, I did deem one other to be self-evident and therefore not very useful (Principle 30) and one more to be helpful only in one of three cases (Principle 36.)

I have determined from this analysis that putting additional careful thought into treatment planning via consideration of this volume's outlined principles of therapeutic change would lead to richer and ultimately more therapeutic clinical interventions and, thus, potentially better treatment outcomes for Phillip, Robert, and Marie. Taken more broadly, my personal conclusion is that I, and my real-life clients, may well benefit if I make the effort to make my treatment decisions more conscious via consideration of many of these principles of change.

References

Castonguay, L. G., Boswell, J. F., Zack, S. E., Baker, S., Boutselis, M. A., Chiswick, N. R., ... Holtforth, M. G. (2010). Helpful and hindering events in psychotherapy: A practice research network study. *Psychotherapy, 47,* 327–344.

Maslow, A. H. (1943). A theory of human motivation. *Psychological Review, 50*(4), 370–396.

Norcross, J. C., Krebs, P. M., & Prochaska, J. O. (2011). Stages of change. *Journal of Clinical Psychology, 67,* 143–154.

Stiles, W. B. (2002). Assimilation of problematic experiences. In J. C. Norcross (Ed.), *Psychotherapy relationships that work: Therapist contributions and responsiveness to patients* (pp. 357–365). New York, NY: Oxford University Press.

11
More Than a Feeling?

Application of Principles of Change to Treatment of Anxiety

Igor Weinberg

The goal of this chapter is to describe how I, as a practicing clinician, might implement a variety of principles of change that have received empirical support. Before doing so, however, it is important for me to present fundamental elements of my understanding and treatment approach to anxiety disorders that provide a conceptual and clinical context to the implementation of these principles.

Writing the chapter brought up a few reactions. I was excited to describe the anticipated course of treatment of the cases and elucidate my own thinking regarding parameters that are likely to make these treatments effective. My own clinical work is guided by a number of principles—some intuitive and some are more explicit. Therefore, the task of thinking about the empirically validated principles described in this book made me want to explicate my own clinical thinking about the treatment of anxiety disorders. I will describe them in the following discussion.

Using treatment principles, rather than session-by-session protocols to guide treatment allows for a flexible approach that is both adherent to these treatment principles and compatible with complex clinical situations. In fact many of the empirically supported therapies for complicated clinical cases, such as dialectical behavior therapy (DBT), are principle-based.

In my discussion of the cases, I will describe a few principles of assessment and treatment that I find helpful in the treatment of anxiety disorders. In these cases, similar to many others in my clinical practice, anxiety does not appear alone. Commonly, it appears as an unwelcome concomitant of other difficulties, and many times it is the ultimate reason that the patient presents to treatment. In other words, anxiety adds an element of unbearable anguish to the patient's suffering that leads the patient to finally seek treatment—sometimes after years of help rejection and denial. Acute personal distress and pervasive avoidance that progressively reinforce each other and trap the patient in an intolerable state are the Phobos and Deimos of anxiety disorders. Like the two moons of Mars, they are present wherever anxiety disorder is. Not only, then, is anxiety a target of treatment, but it is also a motivating factor for change. Productively using anxiety can help engage the patient in collaborative work on the reasons that led to anxiety.

Yet another aspect of treatment of anxiety disorders helps to guide my thinking. That is, their dynamics, meaning, and treatment change depending on characteristics of the patient, such as demographic factors, co-morbid conditions, personality, and cognitive style. Although anxiety is easily identified by the patient as the reason for treatment, it requires thorough assessment of these contextual factors and careful consideration of interventions and priorities. Fortunately, as the following discussion illustrates, some of the contextual factors are addressed by a particular cluster of principles of change (i.e., client prognostic principles). In some cases, anxiety might have to be conceptualized in the context of other aspects of pathology that receive higher priority in treatment. Risks of iatrogenic effects of treatment on anxiety also need to be taken into account. Iatrogenesis can result from styles of interventions (i.e., hyperfocusing on discussion of anxiety), inadequate interventions (i.e., not challenging the cognitions that maintain anxiety), or misguided conceptualization of the problem (i.e., treating anxiety as a primary problem and ignoring the actual cause of it). Finally, another principle that guides my clinical work is that I usually start treatment with assessment and then use my assessment to put together all clinically important information in a concise formulation that helps me decide regarding the recommended treatment as well as anticipate various treatment responses.

Let's turn to the clinical material and see how the treatment and assessment exemplifies important clinical principles described in this book.

Case 1

Case Formulation and Treatment Plan

I usually find it helpful to start treatment by setting a frame. In the case of Philip, I would start with carefully listening to what he wants to accomplish and what he expects from treatment. Growing up in an immigrant family, he is likely to have adopted a style of deferring to the person in the position of authority. Instead, a successful treatment will be sensitive to his experiences and wishes and will encourage his own sense of agency—becoming an authority over his anxiety. Anticipating Philip's sensitivity to power differential in life and, therefore in therapy, it is helpful to adopt an egalitarian collaborative stance. This can be accomplished by taking a genuine interest in Philip's life story and experiences, disclosing personal reactions to his life history and inquiring about his experiences in therapy—requesting feedback and making adjustments if appropriate. From this perspective, coming up with a case formulation and accurate diagnostic assessment is critical to "not missing" what is unique about Philip.

Let's start with the diagnostic case formulation. A number of features make Philip's social anxiety diagnosis presentation quite typical. Clinically, Philip presents with discomfort around others, anxiety around meetings, fear of negative evaluations, and avoidance of personal interactions with most others outside of his family and close friends. History of overprotection in childhood is typical as well, though the history of assignment of a caregiver role is more unique to Philip's past. His somewhat dependent attitude toward others is also a typical characteristic of people with social anxiety disorder. Interestingly, once he became a caregiver as an adult—once his son was born—he became depressed and agoraphobic, as if he could not tolerate being cast in this role again. In contrast to being a caregiver, his functioning at work is plagued by lack of assertiveness and ambition. Whereas lack of assertiveness is typical of someone diagnosed with social anxiety disorder, it is also likely to carry additional meanings. Philip has already been "promoted" once as a child into a caregiver and learned to resent that role. So—not again! Unfortunately, inhibition of ambition comes with a price of remaining in a submissive, inferior role. In this way, he remains dependent on others, which satisfies his need for dependence. A goal of my treatment with Philip would be to help him recognize how his upbringing predisposed him to avoid ambition, fear promotion, and resent caregiving roles, which led to inhibitions, as well as agoraphobia and depression as a way to avoid the experience and expression of anger.

However, it is not possible to fully understand this case without taking into account cultural aspects—coming from an immigrant family. This part of his life will still have strong implications for treatment even if the therapist shares his background. The unspoken part of his history stems from him growing up in an immigrant family and, possibly, having experienced typical hardships related to financial, cultural, and value differences with the "dominant culture." One possible outcome is developing an internal conflict between the family orientation of his family of origin and the push toward self-reliance by the US culture. We do not know what his fantasies or expectations were regarding finding his own place within both cultures. Was he experiencing one culture as inferior, and another as superior? One "dominant" culture and another "passive?" One culture that prioritizes ambition, and another one, family? One culture that prioritizes individual needs, and another, the needs of others? While growing up, not only did Philip have to deal with all of the struggles of an immigrant family and had to take care of his siblings, but also he had to reconcile these questions and dilemmas.

These dilemmas are possible reasons to become socially anxious, to feel different, to actually be different, and to worry about acceptance of and evaluation by others. Philip's life story makes me wonder if being responsible and doing "the right thing" is a central value for him. This creates an important conflict between being responsible, on one hand, and following his heart, on the other. In addition, conflicts between his wishes and family wishes, as well as his needs and family needs, are apparent. Growing up he learned to prioritize family over personal and career needs. However, both "society" and his wife expect him to make his career and ambition a higher priority. This must be confusing, to say the least! Is social anxiety, then, an adaptive response of a person from a subdominant culture to the dominant culture? Is it also an adaptive way to survive in culture with different value systems? In other words, anxiety allowed him to maintain vigilance about differences between him and the society in terms of values, priorities, and needs and in such a way not make assumptions about others based on his own experiences. These considerations are helpful in guiding the treatment and in validating meanings of the social anxiety in Philip's life. Another aspect of the case is a significant family/couple component that might actually require separate intervention. Both Philip and Christina share a cultural background though the acculturation process may have affected them differently.

In my opinion, it is critically important to structure this treatment around a treatment relationship that is sensitive to Philip's upbringing and to his current issues. Such a relationship will offer him an opportunity to explore his relationship with the dominant culture and authority figures. It will also offer him a new type of a relationship where repetitions of old patterns can be acknowledged and new patterns can be learned and "rehearsed." Acknowledging inherent power differences, cultural differences, and limits to mutual understanding of these experiences is important. This is likely to run counter to Philip's prior experiences where differences were not discussed and negotiated but unconditionally and silently accepted, and his subjectivity was suppressed in service of family survival. Once a trusting, genuine, and collaborative relationship is established, I might decide to incorporate behavioral assignments, such exposure exercises or assertiveness training. Framing these interventions as an opportunity, not a requirement, is yet another way in which the therapist will account for the inherent power differential in a treatment like this one.

Implementation of Principles of Change

Let's go back to the principles discussed in the book and see what they have to say about the prognosis. The first cluster of empirically based principles relate to prognostic considerations. What is a likely outcome of therapy for Philip? The following characteristics increase the chances of a good outcome: an only moderate level of baseline impairment (Principle 1), high therapy outcome expectation (Principle 4), high intrinsic motivation (Principle 5), high readiness for change (Principle 6), and middle-class status (Principle 7). These are some of the strengths that Philip brings into therapy. These strengths allow treatment to take a change-oriented direction and become the foundation for the previously outlined treatment goals: exploration of important relationships in his life, development of a new relationship with others, and successful engagement in behavioral assignments.

However, other factors decrease his chances for improvement: insecure attachment (Principle 3), difficult childhood (Principle 8), and high level of negative self-attributions (Principle 9). How can these obstacles be addressed? In my opinion, and as I demonstrate in the following discussion, these difficulties are best understood in terms of development of his self and attachment in the context of immigration and acculturation stress. Changes in these factors are usually slow and likely to follow the development of a trusting and positive relationship with the therapist. In my opinion, building the foundation for such a positive relationship and fostering its development with the therapist both have a high priority in any effective treatment for Philip. Such treatment is likely to take some time before the problems related to self and attachment can be addressed. Thus, in line with Principle 16, Philip may well derive benefits from long-term treatment, even if he shows a relatively low level of baseline impairment. Furthermore, whereas most intrinsically motivated clients who are ready for change are likely to benefit from a more directive and change-oriented approach (Principles 11 and 12), in case of Philip, it is important to understand the effect of acculturation stress in his development. Considering his internalizing coping style and his moderate level of problem assimilation, he is likely to benefit from interventions aimed at fostering self-awareness and understanding (Principles 18 and 10). Therefore, in line with the principle of flexibility (Principle 33), it will be critical to find balance between nondirective and person-centered interventions (Principles 11 and 12) aimed at fostering positive genuine attachment on the one hand and using exposure-based change-oriented interventions on the other.

As previously mentioned, establishing genuine connection is critical for this treatment (Principle 23). A strong alliance will indeed be necessary for Philip to become actively engaged in the exploratory and action-oriented processes as previously mentioned, which, in turn, may foster his improvement (Principle 21). Therapy, however, runs a risk of becoming a "false" treatment if Philip perceives it as yet another acculturation experience where he has to sacrifice his needs in the service of treatment or treatment protocols. Such risk is inherent in the history of Philip and the power differential between him and the therapist. Put in terms of Principles 21 and 22, how can the therapist maximize the likelihood of Philip's active participation in therapy and minimize the risk of triggering resistance/reactance to it? Treatment has to start with the recognition that the power differential inherent in the treatment relationship, including possible differences in cultural backgrounds between the therapist and patient, are likely to play a role in therapy and could perpetuate the type of dynamics that caused Philip's social anxiety. Moreover, a willingness to consider how such differences are enacted and elaborated by both the therapist and Philip is important (Principle 35). Understanding what are (almost) expected enactments is critical for determining how both Philip and I will contribute to them, how he could understand and change such contribution into other relationships in his life and address possible contribution of others to the perpetuation of his repeated roles from the past. A number of features of treatment might invite "false" engagement and/or create alliance ruptures (Principle 27). First, treatment that prioritizes protocol-based sequences of interventions is likely to invite the perception that this treatment is not designed for Philip but yet another demand with which he must comply. Using general language, devoid of references to personal or subjective aspects of Philip's history, is likely to convey a similar message that his experiences do not matter—contradicting relationship-based principles (working alliance, positive regard, empathy, congruence) and possibly running counter to preference principles (Principles 13 and 14). Using language that introduces treatment interventions as "the truth," or treatment assignments as requirements, is likely to repeat his experience of giving up his authority in service of his external needs. Such processes can be subtle enough that they "trigger" old patterns outside of Philip's awareness. Therefore, the therapist is facing a formidable task of offering treatment that is participatory, genuine, and collaborative (Principles 21 and 22, as well as Principles 23–26, are all relevant to this aim).

During such treatment, it would likely be beneficial to inquire about Philip's experiences, including those related to the therapy and the therapist (Principle 32), as well as to invite him to become more aware of and to embrace his own sense of authority and ownership of his therapy, his past, and the present—thereby fostering his self-understanding and emotional deepening (Principles 35 and 36). During this process, incorporating Philip's language and metaphors and avoiding a formulaic approach is critical. Philp's agency can also be a target of exploration. For example, exploring his childhood can be supplemented with validation of how he preserved (agency) his family values by prioritizing his family over his needs (Principle 26). Identifying how his sense of agency is growing and manifesting itself inside and outside therapy session is another avenue for validation. For example, at some point the therapist might say, "I am noticing that you are pointing out today ways in which I misunderstood you—what's that like?" In line with Principle 27, such intervention aimed at an alliance rupture could be beneficial Philip, above and beyond the repair of the relationship breach.

I usually do not use structured outcome measures to track progress in therapy (Principle 31). In my opinion, while routine measurements generate shared knowledge of progress or lack thereof, it also runs a risk of inviting false compliance in a case like Philip's. My preference would be to track progress through open discussion and through noticing spontaneous examples of progress in therapy. In these cases I would be inclined to share my observations with Philip and ask about his perspective.

Based on Principle 15, the use of transference interpretation is not likely to be detrimental to someone with Philip's level of interpersonal functioning. However, if the therapist decides to offer interpretations (transferential or not), they need to be offered as possibilities, not as ultimate "truths." This is to avoid the risk of "erasing" Philip's personal experience through inaccurate interpretation. Interpretations are better offered as hypotheses, alternative perspectives, or summary statements that restate what Philip has started understanding about himself on his own (Principles 29 and 30). The interpersonal dynamic of *offering* interpretations is important. It is better to offer interpretations that validate what the patient is already becoming aware of during close collaborative exploration. Offering interpretations from an interpersonal distance or about material that has not been explored enough is running the risk of repeating his childhood drama of blind compliance.

Another important consideration in conducting such treatment is offering protocol-based treatments for social anxiety, agoraphobia, or depression. Among the primary focus of these treatments are interventions aimed at fostering adaptive interpersonal and behavioral changes (Principles 34 and 38). Those can be helpful, though they run the risk of perpetuating the same problem that is central to Philip's life—sacrificing one's self to the dominant discourse of culture, family needs, and now treatment protocol. This could run the risk of iatrogenically reinforcing maladaptive solutions. Again, guided by a principle of flexibility (Principle 33), I would rather recommend a treatment approach that capitalizes on helping Philip develop a personalized narrative of his past and present. Such a narrative will help with development of his sense of agency that is so critical in this treatment. Whereas, theoretically speaking, one might expect that in itself such a process will be sufficient for the resolution of his symptoms, I would be cautious in expecting that a single intervention will be sufficient to accomplish such a change. Therefore, in addition to using nondirective, self-understanding, and emotional-deepening interventions (Principles 35–37), I would be prepared to introduce others, including exposure and/or assertiveness training.

At times, such narrative includes an intergenerational past, for which he is a likely "container." In many immigrant families, children become such containers once parents feel that they have immigrated "for the sake of their children." Helping Philip develop his own narrative can help him create some separation between himself and his family of origin, as well as his own family, and to think about various aspects of his acculturation and identity—a process reflecting both an increase of self-understanding and adaptive interpersonal functioning (Principles 35 and 36). Such a process is likely not only to require genuineness, nonjudgment, empathic listening, validation (as captured by Principles 23–26), and appropriately disclosing personal reactions to his life history (Principle 28) but also an openness to learning about cultural aspects of Philip's experiences (which is consistent with Principle 13). However, it is also likely to encounter predictable challenges related to the perception of the cultural affiliation of the therapist. This is likely to lead to re-experiencing feelings of fear and inadequacy on the one hand and anger and desire to emulate the dominant culture on the other hand. At some stage in treatment, a different side of Philip might start to surface. Comparison with the therapist, feelings of jealousy, or contempt are likely signs that he is preparing to explore his own motivation that was suppressed during the acculturation process. It is important to find room for these feelings and to help Philip articulate his own narrative of his life. The hope is that this process will "undo" the suppression of various parts of himself that were cast away as a result of the acculturation process, recognize conflicts related to different values, and put into perspective his struggles growing up in his family of origin. Reflected in this complex therapeutic process are different facets of principles of engagement (Principles 21 and 22) and self-exploration (Principles 35–37).

Such a process is also likely to rely on multiple cycles of repairs of expected ruptures in the therapeutic relationship (Principles 23 and 27). One of the challenges for this therapy is noticing signs of alliance ruptures: missed sessions, distancing in therapy, avoiding feelings, avoiding discussion of vulnerability, and using the therapist's language for personal experience—a parallel to his experiences of eschewing his subjectivity in service of his family. Ability to tactfully bring up these experiences and explore their possible relevance to Philip's perception of misalignment in therapy is critical for therapy progress—not only to repair alliance ruptures but also as an opportunity for increased self-understanding. It should be noted, however, that such misalignment is likely to stem from power differential, subtle demonstration of power, and cultural differences of the therapist. Similarly, misunderstanding of the patient by the therapist or misunderstanding of the therapist by the patient can equally bring about such misalignment. In my experience, it is important to discuss *real contributions of both the therapist and the patient* to these developments. Such discussions can be facilitated by a skillful use of relational, nondirective strategies, self-disclosure, and interpretative interventions (a complex integration of Principles 23–26 and 28–30). In this context, however, interpretations can be perceived as false attempts of the therapist to avoid responsibility, not genuine validation of the real experiences of Philip. It is better to reserve interpretations for a "summary statement" of what the therapist and Philip understand together about these misattunements.

Another possibility for intervention is couples therapy that can be conducted adjunctively. This intervention takes into account the importance of the family values, and it destigmatizes Philip as the "identified patient." Such treatment will need to be conducted within the same frame as the individual therapy, with full recognition of cultural and power differences. As a means to foster adaptive interpersonal functioning (Principle 34), it will also have the advantage of helping the couple co-create a narrative that integrates their personal narratives within a larger narrative of them as a family.

Case 2

Case Formulation and Treatment Plan

Robert presents both diagnostic and treatment challenges. Although at first glance he meets criteria for both social anxiety disorder and alcohol use disorder, moderate to severe, one has to wonder if this is the only way to look at his palpable difficulties. First, he meets criteria for alcohol use disorder because of excessive and regular drinking, unsuccessful attempts to stop drinking, some signs of withdrawal, and clear negative consequences in vocational, social, and romantic relationship realms. The diagnosis of social anxiety is more complicated. At first glance, signs of social anxiety disorder can be easily found in his current clinical presentation, including fear of being judged by others, hypervigilance, avoidance of public activities, and physical signs of anxiety. We are also learning that he gets suicidal due to his social isolation, suggesting the possibility of a co-occurring affective disorder. However, the complexity of this case comes from difficulty ascertaining his diagnoses.

From his history, we know that Robert had social difficulties prior to actual onset of either social anxiety or problematic drinking. Does it mean that social anxiety developed secondary to drinking, social consequences of drinking, and pre-existing social difficulties? In this case, is Robert anxious because he is actually realistically aware that social interactions are not his strengths and, thus, when intoxicated he tends to embarrass himself? Is it, then, a realistic assessment of the consequences of his drinking or, alternatively, his pre-existing personality? Robert is likely to be profoundly embarrassed about his drinking and its disastrous and tragic effects on his life. Socially isolated, he is likely to experience an intense sense of failure and shame around the demise of his romantic life, as well as being on verge of a vocational crisis. These feelings are likely to fuel anxiety in interactions with others, fears of judgment, and further avoidance of interpersonal closeness. His externalizing cognitive style and tendency to externalize responsibility or assign blame to others are not just an impediment to engaging Robert in self-exploration but also in him taking responsibility over his behaviors. When coupled with an intense sense of shame, an externalizing cognitive style leads not only to a tendency to assign blame to others but also to expect shaming responses from others. This is likely to promote hypervigilance and an anxious presentation. Instead of dealing with his own self-shaming process, he expects it to come from outside. Consequently, he describes social anxiety signs, though in the context of his externalizing cognitive style, it is more a sign of projected shame.

The role of alcohol use disorder is hard to overestimate. The first issue to consider is that the co-morbid affective component is not just a result of isolation but also a result of heavy drinking. Pharmacologically speaking, alcohol is a sedative. It produces signs of depression, typically after the initial intoxication or elation stage. This is especially likely in Robert's case, given that he reports a violent transformation of his character during intoxication. Having more pronounced mood changes in response to alcohol, whether depressive or angry in nature, is a sign of progression of alcoholism, suggesting that his addiction has to be taken seriously. Another issue to consider is that given his shame around drinking, Robert is likely to downplay the centrality of his difficulties with alcohol and overly emphasize another problem/disorder. For that reason, the extent to which he actually has social anxiety needs to be ascertained using behavioral and longitudinal observations, as well as collateral information.

The treatment will start with a diagnostic assessment. Once these diagnostic dilemmas are identified, a few considerations will guide the next steps. The first treatment recommendation, in line with Principle 38, is to stop drinking to diagnose and address other difficulties. This recommendation will likely require psychoeducation as to reasons why the clinician strongly believes that treatment will not address social difficulties or "depression/suicidal thinking" without establishing a baseline of sobriety. Robert might need little convincing to agree that alcohol is a problem. However, he might have significant ambivalence in actually quitting the behavior.

The possibility of co-occurring posttraumatic stress disorder (PTSD) needs to be assessed. A history of adversity in childhood, specifically a physically abusive father, suggests that Robert might be using alcohol to medicate PTSD. In this case, asking him to give up alcohol is like asking him to face memories of childhood abuse without any numbing mechanism. It is like facing his abusive father without the protection of his mother—experiences that he had too many times in the past to make room for once again. The possibility of PTSD will require additional careful assessment. If present, a number of treatment options can be offered. PTSD and alcohol use disorder can be addressed concurrently using such procedures as the COPE (Back et al., 2014) protocol or using the Seeking Safety (Najavits, 2001) protocol. COPE incorporates working on traumatic memories (including prolonged exposure to traumatic memories) and on beliefs formed because of trauma. I would recommend this intervention if Robert is capable of tolerating such an intensive treatment focus. Seeking Safety would invite Robert to learn behavioral coping skills to manage the effects of trauma and PTSD symptoms without discussing the traumatic memories directly. It is advised for patients who are not able or willing to work on traumatic memories but still want to learn skills to manage the PTSD symptoms.

Implementation of Principles of Change

As I did in the case of Philip, let's first review factors related to the prognostic principles and derive guidelines to address them in treatment. The following factors decrease his chances for improvement: a significant level of baseline impairment (Principle 1), low therapy outcome expectation (Principle 4), lack of intrinsic motivation (Principle 5), low readiness for change (Principle 6), insecure attachment (Principle 3), difficult childhood (Principle 8), high level of negative self-attributions (Principle 9), and low socio-economic status (Principle 7). Robert's ambivalence about sobriety, minimization of drinking, and externalizing style are main roadblocks to successful treatment. This indicates that his prognosis is poor, making his expected treatment outcome less favorable than Philip's prognosis.

How can these obstacles be addressed? Robert's treatment needs to prioritize alcohol dependence over other treatment targets. Further, given the fragility of his self-esteem, his treatment will require a lot of tactful, well-timed interventions that, over time, have the promise of helping him embrace sobriety. Considering the severity of his alcohol and self-esteem problems and his fairly high level of functional impairment, long-term treatment is indicated (Principle 16). Also, considering his levels of resistance and motivation, Robert is likely to benefit from therapy that is, at least initially, geared toward validation of Robert's experiences, rather than encouraging change (Principle 12), especially if such therapy is nondirective (Principle 11). Especially early in treatment, the use of nondirective and client centered intervention would also be attuned to his relatively low level of problem assimilation (Principle 10). Higher order interventions, such as confrontations, interpretations, or analysis of the treatment relationship need to be avoided—at least initially (Principle 15). Due to his externalizing coping style, therapy is more likely to be successful if it is behaviorally focused (e.g., discussing the effects of drinking) rather than insight-oriented (e.g., discussing personal motives; Principle 17). Similarly, addressing interpersonal functioning seems important given social difficulties that Robert experiences (Principle 19). Consistent with Principle 20, the successful implementation of these diverse principles of change, as well as Robert's treatment in general, is not contingent on whether or not the therapist has a personal history of substance use problems.

As treatment progresses from assessment to therapy, establishing a nonjudgmental, collaborative relationship is central to effectiveness. Relying on the principles inherent to such a relationship (Principles 23-26), motivational interviewing (Miller & Rollnick, 2002) was established as a set of empirically based, interviewing techniques that help many patients with addictions develop motivation to stop using substances. This is a treatment that also meets the definition of a therapy that is likely to benefit Robert at least at earlier stages of treatment (see previous discussion). Motivational interviewing in his case will start with validation of his experiences and decisions related to drinking. Validation does not mean agreement—the therapist will walk a fine line of expressing understanding of Robert's drinking without condoning it. One way to accomplish that is to validate the personal function of drinking: "I understand that you are drinking—it helps you make the depression go away." The goal of validation and reflection is establishing a positive relationship and conveying, in a genuine way, that the clinician understands him. Like most patients with alcohol dependence, Robert displays signs of avoidant attachment, marked by social anxiety, fear of interacting with others, avoidance of others, and negative self-image (Brown & Elliott, 2016). Avoidant attachment suggests that Robert tends to withdraw from others as a strategy to regulate emotional distress. This makes alliance with the therapist more tenuous. For Robert, similar to other patients with substance use disorder, attachment to alcohol feels more powerful than anything else, including attachment to the therapist. Since his motivation to stop drinking is low, attachment to alcohol is high, and attachment to the therapist is low, it becomes important to use the type of interventions that strengthen the treatment relationship and avoid provoking anxiety that will propel the patient out of treatment. These interventions are not only fully in line with Principles 23 to 26, they are also consistent with engagement principles (Principles 21 and 22): Robert's high level of resistance/reactance makes him at risk of dropping out, and the therapist must act tactfully to help him to participate and possibly benefit from therapy.

I would use descriptive, nonjudgmental language to convey my understanding of his difficulties (Principles 24 and 26). I would start with validating Robert's difficulties with alcohol, mood, and social interactions. I would express clear concern that his current drinking is not only a significant problem with regard to personal, social, vocational, medical, and possibly legal consequences (note his violent temper!) but also in precluding more diagnostic clarity. Given the recurrent suicidal thinking, I would express concern that drinking is likely to be contributing to this type of thinking and frame drinking as a possibly life-threatening condition. I would do this not only to communicate my empathy and build our alliance (Principles 23 and 26) but also to enhance Robert's expectation, motivation, willingness to change, and active participation in treatment (Principles 4–6 and 21).

It is our intention that the validation of Robert and empathy toward the inherent ambivalence about drinking, conveyed using motivational interviewing techniques, will create sufficient curiosity in Robert to notice the effects of his drinking and to stimulate an intrinsic desire to stop drinking. Taking a directive approach is likely to externalize the internal ambivalence that Robert has about drinking, thereby triggering or reinforcing his already high level of resistance to therapy (Principle 22). In that case, the therapist starts representing the idea of sobriety, and the patient embraces the drinking position. However, if the therapist avoids taking a directive approach (Principle 37), Robert will "discover" his own ambivalence. Motivational interviewing takes one step further, however. It incorporates paradoxical interventions by "siding" with the patient's desire to drink. If "siding" with a position of sobriety is reinforcing the patient's position of drinking, then "siding" with the position of drinking might push the pendulum in the opposite direction and elicit the patient's desire to be sober.

With this rationale in mind, motivational interviewing offers interventions that range from reflection (Principle 26) to strategic amplification of the patient's arguments (Principle 38) in service of tilting ambivalence toward a decision to stop drinking (Principles 17 and 38). For example, the therapist might indicate, using a matter-of-fact tone, that "it seems that drinking is working" for Robert. Such a statement is likely to elicit a disclosure from Robert about how drinking is actually detrimental for him. However, for such a statement to have a good impact (in terms of self-understanding and emotional experience [Principles 35 and 36]), process wise, its timing has to be optimal (Principle 21). Such a statement is likely to be effective when the therapist has already spent some time validating reasons for drinking and Robert seems ready to push the discussion to the next level.

Robert might be underplaying his readiness and/or his ability to quit. This issue will require assessment and an open and empathic discussion. Is he afraid of withdrawal? Is he afraid to lose alcohol, which became for him his best defense mechanism? Is he afraid to find out who he actually is without alcohol? What if not all of his difficulties go away once he is sober? Will he be able to face and take ownership over his problems? This is not an easy dilemma for someone who relies on externalization as a central coping mechanism. Given the paucity of connections in his family, drinking might be the only way to identify with his otherwise absent father. Thus, giving up drinking would mean giving up a part of his connection to his father.

Treatment using motivational interviewing principles is likely to help Robert explore reasons why giving up alcohol is so challenging. This is when Robert will be invited to express his ambivalence about drinking versus staying sober. The therapist is likely to tactfully challenge some myths related to drinking and "social anxiety"—thereby fostering both his self-understanding and adaptive interpersonal change (Principles 34 and 35). Whereas drinking decreases the anxiety, it also diminishes the "performance"—many times drinking leads to acting inappropriately. Drinking also interferes with taking ownership over social success—"Is it me or is it the alcohol?" Drinking also creates an undesirable reputation for the person. In the case of Robert, using motivational interviewing will hopefully help him develop stronger motivation to take necessary steps to stop drinking (Principle 38), such as participating in medically supervised detoxification (if advised), residential, or partial treatment that is likely to be followed by outpatient treatment. When motivational interviewing is working, the therapist will see a clear shift in Robert's statements in therapy ("I think I want to stop drinking"), affect (e.g., displaying anxiety, shame, or helplessness around drinking), and indication of a desire to take steps to stop drinking (e.g., asking for help in identifying next steps, seeking guidance in starting a medical detoxification; Principles 35, 36, and 38). Once that milestone is reached, Robert and the therapist need to develop an action plan for how to become sober (Principle 38).

The motivational interviewing approach will need to take into account both his history (of childhood adversity and abuse, and repeated "failures" in relational and possibly vocational realms), as well his defensive style, which suggests that shame, negative self-evaluation, and fragility of self-esteem are likely inner experiences from which he is running away. The treatment approach will require special sensitivity on the part of the clinician to provide both validation and empathy, that is, an ability to see things from the patient's perspective (Principles 24 and 26). The therapist will need to be patient and to resist the countertransferential need to push the patient to give up alcohol. The therapist also needs to be prepared for a few relapses along the way and help prepare Robert for their possibility. Sometimes I use the metaphor of running a marathon: I might have 100% motivation to run the marathon, but if I still lack the capacity, I will not get to the finish line. Treatment is about gaining both motivation to change *and* developing the capacity (e.g., skills) to stay sober. Each relapse is an opportunity to learn about both motivation and capacity.

Provision of feedback about Robert's progress is critical (Principle 32), given his tendency to externalize responsibility and minimize the effects of alcohol. Incorporating regular discussion about how he thinks he is progressing can help him develop a bird's-eye view of his treatment trajectory and confront externalization, avoidance, and minimization.

If Robert succeeds in establishing significant sobriety, the therapist will have the opportunity to assess the presence of other co-morbid disorders, including social anxiety disorder, major depressive disorder, and PTSD. Treatment of these disorders in a sober patient is important as a form of relapse prevention, as the possibility of future relapses decreases when other psychiatric disorders are being addressed (Kelly, Daley, & Douaihy, 2012). The use of treatment of these conditions should be guided by flexibility (Principle 33), depending on the preferences of the patient (Principle 13) and the therapist, as well as what will transpire diagnostically, once Robert is no longer drinking. For example, if the diagnosis of social anxiety gets confirmed, exposure-based treatment for social anxiety (Heimberg, Heimberg & Turk, 2004) is a likely recommendation for treatment. If he displays clear effects of trauma and maybe PTSD, then treatment approaches such as Seeking Safety or COPE can be suggested. In all of these treatments, it will be important to maintain a dual focus—helping Robert with the co-morbid disorders (social anxiety, PTSD), while carefully monitoring risk and craving for alcohol (Principles 35 and 38). Usually, developing a relapse prevention plan (Principle 38)—an action plan as to what steps to take to avoid drinking (e.g., call a friend, engage in hobbies, go for a walk)—helps in decreasing risks of a relapse. Robert is likely to have a higher risk of relapse during intensive work on anxiety. Therefore, and again in line with Principles 35 and 38, it will be beneficial to anticipate increased risk by discussing it with the patient, developing a coping plan (including a relapse prevention plan) and carefully monitoring whether Robert can tolerate these interventions. In fact, if he is not able to tolerate exposure work without relapses, such interventions need to be postponed until further stages in treatment (Principle 33).

As a part of exposure tasks, Robert might be asked to talk in front of a crowd, such as at an AA meeting, or join an amateur stand-up comedy club. In such a way he can start engaging in activities that provoke his social anxiety and even push these activities beyond his usual social engagements (simultaneously fostering change highlighted in Principles 34 and 38). This is likely to help in eliminating most of his social anxiety. If the PTSD diagnosis gets confirmed, he might be asked to develop a detailed narrative of his childhood experiences of being physically and emotional abused by his father and then go over that narrative numerous times with his therapist until his distress subsides (Principles 35, 36, and 38).

Once again reflecting principles of preference (Principle 13) and flexibility (Principle 33), this treatment can also be based on more traditional psychodynamic therapy to help Robert with emotional suppression, including inhibition of his anger, coming to terms with childhood adversity, and his fragile self-esteem. Such treatment will ask Robert to describe his childhood experiences and explore their effects on his sense of self, perception of others, and his experience in the world (Principle 35). It is possible that he internalized both the feeling of being insignificant and bad and deserving of his father's violent abuse, as well as a sense of responsibility for his father's temper, along with a fear of his own anger grounded in his unconscious identification with his father. Consequently, his social anxiety is yet another way to shield himself against his own anger and fear of becoming savagely violent like his father. Exploring and re-experiencing these feelings in therapy—very much in line with emotional exposure—is likely to help him develop a better self-esteem and a more integrated perception of his own anger, as well as better self-awareness (Principles 35, 36, and 38). Through judicious use of interpretations (as describe by Principles 29 and 30), Robert could start coming to terms with projection of self-shaming and self-criticism as well as with projection of his own feared anger. These will help with decreasing his externalization as well as his tendency to cast others into critical roles—yet another component of social anxiety. Re-experiencing his childhood relationships is likely to color his relationship with the therapist. He might develop an apprehension that the therapist will get angry at him or that he might get angry at his therapist. From that fearful stance, he might project perception of his angry father on the therapist or enact his own identification with his father. The alliance ruptures that are likely to result from such emergence of anger will then need to be attended to and repaired (Principle 27). With skillful and empathic (Principle 26) use of interpretations (Principles 29 and 30) and self-disclosure (Principle 28), the therapist can help Robert identify these patterns, experience them, and put them in the perspective, which, in turn, could free him up from the stifling grip of his past (Principles 34–36). In such a way, psychodynamic therapy is likely to help Robert address his difficulties that made him want to drink. In line with dual-focus treatments for substance use disorder patients with other comorbid disorders, Robert's treatment will not only have to keep an eye on possible relapses to help Robert have a better handle of his sobriety but also to help him understand that alcohol use, social anxiety, depression, and possible PTSD are different reflections of his general vulnerability that came from a combination of genetic predisposition and childhood adversity. Helping him create new and meaningful directions in life, somewhat in line with Hayes's acceptance and commitment therapy is another potential area of intervention.

Case 3

Case Formulation and Treatment Plan

In my opinion, this is a great case to demonstrate the importance of identifying personality pathology in patients with anxiety disorders. Accurately identifying personality disorders helps in guiding the treatment and identifying treatment priorities. Alternatively, and very much in line with a need for therapeutic flexibility (Principle 33), missing personality pathology is likely to lead to stalemates in treatment. What are the signs of personality pathology, most likely borderline personality disorder (BPD)? The patient describes symptoms of emotional instability, relational instability, an unstable sense of self, and suicidality. A number of features associated with the clinical presentation of this patient's history signal that this is not "just an anxiety disorder." The patient describes difficulty with intimacy and sustaining relationships over time, as well as brief affairs and risky choice of partners. These are features that are inconsistent with the avoidance of risks and fear of embarrassment characteristic of typical patients with social anxiety.

Using the language of object relations, these features represent opposite, unintegrated sides of self and object representation and, thus, suggest lack of internal integration. Thus, fear of embarrassment is not the main reason behind the clinical picture of what the patient is describing as "social anxiety." In this formulation, lack of inner integration results in a fragile sense of self. This fragile self appears dependent on a positive relationship with a positively viewed other, which results in anxiety when these positive reactions are absent.

Another issue is the tendency to project negative, aggressive intent on others—a feature of BPD that results from splitting off of unintegrated aggression. This will lead to the coloring of interpersonal relations with sensitivity to criticism. The patient's history suggests difficulty functioning following separations, such as after starting college. This is another pattern that is typical of patients with BPD (Masterson, 1978)

The importance of such assessment is twofold: (1) It allows the clinician to choose effective treatment, and (b) it permits the provision of psychoeducation regarding these difficulties to the patient and explain anxiety as part of BPD pathology. In fact, in my experience, social anxiety in cases such as Marie's is rarely a separate disorder but rather is a manifestation of core BPD issues: rejection sensitivity, projection of aggression, and a nonconsolidated fragile self. Marie is likely to find such explanation validating and it will give her new hope that by treating BPD, the signs of social anxiety will improve as well (see the following discussion of diagnostic disclosure).

In this case, accurate diagnosis of the co-morbid BPD indicates that treatment of social anxiety needs to be conducted in the context of treatment of BPD. However, treatment of BPD should not ignore social anxiety. In fact, it will be helpful to convey that the therapist understands how painful and limiting social anxiety can be for Marie and explain how targeting BPD will also help with her social anxiety (Principle 24 and 26). Studies show that in BPD patients the co-morbid social anxiety improves following improvement of BPD (Keuroghlian et al., 2015). However, if BPD does not improve, social anxiety does not improve either (Keuroghlian et al., 2015). Thus, if BPD is ignored, the social anxiety treatment is not likely to be effective.

Again referring to the principle of flexibility (Principle 33), what will this diagnostic assessment imply in terms of treatment? Treatment will be structured around addressing BPD. A number of treatments were validated to treat BPD (Gunderson, Weinberg, & Choi-Kain, 2013; Stoffers et al., 2012; Weinberg, Ronningstam, Goldblatt, Schechter, & Maltsberger, 2011). Primarily, DBT (Linehan, 1993) was validated in numerous randomized controlled trials. Other treatments such as mentalization-based treatment (MBT; Bateman & Fonagy 2004), transference-focused psychotherapy (TFP; Clarkin et al., 2015), and general psychiatric management (GPM; Gunderson 2008) have shown comparable efficacy as DBT in reducing many symptoms of BPD patients, including their anxiety (Stoffers et al., 2012).

Which one of these treatments is the most appropriate for Marie? In many ways, Marie's presentation is very typically of BPD patients, and therefore, in my opinion, any of the specialized treatments for BPD will be likely to help her. In her case, the nonspecialized treatments are not likely to be as effective as a specialized one. Specialized treatments for BPD are uniquely equipped to reduce suicidality in these patients (Gunderson et al., 2013). Her unique features, however, stem from demoralization and ambivalence, and I will subsequently discuss how these challenging characteristics can be addressed.

Implementation of Principles of Change

Based on the first cluster of principles of change, what can we say about the likely prognosis for Marie? The following characteristics increase chances of a good outcome: only moderate level of baseline impairment (Principle 1), intrinsic motivation (Principle 5), moderate readiness for change (Principle 6), and middle-social class status (Principle 7). However, other factors decrease her chances for improvement: co-morbid personality disorder (Principle 2), insecure attachment (Principle 3), low therapy outcome expectation (Principle 4), and difficult childhood (Principle 8).

In my experience of cases like this one, structuring treatment around BPD is the most effective way to accomplish change, including change in social anxiety. Most of the factors that reduce her prognosis can be seen through the lens of the co-morbid BPD. Reviewing the prognosis for BPD, however, shows that one can be cautiously optimistic regarding her prospects. She is young, has no known history of childhood abuse, no known history of substance use in her family, has a part-time job, takes classes at school, and has no signs of a co-morbid Cluster C personality disorder (Gunderson et al., 2006; Zanarini et al., 2006). Interestingly, she presents with some irritability during the interview. This is a positive prognostic sign: She can access her emotions and is willing to express them. In patients like Marie, anger is predictive of a better treatment alliance (Colson, Eyman, & Coyne, 1994). Therefore, I would feel somewhat optimistic that offering Marie any of the evidence-based treatments for BPD is likely to help her address her personality functioning, which is likely to be accompanied by improvement in signs of social anxiety. That said, her ambivalence is a main roadblock to effective treatment.

After the initial assessment, Marie can benefit from a psychoeducational discussion of her diagnosis, including suggested understanding of the social anxiety symptoms, as well as the recommended treatments. From the perspective of prognosis, it is critical to explain the following points. First, the therapist might explain that BPD is a "good prognosis diagnosis," to use an apt expression coined by Mary Zanarini. With treatment, patients with BPD can get better across most domains (Gunderson et al., 2011; Zanarini et al., 2003). Second, I would add a brief explanation about the nature of BPD, explaining how emotional instability, relational difficulty, impulsivity, and problems with sense of self develop in the context of difficult early attachments. Third, improvement of co-morbid disorders, including social anxiety, often follows improvement in BPD symptoms, not the other way around (Keuroghlian et al., 2015; Zanarini et al., 2003). This means that addressing BPD is a sine qua non of resolution of other disorders, such as anxiety or depression (Gunderson, 2008). When BPD improves symptomatically, relapses of symptoms are not common (Zanarini et al., 2010), though they are certainly possible in time of stress, loss, and exceptional life challenges (McGlashan et al., 1986). Patients can, however, be prepared for such instances. Finally, I would add that treatments are available today to address these difficulties and that I believe I can help her, if she agrees to participate. This explanation is usually well received, so in Marie's case, I would expect her to feel more validated and more hopeful following this explanation. Considering the impairment level associated with personality disorder, however, she would have to accept that her treatment would likely be longer-term (Principle 16) and would have to address her unfulfilled social needs (Principle 19).

An important challenge in Marie's treatment is how to engage her in therapy (Principle 21). Many patients with BPD feel demoralized because they have a history of not being helped in prior therapies. In my experience, many of them start feeling more hopeful once they start specialized treatment for BPD. Such increase in motivation comes from a number of directions, many of them converging along the quality of a good working alliance, including the formation of a bond, and a mutual agreement about the goals and tasks of therapy (Principle 23). First, they receive an explanation about their diagnosis that they experience as validating (Gunderson & Links, 2014). Sometimes, this is the first time that they have received an explanation of all their difficulties that actually makes sense. Second, they participate in treatment with a therapist that understands their psychopathology and the treatment itself and uses interventions that effectively address their problems. Whereas these interventions could potentially work, it is possible that Marie still feels reluctant to embark on therapy. This is understandable given her childhood history. A cold mother, a distant father, lack of close connection with siblings, and an abusive brother are not only suggestive of an invalidating environment but also suggest insecure attachment—a likely reason she continued to feel disconnected from others and lonely in her adult life.

Possibly, Marie internalized the view of others as being abusive (like her brother), distant and cold (like her parents and siblings), or nonprotective (like her whole family who did not protect her from her brother). In line with Principles 11 (resistance) and 12 (motivation), I would be inclined to validate that her ambivalence is an honest self-disclosure that is very understandable, given her history (Principles 26 and 37). This is likely to pave the way to an exploration of how this general attitude of distancing helped her survive as she was growing up (Principle 24–26 and 35). I would be inclined to discuss many of her behaviors, such as distancing, distracting the therapist, cutting, drug use, and reliance on relationships for comfort in terms of efforts to survive in the chaotic, invalidating environment of her childhood. This can take a preliminary stage in treatment that will help Marie feel understood and trusting of the therapist as well as consolidate hope for treatment engagement. At that stage, and hopefully in line with her own preference (Principle 13), Marie might consider engaging in any of the suggested specialized treatments with an explanation offered by the therapist that these treatments are likely to help her accomplish the kind of the changes she is seeking—developing a meaningful life ("life worth living"; DBT), stable relationships, and self-esteem as well as decreasing anxiety and self-destructive behaviors.

What would these treatments look like if delivered to Marie? In DBT, for example, the therapist is likely to rely on a hierarchy of treatment targets, which will prioritize Marie's suicidality (a Stage I target) overavoidance, anxiety, and emotional dysregulation (Stage II or quality-of-life targets). Treatment will expect Marie to attend individual therapy and a DBT skills group, monitor target behaviors, and use skills. In this approach, reduction of BPD symptoms and improvement of social anxiety is attributed to the increased use of skills that are consistent with Principles 34 to 38: emotional regulation, distress tolerance, interpersonal effectiveness, and mindfulness. In DBT, these skills are fostered by the therapist's maintenance of a dialectic balance between acceptance (client-centered, nondirective) and change (directive, behavioral change-oriented) techniques. The responsive use of these various types of interventions is likely to be beneficial considering Marie's relatively low level of problem assimilation (Principle 10), relatively high level of reactance level (Principle 11), and her presentation of both internalizing and externalizing coping styles (Principles 17 and 18). The acceptance techniques, as well as the use of self-disclosure (Principle 28), are particularly emphasized in the repair of alliance ruptures (Principle 27), which are frequent in the treatment of BPD.

In TFP, the risk of suicidality will also be taken up with the patient. Improvement in social anxiety will likely to happen once Marie develops a better integrated and thus less fragile identity and starts recognizing instances of projection of her anger. In TFP, the therapist is likely to explore how her sensitivity recurs in the treatment relationship and help her develop insight into projected anger (Principles 26, 27, 29, 34–36). In GPM, the therapist and Marie will collaborate on pragmatic goals, such as getting and keeping a job, and maintaining functional relationships (Principle 34, 38). Social anxiety becomes understood in the context of "rejection sensitivity," which is a temperamental difficulty of many BPD patients. Accepting and recognizing this difficulty in the context of temperamental factors will hopefully help Marie anticipate it and learn various coping skills to manage it (Principles 38). MBT will help Marie with social anxiety by helping her develop a broader perspective on other people's states of mind (Principle 34, 35). This is usually done by "mentalizing"—thinking through—different possible states of mind of others.

These psychodynamic approaches differ as to what they recommend regarding various principles. Principle 30 applies to TFP treatments but is less likely to play a role in MBT or GPM that, consistent with Principle 15, discourage a transference focus, especially early on in treatment. Use of self-disclosure (Principle 28) is strongly discouraged in TFP but very much present and used strategically in both MBT and GPM.

Although coming from different perspectives, these treatments are likely to look very much alike when delivered. They are all likely to emphasize the emotional focus of therapy, attention to the treatment relationship, a pragmatic focus on treatment goals, respective collaboration, expectations, and keeping Marie in a proactive role (Weinberg et al., 2011). Such similarities in therapeutic focus emphasized by so many of the principles of change identified in this book allow for, if not intrinsically encourage, flexible use of the most appropriate interventions to particular clients (Principle 33). The following vignette illustrates a likely development in any effective treatment of Marie.

After a few months of therapy, Marie comes for a regular appointment; she enters the therapist's office, sits down, and proceeds silently looking at the floor.

THERAPIST: I am noticing you are silent today. Could you share what's on your mind?
MARIE: (shaking her head) I thought . . . I want to stop therapy . . . stop coming here."
THERAPIST: Can you say more about what made you think about stopping therapy?
MARIE: I don't think it is a good fit; I don't feel I am connecting with you.
THERAPIST: I am not sure I understand yet—can you help me understand the way you experience it?
MARIE: I guess . . . I was feeling that for a while . . . for the last few weeks . . . after that time you called and canceled the appointment. I guess, you said you were feeling sick and offered to reschedule, but. . . . After that I started feeling it was not going to work.
THERAPIST: What was on your mind when I called, do you remember?
MARIE: It was just over for me. . . . I thought you are like everyone else, it is like a job for you. And here I am, stupid me, wanting you to care.
THERAPIST: Seems like you are saying that I don't care.
MARIE: No, you don't.

THERAPIST: That must have felt terrible—here we go again, here is another person who does not care.
MARIE: (starting to tear up) Yep, you nailed it. Yet another person.
THERAPIST: What is behind your tears, Marie?
MARIE: I don't know. . . . I feel stupid that I was hoping that maybe it can be different this time, was hoping you could be different. First, my parents, then all these boyfriends I had and then Marc. And now—you.
THERAPIST: I hear you. How would you know that anyone cares?
MARIE: (looking at the therapist now and is sounding angry) They are there for me; they are helping me. And you were not there that day. That means you don't.
THERAPIST: You sound angry now—could you say more?
MARIE: More? What more do you want? You are the one who messed up, you cancelled! And you want ME to talk?
THERAPIST: Ok, now I think I see it. You were really looking forward to seeing me and thought I cared; then I canceled the appointment and your whole world collapsed—you felt that I don't care anymore.
MARIE: I know, it does not make sense. You were sick, you sounded really sick that day. I just never know what to trust. I always have worries that people will betray me, so I don't get close to them. I feel such a terrible person—I yelled at you now.
THERAPIST: No offense taken. But maybe it tells you something about your relationships with other people?
MARIE: That I worry so much that they will leave me that once they disappoint me I say, "That's it, done with you, I am leaving?" (looking at the therapist with a half-smile)
THERAPIST: Well said. I would suggest remembering this thought the next time you feel that people don't care. And I am also noticing you are not looking away anymore?
MARIE: I think I feel better now. I get it—sometimes I go with my worries and feel alone.

In this example the therapist and Marie collaborate closely around their relationship with a clear affective focus. Given her heightened emotional state, the interventions are mostly empathic validation. The therapist is working hard on staying connected with her emotional experience. This helps them work things out between them, repair the alliance, and help Marie develop a new important understanding of herself that is also relevant to her social anxiety and relationships with others (Principles 26, 27, 35, 37).

If specialized treatment for BPD is not effective in reducing the social anxiety, the therapist should include additional focus on social anxiety. In fact, in some cases, DBT requires the addition of a separate attentional focus on using exposure-based interventions (Harned, Korslund, & Linehan, 2014), whereas GPM is "friendly" to the incorporation of additional anxiety focus, if such focus is clinically justified (Principle 38).

Reflection on the Writing Process

In my clinical work I see patients with complex clinical pictures. That means that most of my patients present with multiple disorders, and almost all of them would be excluded from clinical trials that test evidence-based interventions that became a gold standard of clinical care. Treating such a patient population is a likely common practice and possibly not that unique to the clinical settings in which my colleagues and I are working hard on translating effective treatment approaches into effective care for each individual patient with their unique circumstances.

Coming from that perspective, writing my reactions to the three cases was very educational. I found the approach helpful in developing treatment plans for how to extrapolate existing treatments outside the areas of their usual application. For example, how does one apply treatment for social anxiety, commonly treated by exposure-based interventions, to a person with a different cultural background, or a patient with alcohol use disorder, or a patient with BPD? Having explicit treatment principles helps with generalizing treatment interventions in a meaningful way while taking into account the subjective characteristics and circumstances of an individual patient. While some of the of the principles were known to me either based on the literature or clinical experiences, others were not and that was a welcome learning opportunity.

Writing this chapter deepened my thinking about anxiety disorders. In all three cases anxiety does not appear alone but rather in the context of other clinical characteristics that critically affect treatment. In the case of Philip, acculturation stress and its effect on the development of his identity and relationships highlighted the need for altering treatment targets (identity, relationships) and treatment style (genuine connection, awareness of power differential). In the case of Robert, recognition of co-morbid alcohol use emphasized the complexity of a diagnosis of social anxiety in the presence of active drinking as well as difficulty treating social anxiety in the absence of treatment for alcohol use. In the case of Marie, accurate diagnosis of BPD highlighted the importance of addressing BPD and understanding social anxiety in the context of BPD psychopathology. In all of these cases, cultural background or co-morbid disorders (alcohol use, BPD) interact with individual characteristics of the patients, but all of these factors have separate effects on social anxiety symptoms.

Writing this chapter also prompted me to think about explicit or implicit principles I use in my own clinical practice (e.g., using dual-focus treatments in patients with substance use and co-morbid disorders, prioritizing treatment of personality disorders in patients with these conditions, understanding the psychopathology of the patient helps in understanding and validating the patient, anticipating the future course/prognosis, and in developing treatment goals). Thinking in terms of such principles helps not only in translating the literature into practice but also in subjecting my own thinking to more explicit scrutiny and identifying what works, what does not and what, potentially, harms the patient.

References

Back, S. E., Foa, E. B., Killeen, T. K., Mills, K. L., Teesson, M., Dansky Cotton, B., . . . Brady, K. T. (2014). *Concurrent Treatment of PTSD and Substance Use Disorders Using Prolonged Exposure (COPE): Therapist guide*. Oxford, England: Oxford University Press.

Bateman, A., & Fonagy, P. (2004). *Psychotherapy for borderline personality disorder: Mentalization-based treatment*. Oxford, England: Oxford University Press.

Brown, D. P., & Elliott, D. S. (2016). *Attachment disturbances in adults: Treatment for comprehensive repair*. New York, NY: Norton.

Clarkin, J. F., Yeomans, F. E., & Kernberg, O. F. (2015). *Transference-focused psychotherapy for borderline personality disorder: A clinical guide*. Washington, DC: American Psychiatric Publishing.

Colson, D. B., Eyman, J. R., & Coyne, L. (1994). Rorschach correlates of treatment difficulty and of the therapeutic alliance in psychotherapy with female psychiatric hospital patients. *Bulletin of Menninger Clinic, 58*(3), 383–388.

Gunderson, J. G., & Links, P. S. (2014). *Handbook of good psychiatric management for borderline personality disorder*. Washington, DC: American Psychiatric Publishing.

Gunderson, J. G., Daversa, M. T., Grilo, C. M. McGlashan, T. H., Zanarini, M. C., Shea, T., . . . Stout, L. (2006). Predictors of 2-year outcome for patients with borderline personality disorder. *American Journal of Psychiatry, 163*(5), 822–826.

Gunderson, J. G., Stout, R. L., McGlashan, T. H., Shea, M. T., Morey L. C., Grilo, C. M., . . . Skodol, A. E. (2011). Ten-year course of borderline personality disorder: psychopathology and function from the Collaborative Longitudinal Personality Disorders study. *Archives of General Psychiatry, 68*(8), 827–837.

Gunderson, J. G., Weinberg, I., & Choi-Kain, L. (2013). Borderline personality disorder. In G. Gabbard (Ed.), *Gabbard's treatments of psychiatric disorders: DSM-5 edition*. Washington, DC: American Psychiatric Publishing.

Harned, M. S., Korslund, K. E., & Linehan, M. M. (2014). A pilot randomized controlled trial of dialectical behavior therapy with and without the dialectical behavior therapy prolonged exposure protocol for suicidal and self-injuring women with borderline personality disorder and PTSD. *Behavior Research and Therapy, 55*, 7–17.

Hope, D. A., Heimberg, R. G., & Turk, C. L. (2010). *Managing Social anxiety, therapist guide. a cognitive-behavioral therapy approach* (2nd ed.). Oxford, England: Oxford University Press.

Kelly, T. M., Daley, D. C., & Douaihy, A. B. (2012). Treatment of substance abusing patients with comorbid psychiatric disorders. *Addictive Behaviors, 37*(1), 11–24.

Keuroghlian, A. S., Gunderson, J. G., Pagano, M. E., Markowitz, J. C., Ansell, E. B., Shea, M. T., . . . Skodol, A. E. (2015). Interactions of borderline personality disorder and anxiety disorders over 10 years. *Journal of Clinical Psychiatry, 76*(11), 1529–1534.

Linehan, M. M. (1993). *Cognitive-behavior treatment for borderline personality disorder.* New York, NY: Guilford.

Masterson. J. (1978). *Psychotherapy for the borderline adult.* New York, NY: Brunner Mazel.

McGlashan, T. (1986). The Chestnut Lodge follow-up study: III. Long-term outcome of borderline personalities. *Archives of General Psychiatry, 43*(1), 20–30.

Miller, W. R., & Rolnick, S. (2012). *Motivational interviewing: Helping people change* (3rd ed.). New York, NY: Guilford.

Najavits, L. (2001). *Seeking safety: A treatment manual for PTSD and substance abuse.* New York, NY: Guilford.

Stoffers, J. M., Völlm, B. A., Rücker, G., Timmer, A., Huband, N., & Lieb K. (2012). Psychological therapies for people with borderline personality disorder. *Cochrane Database Systematic Reviews, 8*, CD005652.

Weinberg, I., Ronningstam, E., Goldblatt, M. J., Schechter, M., & Maltsberger, J. T. (2011). Common factors in empirically supported treatments for borderline personality disorder. *Current Psychiatric Reports, 13*(1), 60–68.

Zanarini, M. C., Frankenburg, F. R., Hennen, J., Reich, D. B., & Silk, K. R. (2006). Prediction of the 10-year course of borderline personality disorder. *American Journal of Psychiatry, 163*(5), 827–832.

Zanarini, M. C., Frankenburg, F. R., Hennen, J., & Silk, K. R. (2003). The longitudinal course of borderline psychopathology: 6-year prospective follow-up of the phenomenology of borderline personality disorder. *American Journal of Psychiatry, 160*(2), 274–283.

12
Conceptual, Clinical, and Empirical Perspectives on Principles of Change for Anxiety Disorders

Eva D. Papiasvili, Catherine S. Spayd, Igor Weinberg, Larry E. Beutler, Louis G. Castonguay, and Michael J. Constantino

The goal of this chapter, as was the case with the concluding chapter of the depression section (Chapter 7), is to bring together different views about principles of change and future directions to better understand them. To do so, both chapters involve the collaboration of the three clinical authors who have respectively worked on each section of the book and the book editors to (a) delineate convergences and differences in implementing the principles; (b) discuss the clinical importance of using principles in practice; (c) suggest possible combinations principles perceived as redundant; (d) identify additional principles that could be the focus of future research; and (e) offer final thoughts about principles of change. As was done in Chapter 7, the first and predominant voice has been given to the clinical authors; comments from the editors then follow to foster dialogues in addressing these important topics.

Convergences and Complementarities in Implementing Principles of Change

Each therapist/author who contributed to the anxiety disorders section of this book (Papiasvili, Spayd, and Weinberg) read the two chapters in this section that were written by the other two authors who addressed anxiety. They then wrote a brief text in which they compared their chapters to the other two, in terms of how much emphasis each of author gave to each of the 38 empirically based principles (see Box 12.1) and the ways that they are implemented in clinical practice. These texts, or reflections, from each separate clinical author are presented next. They are followed by general comments by the book editors regarding areas convergence and divergence among the three therapists/authors, as well as how these areas are linked to the corresponding therapist profile of therapeutic preference disclosed in Chapter 8.

Dr. Papiasvili's Reflections

In the following comment, I will offer reflections about what I perceive as major convergences between Dr. Spayd, Dr. Weinberg, and me with regard to principles of change that are at the core of our clinical practice. This will be followed by thoughts on related, but less central, similarities and differences between our respective ways of conducting therapy.

Main Convergences
First, the most striking commonality that I see among us, the clinical authors, is the emphasis on the establishment and maintenance of a viable, trusting, and high-quality therapeutic alliance (Principle 23). For the three of us, this also includes the expectation that periodic ruptures are inevitable and that their subsequent repair (Principle 27) is paramount for the treatment to effectively progress (and, in some cases such with Robert, to progress at all). It seems that the expectation of episodes alliance rupture–repair, irrespective of how it is conceptualized and linked to other principles, becomes one of the main motivators for implementing flexibility (Principle 33).

In this context, and again for the three of us, clients like Robert and Marie who present with a more complex diagnostic picture with substantial comorbidity, problematic attachment patterns that are linked to adverse childhood events, lower (and rather extrinsic vs. intrinsic) motivation, and higher resistance (Principles 1–3, 8, 11, and 12) seem to pull for the implementation of a more flexible approach (Principle 33), especially in light of resistance (Principle 11). The most striking example of such flexibility is, in my view, when Dr. Spayd, who otherwise works within the cognitive-behavioral therapy (CBT) model, resorts to an exploratory stance in a situation when Robert resists the assignment to call his brother. Her hypothetical exploratory dialogue addresses the dynamic meaning of the resistance: It reveals the historical underpinnings of Robert's difficulty in making a call, when as a child he called from camp and his father berated him. Implicit here is the assumption that uncovering and understanding how this childhood experience dynamically impacts his inability to make a phone call as an adult will remove the resistance and lead to the therapeutic change. This process possibly involves interpretation and insight into such dynamic connection. In the case of Robert, I, as an analyst, also employ a modified approach that involves a therapeutic "contract," which is essentially behavioral in nature. Implicit here is the assumption that to proceed with the dynamic/exploratory approach the most destructive behavior may need to change first to facilitate the continuation of therapy. In my case, this is also embedded in the exploratory insight-oriented dialogue and my interpretation of specific transferential and historical meaning of resistance.

Moreover, a convergence in terms of clinical content that emerged across our respective chapters is that Robert's drinking may be related to his relationship with his father. Both Dr. Weinberg and I conceptualized this dynamic explicitly as a possible "identification with the aggressor," but it is also discernible in Dr. Spayd's example of a hypothetical dialogue—although, in her case, it is not explicitly conceptualized within dynamically oriented context. My overall point here is that based on the chapters that my two colleagues and I wrote, it is my firm impression that in the face of therapeutic challenges, when the resistance rises to the point of strongly affecting the patient and/or the treatment, therapists of different theoretical orientations will employ clinical flexibility and creativity. The ability to employ such clinical creativity and flexibility, however, needs to be felt as congruent and genuine to be effective.

Further Related Convergences Coupled with Sometimes Divergent Clinical Implementation

Linked to all the previously discussed convergences (i.e., establishment and maintenance of therapeutic alliance and flexibility in face of complicated diagnoses, as well as patient's history and resistance) is the emphasis given to the two principles related to client engagement, or lack of thereof, during treatment (Principles 21 and 22). While we may approach (conceptually and technically) these principles differently, the three of us agree that these principles are of utmost importance. Specifically, we all pay acute attention to engagement in early active collaboration (Principle 21) with the three clients, but especially with Robert and Marie, who are perceived by the three of us as posing more diagnostic and therapeutic challenges due to many factors in the area of prognostic principles. While our methods sometimes differ (Dr. Spayd and, to a lesser degree, Dr. Weinberg, employ more educational approaches than I would), we all pay attention to initial expectations (Principle 4).

The three of us are also aware of the importance of increasing intrinsic motivation (Principle 5), presenting therapy as the patient's choice, rather than recommended (or demanded/required) by circumstances and/or other people. We all view this as being connected to readiness to change stages (Principle 6). Both Dr. Spayd and Dr. Weinberg described their work by referring to specific dimensions of the scale that has been developed to measure this construct. In contrast, not having been familiar with this scale before writing my chapter, I work with this conceptualization in a more fluid way. I do so by exploring how patients perceive themselves as capable/incapable of changing and how such a change in their mind would come about—which I see as also related to the Principles 4 to 6. But even here convergences are present. For example, in the case of Phillip, both Dr. Weinberg and I focus on interactively on addressing his passive compliance (as an impediment to change), rather than a genuinely active participation on his part. Like Dr. Spayd, I am aware of Marie's view of therapist as a "savior." Furthermore, both of us would contemplate engaging with Robert in an indirect dialogue around the usefulness of therapy as a way of fostering possible change, where Dr. Spayd's words ("Maybe you are right. . . . Let's wait and see") sounds similar to mine ("One might as well give it a chance . . ."). The key here is that Robert's low initial expectations (Principle 4) are addressed indirectly, almost (but not completely) paradoxically as "siding with resistance."

Similarities are also noticeable with regard to Phillip. Both Dr. Spayd and I point out his self-view of his core lack of capacity to change as something to be mindful of and to be address in therapy (albeit differently, owing to divergent theoretical and technical tools used). At the same time, Drs. Spayd and Weinberg and I view Phillip as the most intrinsically motivated (Principle 5), self-aware (Principle 18), and ready for change (Principle 10) of the three cases with whom we worked. Dr. Spayd and I explicitly state that Phillip would benefit from an essentially nonmodified application of our preferred clinical model (cognitive-behavioral and psychoanalysis, respectively).

It follows that these three principles (Principles 5, 10, and 18) are perceived by the three of us as very important indicators of the way that we each implement our own therapeutic system—in a modified or more-or-less standard way (speaking relatively, as there is no such a thing as a "standard" patient). But even Dr. Spayd's "straightforward," or my own relatively nonmodified "standard," use of any particular therapeutic model will always be implemented in a unique way—attuned to each particular patient. This adaptive-individualized way of practicing therapy is in part reflective of ongoing feedback (Principle 32), and although we diverge on the use of standardized measures (Principle 31), the three of us stress the importance of feedback as a general principle of change.

While two of the therapeutic relationship principles (therapeutic alliance and repair of alliance ruptures) were presented as main convergences, others are also viewed as important by the three writers. This is certainly the case for therapist regard (Principle 24), therapist congruence (Principle 25), and therapist empathy (Principle 26). Interesting nuances emerged with respect to the use of self-disclosure (Principle 28). Dr. Weinberg utilizes this principle as a tool to strengthen authenticity of the therapeutic exchange and for other specific purposes, as exemplified in his work with Phillip (to foster a nonauthoritarian atmosphere where Phillip may feel freer to assert himself and share his experience). In contrast, the principle is used more sparingly by both Dr. Spayd (to demonstrate that she can identify/empathize with and or to mitigate the client' shame) and myself (when offering associations to help bridge the client's lack of words for describing his or her experience).

In terms of usage of therapist intervention principles, the three chapters reveal convergences but also important divergences. I will briefly state some of them here. As a psychoanalyst, I believe that my work relies more heavily on the use of (hopefully) high-quality and individually tailored psychodynamic interpretations (Principles 29 and 30) than Dr. Weinberg's and Dr. Spayd's work. Both Dr. Weinberg and Dr. Spayd implement these principles when they assess whether the client is in particular need of them, especially when the client's behavior presents resistance to further progress of treatment. As a point of divergence, however, the whole methodology of my therapeutic approach could be viewed as a broad inquiry, accompanied by a kind of rolling, affectively laden interpretative process, including transference interpretations in the here-and-now context, the there-and-now context of the client's present life (work, relationships), and the there-and-then context of historical-archaic underpinnings.

Both Dr. Spayd and I stress explicitly the importance of being responsive to the clients' adaptive interpersonal changes (Principle 34; e.g., saying to Robert, "It is hard but you can do it. . . . You are doing it . . ."); while it is implied in Dr. Weinberg's write up. With regard to fostering self-understanding (Principle 35) and deepening of emotional experiencing (Principle 36), Dr. Weinberg and I seem to do this more explicitly than Dr. Spayd. The implementations of these principles, however, has to be responsive to the clients' therapeutic needs. As noted by Dr. Spayd, indiscriminate deepening of emotional understanding can potentially have a harmful effect.

Selective fostering of behavioral change (Principle 38) is part of a standard clinical methodology for Dr. Spayd, and it is sometimes emphasized by Dr. Weinberg. In comparison, I employ it very infrequently, as this represents a rare modification of usual analytic technique. However, there are times when I encourage behavioral change (as when I contracted with Robert), while concomitantly exploring it dynamically.

Overall, reading and comparing our convergences and divergencies was challenging, yet an immensely rewarding and highly educational process. I learned so much! I am thankful to the editors and to Dr. Spayd and Dr. Weinberg for this unique opportunity.

Dr. Spayd's Reflections

My initial reaction to reading Drs. Papiasvili's and Weinberg's chapters on applying the therapeutic principles of change to the three cases of social anxiety that I had just (virtually) treated was simply "Wow!" Three PhD-level clinical psychologists with presumably equitable graduate school, internship and postdoctoral training, all with years of clinical experience, had interpreted the same clinical data but had then developed very different case formulations and proposed very different treatment plans for these same three individuals! As I read and reread the three chapters, however, I came to also see points of convergence and divergence that further challenged my thinking about Phillip's, Robert's, and Marie's best mental health care.

In Phillip's case, for example, all three of us conceptualized his social anxiety as developing in response to childhood experiences, in particular his father's highly critical statements (Drs. Papiasvili and Spayd). However, I did not consider his status as a first-generation immigrant to be critical, but both Drs. Papiasvili and Weinberg provided persuasive arguments that it is likely an important demographic component to consider and address in therapy. Both Drs. Papiasvili and Weinberg also focused more on exploring Phillip's life roles and intimate relationships, which I addressed more peripherally within the context of improved interpersonal communications. And, while Dr. Papiasvili focused more on the treatment goal of emotional deepening and developing an independent sense of self, both Dr. Weinberg and I emphasized a primary treatment goal of behavioral change as a central component in effectively decreasing his distressing anxiety symptoms.

Not surprisingly, our three treatment plans thus also varied considerably, in line with these differing case conceptualizations. As a cognitive-behaviorist, I, of course, focused Phillip's treatment plan around the strategies of psychoeducation, identifying and replacing the distorted cognitions that perpetuate his anxiety, his development of skills for nonanxious social interactions (Principle 34), and anxiety reduction behavioral change techniques (Principle 38). Dr. Weinberg, however, emphasized the need to first explore and validate Phillip's life story, helping him to develop an understanding of how cultural differences in values may have contributed to his anxiety (Principle 18), while simultaneously emphasizing a collaborative, versus authoritative, therapist-patient stance. I see this latter point, in particular, as likely being an important component of Robert's but not necessarily Phillip's therapy. Dr. Papiasvili's approach was clearly more psychoanalytic, using her therapeutic relationship with Phillip as the primary vehicle to explore his important life relationships and how he might view them more productively (Principle 30). Of note, she predicted this approach would require more intensive (frequency and number of sessions) treatment than I anticipated being necessary for Phillip's positive treatment outcome.

There appears to have been one overlapping principle of therapeutic change that all three authors emphasized in our work with Phillip, Principle 21, which identifies the importance of a patient's active participation in the treatment process. But my implementation of this concept (completing cognitive and behavioral exercises) varied significantly from both Dr. Weinberg's (the patient's participation in a collaborative therapy process) and Dr. Papiasvili's (his participation in exploring, accepting, or refuting the therapist's interpretive statements). Note that several other therapeutic principles were strongly emphasized in Phillip's care by both Drs. Weinberg and Papiasvili but not by me: the importance of a high-quality therapeutic alliance (Principle 23), fostering increased self-understanding (Principle 35), and, for Dr. Papiasvili, emotional deepening (Principle 36). While I, of course, advocate for developing a positive therapeutic alliance with all of my patients, I did not see that as a primary focus of Phillip's treatment plan; from my understanding of his case, I did not anticipate there would be unusual barriers to the formation of a positive alliance. Similarly, while I endorsed the value of increasing Phillip's self-understanding of childhood causes for the development of his anxiety, it was not a central tenet of my treatment plan. In considering Principle 36, however, I proposed that Phillip would benefit more from focusing on interactions with the world and less on staying "stuck in his head," given his described historical tendency to overly emote versus act; Dr. Papiasvili simply saw the benefit versus risk of this principle differently than I did.

When comparing our three case formulations for Robert, I again found some similarities but also notable differences. I viewed social anxiety as Robert's primary treatment focus, with alcohol abuse as a complicating variable he developed in an effort to manage that anxiety. Conversely, Dr. Weinberg proposed alcohol abuse as the first treatment consideration, even suggesting that it may have been the root issue that caused, versus developed secondary to, his social anxiety. Dr. Papiasvili presented a third conceptualization—that Robert's experience of abuse and neglect in childhood resulted in his inability to function effectively in adulthood, to the point of regressing to a helpless child stance in the face of his increasing life stressors; she proposed that these struggles were the root cause of his social anxiety. As understandably follows, while my approach focused first on reducing his social anxiety symptoms and then moved on to alcohol reduction strategies, Dr. Weinberg's treatment plan prioritized sobriety from alcohol; he also very astutely promoted the therapy strategy of providing feedback to Robert regarding his treatment progress as an effective way to facilitate shifting his world view to one of accepting more personal responsibility for his life outcomes versus externalizing and blaming others (Principle 32).

Dr. Papiasvili's approach, instead, focused initially on monitoring and mutually examining the therapeutic relationship (Principle 30), leading to an increase in Robert's self-awareness (Principle 35) and, thus, self-determination, thereby reducing his anxiety as he became more "adult" (accepting responsibility for his own behaviors) in his world view. She proposed later contracting with Robert in an effort to help him more effectively manage his alcohol intake.

Despite these divergent views of his psychological situation, there was more overlap in our preferred principles of therapeutic change in Robert's case. For example, we all emphasized the importance of Principle 11, which suggests the use of nondirective approaches in patients such as Robert who exhibit high resistance to treatment. However, my behavioral manifestation of that principle was to emphasize to Robert that he is in control of accepting or rejecting psychotherapy treatment. Conversely, Dr. Weinberg's approach in this regard was to validate Robert's life experiences, as he exemplified so well in his description of applying motivational interviewing techniques with Robert. And Dr. Papiasvili's approach was to use their therapeutic relationship as a means to identify Robert's tendency to act out upon, rather than verbally describe, his emotional experiences and thus lead him to awareness of these actions' hidden (emotional) meanings (Principle 36). Additionally, she suggested the brilliant interpretation that Robert's alarm regarding his recent behaviors (leading to the loss of his girlfriend and possible loss of his job) was actually a sign of his emotional strength—a way to reinforce his movement toward considering change and thus away from resisting change.

In response to our shared awareness of Robert's tenuous treatment compliance, all three of us also emphasized the use of Principle 23 in his care, the development of a strong therapeutic alliance, though again we varied somewhat in the enactment of this principle. While Drs. Papiasvili and Weinberg and I all proposed empathizing with Robert's history of difficult life events and affirming his recent distress, Dr. Weinberg also added the likely very effective strategy of empathizing with Robert's ambivalence regarding giving up alcohol. There were several other principles of therapeutic change that both Dr. Weinberg and I emphasized in our work with Robert, but Dr. Papiasvili did not. These included the complementary Principle 17 (focusing more on behavioral change and less on insight in patients with externalizing coping styles) and Principle 38 (focusing on behavioral change). Dr. Weinberg's behavioral approach focused primarily on changing Robert's drinking behaviors. Conversely, my plan's behavioral interventions included relaxation strategies and techniques to improve the quality and quantity of his social interactions, in addition to behavioral experiments with changes in his alcohol consumption. Finally, both Dr. Weinberg and I emphasized therapeutic Principle 19 (addressing more impaired and/or less supported patients' social and medical needs). My treatment plan in this regard was to employ graduated structured exercises to increase Robert's positive social interactions. Although Dr. Weinberg briefly mentioned the importance of increasing Robert's support system, he focused instead on addressing medical concerns related to drinking (e.g., referring to it as a sedative and framing it as potentially life-threatening in terms of increasing his depression and, thus, his suicide risk). I believe both of these treatment approaches have strong merit.

In the case of Marie, all three of us clearly identified her borderline personality disorder (BPD) characteristics, especially her fear of rejection, as issues of major significance to be addressed in her course of psychotherapy. Both Dr. Papiasvili and I identified the root cause of this BPD as her parent's lack of support and emotional absence during her childhood, but I further suggested her mother's modeling of socially anxious behaviors as an additional causal variable of Marie's anxiety. Dr. Weinberg, however, went further to propose that Marie's social anxiety was not a separate disorder, but rather a trait of her BPD; thus, the effective treatment of the BPD would by itself mitigate this social anxiety. His proposed treatment plan was thus to apply one of several structured therapy programs for BPD, such as dialectical behavior therapy. Alternately, my proposed therapy approach was to use cognitive and behavioral strategies directly applicable to social anxiety but only after carefully constructing our positive therapeutic alliance and helping Marie to clarify her values regarding healthy relationships. Dr. Papiasvili again focused on primary use of the therapeutic relationship as a vehicle to explore and improve both Marie's sense of self (and thus her self-determination) and her healthy interactions in other present and future relationships, all as ways to mitigate her social anxiety.

Despite these differing case formulations and treatment plans, I again identified several areas of convergence in our most prominently used therapeutic principles. Presumably due to our shared awareness of the BPD trait of splitting, which leads to disastrous interpersonal relationships (e.g., her chaotic relationship with ex-boyfriend Mark), all three of us focused on the importance of using Principle 27, the importance of attending to and repairing anticipated alliance ruptures, and Principle 34, fostering adaptive behavioral change. In this case, Dr. Papiasvili's and my specific means of implementing Principle 27 were fairly similar. Dr. Papiasvili proposed careful monitoring of Marie's verbal and nonverbal communications and addressing perceived ruptures quickly. I proposed much the same plan, though also included deliberately predicting such "bumps" in our relationship at the start of therapy, to facilitate Marie's acceptance of this concept when I later identified them. Dr. Weinberg implemented this principle somewhat, but not drastically, differently by using DBT-based acceptance and self-disclosure techniques to address alliance ruptures. Our therapeutic interventions based on Principle 34 were more discrepant. Dr. Papiasvili proposed facilitating such adaptive behavioral change via the use of the therapeutic relationship, particularly by demonstrating respect for Marie's boundaries and helping increase her self-understanding and emotional experiencing. Conversely, Dr. Weinberg proposed the use of a DBT skills group to meet this goal, while I suggested helping Marie to clarify her own values about healthy relationships and then using this template to monitor and manage her behavior in future relationships.

A principle that was uniquely emphasized by Dr. Papiasvili in discussing Marie's treatment was Principle 33, the importance of flexibility in treatment techniques. She made the excellent point that, given her fragile ego, Marie would benefit (feel safer) by explicitly informing her that she could use a "stop signal" if she became uncomfortable about a treatment topic to improve Marie's sense of self-control over her boundaries. Finally, unique to Dr. Weinberg's treatment plan for Marie was his emphasis on Principle 21, promoting a patient's active participation in the treatment process, increasing her buy-in to treatment by providing thorough, ego-syntonic explanations of both her BPD diagnosis and empirically validated BPD-specific treatment.

My conclusions from this compare and contrast exercise? At the risk of appearing immodest, I believe that our three patients would have received high-quality psychotherapy from any of the three of us. But if we could meld the unique contributions of each author's use of the therapeutic principles of change into a single Dr. Papiasvili–Spayd–Weinberg (and wouldn't that be a mouthful), I feel confident that our patients would have had amazing treatment success!

Dr. Weinberg's Reflections

Reading the chapters was an exhilarating experience. I felt privileged to learn from Drs. Spayd and Papiasvili about their approaches and from what at times felt like very personal disclosures of their ways of intervening. While noticing and learning from the differences, I could not help recognizing substantial similarities in our approaches. All three of us use principles from all five clusters as we move from assessment to formulation of the cases, treatment planning, and implementation of the treatment. While richness of the cases and the commentaries invites a much longer response, I would like to illustrate how our approaches converge and differ in a few specific clinical dilemmas and how such differences and similarities are actually interwoven. What appears to be different in terms of treatment interventions is similar in terms of treatment style, and what is different in terms of style sometimes is aiming to accomplish a very similar treatment goal.

Let's start with assessment and case formulation. First, whether using psychoanalytic model (Dr. Papiasvili), cognitive behavior model (Dr. Spayd), or a mixed pragmatic model (Dr. Weinberg) all three of us rely on case formulations and utilize those as a compass for treatment. Second, those case formulations explain current difficulties of the patient in terms of the past—namely, significant life events and relationships. Third, these formulations, while using different concepts, highlight role of factors that perpetuate the patients' difficulties in the present. Fourth, these case formulations are commonly shared and even collaboratively developed (Dr. Papiasvili) with the patient. However, at times our formulations differ regarding priorities in treatment. In the treatment of Robert, for example, I prioritize treatment of alcohol use disorder while Dr. Spayd suggests treating social anxiety first. In my experience, prioritizing treatment of addiction by either treating it first or maintaining a dual or concurrent focus on addiction and co-morbid disorders prevents treatment stalemates, especially concurrent drinking is likely to compete with skills acquisition or deepening of exploratory work.

Interestingly, while I formulated the case of Phillip primarily around identity formation with a conflict between affiliation and identity, Dr. Papiasvili's formulations centered around a conflict between affiliation and self-assertion. Dr. Spayd is using learning theory and CBT principles to explain Phillip's difficulties in terms of negative core beliefs, cognitive processing biases, and reinforcement of maladaptive behaviors. These formulations, as hypothetical as these cases are, have differential implications for the treatment approach. In fact, both Dr. Spayd and Dr. Papiasvili are optimistic that treatment can proceed without major changes in technique, whether it is CBT (Dr. Spayd) or psychoanalysis (Dr. Papiasvili). On the other hand, I advocate for significant changes, especially along the lines of higher attunement to power differential and risks of silencing the authentic self and of the genuine engagement in therapy, resulting in a more participatory, interpersonal approach (Fiscalini & Grey, 1993). In staying sensitive to these issues, I hope that in addition to helping Phillip recognize repetition of the past, challenge negative automatic thoughts, or engage in successful exposure interventions, such approach would help Phillip develop a new relationship (Loewald, 1971)—a relationship that is open, collaborative, and supportive. Such relationship is more genuine and is not based on misuse of power and dismissal of Phillip's subjectivity and identity, allowing him to grow from these experiences.

In case of Robert, all three of us agree that this is complex, difficult case with a more guarded prognosis. However, we take different approaches in addressing the difficulties. All three of us address Robert's drinking, and each one of us remains loyal to our respective general clinical approach. In line with general psychoanalytic model, Dr. Papiasvili sets a limit, suggests an alternative to drinking, and takes and interpretive-confrontational stance, conceptualizing drinking as a form of acting out. Dr. Spayd is using classical CBT techniques of sampling sobriety and identifying pros and cons of alcohol consumption (Barlow, 2001). I, mostly swayed by the empirical basis supporting effectiveness of motivational interviewing, rely on that approach in shifting Robert's motivational balance toward sobriety.

All three of us seem to emphasize the importance of validation and alliance building in this case either as a part of a pragmatic approach to keep Robert in therapy (Dr. Spayd) or as a part of motivational interviewing techniques to target drinking (Dr. Weinberg) or through attention to expression of negative feelings through nonverbal behaviors (Dr. Papiasvili). Dr. Papiasvili is especially sensitive in this case to how past experiences of violence in the family affect treatment interactions. She suggests specific ways to intervene: inviting Robert to share his experience of the therapist's interventions, staying sensitive to the possibility that these interventions get experiences through the lenses of the past adversity and are being viewed as criticism or attacks. These interventions are powerful ways to convey respectful validation of his experiences and help Robert stay in treatment.

Interventions that address Robert's traumatic past vary between cognitive behavior and psychoanalytic approaches. However, regardless of a specific model, these approaches emphasize the importance of processing past trauma (if Robert is capable of tolerating such endeavor; if not, a more here-and-now skills-based approach is more advisable) with the recognition that such processing is likely to surface in therapeutic relationship (Drs. Papiasvili and Weinberg).

In Marie's case, the three of us agreed regarding most aspects of her treatment, though I seem to be more optimistic regarding her prognosis. I have to acknowledge that my optimism is likely to result from comparing the prognosis of patients like Marie to those who suffer from more severe personality disorders that I typically see in my practice. It seems that while we agree that it is critical to address Marie's hesitant and ambivalent approach to therapy, we intervene differently. Dr. Papiasvili interprets expressions of such hesitation in context of what appears to be negative transference. I take a different approach by providing psychoeducation about BPD and the treatment and by validating her adaptations in terms of their survival role in the past.

It seems that we all conceptualize her treatment in terms of stages with more "supportive" interventions earlier in its course and more "expressive" interventions later in its course, to use an apt continuum described by Horwitz et al. (1996). For example, earlier in treatment, all three of us suggest using empathic validations of her difficulties in context of her childhood, psychoeducation

(Drs. Spayd and Weinberg), expression of praise and reminding Marie of her strengths (Drs. Spayd and Papiasvili) or "giving" Marie the right to use the stop sign (Dr. Papiasvili), focusing first on extratherapeutic relationships (Dr. Papiasvili). However, later in treatment we advocate for more "expressive" interventions, such as direct transference interpretations (Dr. Papiasvili) or exploration and repair of alliance ruptures (Dr. Weinberg). Dr. Spayd also is suggesting differential use of treatment principles depending on the stage of therapy. She is writing that she is likely to be more directive early in treatment with Marie regarding boundaries and more open-ended later in treatment, for example, when she advises Marie to explore her values about relationships. This progression, though using different types of interventions, acknowledges Marie's fragility of self and tenuousness of her attachment at the outset of treatment and strengthening of her sense of self and connection with the therapist and the deepening of the therapeutic relationship. It seems that coming from different perspectives, we all take an empathic, validating stance in Marie's treatment, a stance that also invites sensitivity to her strengths and weaknesses, strength of the alliance, and her overall progress.

One advantage of formulating Marie's difficulties along the lines of BPD is the recognition that one needs to make modifications in technique. Typical characterological limitations related to tenuousness of alliance, limited ability for emotional and not just intellectual insight, impulsivity and black-and-white thinking (splitting) of BPD patients led to specialized approaches such as DBT, mentalization-based therapy, transference-based therapy, or general psychiatric management. These approaches not only take into account the typical conflictual themes (e.g., expectation of lack of availability of others), but also they emphasize structural characterological deficits (e.g., difficulty utilizing deep interpretations), which require technical adaptations. All three of us illustrate such modifications. For example, Dr. Spayd, emphasized clear boundaries and anticipation of "bumps." Dr. Papiasvili suggests proactive monitoring of signs of the negative transference, while both she and I use "experience-near" interventions, which are more likely to be experienced as validating by Marie. All of us emphasize a prolonged "preparatory phase" in treatment that defines a safe and workable frame.

At the same time, it seems that there are some differences among us in terms of the expected mutative role therapeutic relation versus relationships and events outside of treatment. It seems that in line with psychoanalytic model Dr. Papiasvili is almost exclusively focusing on the therapeutic relationship and promoting change by transference analysis or analysis of resistance to change (Robert). On the other hand, Dr. Spayd is focusing on the patients' symptoms both in therapy and outside of therapy (Phillip, Robert, Marie) and the focus on therapeutic relationship is mostly strategic in promoting collaboration, rather than mutative in and of itself, as psychoanalytic model would emphasize. This includes more directive interventions, such as skills practice, homework assignments, exposure practice, and instructing the clients to implement learned skills outside of therapy—interventions that are inconsistent with the psychoanalytic model. I adopt a pragmatic approach that tailors treatment to the patient's strengths and weaknesses and also takes into account evidence-based treatments.

Emphasizing perspective and agency of the client—an important goal of treatment—seems to be present in all of our approaches. However, we use somewhat different interventions to accomplish that. For example, Dr. Spayd is suggesting that Robert should be instructed to decide effectiveness of nondrinking experiment and asking him to monitor his own drinking behaviors. Dr. Papiasvili is inviting Marie to use a stop sign, and I emphasize awareness of power differential in treatment of Phillip.

Targeting symptoms versus targeting underlying problems (e.g., conflicts) is another controversy. Dr. Papiasvili is more inclined to target conflicts and developmental antecedents (and expect that symptoms will change as a result of these interventions) and Dr. Spayd is more likely to target symptoms (and view conflicts and developmental factors as reasons that explain the symptoms). However, these differences seem to result from these clinicians' affiliations with the psychoanalytic versus cognitive behavior models.

The role of emotional deepening is another point of controversy. Dr. Spayd is advising to minimize such deepening in cases of Phillip and Marie, while Dr. Papiasvili and I suggest that such deepening is likely to be beneficial (if the client can tolerate it). I think this disagreement is illustrative of understanding of what such deepening entails. I usually assume that if the patient is already experiencing an emotion but is not expressing it, it is important to validate it and make room for it in treatment so that the patient can process the emotion together with the therapist. Other clients avoid painful experiences through different strongly expressed emotions. In these cases, they need to be helped to identify, experience, and process the original emotions.

Thank you for the opportunity to comment on the chapters. This has been a very inspiring and educational experience for me.

Editors' Comments

While the three therapist/authors recognized clear differences among their respective understanding of, and general approach to, the clinical cases (sometimes with astonishment, as expressed by Dr. Spayd's evocative "Wow!"), their conceptually rich and clinically helpful comments also highlight several commonalities in the use of empirically derived principles of change. A number of these convergences were noted by at least two of them, such as the importance of the principles related to the client engagement (e.g., active participation), and the therapeutic relationship (e.g., working alliance, repair of alliance ruptures, and therapist's empathy). Two prognostic principles were also identified as common principles by at least two authors: the role of childhood traumatic experiences in the etiology and treatment of social phobia and the therapeutic value of increasing intrinsic motivation or client's agency. In addition, two interventions principles were reported as convergences by two of the three therapists/authors: fostering adaptive interpersonal changes and therapeutic flexibility. Other principles were identified as common practice by one author, including the provision of feedback and the use of nondirective interventions with highly resisting clients. Dr. Weinberg also points to shared developmental stages in the treatment of Marie, with the use of supportive interventions early and expressive techniques later in therapy.

Interestingly, the degree of convergence for specific principles appear to vary with different cases. For Dr. Spayd, for example, the clinical relevance of the alliance is less crucial for the treatment of Phillip (a less complex case) than for her colleagues. As noted by Dr. Papiasvili, more flexibility and creativity in the implementation of one's preferred model (CBT or psychodynamic) might be called for when working with clients, like Robert and Marie, presenting with more severe and difficult problems (although Dr. Weinberg argued for the modification of usual treatment for Phillip).

What the three previous comments also convey is that principles of change can be implemented in different ways—even those principles that are perceived by therapists as sources of convergence. This is illustrated, for example, in diverse methods described to establish a good therapeutic alliance, to deal with high level of resistance, to meet similar goals at different stages of treatment, as well as to promote client active participation, intrinsic motivation or agency, and adaptive interpersonal changes. As Dr. Spayd pointed out, however, very similar strategies can be used in divergent theoretical approaches in identifying and working with alliance ruptures.

What also emerged from the previous comments are differences in terms of reliance on some principles. Many of these differences (such as the use of transference interpretations, emotional deepening, behavioral activation, and symptom reduction techniques) are consistent with self-identified theoretical allegiance (e.g., psychodynamic or CBT), as well as with the unique profile of intervention of each therapist presented in Chapter 8. Interestingly, as illustrated by Dr. Papiasvili with regard to self-disclosure, a principle can be implemented with various level of frequency and for different (although not irreconcilable) therapeutic purposes.

Despite, or perhaps because of, differences in how to apply principles or how much to rely on some of them, all three therapists/authors made it clear that they benefited from reading the work of their colleagues. Specific lessons that they derived involve insights and/or strategies related to subtle, complex, but crucial issues, such as paying attention to ethnic (generational) status of client, creating collaborative rather than authoritative therapeutic relationship, validating client's experience, fostering his or her sense of responsibility, addressing resistance or ambivalence toward change, and helping clients with BPD to develop self-control over boundaries with therapist.

Clinical Importance of Principles in Practice

After having completed their respective chapters, therapists/authors were asked to rate the helpfulness (on a 10-point scale, with 10 being most helpful and 1 being least helpful) of each of the 38 empirically based principles retained for this book (see Box 12.1). The following discussion provides a summary of these ratings (organized within each of the five clusters of principles)—ratings that were complemented with notes provided by the therapists/authors (or statements made in their chapter) related to the usefulness or clinical validity of particular principles.

As indicated in Box 12.1, four of the nine prognostic principles were viewed as reflecting clinically important information by the three therapists/authors (with a mean rating of close to or above 8): level of baseline impairment (Principle 1), initial expectations (Principle 4), intrinsic/autonomous motivation (Principle 5), and stages of change readiness (Principle 6). Four other principles were rated high (>7) by both Drs. Papiasvili and Weinberg but low (≤3) by Dr. Spayd. For two of these principles (attachment [Principle 3] and adverse childhood events [Principle 8]), the discrepancy appears to reflect differential affinity (toward or away from) psychodynamic assumptions about psychopathology. Consistent with her cognitive behavioral leaning, Dr. Spayd views Principle 9 (negative self-attribution) relevant to the treatment of social phobia, but she disagrees with the way the principle is formulated: In her experience, clients with higher levels of negative self-attributions will benefit more rather than less from treatment, as extremely negative thoughts can be easier to identify and change. Her low rating of this principle therefore reflects an issue of perceived validity rather than helpfulness.

Box 12.1 Rating of Helpfulness of Empirically Based Principles

Anxiety Disorders Section
Client Prognostic Principles

1. Clients with higher levels of baseline impairment may benefit less from psychotherapy than clients with lower levels of impairment.
   Dr. Papiasvili: 8; Dr. Spayd: 7; Dr. Weinberg: 8
   Mean: 7.67
2. Clients whose primary presenting problems are complicated by a co-morbid secondary personality disorder diagnosis may benefit less from psychotherapy than clients without a co-morbid personality disorder diagnosis.
   Dr. Papiasvili: 8; Dr. Spayd: 5; Dr. Weinberg: 5
   Mean: 6
3. Clients with more secure attachment may benefit more from psychotherapy than clients with less secure attachment (i.e., more attachment anxiety).
   Dr. Papiasvili: 9; Dr. Spayd: 1; Dr. Weinberg: 10
   Mean: 6.67
4. Clients with higher initial expectations for benefitting from psychotherapy may benefit more from it than clients with lower initial outcome expectations.
   Dr. Papiasvili: 9; Dr. Spayd: 10; Dr. Weinberg: 10
   Mean: 9.67
5. Clients who are more intrinsically (or autonomously) motivated to engage in psychotherapy may benefit more from it than clients who are less intrinsically (or autonomously) motivated.
   Dr. Papiasvili: 9; Dr. Spayd: 7; Dr. Weinberg: 10
   Mean: 8.67
6. Clients in advanced stages of change readiness (i.e., they are actively preparing for or currently taking action toward healthy behavior) may benefit more from psychotherapy than clients at lower stages of change readiness.
   Dr. Papiasvili: 8; Dr. Spayd: 9; Dr. Weinberg: 10
   Mean: 9

7. Clients with low socio-economic status and employment problems may benefit less from psychotherapy than clients with higher socio-economic status and no employment problems.
Dr. Papiasvili: 7; Dr. Spayd: 3; Dr. Weinberg: 8
Mean: 6

8. Clients who have experienced adverse childhood events may benefit less from psychotherapy than clients who did not experience adverse childhood events.
Dr. Papiasvili: 8; Dr. Spayd: 1; Dr. Weinberg: 8
Mean: 5.67

9. Anxious clients with more negative self-attributions may benefit less from psychotherapy than clients with fewer negative self-attributions.
Dr. Papiasvili: 7; Dr. Spayd: 1; Dr. Weinberg: 10
Mean: 6

Treatment/Provider Moderating Principles

10. Clients whose therapist uses interventions consistent with the client's level of problem assimilation may benefit more from psychotherapy than patients whose interventions are not consistent with their assimilation level.
Dr. Papiasvili: 8; Dr. Spayd: 7; Dr. Weinberg: 10
Mean: 8.33

11. Clients with higher levels of resistance may benefit more from psychotherapy that is more nondirective compared to clients with lower levels of resistance who may benefit more from psychotherapy that is more directive.
Dr. Papiasvili: 8; Dr. Spayd: 7; Dr. Weinberg: 10
Mean: 8.33

12. Clients with lower motivation for, or higher ambivalence about, change may benefit more from psychotherapy when their therapist is responsive and person-centered versus more directive and change-oriented.
Dr. Papiasvili: 8; Dr. Spayd: 7; Dr. Weinberg: 10
Mean: 8.33

13. Clients who are matched to their preferred therapy role, therapist demographics, or treatment type may benefit more from psychotherapy than clients unmatched on these preferences.
Dr. Papiasvili: 6; Dr. Spayd: 7; Dr. Weinberg: 10
Mean: 7.67

14. Clients whose preference for religiously or spiritually oriented psychotherapy is accommodated may benefit more from treatment than clients whose preference is unmet.
    Dr. Papiasvili: 5; Dr. Spayd: 2; Dr. Weinberg: 10
    Mean: 5.67
15. Clients who present with poorer interpersonal functioning are likely to benefit less from psychotherapy when their therapist uses a higher versus lower proportion of *transference* interpretations.
    Dr. Papiasvili: 8; Dr. Spayd: 5; Dr. Weinberg: 8
    Mean: 7
16. Clients higher in baseline impairment may benefit more from psychotherapy that is longer-term and/or more intensive compared to clients lower in baseline impairment who may benefit equally well from psychotherapy that is long- or short-term and/or more or less intensive.
    Dr. Papiasvili: 8; Dr. Spayd: 7; Dr. Weinberg: 10
    Mean: 8.33
17. Clients with externalizing coping styles may benefit more from psychotherapy that is more focused on behavior change and symptom reduction than fostering insight and self-awareness.
    Dr. Papiasvili: 7; Dr. Spayd: 7; Dr. Weinberg: 10
    Mean: 8
18. Clients with internalizing coping styles may benefit more from psychotherapy that is more focused on fostering insight and self-awareness than behavior change and symptom reduction.
    Dr. Papiasvili: 10; Dr. Spayd: 5; Dr. Weinberg: 10
    Mean: 8.33
19. Clients with moderate to severe impairment and/or fewer social supports will benefit more from psychotherapy when their therapist helps them address their social or medical needs.
    Dr. Papiasvili: 7; Dr. Spayd: 9; Dr. Weinberg: 10
    Mean: 8.67
20. Clients with substance use problems may be equally likely to benefit from psychotherapy delivered by a therapist with or without his or her own history of substance use problems.
    Dr. Papiasvili: 8; Dr. Spayd: 2; Dr. Weinberg: 10
    Mean: 6.67

Client Process Variables

21. Clients who more actively participate in the treatment process may benefit more from psychotherapy than clients who less actively participate.
    Dr. Papiasvili: 10; Dr. Spayd: 9; Dr. Weinberg: 10
    Mean: 9.67
22. Clients who are more resistant to the therapist or therapy may benefit less from psychotherapy than clients who are less resistant.
    Dr. Papiasvili: 9; Dr. Spayd: 7; Dr. Weinberg: 10
    Mean: 8.67

Therapy Relationship Principles

23. Clients experiencing a higher quality therapeutic alliance in group psychotherapy (group cohesion) or individual psychotherapy (bonding/collaboration) may benefit more than clients experiencing a lower quality alliance.
    Dr. Papiasvili: 10; Dr. Spayd: 8; Dr. Weinberg: 10
    Mean: 9.33
24. Clients experiencing more therapist regard and affirmation may benefit more from psychotherapy than clients experiencing less therapist regard and affirmation.
    Dr. Papiasvili: 10; Dr. Spayd: 9; Dr. Weinberg: 10
    Mean: 9.67
25. Clients experiencing more therapist congruence may benefit more from psychotherapy than clients experiencing less therapist congruence.
    Dr. Papiasvili: 9; Dr. Spayd: 9; Dr. Weinberg: 9
    Mean: 9
26. Clients experiencing more therapist empathy may benefit more from psychotherapy than clients experiencing less therapist empathy.
    Dr. Papiasvili: 10; Dr. Spayd: 9; Dr. Weinberg: 9
    Mean: 9.33
27. Clients who experience alliance rupture–repair episodes and/or who work with therapists trained to repair alliance ruptures may benefit more from psychotherapy than clients who experience no or unrepaired ruptures and/or work with therapists not trained specifically on rupture–repair interventions.
    Dr. Papiasvili: 10; Dr. Spayd: 7; Dr. Weinberg: 10
    Mean: 9

28. Clients whose therapist uses more supportive self-disclosures may benefit more from psychotherapy than clients whose therapist uses less supportive self-disclosures (or does not disclose at all).
Dr. Papiasvili: 9; Dr. Spayd: 1; Dr. Weinberg: 5
Mean: 5

Therapist Intervention Principles

29. Clients whose therapist uses a higher proportion of general psychodynamic interpretations may benefit more from psychotherapy than clients whose therapist uses a lower proportion of general psychodynamic interpretations.
Dr. Papiasvili: 10; Dr. Spayd: 1; Dr. Weinberg: 7
Mean: 6

30. Clients whose therapist uses higher quality psychodynamic interpretations may benefit more from psychotherapy than clients whose therapist uses lower quality psychodynamic interpretations (see glossary for definition of quality of psychodynamic interpretation).
Dr. Papiasvili: 10; Dr. Spayd: 4; Dr. Weinberg: 10
Mean: 8

31. Clients whose therapist receives feedback based on a routinely delivered outcome measure may benefit more from psychotherapy than clients whose therapist does not receive feedback.
Dr. Papiasvili: Not applicable; Dr. Spayd: 7; Dr. Weinberg: 10
Mean: 8.5

32. Clients who receive feedback from their therapist on their performance in treatment may benefit more from psychotherapy than clients who do not receive feedback
Dr. Papiasvili: 8; Dr. Spayd: 9; Dr. Weinberg: 10.
Mean: 9

33. Clients may benefit more from psychotherapy when their therapist is more versus less flexible in their administration of, or adherence to, a given treatment approach.
Dr. Papiasvili: 9; Dr. Spayd: 9; Dr. Weinberg: 10
Mean: 9.33

34. Clients whose therapist selectively/responsively fosters more adaptive interpersonal changes may benefit more broadly from psychotherapy than those whose therapist fosters fewer adaptive interpersonal changes.
Dr. Papiasvili: 8; Dr. Spayd: 10; Dr. Weinberg: 10
Mean: 9.33

35. Clients whose therapist selectively/responsively fosters more self-understanding may benefit more broadly from psychotherapy than clients whose therapist fosters less self-understanding.
Dr. Papiasvili: 10; Dr. Spayd: 7; Dr. Weinberg: 10
Mean: 9

36. Clients whose therapist selectively/responsively fosters more emotional experiencing and/or deepening may benefit more broadly from psychotherapy than clients whose therapist fosters less emotional experiencing and/or deepening.
Dr. Papiasvili: 10; Dr. Spayd: 7; Dr. Weinberg: 10
Mean: 9

37. Clients whose therapist selectively/responsively uses nondirective interventions skillfully may benefit more from psychotherapy than clients whose therapist uses nondirective interventions unskillfully.
Dr. Papiasvili: 10; Dr. Spayd: 7; Dr. Weinberg: 10
Mean: 9

38. Clients whose therapist selectively/responsively fosters more behavior changes may benefit more broadly from psychotherapy than clients whose therapist fosters fewer behavior changes.
Dr. Papiasvili: 7; Dr. Spayd: 10; Dr. Weinberg: 10
Mean: 9

Note. Ratings of helpfulness is based on a 10-scale with 10 being most helpful and 1 being least helpful.

Dr. Spayd also disagrees with Principle 7 (that low socio-economic status [SES] and employment problems may put clients at a disadvantage in terms of benefiting from therapy). Despite rating this principle rather highly, her colleagues also see flaws in the way it is formulated, with Dr. Papiasvili pointing out that level of education does not necessarily coincide with SES and/or employment problems, and Dr. Weinberg arguing that SES is likely to have an inverted U-shaped relationship with the outcome (in the same way that low SES limits clients' resources, an exceptionally high SES creates opportunities for misuses of fortune—secondary gain, not needing to work, being able to pay their way through life and difficulties). Lastly, the prognostic principle regarding personality disorder (Principle 2) was perceived as relatively more helpful by Dr. Papiasvili (who gave it a score of 8) than by her two colleagues (who both rated it as 5). Interestingly, however, she believes that the principle is too general, as different personality disorders may have different prognosis.

Interestingly, the idea that this principle is helpful for some, but not all types of personality disorders is the reason why both Drs. Spayd and Weinberg rated it as a 5 (an average score, literally).

Most of the eleven treatment/provider moderating principles were rated high on average. The mean for 10 of them was higher than 6, and 7 of those reached a mean of 8 or above. Yet, noteworthy observations were made regarding the validity or at least generalizability of some of these principles. In contrast with Principle 15 (which stipulate that clients who present with poorer interpersonal functioning are likely to benefit less from psychotherapy when their therapist uses a higher versus lower proportion of transference interpretations), Dr. Spayd argues in her chapter that her work with Marie (a case with personality disorder) would focus on their relationship and Marie's transferential reactions to help her develop more adaptive interpersonal relationships. Providing a complementary perspective, Dr. Weinberg notes that transference interpretations can be helpful, even when provided to clients with severe interpersonal problems, if they are offered in a nonjudgmental, nonblaming way. Such interpretations can be helpful for clients who have enough curiosity about their own processes and have the capacity to make use of them. This is especially true when such interpretations are preceded by a long period of collaborative explorations.

In her chapter, Dr. Spayd also questioned the validity of Principle 18 (clients with internalizing coping styles may benefit more from psychotherapy that is more focused on fostering insight and self-awareness than behavior change and symptom reduction). She warns that a primary focus on thinking rather than on doing with an internalizing client (Phillip) would reinforce his maladaptive ruminative and avoidance coping styles.

It is also noteworthy that Dr. Spayd's rating of Principle 20 (clients with substance use problems may be equally likely to benefit from psychotherapy delivered by a therapist with or without his or her own history of substance use problems) is much lower than the rating of her two colleagues. Dr. Spayd questioned why one's experience with this issue (substance abuse) be any different than if a therapist has experience with any other difficulty being addressed in treatment (e.g., divorce, racial discrimination, being of a certain religion, being homosexual vs. heterosexual). As psychotherapists, she believes that we are trained to listen to and learn from the patient's expressed experience and not to use our own past experience as a gage of their functioning, perceptions, emotions, etc. The only difference she can see being relevant with substance abuse is the known phenomenon of such patients being dishonest with the therapist about continuing usage of the substance, with the clinical wisdom being that another individual with a substance abuse history would have more finely tuned radar for such dishonesty. But, being untruthful with one's therapist (and even oneself) is certainly a common therapeutic phenomenon for many different issues, and, again, a skilled therapist should know how to discern and address this.

Like Dr. Spayd, Drs. Weinberg and Papiasvili believe that therapists with or without history of substance use problems can be equally efficient in treatments with clients with these problems. For both of them, however, the principle is clinically helpful because it points to a key issue—whether or not a therapist with past problems with substance abuse has been able to resolve and integrate such difficulties. Dr. Weinberg notes that prior history could serve as a source of empathy, but, if not fully worked through, it can become a source of countertransference enactment. In these cases, therapist might take either an overly forgiving position or a judgmental one, to name just a few such attitudes.

A discrepancy is also observed for Principle 14 (clients whose preference for religiously or spiritually oriented psychotherapy is accommodated may benefit more from treatment than clients whose preference is unmet), the only principle with a mean lower than 6. Dr. Spayd gave a rating of 2 for this and Principle 20 for a very similar reason—her belief that psychotherapists should be open and responsive to their clients' experience. She also stated that this principle would only be relevant if a client wishes to hear therapeutic concepts presented through a spiritual "lens." However, she noted that very few individuals have expressed such wish in her career and that, in such cases, she referred them to another therapist. Dr. Weinberg gave a rating of 10 to this principle because of his belief that therapy is likely to be most efficient when there is a match between the language of the therapy and the language of the client. Therapists who listen to their clients about what they see as working for them are more likely to establish a collaborative and effective working alliance. This principle is also clinically important for Dr. Papiasvili, but her relatively low rating (5) reflects her misgiving about the way it is formulated. What matters in her eyes is that the dynamic meaning of religious or spiritual preferences be considered and explored during therapy—not that they are accommodated at face value.

Box 12.1 also shows that the two principles related to client process variables, as well as five of the six therapy relationship principles were scored very highly, all with an average above 8. The other relationship principle on self-disclosure (Principle 28) was rated highly by Dr. Papiasvili (9), but much less so by Dr. Weinberg (5) and Dr. Spayd (1). Dr. Weinberg's score reflects the fact that he distinguishes between two types of disclosures: (a) disclosures about himself in response to what the client is sharing and (b) disclosures of how the client is affecting him, such as effects of the client's interpersonal behaviors. While he found that there are numerous risks associated with the first type, he believes that there are numerous benefits that can come out of the second one. In contrast, Dr. Spayd's low score reflects that she generally does not use self-disclosure during therapy.

Similarly, all but one of the 10 interventions principles were rated, on average, 8 or above. The mean of the other principle (Principle 29) was lower due to Dr. Spayd's infrequent use of psychodynamic interpretations. Interestingly, Dr. Weinberg, who has a closer affinity with the psychodynamic tradition, notes that he tends to use a lot of explorations and empathic validations before he uses interpretation and (in line with Principle 15) an even higher proportion of explorations, clarifications, and empathic validation over interpretations with patients with lower level offunctioning. It is also worth noting that while Dr. Spayd rated Principle 36 (fostering emotional experiencing and/or deepening) fairly highly (7), she views this principle as applicable to some, but not all clients.

Lastly, it should also be noted that Principle 31 (use of routine outcome measure) was not rated by Dr. Papiasvili, as she does not use psychometrically based feedback in her practice.

Editors' Comments

As it was the case for the concluding chapter of the depression section (Chapter 7), the majority of the principles were rated highly in terms of helpfulness, but a number of them were not perceived as helpful and/or clinically valid by some therapists/authors. Yet, some of the latter principles have been shown to have a robust effect on clinical outcomes ($d = 0.55$ for both Principles 17 and 18 combined; Beutler, Harwood, Kimpara, Verdirame, & Blau, 2011). Of course, none of the principle, even the ones with the highest effect size, fully capture all the nuances of the process of change. It may thus be possible that, as feared by Dr. Spayd, a focus on insight would reinforce a pattern of avoidance for a client like Phillip with internalizing tendency. But it may also be that this would primarily be the case if focusing on cognitive appraisal was done rigidly and/or throughout the entire treatment. We would certainly not argue that the behavior changes aimed by Dr. Spayd would be countertherapeutic. Considering the current empirical evidence, however, it might be that she could improve her effectiveness with internalizing clients if she were to use, particularly early in therapy, interventions that would be consistent with the way they have coped with previous stress. In the case of Phillip, for example, relying on his introspective and intellectual abilities to acquire a new perspective of self and the world might be comforting, even validating. Such shift in understanding might possibly enhance a sense of self-efficacy and working alliance, which, in turn, might provide solid foundations to help him engage in what could be, in his case, highly beneficial, but also highly stressful, interpersonal changes.

The difficult question is how to best examine and possibly reduce discrepancies between therapists' subjective perspective and current available evidence, as well as some of the discrepancies between clinicians that are highlighted in the previous discussion. Although beyond the scope of this book, this could involve discussions between clinicians and researchers anchored in multiple sources of information and experiences, such as (a) reading of journal articles that summarize empirical data and effects size; (b) observations of taped therapy sessions illustrating both the implementation and impact (positive, neutral, harmful) of interventions consistent and inconsistent with particular principles; and (c) training of clinicians by researchers (and vice versa!) focused on principles that are sources of discrepancies.

Possible Combinations of Separate Principles

The three therapists/authors who contributed to the anxiety section have described many situations in their respective chapters where principles are intertwined. As eloquently captured by Dr. Papiasvili, no principle is implemented "on its own merit or in isolation." However, neither she nor Dr. Weinberg has suggested the deletion or combination of some principles because of high levels of similarity. In contrast, Dr. Spayd offered suggestions for collapsing some overlapping principles.

In Dr. Spayd's view, Principle 3 (secure attachment) is fundamentally an example or an outcome of Principle 8 (adverse childhood events), though a particularly important one in clients with social anxiety. On that basis, she suggested the possibility of combining both principles as follow: "Clients who have experienced adverse childhood events, at times resulting in less secure attachment, may benefit less from psychotherapy than clients who did not experience adverse childhood events." She did, however, express ambivalence about the merit of combining them, as doing so takes the emphasis off the secure attachment issue.

For Dr. Spayd, one's expectations are likely to correlate strongly with, or perhaps even cause, the level of one's intrinsic motivation to engage in the treatment process. Accordingly, she suggested the possibility of combining Principles 4 and 5 into the following: "Clients with higher initial expectations and intrinsic motivation to engage in psychotherapy may benefit more than clients with lower initial expectations and/or less intrinsic motivation." While arguing that the two original principles greatly overlap, she also recognized that a client might initially have high expectations but once actually "in the trenches" of therapy may not be motivated to fully engage—perhaps because he or she had no idea of how much mental work would be involved.

In addition, Dr. Spayd views the main concepts of Principles 11 and 12 ("resistance" vs. "lower motivation for, or higher ambivalence about") to have a similar meaning. She therefore suggested combining these principles into a single one: "Clients with lower motivation for, higher levels of ambivalence about, or resistance to change may benefit more from a psychotherapeutic approach that is responsive and person-centered, rather than directive and change-oriented." In her chapter, she also commented that Principle 5 (which refers to motivation as a prognostic characteristic) and Principle 22 (which refers to resistance as a client process variable) are redundant.

Editors' Comments

We appreciate Dr. Spayd's careful considerations of the advantages and disadvantages of combining some overlapping principles (i.e., Principles 3 and 8 and Principles 4 and 5). As we also mentioned in Chapter 7, there are benefits (in terms of conceptual efficiency) and costs (in terms of loss of clinically meaningful information) in aggregating concepts that have been found to be empirically reliable, valid, and distinctly predictive on their own. From our research standpoint, we are inclined to think that with more empirically derived information presented to them, more potentially useful heuristics will be available to clinicians when building broad case formulations, as well as when developing comprehensive and precise treatment plans. How this information is used obviously depends on particular clients: For some cases, the integration of several principles might lead to cohesive and insightful clinical pictures; for others, keeping some principles distinct may be helpful in determining what change to target, what resources to count on, and how and when to work with diverse problematic issues.

We would also like to express concerns about Dr. Spayd's suggestion to combine principles related to motivation and resistance (i.e., Principles 11 and 12 and Principles 5 and 22). These two constructs are related, yet they are not synonymous. Ambivalence, or lack of motivation, is an internal process, whereas resistance is interpersonal. And while poor motivation generally reflects passivity, resistance is frequently an active process, one that connotes a competition, usually for control and to avoid change. As one illustration of the distinct nature of these constructs, some clients who are motivated to begin therapy end up being uninterested in working with a particular therapist and/or disagreeing with specific treatment tasks. And, as illustrated in most if not all clinical chapters of this book, one of the most difficult, but important goals of the therapist is to help clients with initially low motivation to become engaged in therapy.

Future Research Directions about Principles

As was done in the depression section of this book, directions for future research on principles of change were generated from therapists/authors via two strategies. First, after they had completed their respective chapter, the authors were asked if they were aware of principles or strategies of intervention guiding their treatment that were not covered in the list of 38 empirically based principles. They were later invited to rate the helpfulness of nine principles that had not been presented to them prior to and while they wrote their chapter. These principles, as described in Chapter 2, were not included in the list retained for this book because our review of the literature indicated a lack of sufficient empirical support. The goal was to assess whether these deleted principles deserved, from the therapist/authors perspective, to be further investigated.

Clinically Based Principles

We first present principles that were initially generated by each of the clinical authors and then formulated as tentatively worded principles, co-constructed with the editors.

Dr. Papiasvili's Suggestions

- Clients who are more able to form a therapeutic/working alliance are more likely to benefit from therapy than clients who are less able to do so.
- Clients who are more able to form a transference with their therapist are more likely to benefit from therapy than clients who are less able to do so.
- Clients who have a greater ability for delay of gratification are more likely to benefit from therapy than clients who have a lesser ability to do so.

Dr. Spayd's Suggestions

- Clients who explicitly define and state their psychotherapy outcome goals early in treatment may benefit more than clients who do not complete this task.

Dr. Weinberg's Suggestions

- Clients are more likely to benefit from therapy, if their therapist conducts a thorough assessment, comes up with a formulation (meaningful summary that explains problems of the client in terms of meaningful psychological process, prior experiences, and contextual variables) and shares this formulation in experience-near terms.
- Clients are more likely to benefit from therapy if their therapist identifies and anticipates treatment-interfering behaviors.
- Clients whose therapist identifies realistic treatment goals are more likely to benefit from therapy than clients whose therapist does not.
- Clients who are engaged in meaningful activities outside of therapy (work, school) are more likely to benefit from treatment than those who are not.
- Clients who are sensitive to criticism, blame, or shame are more likely to benefit from therapy when their therapist explores issues of transference in relation with others in the client's life rather than in relation with the therapist (working in transference in displacement rather than working with transference within the therapeutic relationship).
- Clients with externalizing style and sensitivity to shame are more likely to benefit from treatment when interpretations are provided after longer periods of explorations of transferential feelings rather than after shorter periods.
- Clients with significant narcissistic or paranoid characteristics are likely to benefit more from a moderate use of empathic statements than from a limited or excessive use of such empathic statements (inverted U curve phenomena).
- Clients whose therapist has a more thorough understanding of their psychopathology (a clinical and theoretical knowledge about the disorders that the patient has) will benefit more from treatment than clients whose therapist's understanding is less thorough.

Principles Deleted from Empirically Based List

Box 12.2 presents each therapist helpfulness scores and mean (using the same 10-scale as before, with 10 being most helpful and 1 being least helpful) for nine principles, which, as the result of the literature reviewed conducted as part of this book, were not deemed to have a sufficiently strong empirical base to include them in the primary list of principles. Two of these principles did not earn a helpfulness score above 6 by any of the three therapists/authors (Deleted Principle 4, "If patients and therapists come from the same or similar racial/ethnic backgrounds, dropout rates are positively affected and improvement is enhanced," and Deleted Principle 9, "Younger clients may benefit more from psychotherapy than older clients"), suggesting that more research on these factors might not be viewed as particularly relevant—at least for some practitioners.

In contrast, four principles were rated 6 or above by the three therapists (Deleted Principle 2, "The therapist is likely to be more effective if he or she is patient"; Deleted Principle 3, "If psychotherapists are open, informed, and tolerant of various religious views, treatment effects are likely to be enhanced"; Deleted Principle 7, "Therapists working with a specific disorder may increase their effectiveness if they receive specialized training with this population"; and Deleted Principle 8 "The positive impact of therapy is likely to be increased if the therapist is comfortable with long-term, emotionally intense relationships").

The other three deleted principles, interestingly, show discrepancies among the therapists' ratings. In contrast with Dr. Spayd, Drs. Papiasvili and Weinberg rated very highly Deleted Principle 1 ("The benefits of therapy may be enhanced if the therapist is able to tolerate his or her own negative feelings regarding the patient and the treatment process"). Because this principle is related to the construct of countertransference, the rating discrepancy most likely reflects the authors respective affinity (or lack of thereof) with a psychodynamic perspective. Compared to her colleagues, Dr. Spayd also gave a low rating (4) to Deleted Principle 6 ("Positive change is likely if the therapist provides a structured treatment and remains focused in the application of his or her interventions"). This discrepancy, however, may, in part, be due to a lack of clarity of the principle, as it is currently formulated. Dr. Papiasvili noted her rating of 10 is based on the assumption that the construct of "structure" is defined as keeping an overall viable frame/setting, assuring both participants' safety and freedom to explore anything that is meaningful in the context of the patient's problems. She would, however, rate this principle as a 5 if "structure" is defined by restriction to specific proscribed topics. This rating is similar to

Box 12.2 Deleted Principles Based on Lack of Sufficient Evidence

Anxiety Disorders Section

1. The benefits of therapy may be enhanced if the therapist is able to tolerate his or her own negative feelings regarding the patient and the treatment process.
   Dr. Papiasvili: 10; Dr. Spayd: 5; Dr. Weinberg: 10
   Mean: 8.33
2. The therapist is likely to be more effective if he or she is patient.
   Dr. Papiasvili: 10; Dr. Spayd: 9; Dr. Weinberg: 10
   Mean: 9.67
3. If psychotherapists are open, informed, and tolerant of various religious views, treatment effects are likely to be enhanced.
   Dr. Papiasvili: 10; Dr. Spayd: 7; Dr. Weinberg: 10
   Mean: 9
4. If patients and therapists come from the same or similar racial/ethnic backgrounds, dropout rates are positively affected and improvement is enhanced.
   Dr. Papiasvili: 5; Dr. Spayd: 3; Dr. Weinberg: 5
   Mean: 4.33
5. Patients representing underserved ethnic or racial groups achieve fewer benefits from conventional psychotherapy than Anglo-American groups.
   Dr. Papiasvili: 5; Dr. Spayd: 2; Dr. Weinberg: 8
   Mean: 5
6. Positive change is likely if the therapist provides a structured treatment and remains focused in the application of his or her interventions.
   Dr. Papiasvili: 10; Dr. Spayd: 4; Dr. Weinberg: 8
   Mean: 7.33
7. Therapists working with a specific disorder may increase their effectiveness if they receive specialized training with this population.
   Dr. Papiasvili: 9; Dr. Spayd: 7; Dr. Weinberg: 10
   Mean: 8.67
8. The positive impact of therapy is likely to be increased if the therapist is comfortable with long-term, emotionally intense relationships.
   Dr. Papiasvili: 10; Dr. Spayd: 6; Dr. Weinberg: 10
   Mean: 8.67

> 9. Younger clients may benefit more from psychotherapy than older clients.
> Dr. Papiasvili: 6; Dr. Spayd: 2; Dr. Weinberg: 5
> Mean: 4.33
>
> *Note.* Ratings of helpfulness is based on a 10-scale with 10 being most helpful and 1 being least helpful.

Dr. Spayd, who read the construct of "structure" as close adherence to a treatment manual. Finally, Deleted Principle 5 ("Patients representing underserved ethnic or racial groups achieve fewer benefits from conventional psychotherapy than Anglo-American groups") was rated higher by Dr. Weinberg than by Drs. Papiasvili and Spayd.

Editors' Comments

The two strategies used to generate insights and input from clinicians have led, in our opinion, to interesting new directions for research. New principles derived from the three therapists/authors' experience, as well as seven of the nine deleted principles are promising candidates for studies that could be conducted to expand the current empirically based principles, as well as clarify the lack of consistency between the current state of research and the views of some therapists and/or between the perspective of various clinicians.

Final Thoughts

Concluding this chapter are final thoughts offered by therapists/authors and editors. Therapists/authors were invited to bring up new ideas related to principles of change, further highlight points that they presented in their chapter, react to the editors comments in the previous sections of the current chapter, as well as to discuss what they think we can learn from the principles of change with regard to two important issues: (a) what makes some therapists more effective than others, and (b) how we could improve therapist training. It was also an opportunity for the editors to contribute to a closing discussion about the role and implementation of principles of change.

Dr. Papiasvili's Closing Remarks

Reflecting on all of the authors' writings, it is my firm impression that in the face of therapeutic challenges, at a point of urgency, when resistance threatens to impede the patient and/or the treatment, therapists of different theoretical orientations will employ clinical flexibility and creativity. The ability to employ such clinical creativity and flexibility, however, needs to be felt as congruent and genuine to be effective. In fact, I will go out on a limb and hypothesize that it may be this very openness to expand one's technical repertoire, when genuinely felt that this is in the best interest of a patient, that differentiates effective therapists from not-so-effective ones. It may be this very dimension of the clinical work that is sometimes designated as clinical art.

This is also the very dimension of clinical work that may lead to the expansion of current models of psychotherapy and the construction of clinically substantiated theories. I believe that the divisions between theories are not absolute. Rather they are supported by diverse clinical needs of patients and different clinical–theoretical explanatory modes (and congruent technical arsenal) espoused by the therapists. Put simply, different theories recognize and focus on different dimensions of personality and different aspects of change. The complementarity and interconnectedness of clinical approaches, in line with the variety of patients' needs, may ultimately lead to more nuanced and more internally integrated clinical theory.

Dr. Spayd's Closing Remarks

In reviewing the editors' comments regarding the three author/therapists' divergences in helpfulness ratings, I wish to further explain my low rating of Principle 7 ("Clients with low SES and employment problems may benefit less from therapy"). It is not that I fully disagree with this concept (hence my rating of 3 as opposed to 1), but rather that I just do not find information about a client's SES is all that helpful in conducting therapy. I have developed a fairly automatic response of adjusting my vocabulary and communication style to match a client's level of comprehension; aside from this issue, our clients' (and our own) emotional problems seem to me to be universally experienced across all levels of SES.

I thought several times while writing my chapter that I would like to have reviewed a summary of the relevant empirically based literature that supported the principle I was addressing at the time. I therefore believe that educating psychotherapists (both those in graduate school training and practicing clinicians engaged in continuing education efforts) about these therapeutic principles of change could be a very rewarding endeavor. Goals of such an educational program would be to augment the clinicians' current therapeutic skills and thus, of course, hopefully improve their clients' therapeutic outcomes. I would envision such training first introducing one specific principle (or perhaps, in some cases, two related or opposing principles of change, such as Principles 17 and 18), presenting the research that supports the principle(s), and then providing structured opportunities to practice applying the principle(s) within varying theoretical orientations, via, for example, a role-play therapy format. Now *that's* a CE program I would rate as helpful in continuing my ongoing therapist education!

Although my last comments indicate the value that I see in receiving systematic training regarding principles of change, I want to end with what emerged for me as the "$64,000 question" when I was writing my chapter: Why does a clinician, at times, adhere to certain theoretical principles and resultant treatment strategies, while, at other times, follow his or her clinical intuition to deviate from his or her typical approach, with the goal of using more effective psychotherapeutic interventions to foster patient change?

Dr. Weinberg's Closing Remarks

In the age when the science of psychology is offering hope through empirically supported manualized treatments, the reality of clinical practice teaches us that the majority of our clients do not fit the inclusion criteria of the studies that validated these treatments in the first place (Lorenzo-Luaces et al., 2018). On the other hand, the art aspect of psychotherapy offers its promise through practices that are next to impossible to validate. Respectful attitude, deep listening, therapist's ability to relate to the client, and the therapist's ability to introduce new perspectives and behaviors are among the cornerstones of effective clinical engagement and most of them are related to the talent of the therapist. And yet, similar to parachutes that nobody tried to validate in a randomized controlled trial (Smith & Pell, 2003), we rely on them with the same tenacity. The dialectic between the science of clinical interventions and the art of the clinical engagement is what seems to be at the basis of identifying principles of change. They bridge the gap between the general treatment protocols and the individual client, as well as between the science and the art of therapy.

Therapists differ in their ability to engage and treat individual clients. Sometimes it is a matter of general effectiveness and sometimes, of a goodness-of-fit with a specific client. Implementation of principles of changes offers a promise that implementing these principles will create a better fit between the therapist and the client, thus paving the way for more effective therapies. This could mean that certain principles are more relevant for some clients than others, and, by extension, some therapists or even therapist–client dyads are better at implementing some principles than others. In fact, each therapist–client dyad is discovering, if not creating, these principles as they work together. Relying on principles, not on manualized protocols helps to develop a more integrated perspective on individual clients, even if they don't "fit" into a single protocol. Principles are also easier to teach. In my experience, clinicians in training usually perk up when I discuss treatment principles because those are easier to learn and implement while remaining thoughtful and flexible. Principles also leave room for therapists' own personal touch in their delivery and so they feel less confined and more creative in their clinical work. Instead of asking the question of who fits the treatment, we learn to ask the question what principles fit this client. And this is a more inclusive message.

Editors' Closing Remarks

We want to begin our final comment by stating that we greatly appreciate Dr. Spayd's take on the Principle 7 related to client's SES and employment. As we have also suggested in the concluding chapter of the depression section, if this and other principles fail to provide heuristics for responsive interventions to client's particular characteristics, they should be considered for removal in future revisions of principles of change. We are also in total agreement with her proposal for training. We think it is a great idea for therapists to be provided with summaries of literature supporting specific principles. In line with the recommendation made by one of authors (Dr. Johnson) in the depression section, we would even go one step further: Especially for principles that raise discrepancies between researchers and clinicians, discussions of original empirical papers upon which the principles are based should be part of training initiatives. This could lead to revisions of principles—hopefully make them more precise in terms of when, how, and/or for and by whom they are best applied. We also fully agree with Dr. Spayd that the rehearsal of strategies associated with particular principles would be optimal. Direct exposure to and feedback-based implementation of principles could be taught by academicians that have been involved in research on particular principles. The same could also be done by expert practitioners. For example, Dr. Weinberg could administer a workshop based on the way he teaches his supervisees about principles—now *that's* a continuing education program we would take to learn more, both clinically and empirically! As mentioned in Chapter 7, we (e.g., Holt et al., 2015) agree with him and Dr. Johnson (who wrote a chapter in the depression section of the book) that practice and training based on principles is more flexible and cost-effective than on treatment manuals.

We also believe that much can be derived from the therapists/authors remarks to better understand therapist effects. Dr. Weinberg identified a number of complex skills that have not been the primary focus of randomized controlled trials but that appear to us noteworthy candidates to explain why some therapists are better than others (Castonguay & Hill, 2017). Also highlighted by the three clinical authors is the therapist's flexibility and creativity (in using principles that are inconsistent with one's preferred theoretical orientation, in using different principles with different clients, or in deviating from principles to rely on one's intuition). For Dr. Papiasvili, the skillful actualization of such flexibility and creativity is what defines clinical art; for Dr. Spayd, figuring out the ins and out of this issue would be worth a lot of money!

As integrative scholars, we resonate with Dr. Papiasvili's idea that theoretical flexibility and openness is likely to enhance our conceptualization of the therapeutic process. As researchers, we also find interesting her observation that such flexibility and creativity were required (in her work and the work of her two colleagues) when confronted with difficult and challenging clients. This is because research tells us that therapist effects are particularly strong with highly distress and impaired clients (Barkham et al., 2017). In other words, who the therapist is makes a big difference in terms of the probability for very severe clients to improve. But what the research is not telling us is how this happens. The remarks of our clinical colleagues are providing us with some insightful cues as to what *generally* makes some therapists outperform others. As noted in our comments in the depression section, though, this only scratches the surface of the therapist effect. To us, our field far too often conceptualizes training as the dissemination of principles or strategies as though each therapist who received such training could be equally helpful when applying it. As we noted in Chapter 7, as the research advances on the therapist, we will surely see that, at least in some cases, different therapists will use similar strategies to different effects. Thus, training and dissemination becomes much more layered and much more about fit and matching *both* at the provider and recipient level. This is an acknowledgement that psychotherapy is not just about *what* works for whom (i.e., principles and strategies) but also *who* works for whom (i.e., providers in interaction with certain types of the patients or problems; Constantino, Boswell, Coyne, Kraus, & Castonguay, 2017). And, of course, we need to know *how* these things happen—yet another $64,000, or more, question!

As a final note, we have not talked about the interdiagnostic differences in how anxious and depressed patients were conceptualized and treated.

For example, while the three anxiety cases were virtually identical to the three depression cases, except for the primary symptom, all three therapists diagnosed one of the three anxious patients as BPD while such a diagnosis was not mentioned with respect to depressed patients. It was also interesting that the presentation of co-morbid social anxiety and alcohol abuse stimulated a discussion of how to pattern treatments in this chapter, whereas the co-morbidity of depression and substance abuse stimulated no such discussion among the therapist/authors who reviewed patients with depression. Anxiety as a symptom is clearly given a different meaning than depression both in the diagnostic and treatment processes that are independent of the principles. Such differences are food for scientific investigation. which we hope will lead to the clarification and addition of effective principles of change.

References

Barkham, M., Lutz, W., Lambert, M. J., & Saxon, D. (2017). Therapist effects, effective therapists, and the law of variability. In L. G. Castonguay & C. E. Hill (Eds.), *Therapist effects: Toward understanding how and why some therapists are better than others* (pp. 13–36). Washington, DC: American Psychological Association Press.

Barlow D. H. (Ed.). (2001) *Clinical handbook of psychological disorders* (3rd ed.). New York, NY: Guilford.

Beutler, L. E., Harwood, T. M., Kimpara, S., Verdirame, D., & Blau, K. (2011). Coping style. In J. C. Norcross (Ed.). *Psychotherapy relationships that work: Evidence-based responsiveness* (2nd ed., pp. 336–353). New York, NY: Oxford University Press.

Castonguay, L. G., & Hill, C. E. (Eds.). (2017). *How and why some therapists are better than others: Understanding therapist effects.* Washington, DC: American Psychological Association.

Constantino, M. J., Boswell, J. F., Coyne, A. E., Kraus, D. R., & Castonguay, L. G. (2017). Who works for whom and why? Integrating therapist effects analysis into psychotherapy outcome and process research. In L. G. Castonguay & C. E. Hill (Eds.), *Why are some therapists are better than others? Understanding therapist effects* (pp. 55–68). Washington DC: American Psychological Association. doi:10.1037/0000034-004

Fiscalini, J., & Grey, J. (Eds.). (1993). *Narcissism and interpersonal self.* New York, NY: Columbia University Press.

Holt, H., Beutler, L. E., Kimpara, S., Macias, S., Haug, N. A., Shiloff, N., . . . Stein, M. (2015). Evidence-based supervision: Tracking outcome and teaching principles of change in clinical supervision to bring science to integrative practice. *Psychotherapy, 52,* 185–189.

Horwitz, L., Gabbard, G. O., Allen, J. G., Frieswyk, S. H., Colson D. B., Newsom G. E., & Coyne, L. (1996). *Borderline personality disorder. Tailoring the psychotherapy to the patient.* Washington, DC: American Psychiatry Press.

Loewald, H. W. (1971). The transference neurosis: comments on the concept and the phenomenon. *Journal of the American Psychoanalytic Association, 19,* 54–66.

Lorenzo-Luaces, L., Zimmerman, M., & Cuijpers, P. (2018). Are studies of psychotherapies for depression more or less generalizable than studies of antidepressants? *Journal of Affective Disorders, 234,* 8–13. doi:10.1016/j.jad.2018.02.066

Smith, G. C., & Pell, J. P. (2003). Parachute use to prevent death and major trauma related to gravitational challenge: Systematic review of randomised controlled trials. *BMJ, 20,* 1459–1461. doi:10.1136/bmj.327.7429.1459

PART IV

CONCLUSION

13
Harvesting the Fruits of a Clinician-Researcher Collaboration and Planting Seeds for New Partnerships

Louis G. Castonguay, Michael J. Constantino, and Larry E. Beutler

The overarching goal of this book was to create a new pathway of collaboration between researchers and clinicians through the presentation of, and discussion about, unique and complementary types of knowledge. The first type of knowledge, provided by researchers, was a list of empirically based principles of change that could serve to improve the efficacy and efficiency of psychotherapy. The second type of knowledge, delivered by practitioners, was descriptions of how these principles are implemented in day-to-day clinical practice. Exchanges of perspectives between clinicians and researchers were then presented to better understand the place and helpfulness of the principles across different treatment approaches, as well as to generate suggestions about possible combinations of principles and future research.

The aims of this concluding chapter are to provide a brief summary of the specific steps that we pursued, what was achieved through these steps, and what were the experiences of both clinicians and researchers regarding the process and outcome of our collaborative venture, as well as to offer some suggestions to solidify and guide the future collaboration between clinicians and researchers.

Identification of Empirically Based Principles of Change

As described in Chapter 2, a list of principles published in an earlier book (Castonguay & Beutler, 2006) was first revised and updated by us, the editors. This revised list was used for an extensive review of empirical literature conducted by six graduate students. The results of this review led us to retain and formulate 38 principles, which were organized within the following five clusters or categories:

- Prognostic principles, which tell us about types of clients that are more or less likely to benefit from treatment.
- Moderating principles, which inform us about how to adjust our interventions to maximize efficacy based on certain client characteristics and prognostic factors, some of which are also identified in particular prognostic principles.
- Process principles, which describe ways of client being, feeling, or acting in sessions that either facilitate or interfere with change.
- Relationship principles, which describe elements of the client–therapist relationship that either facilitate or interfere with change.
- Intervention principles, which describe therapist behaviors and strategies that either facilitate or interfere with change.

Implementation of Empirically Based Principles of Change in Clinical Routine

Based on the recommendations of expert members of an advisory board, six experienced therapists representing a range of theoretical orientations were invited to describe if, how, when, and with whom they implement each of the retained principles of change in their day-to-day practice. In writing about such implementation, the authors were asked to refer to three cases (one with substance abuse, one with personality disorder, and another without either of these co-morbidities) presenting with a primary symptom of either depression or social phobia. They were encouraged to describe specific clinical situations and to do so as if they were talking to clinical supervisees or colleagues. Using hypothetical dialogues, quotes, and therapeutic events, they were asked to illustrate how they would make the principles work. This could entail giving examples of contexts that might call for or be indicative of a principle, describe specific interventions that might be used in these contexts, anticipate obstacles that might emerge, and discuss the way that they might address them.

As a result, the clinical authors not only brought the principles to life, but they also painted insightful pictures of how to conduct therapy. For each principle cluster, they provided concrete illustrations of how to make use of evidence-based information in ways that are responsive to particular clients. For example, rather than seeing prognostic principles as therapeutic contraindications or otherwise unactionable predictions, the clinical authors showed how clients' personal characteristics can help them foresee and prepare for difficulties of therapeutic involvement, as well as to adjust treatment to the particular strengths of a client.

This type of clinical knowledge is complementarity to, and greatly enrich, information that is provided by research evidence. Although the prognostic principles identify clients who are more or less likely to benefit from treatment, they do not tell us what to do with clients who vary in terms of the constructs that each of these principles define. Aside from showing that clinicians frequently do work with clients whom they know might not improve substantially (those who have high levels of impairment or low level of motivation, for example), the clinical chapters illustrate how the pace of therapy, the way of being with a client, the focus of treatment, and the manner of conducting therapy can differ based on prognostic characteristics.

The same type of knowledge is necessary, we believe, to provide broad and in-depth roadmaps of intervention vis-à-vis other principles of change. As one of us lamented a number of years ago (Castonguay, 2000), how helpful would it be for a therapist in training to be told by his or her supervisor, "Now, for your first session, make sure to build a good therapeutic alliance, as the research indicates that this is important." What a trainee will find in the clinicians' writing in this volume are not only depictions of different ways (based on various theoretical preferences) to establish and maintain a therapeutic relationship in general but also examples of obstacles he or she might expect (based on his or her assessment, case formulation, and/or treatment plan) for different cases, how these challenges may manifest themselves, and how he or she might anticipate, prevent, or address these challenges.

The same trainee, as well as more experienced therapists, will also find the same type of clinical "meat" to enrich the empirical "bones" of principles related to moderator, process, relationship, and technical variables, providing them with a wide range of specific lessons to deal with clinical questions such as, How do you adjust your way of conducting therapy based on the client's typical patterns of coping with stressful events? What are some of the client's ways of being in session that tells you that he or she is engaged in therapy? What are the different ways that you attempt to foster the engagement of particular clients? When, how, and for what purposes might you apply interventions to help these clients to explore their emotional experiences, explore their views of self and others, and change their behavior outside of psychotherapy?

We believe that the six clinical chapters of this book have succeeded in illustrating that principles are not guiding therapists on what to do in a uniform manner. Rather, they help therapists formulate their own general strategies that can be quite different from therapist to therapist, as well as for different clients and across a variety of contexts or markers of interventions. These principles manifest themselves via different strokes for different folks at different times. We also believe that what therapists do in implementing principles is not typically found in treatment manuals or usual textbooks about psychotherapy. As such, by relying on their clinical experience and rich knowledge, these clinicians provide a type of expertise that is beyond what is found in the current field of psychotherapy.

Reflections, Recommendations, and Exchanges about Empirical Principles of Change

After completing their chapters, the clinical authors were invited to provide thoughts on a diversity of issues regarding the principles and their implementation. As an effort to stimulate exchanges between research and clinical perspectives, the editors offered comments on these issues in the concluding chapters of both the depression and anxiety sections of the book. The following discussion identifies some of the ideas, questions, and recommendations for future directions (conceptual, clinical, and empirical) that have emerged from these of reflections and attempts (albeit initial and limited) at dialogue.

Convergences and Complementarities in the Implementation of Principles of Change

Rather than assuming that all principles play a role in different orientations and that such commonalities are more clearly and accurately captured from a bird's eye view (with us, the three editors, perched at the top of our academic Babel tower), we asked clinicians to read the chapters of their peers and to delineate, with their boots on the grounds, points of convergences and divergences among them.

In the two sections of the book, a number of principles in each of the five clusters were perceived as being common elements of effective clinical practice. Prominent among them were qualities of the therapeutic relationship and evidence of client engagement. Divergences in terms of emphasis given to some principles, as well as interventions use to implement them, were identified, with these differences predominantly viewed as viable alternatives of interventions and/or strategies to improve one's clinical model or technical repertoire. Considering the integrative perspective espoused by each of us (the editors), reading about the complex and nuanced level convergence and complementary detected by our clinical colleagues was, to say to least, gratifying.

Clinical Importance of Principles in Practice

Rather than assuming that all principles, including those that are perceived as common, are equal, clinically speaking, the clinical authors were invited to rate them in terms of helpfulness, as well as to voice any concerns, about their clinical validity. The therapists ratings, across both sections of the book, indicate that the majority of the principles were perceived as clinically helpful. Interestingly, however, some of them were not viewed as helpful and/or valid (sometimes by one therapist, sometime by more) for a number of reasons, including the absence of salient clinical information, failure to take into account the therapist's ability to adapt the client's needs and situations, too general (not applicable to all clients) or an otherwise flawed formulation, incompatibility with clinical observations, and inconsistency with clinical practice and/or theoretical affinity.

All of these critical arguments were viewed by us, the editors, as having clear merit. In our opinion, they could provide fertile grounds for meaningful dialogues about the role and place of theory and research in guiding practice. We also believe that they should inform revisions of the current list of principles. For example, it was proposed that principles being viewed as not informative in guiding responsive treatment might be removed. Notably, the possibility of removing prognostic variables was raised until hidden moderators are identified in future research to guide their use. In addition, suggestions were made to address discrepancies between clinical perception and empirical data regarding the validity and impact of some principles, including discussions of the empirical evidence, observations of clinical material, and bidirectional training experiences.

Possible Combinations of Separate Principles

Rather than assuming that each principle represents a unique and distinct heuristic to guide therapists' work, clinicians were asked if they believe that some of them should be combined. The suggestions of the clinical authors and the comments of the editors related to them have led to a number of propositions—none of them, in our opinion, irreconcilable:

- No principle is implemented in isolation. From a clinical standpoint, the principles are in a constant state of interaction and interdependence.
- Several principles highly overlap. The combination of pairs among them have been suggested (e.g., childhood adverse events and insecure attachment), but this could come at the cost of de-emphasizing valuable clinical information.
- A number of principles can be grouped into theoretically driven constructs (e.g., interventions for clients with high severity of impairment). The benefits of such aggregation, in terms of communication and dissemination, can serve important functions (e.g., training, supervision). Yet, promulgating a list of distinct principles, each based on empirically reliable and valid constructs, allows clinicians with an extensive basis of knowledge to guide their responsive assessment and interventions to a wide range of clients.

Future Research Directions about Principles

Rather than relying on our knowledge, as full-time academicians, regarding what has and has not been studied, we wanted to give clinicians an opportunity to have a voice in setting up a research agenda (Zarin, Pincus, West, & McIntyre, 1997) regarding principles of change. As a result, a wide range of directions for future investigations were generated, based on clinicians' own observations and/or their input on a number of principles previously investigated. Because some of these directions are consistent with the interest of many researchers (thus providing clinical credibility to their empirical pursuits) and others reflect new and bold ideas, it is difficult to think of more precious gifts to the field of research.

Clinicians and Researchers' Experience

Reflecting the collaborative nature of this project, clinicians were involved in designing the chapters they were invited to contribute. It was their idea to write a case formulation and treatment plan for each of the three cases they were presented with. In retrospect, we (the editors) fully appreciate how such foundational elements of clinical practice provided necessary context (above and beyond the rather lengthy case descriptions that we had already provided) to explain why and to illustrate how and when they implement particular principles for each individual cases. It was also clinicians who suggested that they begin each of their chapters by sharing their initial reactions toward the principles and their task of writing about them, as well as to end their chapter by describing their experience in writing them. As these might provide helpful lessons for future efforts of collaboration aimed at better understanding and improving psychotherapy, key elements of these reactions and experiences (as well as those capture in the "final thoughts" provided by the clinical authors and the editors in the concluding chapters of the depression and anxiety disorders sections) are highlighted here.

- No doubt explaining part of the reasons why they agreed to join this project, several clinical authors stated that the concept of principles is consistent, conceptually, with the way they view the process of change and, clinically, with the way they practice therapy. Relatedly, the principles were perceived as valid components of the empirical foundations of psychotherapy. For Drs. Johnson and Weinberg, they provide a more flexible approach to treatment manuals, which are frequently viewed as the most legitimate pillar of evidence-based practice.
- Describing how principles are implemented in day-to-day routine, however, was expected to be difficult—and it was. Two major difficulties stood out. First, how does one use a set of guidelines that has been derived from an aggregation of individuals when working with a particular client? Several authors indeed wrote about the challenge of illustrating in their chapter idiographic applications of nomothetic knowledge that reflect the complexity of the therapeutic process—using what, how, and when. Both the difficulty at hand and the prize that could be reached by mastering it was eloquently summed up by Dr. Wolf: "How the principles can provide a heuristic that informs appropriate contextual responsiveness represents the bridge from science to practice." Second, several clinicians felt that it would be impossible to write about one principle without writing about its connection with many others, within and across the five clusters—and they were correct. While these principles were presented as a list of separate guidelines, they are, in fact, interconnected. These two difficulties are, of course, related. As aptly stated by Dr. Papiasvili, "while for research and theory purposes it is extremely valuable to formulate abstract generalizable principles, in an 'alive' clinical work there is a complex, unique configuration of interactively connected principles applicable to each patient–therapist dyad, rather than any principle being implemented on its own merit or in isolation."

- Although the task was difficult, the authors described its completion as being worthwhile and gratifying. It helped them bring into awareness strategies that guide, most often implicitly, the way they think and work clinically. In doing so, it made those strategies more actionable. For example, reflecting on each of the principles made Dr. Johnson more appreciative of their respective role and provided him with ideas about how to make greater use of them. Dr. Spayd anticipates that conscious efforts to integrate principles in her treatment plan is likely to result in more effective interventions—by shaking her off of an "automatic pilot" mode of practicing therapy! Above and beyond making explicit what was implicit, writing about the 38 principles created new knowledge. For Dr. Papiasvili, some of what she learned emerged as a corrective experience—"as the work proceeded," she wrote, "I found what I initially feared as constricting and reductive to be actually expansive and creative, increasing the range of my clinical voice in many directions." Dr. Weinberg derived strategies to expend current treatments beyond their defined targets or scope of interventions—strategies that could be beneficial for the broadening of evidence practice. In addition to the learning that she gained for her own work, Dr. Vivan used her chapter to developed a training protocol that she has begun to test with her supervisees. Such an initiative shows that writing about the implementation of principles not only increases their actionability, it can potentially make them more retainable—for the authors involve and future generation of clinicians. Writing about principles also brought to light unfinished business. As noted by Dr. Wolf, for instance, a conceptual model capable of integrating these guidelines cohesively is needed, as are efforts to connect them with knowledge from other scientific domains (such as psychopathology, social psychology, developmental psychology, and neuroscience).
- With regard to our own experience, as editors and researchers, the best way to characterize it is that we learned a lot! Process-wise, it was exciting and gratifying to see our clinical colleagues gradually infusing, draft after draft, motions and sounds into a list of formal, rather stale descriptions of general guidelines. Outcome-wise, we are convinced that the type of information that one can find in each of the six clinical chapters could only have come from the expertise, observations, reflections, and insights of clinicians—not from researchers, administrators, nor policymakers. It is not that the experience of these other stakeholders of mental health services, let alone patients, is not pertinent. Like Kazdin (2008), however, we believe that knowledge of clinicians has not been fully harvested amidst the field's efforts to establish evidence-based foundations to the practice, training, and dissemination of psychotherapy. By seeking clinicians' views

about how to implement, revise, and investigate empirically based principles and by setting up exchanges on these views, we aimed to go further than the unidirectional exportation of information that typifies the connections between researchers and clinicians. We hope that this is a right step in building new territories of knowledge and action.

What's Next?

We would like to end with a few suggestions for future initiatives related to this book. First, at a content level, we think that the time is ripe to consolidate knowledge that has been derived from this and other efforts to identify principles of change, from a theoretical (e.g., Goldfried, 1980), quantitative (e.g., Beutler, Clarkin, & Bongar, 2000), and qualitative research perspective (Levitt, Pomerville, & Surace, 2916). Delineations of convergences and complementarity between and among these different epistemological sources could increase the robustness and breadth of these principle—and thus the contributions they can make to evidence-based practice. In line with Dr. Wolfe's recommendation, this could also lead to a new conceptualization of the process of change.

Although the current book was aimed at generating collaboration between clinicians and researchers, more elaborated and direct communication and partnerships are needed. This could take the form of a task force sponsored by organizations devoted the growth of the scientific-practitioners model, such as the Society for Psychotherapy Research, the Society for the Advancement of Psychotherapy, and the Society for the Exploration of Psychotherapy Integration. Connected or parallel to such a task force could be regularly planned meetings between researchers and clinicians to examine further questions, discrepancies, and recommendations raised in this book. In particular, we would find interesting to see such meetings focused on two issues that were given particular attention in the final thoughts sections of the concluding chapters of the depression and anxiety disorders sections—how to explain why some therapists are better than others and how to select and train effective therapists. Such meetings would complement an already-established "think tank" of researchers (the Penn State Conferences on the process of change), which has recently examined therapist effects (Castonguay & Hill, 2017) and is now addressing training.

We also believe that these task force and meetings can be a forum to design or promulgate single case studies in naturalistic settings to define specific principles and implement them in training (e.g., Beutler et al., 2014). While avoiding unrealistic burdens to clinical routine (see Koerner & Castonguay,

2015), such studies could investigate the impact of training programs aimed at learning how to implement specific principles of change. With increased knowledge in this realm, it is possible that traditional training models, which have gone largely unchanged through the history of the psychotherapy research field, could begin to be revised in a manner consistent with evidence (broadly generated). As one example, although every author involved in this book rated highly the importance of therapeutic alliance development, maintenance, and repair, a survey of graduate training programs indicated that explicit evidence-informed training in effective elements of the therapy relationship remain virtually nonexistent in graduate curricula (Constantino, Morrison, Coyne, & Howard, 2017). We hope that the future holds *disruptive innovation* in training models, not just for relationship elements but for all principles for which training can guide effective practice beyond, or complementary to, the top–down dissemination of sequenced treatment packages from self- or peer-nominated "experts" (Constantino, Coyne, & Gomez Penedo, 2017).

Take another example that emerged in the present book—resistance. Research is telling us that therapists delivering a formal treatment package can do better by their patients by responding to emergent resistance with principled-based motivational interviewing that appears to causally reduce resistance with the therapist's privileging of empathy, emotional evocation, and interpersonal autonomy-granting in moments when patients may question the utility of a given treatment or provider (Constantino, Westra, Antony, & Coyne, 2017; Westra, Constantino, & Antony, 2016). This is but one additional example where evidence can inform ways of dealing with commonly occurring therapy processes (like resistance) in a way that complements whatever approach from which a therapist operating. The present dialogues between clinicians and researchers tells us that this is stakeholder-driven research agenda, as all clinician authors discussed the potential threats that resistance can pose and the importance of addressing resistance effectively (even if it means operating outside of one's typical mode or sequence).

The aforementioned tasks forces and meetings could also examine divergence of perspectives highlighted in the book, such as the impact of using interventions consistent with or contrary to some principles of change. The same type of partnerships could guide or set up large studies, ideally via practice–research networks (Castonguay, 2011), to examine principles that were generated (or those viewed as deserving more empirical attention) by clinicians who participated in this project.

More important, however, we hope that this book will stand as a chain component of recent and future initiatives that were referred elsewhere as "Ask and tell" (Castonguay et al., 2013). These initiatives have been aimed at making public clinicians' knowledge about different aspects of the relationship between science and practice, whether it is their experience in using research-based interventions (Goldfried et al., 2014; Martin, Hess, Ain, Nelson, & Locke, 2012) or conducting research (Castonguay et al., 2010; Garland, Plemmons, & Koontz, 2006) or their views about the types of research that need to be conducted (Adam-Term et al., 2010; Taska et al., 2015; Youn et al., 2019). Such knowledge is crucial, in our opinion, to make psychotherapy research more clinically valid, actionable, and retainable.

References

Adam-term, R., Castonguay, L. G., Cavanagh, T., Hill, B., Johnson, B., Magnavita, J., . . . Spayd, C. (2010, June). *What do clinicians think about research?* Structured discussion presented at the meeting of the Society for Psychotherapy Research, Asilomar, CA.

Beutler, L. E., Clarkin, J. E., & Bongar, B. (2000). *Guidelines for the systematic treatment of the depressed patient*. New York, NY: Oxford University Press.

Beutler, L. E., Haug, N., Kimpara, S., Macias, S., Shiloff, N., Goldblum, P., . . . Temkin, R. (2014, August). *Systematic treatment selection (STS): Evidence based principles in supervision training*. Paper presented at the annual meeting of the American Psychological Association, Washington, DC.

Castonguay, L. G. (2000). A common factors approach to psychotherapy training. *Journal of Psychotherapy Integration, 10*, 263–285.

Castonguay, L. G. (2011). Psychotherapy, psychopathology, research and practice: Pathways of connections and integration. *Psychotherapy Research, 21*, 125–140.

Castonguay, L. G., Barkham, M., Lutz, W., & McAleavey, A. A. (2013). Practice-oriented research: Approaches and application. In M. J. Lambert (Ed.), *Bergin and Garfield's handbook of psychotherapy and behavior change* (6th ed., pp. 85–133). New York, NY: Wiley.

Castonguay, L. G., & Beutler, L. E. (Eds.). (2006). *Principles of therapeutic change that work*. New York, NY: Oxford University Press.

Castonguay, L. G., & Hill, C. E. (Eds.). (2017). *How and why some therapists are better than others: Understanding therapist effects*. Washington, DC: American Psychological Association.

Castonguay, L., Nelson, D., Boutselis, M, Chiswick, N., Damer, D., Hemmelstein, N., . . . Borkovec, T. (2010). Clinicians and/or researchers? A qualitative analysis of therapists' experiences in a practice research network. *Psychotherapy, 47*, 345–354.

Constantino, M. J., Coyne, A. E., & Gomez Penedo, J. M. (2017). Contextualized integration as a common playing field for clinicians and researchers: Comment on McWilliams. *Journal of Psychotherapy Integration, 27*, 296–303. doi:10.1037/int0000067

Constantino, M. J., Morrison, N. R., Coyne, A. E., & Howard, T. (2017). Exploring therapeutic alliance training in clinical and counseling psychology graduate programs. *Training and Education in Professional Psychology, 11*, 219–226. doi:10.1080/10503307.2017.1301689

Constantino, M. J., Westra, H. A., Antony, M. M., & Coyne, A. E. (2017). Specific and common processes as mediators of the long-term effects of cognitive-behavioral therapy integrated with motivational interviewing for generalized anxiety disorder. *Psychotherapy Research, 5*, 1–13. doi:10.1080/10503307.2017.1332794

Garland, A. F., Plemmons, D., & Koontz, L. (2006). Research-practice partnership in mental health: Lessons from participants. *Administration and Policy in Mental Health, 33*, 517–528.

Goldfried, M. R. (1980). Toward the delineation of therapeutic change principles. *American Psychologist, 35*, 991–999.

Goldfried, M. R., Newman, M., Castonguay, L. G., Fuertes, J. N., Magnavita, J. J., Sobell, L. C., & Wolf, A. W. (2014). On the dissemination of clinical experiences in using empirically supported treatments. *Behavior Therapy, 45*, 3–6.

Kazdin, A. E. (2008). Evidence-based treatment and practice: New opportunities to bridge clinical research and practice, enhance the knowledge base, and improve patient care. *American Psychologist, 63*, 146–159.

Koerner, K., & Castonguay, L. G. (2015). Practice-oriented research: What it takes to do collaborative research in private practice. *Psychotherapy Research, 25*, 67–83.

Levitt, H. M., Pomerville, A., & Surace, F. I. (2016). A qualitative meta-analysis examining client's experiences of psychotherapy: A new agenda. *Psychological Bulletin, 142*, 801–830.

Martin, J. L., Hess, T. R., Ain, S. C., Nelson, D. L., & Locke, B. D. (2012). Collecting multi-dimensional client data using repeated measures: Experiences of clients and counselors using the CCAPS-34. *Journal of College Counseling, 15*, 247–261.

Tasca, G. A., Sylvestre, J., Balfour, L., Chyurlia, L., Evans, J., Fortin-Langelier, B., . . . Wilson, B. (2015). What clinicians want: Findings from a psychotherapy practice research network survey. *Psychotherapy, 52*, 1–11.

Westra, H. A., Constantino, M. J., & Antony, M. M. (2016). Integrating motivational interviewing with cognitive-behavioral therapy for severe generalized anxiety disorder: An allegiance-controlled randomized clinical trial. *Journal of Consulting and Clinical Psychology, 84*, 768–782. doi:10.1037/ccp0000098

Youn, S. J., Xiao, H., McAleavey, A., Scofield, B. E., Pedersen, T. R., Castonguay, L. G., Locke, B. D. (2019). Assessing and investigating clinicians' research interests: Lessons on expanding practices and data collection in a large practice research network. *Psychotherapy, 56*, 67–82. doi.org/10.1037/pst0000192

Zarin, D. A., Pincus, H. A., West, J. C., & McIntyre, J. S. (1997). Practice-based research in psychiatry. *American Journal of Psychiatry, 154*, 1199–1208.

Author Index

Abreu, I., 3
Ackert, M., 33
Adamson, S. J., 27
Adam-Term, R., 374–75
Addis, M. E., 36–37
Ain, S. C., 374–75
Alimohamed, S., 24
Alonso, J., 33
Ametrano, R. M., 26
Amsterdam, J. D., 25
Angtuaco, L., 24
Antony, M. M., 210, 374
Arnkoff, D. B., 26
Arnow, B. A., 25–26
Arntz, A., 25
Aust, C., 24
Austin, S. B., 33

Baardseth, T. P., 25
Bachelor, A., 27
Back, S. E., 309
Bagby, R. M., 25, 35–36
Barkham, M., 3, 29, 360
Barlow, D. H., 335–36
Barrett, M. S., 36
Bartels, C., 24
Basden, S. L., 37
Bateman, A., 316
Bauer, S., 35
Beail, N., 31
Beauregard, A. M., 27, 33
Beck, A., 36
Beckham, E., 26
Beckham, J. C., 23
Bell, L., 24
Berant, E., 28
Bergin, A. E., 231–32
Berne, Eric, 161–62
Bernecker, Samantha, x
Bernecker, S. L., 26, 28, 209
Best, J. R., 31–32
Beutler, Larry E., 3, 4–5, 7, 13, 15, 22, 24, 28–29, 31, 33, 42, 129, 194, 208–9, 215, 349–50, 365–66, 373
Blatt, S., 24
Blau, K., 28, 31, 349–50

Bohart, A. C., 34
Bohman, H., 24
Bond, M., 28
Bongar, B., 42, 194, 373
Boswell, J. F., 208–9, 360
Bottlender, R., 23
Bowen, E., 27, 32
Bradizza, C. M., 25
Brancu, M., 23
Bressi, C., 35
Brown, D. P., 310–11
Brown, S., 27, 32
Brownell, C., 30
Bruce, K. R., 25
Bruce, S. E., 24
Brunett, Hanna, x
Buddeberg, C., 31
Budge, S. L., 25
Burke, B. L., 30
Burlingame, G. M., 33
Butler, A., 36

Caesar, S., 24
Calhoun, P. S., 23
Callahan, J. L., 30
Calvert, S. J., 29
Cardenas, V., 27, 32
Carter, J. D., 28
Castonguay, Louis G., 3, 4–5, 10–11, 13, 15, 41–42, 129, 208–9, 292, 360, 365–66, 367, 373–75
Chapman, J., 36
Choi-Kain, L., 316
Claiborn, C. D., 35
Clark, L. A., 36
Clarkin, J. E., 42, 194, 373
Clarkin, J. F., 316
Clerkin, E. M., 215
Cohen, L. H., 3
Collins, J. F., 26
Colson, D. B., 317
Constantino, Michael J., 4–5, 26, 208–9, 210, 360, 373–74
Cooper, C., 24
Cooper, M., 4
Coyne, A. E., 4–5, 208–9, 210, 360, 373–74

Coyne, L., 317
Craddock, N., 24
Crago, M., 29
Crameri, A., 31
Crane, A. M., 25
Crits-Christoph, P., 23, 26, 30–31, 34–35, 36
Culpepper, L., 24
Curry, J., 23–24

Daley, D. C., 313–14
Dalgleish, T., 32
Danese, A., 28
Davies, M., 32
Davis, D. E., 30
De Bolle, M., 25
Deckersbach, T., 31
Decuyper, M., 25
Dekker, J., 25
Del Re, A. C., 25, 33
DeMaria, A., 3
Derkzen, D. M., 27, 33
DeRubeis, R. J., 25
Detert, N. B., 29
Diener, M. J., 28
Dimidjian, S., 36–37
Dobson, K. S., 36–37
Docherty, J. P., 26
Doolin, E. M., 33
Douaihy, A. B., 313–14
Dreessen, L., 25
Dreyfus, H. L., 208
Dreyfus, S. E., 208
Dutra, L., 37
Dweck, Carol, 89

Eckert, J., 28
Edwards, C. J., 24, 194
Ehrenreich, H., 24
Elbogen, E. B., 23
Elkin, I., 26
Elliott, D. S., 310–11
Elliott, R., 3, 34, 36, 161–62
Ellison, W. D., 26, 28
Engle, D., 28
Entwhistle, S. R., 3
Epstein, L. H., 31–32
Erickson, T. M., 26
Eskildsen, A., 25
Eubanks-Carter, C., 34
Eyman, J. R., 317

Farber, Barry, x–xi, 7–8, 28, 33
Ferguson, B., 26

Fiscalini, J., 335
Flückiger, C., 33
Fonagy, P., 316
Forman, E., 36
Forty, L., 24
Fournier, J. C., 25
Frampton, C. M. A., 27, 28
Freire, E., 36
Fruyt, F. de, 25

Gallagher-Thompson, D., 28
Gallop, R., 25, 35
Gamache, D., 27
Garfield, E. S., 231–32
Garland, A. F., 4, 374–75
Geffken, G. R., 24, 25
Gelso, Charles, x–xi, 7–8
Gibbons, M. B. C., 23, 26, 30–31, 34–35, 36
Girardi, P., 26
Glass, C. R., 26
Goldblatt, M. J., 316
Goldfried, Marvin, x–xi, 7–8, 126–27, 129, 197, 205–6, 208, 215, 373, 374–75
Goldschmidt, A. B., 31–32
Gomez Penedo, J. M., 4–5, 373–74
Goodman, W. K., 24
Goodyear, R. K., 35
Górna, K., 24
Green, K. T., 23
Greenberg, Leslie, 34, 36, 87–88, 161–62, 177
Greenberg, R. P., 26, 27
Grey, J., 335
Groth-Marnat, Gary, x–xi, 7–8
Gunderson, J. G., 279, 316–18

Haaga, D. A. F., 25, 32
Haas, A., 25
Hall, K. L., 30
Hall, S. M., 25
Hardy, G. E., 29
Härkänen, T., 29
Harned, M. S., 321–22
Harricharan, R., 32
Harrington, Sarah, ix
Harwood, T. M., 22, 28, 29, 31, 33, 349–50
Hatfield, J. P., 32
Hawley, K. M., 4
Hays, R. D., 32
Heatherington, Laurie, x–xi, 7–8
Heimberg, R. G., 313–14
Hess, T. R., 374–75
Hettema, J., 30
Hill, C. E., 34, 360, 373

Hilsenroth, M. J., 35
Hirsch, J. K., 32
Hoffman, S. G., 37
Höger, D., 28
Holdsworth, E., 27, 32
Hollon, S. D., 25, 36–37
Holman, J., 22, 29, 33
Holt, H., 359–60
Hook, J. N., 30
Hope, D. A., 313–14
Horner, P. A., 35
Horvath, A. O., 33
Horwitz, L., 336
Hougaard, E., 25
Howard, T., 373–74
Howat, D., 27, 32
Hulburt, M. S., 4

Jääskeläinen, T., 32
Jacob, M. L., 24
Jacobson, N. S., 36–37
Janeck, A., 35
Jaracz, J., 24
Jaracz, K., 24
Jarrett, R. B., 36
Johnson, A. L., 26
Johnson, Benjamin, x–xi, 41, 55, 167–82, 183, 189–91, 192–93, 198, 201, 202–4, 205, 208–9, 359–60, 371, 372
Johnson, T., 26
Jones, I., 24
Jones, L., 24
Jonsson, U., 24
Joorman, J., 41–42
Jordan, J. R., 157
Joyce, P. R., 28

Karno, M. P., 29
Katon, W., 31
Kazdin, A. E., 4, 372–73
Keeley, M. L., 24, 25
Keller, M. B., 24
Kellett, S., 31
Kelly, T. M., 313–14
Keuroghlian, A. S., 316, 317–18
Kiejda, J., 24
Kimpara, S., 7, 28, 31, 42, 194, 215, 349–50
Kirchmann, H., 28
Klein, D. N., 25–26
Klein, M. H., 33
Kliem, S., 37
Knekt, P., 29, 32
Knorring, A. V., 24

Knorring, L. V., 24
Knox, S., 34
Koerner, K., 373–74
Kohlenberg, R. J., 36–37
Kolden, G. G., 33
Kool, S., 25
Koontz, L., 374–75
Kornreich, M., 231–32
Korslund, K. E., 321–22
Kosfelder, J., 37
Kraft, S., 35
Krampe, H., 24
Kranzler, H., 26
Kratochvil, C., 23–24
Kraus, D. R., 157, 208–9, 360
Krebs, P. M., 21, 27, 30, 277–78
Kröger, C., 37
Kunz, C., 30

Laaksonen, M. A., 29
Lambert, M. J., 14, 15, 35, 57–58
Lamis, D. A., 26
Larson, M. J., 24
Laverdiére, O., 27
Lazarus, Arnold, 80, 175
Lebow, J., 32
LeMoult, J., 41–42
Levendusky, Phillip, x–xi, 7–8
Levenson, Hanna, x–xi, 7–8
Levitt, Heidi, x–xi, 7–8, 373
Levy, K. N., 24, 26, 28
Leyro, T. M., 37
Lindfors, O., 29, 32
Linehan, M. M., 316, 321–22
Links, P. S., 318
Litt, M. D., 29
Littlejohn, C., 27
Llewelyn, S., 29
Lobo-Drost, A., 28
Locke, B. D., 374–75
Loewald, H. W., 335
Lorenzo-Luaces, L., 358
Lundahl, B. W., 30
Luty, S. E., 28
Lutz, W., 3
Lyness, J. M., 32

Maat, S. de, 25
Machado, P. P. P., 28
Maddux, R. E., 25–26
Magalhães, P. V., 31
Magri, L., 35
Mainland, B. J., 35–36

Malik, M., 28
Maltsberger, J. T., 316
Manchanda, R., 32
March, J., 23–24
Marinaccio, P. M., 35
Markowitz, J. C., 25–26
Marks, I., 32
Marquet, A., 28
Martin, J. L., 374–75
Marttunen, M., 29
Maslow, A. H., 287
Masterson, J., 315–16
Mausbach, B. T., 27, 32
McAleavey, Andrew, x, 3, 41–42, 209
Mcbride, C., 35–36
McClendon, D. T., 33
McCrady, B. S., 32
McCullough, J. P. Jr, 130, 161
McDaniel M. A., 30
McGlashan, T., 317–18
McIntyre, J. S., 370
Mckenzie, J. M., 28
McWilliams, N., 3
Meltzoff, J., 231–32
Merlo, L. J., 24, 25
Meunier, G., 27
Michelson, A., 22, 29, 33
Mikulincer, M., 134–35
Miller, K., 194
Miller, W. R., 30, 310–11
Milos, G. F., 31
Milrod, B., 29
Modesto-Lowe, V., 26
Mohr, D., 28
Moleiro, C., 28
Molenaar, P., 25
Möller, H., 23
Monroe, J. M., 28
Moore, J. T., 25
Moore, R., 27, 32
Morant, N., 32
Morrison, Nicholas, x, 373–74
Morrow-Bradley, C., 3
Mufson, L., 32
Mukherjee, D., 30–31, 34–35, 36
Mulder, R. T., 25, 26, 28
Muran, C. M., 126–27
Muran, J. C., 34, 208
Murphy, S., 26

Najavits, L., 309
Nanni, V., 28
Narducci, J., 35
Nelson, D. L., 374–75

Neudeck, P., 161
Newman, D. W., 31
Newman, M. G., 26, 35
Newton-Howes, G., 26
Nienhuis, J. B., 25
Nierenberg, A., 31
Nocito, E. P., 35
Norcross, J. C., 14, 15, 21, 27, 30, 277–78
Norman, R., 32
Northcott, S., 32

Obegi, J. H., 28
Ogilvie, J., 3
Ojanen, S., 32
Olsson, G., 24
Osatuke, K., 29
Otto, M. W., 31, 37
Ougrin, D., 37
Owen, J., 35

Paaren, A., 24
Paas, N. D., 25
Palermo, M., 26
Papenhausen, R., 28
Papiasvili, A., 231–32
Papiasvili, Eva D., x–xi, 215, 230, 231–33, 325–38, 339, 340–47, 348–49, 350, 352, 354–56, 357, 360, 371–72
Parhar, K. K., 27, 33
Pascual-Leone, A., 36
Patterson, T. L., 27, 32
Pekarik, G., 27
Pell, J. P., 358
Perry, J. C., 28
Peters, A. T., 31
Pilkonis, P. A., 26
Pincus, H. A., 370
Plemmons, D., 374–75
Pochaska, J. O., 277–78
Pomerville, A., 373
Pompili, M., 26
Porcellana, M., 35
Power, M., 32
Powers, M. B., 37
Prochaska, J. O., 21, 27, 30
Puschner, B., 35

Quilty, L. C., 25, 35–36

Regner, E., 7, 42, 215
Renner, F., 36
Rice, L. N., 161–62
Riso, L. P., 25–26
Roberts, M. E., 25

Rodriguez, B. F., 24
Roesch, S., 27, 32
Rogers, Carl, 60, 105, 154
Rohde, P., 23–24
Rolland, J.-P., 25
Rollnick, S., 30, 310–11
Romanelli, R., 28
Ronningstam, E., 316
Rosenberg, N. K., 25
Rossi, J. S., 30
Rothbaum, B. O., 25–26
Roy, C., 28
Russo, J., 31
Ruther, E., 24
Rybakowski, J., 24

Saelens, B. E., 31–32
Safran, Jeremy, 3, 34, 87–88
Santoso, Patricia, x
Sargent, M. M., 3
Saypol, E., 28
Schamberger, M., 35
Schechter, M., 316
Schedler, J., 231–32
Schepf, D., 161
Schmaling, K. B., 36–37
Schoevers, R., 25
Scott, L. N., 26, 28
Sechrest, L. B., 3
Seivewright, N., 26
Seligman, D. A., 157
Seligman, M., 98
Sellman, J. D., 27
Seretti, M. E., 26
Shaver, P. R., 134–35
Shea, M. T., 26
Shelton, R. C., 25
Sherbourne, C. D., 32
Shimokawa, K., 35
Silva, S., 23–24
Simons, A., 23–24
Singer, Hayley, x
Smith, D., 24
Smith, G. C., 358
Smith, J. Z., 26
Smits, J. A., 37
Someah, K., 24
Song, X., 22, 29, 33
Sotsky, S. M., 26
Spayd, Catherine S., x–xi, 215, 230, 325–29, 330–39, 340–52, 353, 354–56, 357–58, 359–60, 372
Spencer, M. A., 24
Spindler, A. M., 31

Stasiewicz, P. R., 25
Stathopoulou, G., 37
Stawicki, S., 24
Steele, J., 30
Stefani, H., 26
Steiger, H., 25
Stein, Mickey, x, 24
Stein, R. I., 31–32
Steiner, C. M., 161–62, 177
Stiles, W. B., 21–22, 29, 35, 280–81
Stoffers, J. M., 316
Storch, E. A., 24, 25
Strauß, A., 23
Strauss, B., 28
Surace, F. I., 373
Swift, J. K., 26, 27, 30
Sylvia, L., 31
Symonds, D., 33

Taska, G. A., 374–75
Teachman, B. A., 215
Thase, M. E., 25–26, 36
Thompson, L., 28
Thompson, N. L., 23
Thompson-Brenner, H., 31
Thrasher, S., 32
Timulak, L., 36
Tollefson, D., 30
Treasure, J., 25
Tryon, G. S., 33
Turk, C. L., 313–14
Tyrer, P., 26

Uher, R., 28
Unützer, J., 31
Urdahl, A., 31
Usami, S., 7, 42, 215

Välikoski, M., 29
Van, R., 25
Venturini, P., 26
Verdirame, D., 28, 31, 349–50
Vink, A., 25
Virtala, E., 29
Vitiello, B., 23–24
Vittengl, J. R., 36
Vivian, Dina, x–xi, 41, 55, 167–68, 169–70, 171–82, 183, 189–91, 192, 194, 196–97, 198–99, 201, 203, 204–7, 208–9, 372
Vollmer, B. M., 30

Wagner, H. R:, 23
Wagner, T., 24
Wakefield, P. J., 3

Wampold, B. E., 25, 33
Wang, C., 33
Warden, S., 31
Watson, J. C., 34, 36
Weinberg, Igor, x–xi, 208–9, 215, 230, 316, 320, 325–26, 327–39, 340–47, 348–49, 350, 353, 354–56, 358–60, 371, 372
Weisberg, R. B., 24
Wells, K. B., 32
West, J. C., 370
Westen, D., 31
Westra, H. A., 210, 374
Wierzbicki, M., 27
Wilfley, D. E., 31–32
Wilkiewicz, M., 24
Williams, R. E., 3
Windell, D., 32
Winograd, G., 33

Wlater, H., 161
Wolf, Abraham W., x–xi, 41, 56, 126–27, 167–68, 170–82, 183–91, 192–94, 199, 201, 205, 207–10, 371–72, 373
Woody, S. R., 35
Wormith, J. S., 27, 33
Worthington, E. L. Jr., 30

Xiao, Henry, x, 209

Youn, Soo Jeong, x, 374–75
Young, J. F., 32

Zanarini, Mary, 317–18
Zarin, D. A., 370
Zekus, Andrea, ix
Zilcha-Mano, S., 210
Zlotnick, C., 24

Subject Index

Note: References to boxes are denoted by an italic *b* following the page number.

For the benefit of digital users, indexed terms that span two pages (e.g., 52–53) may, on occasion, appear on only one of those pages.

acculturation stress. *See* cultural aspects, in social anxiety disorder treatment
action stage of change, 21. *See also* change readiness
active avoidance, 22, 281. *See also* assimilation of problematic experiences
active participation (principle 21), 17*b*, 21, 22
   clinical helpfulness of principle, 186*b*, 344*b*
   convergence and divergence in implementation, 327, 331, 334
   defined, 23
   in depression treatment, 53
      CBASP application, 150–51
      with comorbid personality disorder, 66, 89–90, 122, 150–51
      with comorbid substance abuse, 79–80, 113, 115–16, 150–51
      convergence and divergence in implementation, 174–75
      without co-morbidity, 65, 66, 104–5, 150–51
   possible combinations of principles, 195
   references supporting, 32–33
   in social anxiety disorder treatment, 228, 288–90
      with comorbid personality disorder, 261–63, 289–90, 318
      with comorbid substance abuse, 252, 264–65, 289, 310–12
      comparisons between cases, 256–57
      without co-morbidity, 239–41, 242, 288–89, 304, 306
actual outcomes (AOs), in situational analyses, 140
adaptive interpersonal changes, fostering (principle 34), 19*b*, 229. *See also* behavior changes, fostering; impairment level, and attention to social or medical needs
   clinical helpfulness of principle, 188*b*, 345*b*
   convergence and divergence in implementation, 329, 330–31, 333–34
   in depression treatment, 54
      CBASP application, 159–60
      with comorbid personality disorder, 71, 92, 125, 160
      with comorbid substance abuse, 82, 83, 84, 114–15, 117, 159–60
      without co-morbidity, 70, 107–9, 159
   possible combinations of principles, 196
   references supporting, 35–36
   in social anxiety disorder treatment, 294–95
      with comorbid personality disorder, 260, 262–63, 295, 319–20
      with comorbid substance abuse, 249–50, 252, 294–95, 312, 314–15
      without co-morbidity, 236, 246, 294, 305–6, 307
adverse childhood events (principle 8), 16*b*
   and attachment, 141, 350
   clinical helpfulness of principle, 183, 185*b*, 340, 342*b*
   and depression treatment, 52
      CBASP application, 141–42
      with comorbid personality disorder, 85, 87, 92, 119, 134, 141–42
      with comorbid substance abuse, 74–75, 77, 110, 132–33, 141–42
      convergence and divergence in implementation, 173
      without co-morbidity, 58, 61, 101–2, 131, 141–42
   references supporting, 27–28
   and social anxiety disorder treatment, 227, 275–76
      with comorbid personality disorder, 257–58, 317
      with comorbid substance abuse, 250–51, 309
      comparisons between cases, 256, 263–64
      without co-morbidity, 236–37, 238, 242, 303–4
affirmation, therapist (principle 24), 18*b*, 228
   clinical helpfulness of principle, 187*b*, 344*b*
   convergence in implementation, 328–29

384 SUBJECT INDEX

affirmation, therapist (principle 24) (*cont.*)
  and depression treatment, 54
    CBASP application, 154–56
    with comorbid personality disorder, 72–73, 90, 122–23
    with comorbid substance abuse, 77, 80–81, 113–14
    convergence and divergence in implementation, 169
    and depression treatment, 154–56
    without co-morbidity, 66–67, 105
  possible combinations of principles, 195
  references supporting, 33
  and social anxiety disorder treatment, 275–76, 282–83
    with comorbid personality disorder, 261–62, 266, 275–76, 316, 318–19
    with comorbid substance abuse, 251–52, 264–65, 275–76, 310–11, 312–13
    comparisons between cases, 256–57
    without co-morbidity, 239, 240–41, 242–43, 304, 306–7
agoraphobia, 42, 44, 59, 132, 216, 217, 234, 235, 301
alcohol abuse. *See* substance abuse
alliance, therapeutic. *See* therapeutic alliance
ambivalence about change (principle 12), 17*b*
  clinical helpfulness of principle, 185*b*, 342*b*
  and depression treatment, 52
    CBASP application, 146–47
    with comorbid personality disorder, 88, 120–21, 146
    with comorbid substance abuse, 78, 81, 111, 146–47
    without co-morbidity, 63–64, 66, 73–74, 103, 146
  and resistance, 351–52
  and social anxiety disorder treatment, 227, 282–83
    with comorbid personality disorder, 258–59, 260–61, 265–66, 282–83, 318–19
    with comorbid substance abuse, 249–50, 251, 256, 282–83, 310
    comparisons between cases, 256–57, 263–64
    without co-morbidity, 238, 240, 303–4
anxiety, interaction of depression and, 98–99. *See also* attachment; negative self-attributions
anxiety disorders, 6–7, 299–300, 322–23. *See also* social anxiety disorder cases
anxious attachment. *See* attachment
AOs (actual outcomes), in situational analyses, 140

approach behavior, 72–73
assimilation of problematic experiences (principle 10), 16*b*
  clinical helpfulness of principle, 185*b*, 342*b*
  convergence in implementation, 328
  defined, 21–22
  and depression treatment, 52
    CBASP application, 143–44
    with comorbid personality disorder, 87, 91, 92, 120–21, 143–44
    with comorbid substance abuse, 77, 111, 143–44
    without co-morbidity, 61, 65, 102–3, 108–9, 130
  possible combinations of principles, 194–95
  references supporting, 29
  and social anxiety disorder treatment, 227, 280–81
    with comorbid personality disorder, 258–59, 261–62, 265–66, 281, 319
    with comorbid substance abuse, 249–50, 251, 255, 281, 310
    comparisons between cases, 256–57, 263–64
    without co-morbidity, 239, 240–41, 264, 280–81, 303–4
Assimilation of Problematic Experiences Scale (APES), 21–22, 240
attachment (principle 3), 16*b*
  and adverse childhood events, 141, 350
  clinical helpfulness of principle, 184*b*, 340, 341*b*
  and depression treatment, 51
    CBASP application, 137–38
    with comorbid personality disorder, 86, 119, 137–38
    with comorbid substance abuse, 76, 110, 137–38
    convergence and divergence in implementation, 170, 173
    without co-morbidity, 60, 101–2, 137–38
  references supporting, 26
  and social anxiety disorder treatment, 226, 275–76
    with comorbid personality disorder, 258–59, 260–61, 275–76, 317
    with comorbid substance abuse, 250–51, 275–76, 309
    comparisons between cases, 256, 263–64
    without co-morbidity, 236–37, 238, 242, 275, 303–4
attributions. *See* negative self-attributions
authenticity, therapist. *See* congruence, therapist

SUBJECT INDEX 385

autonomous motivation. *See* intrinsic motivation
avoidance, 72–73, 137, 140–41, 203, 269–71, 281
awareness interventions. *See* externalizing coping styles; internalizing coping styles

baseline impairment
  and benefits of psychotherapy (principle 1), 16*b*
    and assimilation of problematic experiences, 280–81
    CBASP application, 135–36
    clinical helpfulness of principle, 184*b*, 340, 341*b*
    convergence and divergence in implementation, 170
    depression with comorbid personality disorder, 50–51, 86, 119, 136
    depression with comorbid substance abuse, 50–51, 75, 110, 136
    depression without co-morbidity, 50–51, 59, 101, 136
    references supporting, 23–24
    social anxiety case comparisons, 263–64
    social anxiety with comorbid personality disorder, 225–26, 258, 260–61, 274, 317
    social anxiety with comorbid substance abuse, 225–26, 247, 250–51, 273–74, 309
    social anxiety without co-morbidity, 225–26, 236–38, 273, 303
  relation to length and intensity of therapy (principle 16), 17*b*
    CBASP application, 135–36
    clinical helpfulness of principle, 186*b*, 343*b*
    depression with comorbid personality disorder, 53, 89, 120–21, 136
    depression with comorbid substance abuse, 53, 78, 112, 136
    depression without co-morbidity, 64, 104, 136
    references supporting, 31
    social anxiety case comparisons, 257
    social anxiety with comorbid personality disorder, 227, 258–59, 262–63, 265, 266, 274–75, 317–18
    social anxiety with comorbid substance abuse, 227, 253–54, 255, 264–65, 274–75, 310
    social anxiety without co-morbidity, 274–75, 303–4
behavior changes, fostering (principle 38), 19*b*, 229. *See also* adaptive interpersonal changes, fostering

clinical helpfulness of principle, 189*b*, 192–93, 346*b*
convergence and divergence in implementation, 329, 330–31, 332–33
in depression treatment, 55
  CBASP application, 159–60
  with comorbid personality disorder, 92, 125, 160
  with comorbid substance abuse, 76, 82–84, 114–15, 116, 159–60
  convergence and divergence in implementation, 180–81
  without co-morbidity, 71–73, 107–9, 159
possible combinations of principles, 196
references supporting, 36–37
in social anxiety disorder treatment, 286–87
  with comorbid personality disorder, 260, 263, 295, 319–20, 321–22
  with comorbid substance abuse, 249–50, 252, 294–95, 308–9, 311–12, 313–15
  without co-morbidity, 236, 246, 294, 305–6
borderline personality disorder (BPD), 117, 120, 134, 315–17. *See also* personality disorders

case formulation
  depression cases
    with comorbid personality disorder, 85–86, 117–18, 134–35
    with comorbid substance abuse, 74–75, 109–10, 132–33
    convergence and divergence in, 172–73
    without co-morbidity, 58–59, 99–100, 131
  social anxiety disorder cases
    with comorbid personality disorder, 257–59, 272–73, 315–17
    with comorbid substance abuse, 247–49, 271–72, 307–9
    without co-morbidity, 234–36, 269–71, 300–3
caseload management, 203
CBASP. *See* Cognitive-Behavioral Analysis System of Psychotherapy
CBT. *See* cognitive-behavioral therapy
change, motivation for (principle 12), 17*b*
  clinical helpfulness of principle, 185*b*, 342*b*
  and depression treatment, 52
    CBASP application, 146–47
    with comorbid personality disorder, 88, 120–21, 146
    with comorbid substance abuse, 78, 81, 111, 146–47
    without co-morbidity, 63–64, 66, 73–74, 103, 146

change, motivation for (principle 12) (*cont.*)
references supporting, 29–30
and resistance, 351–52
and social anxiety disorder treatment,
227, 282–83
with comorbid personality disorder, 258–
59, 260–61, 265–66, 282–83, 318–19
with comorbid substance abuse, 249–50,
251, 256, 282–83, 310
comparisons between cases,
256–57, 263–64
without co-morbidity, 238, 240, 303–4
change-oriented approaches, 145–46, 282–
83. *See also* change, motivation for;
directive psychotherapy; resistance/
reactance
change readiness (principle 6), 16*b*
and assimilation of problematic experiences,
143–44, 280–81
clinical helpfulness of principle, 184*b*,
340, 341*b*
convergence in implementation, 327–28
and depression treatment, 52
CBASP application, 139–41
with comorbid personality disorder, 86–87,
92, 119, 139–41
with comorbid substance abuse, 76, 79,
110, 111–12, 114–15, 139–41
without co-morbidity, 61, 65, 102–3,
108–9, 139–41
possible combinations of principles, 194–95
references supporting, 27
and social anxiety disorder treatment,
226, 277–78
with comorbid personality
disorder, 262–63, 278, 317
with comorbid substance abuse, 250–51,
255, 278, 309, 311
without co-morbidity, 236–37, 239–40,
277–78, 303
stages of, 21
childhood. *See* adverse childhood events; family
relationships
client moderating principles. *See* treatment/
provider moderating principles
client process principles, 366. *See also* principles
of change; *specific principles*
clinical helpfulness of, 186–87*b*, 191–92,
344*b*, 348–49
clinician reactions to, 95, 296–97
convergence in implementation, 327
defined, 8
in depression treatment, 53

CBASP application, 150–51
with comorbid personality disorder, 89–90,
122, 150–51
with comorbid substance abuse, 79–80,
113, 150–51
convergence and divergence in
implementation, 174–75
without co-morbidity, 65, 104–5, 150–51
references supporting, 32–33
revised list, 17–18*b*
in social anxiety disorder treatment, 228
with comorbid personality disorder,
261–62, 288–90
with comorbid substance abuse,
252, 288–90
without co-morbidity, 239–41, 288–90
suggestions for implementing in practice, 94
client prognostic principles, 210, 239–40, 366.
See also principles of change; *specific
principles*
clinical helpfulness of, 183–90, 184–85*b*,
340–47, 341–42*b*
clinical knowledge related to, 366–67
clinician reactions to, 95, 164, 296–97
defined, 8
in depression treatment, 50–52
CBASP application, 135–43
with comorbid personality disorder, 86–87,
119–20, 135–43
with comorbid substance abuse, 75–77,
110–11, 135–43
convergence and divergence in
implementation, 170, 171–72, 173, 179
without co-morbidity, 59–61,
100–2, 135–43
references supporting, 23–29
revised list, 16*b*
in social anxiety disorder treatment,
225–27, 233
with comorbid personality disorder, 260–61,
273–80, 317–18
with comorbid substance abuse, 250–51,
273–80, 309
comparisons between cases, 263–65
without co-morbidity, 236–40,
273–80, 303–4
suggestions for implementing in practice, 94
clients, matching to therapy preferences
(principles 13 and 14), 17*b*
clinical helpfulness of principles, 185*b*, 190,
342–43*b*, 348
in depression treatment, 52–53
CBASP application, 147

with comorbid personality disorder, 88,
103, 121, 147
with comorbid substance abuse, 78,
111–12, 147
without co-morbidity, 63–64, 147
references supporting, 30
in social anxiety disorder cases, 227,
277, 283–84
with comorbid personality disorder,
284, 318–19
with comorbid substance abuse,
283–84, 313–15
without co-morbidity, 241–42, 283, 304, 306
clinical implementation of principles. *See also*
depression cases; social anxiety disorder
cases; *specific categories of principles;
specific principles*
clinical helpfulness of principles, 200b, 369
convergence and divergence in, 368–69
in depression cases
clinical helpfulness of principles,
183–94, 184b
convergence and divergence in, 167–83
final thoughts on, 202–10
future research directions, 198–202
possible combinations of principles, 194–97
fostering, 203, 205, 207–8
general discussion, 366–68
in social anxiety disorder cases
clinical helpfulness of principles,
340–50, 341b
convergence and divergence in, 325–40
final thoughts on, 356–61
future research directions, 352–56
possible combinations of
principles, 350–52
clinicians. *See also specific principles of change;
therapist intervention principles; therapy
relationship principles; treatment/
provider moderating principles*
collaboration between researchers and,
3–5, 365–75
contributing to book, 6–8
final thoughts on principles of change, 202–10
future research on principles suggested by,
198–202
with history of substance use problems
(principle 20), 17b
CBASP application, 150
clinical helpfulness of principle, 186b,
190–91, 343b, 347–48
and depression with comorbid personality
disorder, 89, 150

and depression with comorbid substance
abuse, 53, 79, 83–84, 111–12, 150
and depression without co-morbidity,
63–64, 150
references supporting, 32
and social anxiety treatment, 228, 248–49,
288, 310
personal emotional reactions of, 126–27
possible combinations of principles
by, 194–97
reactions to writing about depression
cases, 57–58, 95–96, 97–98, 125–27,
129–31, 162–65
reactions to writing about social anxiety
cases, 231–32, 266–67, 299–300, 322–23
therapist effects, 202, 204, 207, 208, 360
Therapy Process Rating Scale, 42, 55–56,
215, 229–30
unified landscape of science and
practice, 10–11
writing guidelines for, 8–10
Cognitive-Behavioral Analysis System of
Psychotherapy (CBASP), 181
application to treatment of
depression, 190–91
case formulations and treatment
plans, 131–35
client process principles, 150–51
client prognostic principles, 135–43
convergence and divergence in
implementing principles, 169–70
therapist intervention principles, 156–62
therapy relationship principles, 151–56
treatment/provider moderating
principles, 143–50
overview, 130–31
cognitive-behavioral therapy (CBT)
convergence and divergence in implementing
principles, 181
for depression without co-morbidity, 62, 65–66,
69, 71–72, 73–74
social anxiety disorder treatment
case formulations and treatment
plans, 269–73
client process principles, 288–90
client prognostic principles, 273–80
versus other therapy approaches, 326–40
therapist intervention principles
in, 290–96
therapy relationship principles in, 290
treatment/provider moderating
principles, 280–88
top-down approach of, 73–74

388 SUBJECT INDEX

collaboration between clinicians and researchers, 3–5, 365–75
co-morbidity
  depression and personality disorder, 41, 47–49, 51, 117–18
    case formulation and treatment plan, 85–86, 134–35
    client process principles, 89–90, 122, 150–51
    client prognostic principles, 86–87, 119–20, 135–43
    convergence and divergence in implementing principles, 167–83
    therapist intervention principles, 91–93, 123–25, 156–62
    therapy relationship principles, 90–91, 122–23, 151–56
    treatment/provider moderating principles, 87–89, 120–21, 143–50
  depression and substance abuse, 41, 45–47, 51, 109–10
    case formulation and treatment plan, 74–75, 109–10, 132–33
    client process principles, 79–80, 113, 150–51
    client prognostic principles, 75–77, 110–11, 135–43
    convergence and divergence in implementing principles, 167–83
    therapist intervention principles, 81–85, 114–17, 156–62
    therapy relationship principles, 80–81, 113–14, 151–56
    treatment/provider moderating principles, 77–79, 111–13, 143–50
  of PDs, and benefits of psychotherapy (principle 2), 16b
    CBASP application, 136–37
    clinical helpfulness of principle, 183, 184b, 341b, 346–47
    and depression treatment, 51, 59, 75, 86, 101, 119–20, 137
    possible combinations of principles, 196
    references supporting, 24–26
    and social anxiety disorder treatment, 226, 236–37, 250–51, 258–59, 260–61, 274, 317
  social anxiety disorder and personality disorder, 221–24, 225, 260–63, 317–22
    case formulation and treatment plan, 257–59, 272–73, 315–17
    client process principles, 288–90
    client prognostic principles, 273–80
    compared to other social anxiety disorder cases, 263–66
    convergence and divergence in implementing principles, 326–27, 333–34, 336–37
    therapist intervention principles, 290–96
    therapy relationship principles, 290
    treatment/provider moderating principles, 280–88
  social anxiety disorder and substance abuse, 219–21, 225, 249–55, 309–15
    case formulation and treatment plan, 247–49, 271–72, 307–9
    client process principles, 252, 288–90
    client prognostic principles, 250–51, 273–80
    compared to other social anxiety disorder cases, 256–57, 263–66
    convergence and divergence in implementing principles, 326–28, 331–33, 335–36
    therapist intervention principles, 252–55, 290–96
    therapy relationship principles, 251–52, 290
    treatment/provider moderating principles, 251, 252, 280–88
congruence, therapist (principle 25), 18b, 228
  clinical helpfulness of principle, 187b, 344b
  convergence in implementation, 328–29
  and depression treatment, 54
    CBASP application, 154–56
    with comorbid personality disorder, 90, 122–23
    with comorbid substance abuse, 80–81, 113–14
  convergence and divergence in implementation, 169
  without co-morbidity, 67–68, 105
  possible combinations of principles, 195
  references supporting, 33
  and social anxiety disorder treatment, 275–76, 282–83
    with comorbid personality disorder, 261–62, 266, 275–76, 318–19
    with comorbid substance abuse, 264–65, 275–76, 310–11
    without co-morbidity, 242–43, 304, 306–7
contemplation stage of change, 21, 278. *See also* change readiness
contingent personal responsivity (CPR), 130–31, 141–42, 143, 145, 146–47, 152–53
contracts, therapeutic, 252–53, 264–65

SUBJECT INDEX 389

COPE protocol, 309
coping styles. *See* externalizing coping styles; internalizing coping styles
countertransference, 126–27, 141–42, 155, 156, 199, 201, 209, 354–56
couples therapy, 159, 307
cultural aspects, in social anxiety disorder treatment, 301–4, 306

DBT. *See* dialectical behavior therapy
demographics, therapist–patient. *See* clients, matching to therapy preferences
depression cases, 6–7, 57
   CBASP application to, 190–91
      case formulations and treatment plans, 131–35
      client process principles, 150–51
      client prognostic principles, 135–43
      therapist intervention principles, 156–62
      therapy relationship principles, 151–56
      treatment/provider moderating principles, 143–50
   clinical implementation of principles
      clinical helpfulness of principles, 183–94, 184*b*
      convergence and divergence in, 167–83
      final thoughts on, 202–10
      future research directions, 198–202
      possible combinations of principles, 194–97
      suggestions for, 94–95
   clinician reactions to writing about, 57–58, 95–96, 97–98, 125–27, 129–31, 162–65
   with comorbid personality disorder, 47–49, 117–18
      case formulation and treatment plan, 85–86, 134–35
      client process principles, 89–90, 122, 150–51
      client prognostic principles, 86–87, 119–20, 135–43
      convergence and divergence in implementing principles, 167–83
      therapist intervention principles, 91–93, 123–25, 156–62
      therapy relationship principles, 90–91, 122–23, 151–56
      treatment/provider moderating principles, 87–89, 120–21, 143–50
   with comorbid substance abuse, 41, 45–47, 109–10
      case formulation and treatment plan, 74–75, 109–10, 132–33
      client process principles, 79–80, 113, 150–51
      client prognostic principles, 75–77, 110–11, 135–43
      convergence and divergence in implementing principles, 167–83
      therapist intervention principles, 81–85, 114–17, 156–62
      therapy relationship principles, 80–81, 113–14, 151–56
      treatment/provider moderating principles, 77–79, 111–13, 143–50
   deleted principles, helpfulness ratings of, 200*b*
   overview, 41–42
   principles of change related to, 41–42, 50–55
   similarities and differences in, 93–94
   understanding depression, 98–99
   without co-morbidity, 42–44, 99–100
      case formulation and treatment plan, 58–59, 131–32
      client process principles, 65, 104–5, 150–51
      client prognostic principles, 59–61, 100–2, 135–43
      convergence and divergence in implementing principles, 167–83
      therapist intervention principles, 69–74, 106–9, 156–62
      therapy relationship principles, 65–69, 105–6, 151–56
      treatment/provider moderating principles, 61–64, 102–4, 143–50
desired outcomes (DOs), in situational analyses, 140
dialectical behavior therapy (DBT), 316–17, 319, 320, 321–22, 333–34, 337
directive psychotherapy, 52, 282–83.
      See also ambivalence about change; change, motivation for
   for depression without co-morbidity, 106, 107–9
and resistance/reactance (principle 11), 17*b*, 22
   CBASP application, 144–46
   clinical helpfulness of principle, 185*b*, 342*b*
   convergence and divergence in implementation, 326–27, 332
   depression with comorbid personality disorder, 52, 87–88, 120–21, 144–46
   depression with comorbid substance abuse, 52, 77–78, 80, 81, 111, 112, 144–45
   depression without co-morbidity, 52, 61–63, 71–72, 103, 145
   and motivation for change, 351–52
   possible combinations of principles, 351–52
   references supporting, 29

directive psychotherapy (*cont.*)
  social anxiety with comorbid personality disorder, 227, 258–59, 261, 262–63, 265–66, 282, 318–19
  social anxiety with comorbid substance abuse, 227, 232–33, 248–50, 251, 252, 281–82, 310
  social anxiety without co-morbidity, 227, 238, 239–40, 241, 282, 303–4
  for social anxiety disorder without comorbidity, 283
  for social anxiety with comorbid substance abuse, 311
  Socratic nondirective/directive methods, 144, 152
disciplined personal involvement (DPI), in CBASP, 130–31
DOs (desired outcomes), in situational analyses, 140

early traumas. *See* adverse childhood events
economic status. *See* socio-economic status
education. *See also* socio-economic status
emotional experiencing/deepening, fostering (principle 36), 19*b*, 229
  clinical helpfulness of principle, 189*b*, 346*b*, 349
  convergence and divergence in implementation, 329, 331, 332, 338
  and depression treatment, 55
    CBASP application, 161–62
    with comorbid personality disorder, 92, 123–24, 161–62
    with comorbid substance abuse, 82, 111, 115–16, 161–62
    convergence and divergence in implementation, 169, 177
    without co-morbidity, 62, 71, 73–74, 106, 107–8, 161–62
  in psychoanalytical therapy, 232–33
  references supporting, 36
  and social anxiety disorder treatment, 296
    with comorbid personality disorder, 260, 261, 262–63, 296, 319–20
    with comorbid substance abuse, 248, 249–50, 252, 254, 255, 296, 311–12, 314–15
    without co-morbidity, 236–37, 238–39, 240–42, 246, 296, 304–6
emotional reactions, clinician, 126–27
empathic attunement, 151, 154–55
empathy, therapist (principle 26), 18*b*, 228
  clinical helpfulness of principle, 187*b*, 344*b*
  convergence in implementation, 328–29
  and depression treatment, 54
    CBASP application, 154–56
    with comorbid personality disorder, 72–73, 90, 122–23
    with comorbid substance abuse, 80–81, 113–14
    convergence and divergence in implementation, 171
    without co-morbidity, 65–66, 68, 103, 105
  possible combinations of principles, 195
  references supporting, 34
  and social anxiety disorder treatment, 275–76
    with comorbid personality disorder, 262–63, 266, 275–76, 316, 318–21
    with comorbid substance abuse, 248, 251–52, 254–55, 264–65, 275–76, 310–13, 314–15
    without co-morbidity, 238, 242–43, 304–5, 306–7
empirically based principles of therapeutic change. *See* principles of change
employment problems, and psychotherapy benefits (principle 7), 16*b*
  clinical helpfulness of principle, 184*b*, 189, 342*b*, 346–47, 357
  and depression treatment, 52
    CBASP application, 141
    with comorbid personality disorder, 87, 119, 141
    with comorbid substance abuse, 76–77, 110, 141
    without co-morbidity, 61, 101–2, 141
  references supporting, 27
  and social anxiety disorder treatment, 226, 278–79
    with comorbid personality disorder, 317
    with comorbid substance abuse, 250–51, 278–79, 309
    without co-morbidity, 241, 303
empty-chair technique, 161–62
engagement in treatment. *See* active participation
evidence-based principles of therapeutic change. *See* principles of change
expectations for therapy (principle 4), 16*b*
  and assimilation of problematic experiences, 143–44
  clinical helpfulness of principle, 184*b*, 340, 341*b*
  convergence in implementation, 327–28
  and depression treatment, 51
    CBASP application, 138
    with comorbid personality disorder, 86, 119–20, 124–25, 138

SUBJECT INDEX 391

with comorbid substance abuse, 76,
110–11, 138
without co-morbidity, 60, 102–3, 138
and intrinsic motivation, 350–51
possible combinations of principles, 194–95
references supporting, 26
and social anxiety disorder treatment,
226, 276–77
with comorbid personality disorder, 260–61,
265–66, 277, 317
with comorbid substance abuse, 250–51,
256, 276–77, 309, 311
comparisons between social anxiety
cases, 263–64
without co-morbidity, 236–37, 238, 239–40,
276, 303
exposure-based treatment, 313–14
expressive interventions, 336–37
externalizing coping styles (principle 17),
17b, 22–23
clinical helpfulness of principle, 186b, 191,
193–94, 343b
convergence and divergence in
implementation, 332–33
and depression treatment, 53
CBASP application, 148–49
with comorbid personality disorder,
89, 149
with comorbid substance abuse, 78–79,
83–84, 112, 148–49
without co-morbidity, 64, 73–74,
104, 108–9
possible combinations of principles, 195
references supporting, 31
and social anxiety disorder treatment, 228
with comorbid personality disorder, 258–59,
261, 286–87, 319
with comorbid substance abuse, 248, 286,
310, 311–12
comparisons between cases, 256–57, 263–64
without co-morbidity, 242
extrinsic motivation, 21, 138–39

family relationships. *See also* adverse
childhood events
in depression cases, 43, 46–47, 49, 58, 74–75
in social anxiety disorder cases, 216–17, 218,
220, 221, 224
feedback (principles 31 and 32), 18–19b, 229
clinical helpfulness of principles, 188b, 192,
331–32, 345b, 349
convergence and divergence in
implementation, 328

and depression treatment, 54, 140
CBASP application, 157–58
with comorbid personality disorder, 91,
124, 157–58
with comorbid substance abuse, 77, 81–82,
116, 157–58
convergence and divergence in
implementation, 169
without co-morbidity, 69–70, 109,
157–58
possible combinations of principles, 196
references supporting, 35
and social anxiety disorder treatment, 292–93
with comorbid personality disorder,
261–63, 292–93
with comorbid substance abuse, 255, 264–65,
292, 313
comparisons between cases, 256–57
without co-morbidity, 245–46, 292, 304–5
flexibility, therapist (principle 33), 19b, 229
clinical helpfulness of principle, 188b, 345b
convergence and divergence in
implementation, 326–27, 334
and depression treatment, 54
CBASP application, 158–59
with comorbid personality disorder, 91,
123, 158–59
with comorbid substance abuse, 82, 112,
115–16, 158–59
without co-morbidity, 70, 106,
108–9, 158–59
references supporting, 35
and social anxiety disorder treatment, 293–94
with comorbid personality disorder, 260,
261–63, 293, 315, 316, 320
with comorbid substance abuse, 255,
293–94, 313–15
comparisons between cases, 263–64
without co-morbidity, 244–45, 293,
303–4, 305–6
free association, 232–33, 246–47

generalized anxiety disorder (GAD), 42, 59,
99, 132
general psychiatric management (GPM), 316–17,
319–20, 321–22, 337
general psychodynamic interpretations.
See psychodynamic interpretations
global functioning, 51, 225–26, 250–51

*Handbook of Psychotherapy and Behavior
Change* (Lambert), 14, 15
homework assignments, 288–89

SUBJECT INDEX

IDE (interpersonal discrimination exercise), 130–31, 141–42, 145, 152–53, 155
impairment level, and attention to social or medical needs (principle 19), 17b See also baseline impairment
  clinical helpfulness of principle, 186b, 332–33, 343b
  and depression treatment, 53
    CBASP application, 150
    with comorbid personality disorder, 89, 92, 121, 150
    with comorbid substance abuse, 79, 83, 84, 112–13, 150
    without co-morbidity, 64, 104, 150
  possible combinations of principles, 196
  references supporting, 31–32
  and social anxiety disorder treatment, 228, 287–88
    with comorbid personality disorder, 287–88, 317–18
    with comorbid substance abuse, 252–53, 287, 310
    comparisons between social anxiety cases, 256–57
    without co-morbidity, 287
indirect/direct Socratic methods, 144, 152
Innerlife STS, 41–42
insecurity, attachment. See attachment
insight/awareness interventions. See externalizing coping styles; internalizing coping styles
integrative approach to psychotherapy, 4–5, 6, 62, 126, 158–59. See also flexibility, therapist
intensity of psychotherapy. See baseline impairment: relation to length and intensity of therapy
internalizing coping styles (principle 18), 17b, 23
  clinical helpfulness of principle, 186b, 191, 193–94, 343b, 347
  convergence and divergence in implementation, 328, 330–31
  and depression treatment, 53
    CBASP application, 148–49
    with comorbid personality disorder, 89, 90–91, 92, 120–21, 149
    with comorbid substance abuse, 78–79, 112
    without co-morbidity, 64, 73–74, 104, 108–9, 149
  possible combinations of principles, 195
  references supporting, 31
  and social anxiety disorder treatment, 228
    with comorbid personality disorder, 262–63, 286–87, 319
    with comorbid substance abuse, 255
    without co-morbidity, 239, 242, 286, 303–4
interpersonal changes. See adaptive interpersonal changes, fostering
interpersonal discrimination exercise (IDE), 130–31, 141–42, 145, 152–53, 155
interpersonal functioning. See also adaptive interpersonal changes, fostering
  in depression cases, 51
  in social anxiety cases, 226
  and transference interpretations (principle 15), 17b
    CBASP application, 148
    clinical helpfulness of principle, 186b, 190–91, 192–93, 343b, 347
    comparisons between social anxiety cases, 256–57
    convergence and divergence in implementation, 181
    in depression with comorbid personality disorder, 53, 88, 121, 123–24, 148
    in depression with comorbid substance abuse, 53, 78, 112, 148
    in depression without co-morbidity, 53, 63–64, 104, 105–6, 148
    possible combinations of principles, 196
    references supporting, 30–31
    in social anxiety with comorbid personality disorder, 227, 258–59, 261–63, 285–86, 320
    in social anxiety with comorbid substance abuse, 227, 248–49, 285, 310
    in social anxiety without co-morbidity, 227, 238, 284–85, 305
interpretations. See psychodynamic interpretations; transference interpretations
Inter-Regional Encyclopedic Dictionary of Psychoanalysis (IRED), 232
intervention principles. See therapist intervention principles
intrinsic (autonomous) motivation (principle 5), 16b, 21, 351–52
  and assimilation of problematic experiences, 143–44
  clinical helpfulness of principle, 184b, 340, 341b
  convergence in implementation, 327–28
  and depression treatment, 52
    CBASP application, 138–39

with comorbid personality disorder, 86, 119–20, 139
with comorbid substance abuse, 76, 110, 139
without co-morbidity, 60–61, 65, 102–3, 139
and expectations for therapy, 350–51
possible combinations of principles, 194–95
references supporting, 26–27
and social anxiety disorder treatment, 226, 277
with comorbid personality disorder, 260–61, 262–63, 317
with comorbid substance abuse, 250–51, 255, 277, 309, 311
comparisons between cases, 256
without co-morbidity, 239–40, 241, 242, 303

long-term therapy. *See* baseline impairment: relation to length and intensity of therapy

maintenance stage of change, 21.
    See also change readiness
major depressive disorder. *See* depression cases
medical needs, attention to. *See* impairment level, and attention to social or medical needs
mentalization-based treatment (MBT), 316–17, 319–20, 337
mindfulness, 120–21, 125
moderating principles. *See* treatment/provider moderating principles
motivation. *See* change, motivation for; intrinsic motivation
motivational interviewing (MI), 65, 111, 139, 149, 310–13

negative self-attributions (principle 9), 16*b*
clinical helpfulness of principle, 185–87*b*, 189–90, 340, 342*b*
and depression treatment, 52
CBASP application, 142–43
with comorbid personality disorder, 86, 142–43
with comorbid substance abuse, 77, 110, 142–43
without co-morbidity, 61, 101–2, 142–43
references supporting, 28–29
and social anxiety disorder treatment, 227, 279–80
with comorbid personality disorder, 261, 265–66

with comorbid substance abuse, 250–51, 280, 309
without co-morbidity, 238–40, 280, 303–4
nondirective psychotherapy, 106, 283–84
and resistance/reactance (principle 11), 17*b*, 22
CBASP application, 144–46
clinical helpfulness of principle, 185*b*, 342*b*
convergence and divergence in implementation, 326–27, 332
depression with comorbid personality disorder, 52, 87–88, 120–21, 144–46
depression with comorbid substance abuse, 52, 77–78, 80, 81, 111, 112, 144–45
depression without co-morbidity, 52, 61–63, 71–72, 103, 145
and motivation for change, 351–52
possible combinations of principles, 351–52
references supporting, 29
social anxiety with comorbid personality disorder, 227, 258–59, 261, 262–63, 265–66, 282, 318–19
social anxiety with comorbid substance abuse, 227, 232–33, 248–50, 251, 252, 281–82, 310
social anxiety without co-morbidity, 227, 238, 239–40, 241, 282, 303–4
skillful use of (principle 37), 19*b*, 55, 229, 282–83
CBASP application, 162
clinical helpfulness of principle, 189*b*, 346*b*
depression with comorbid personality disorder, 92–93, 123, 162
depression with comorbid substance abuse, 84–85, 114–15, 162
depression without co-morbidity, 74, 107–8, 162
references supporting, 36
social anxiety case comparisons, 257
social anxiety with comorbid personality disorder, 265–66, 318–19, 320–21
social anxiety with comorbid substance abuse, 252–54, 255, 311
social anxiety without co-morbidity, 239–40, 246, 305–6
Socratic nondirective/directive methods, 144, 152

objective countertransference, 155
objective feedback, 292
outcome assessment. *See* feedback
outcome expectations. *See* expectations for therapy

parenting. *See* adverse childhood events; family relationships
patient demographics. *See* clients, matching to therapy preferences
patient process principles. *See* client process principles
patient prognostic principles. *See* client prognostic principles
performance feedback. *See* feedback
personal emotional reactions, clinician, 126–27
personality disorders (PDs), 6
   comorbid, and benefit from psychotherapy (principle 2), 16*b*
      CBASP application, 136–37
      clinical helpfulness of principle, 183, 184*b*, 341*b*, 346–47
      and depression treatment, 51, 59, 75, 86, 101, 119–20, 137
      possible combinations of principles, 196
      references supporting, 24–26
      and social anxiety disorder treatment, 226, 236–37, 250–51, 258–59, 260–61, 274, 317
   depression case comorbid with, 41, 47–49, 51, 117–18
      case formulation and treatment plan, 85–86, 134–35
      client process principles, 89–90, 122, 150–51
      client prognostic principles, 86–87, 119–20, 135–43
      convergence and divergence in implementing principles, 167–83
      therapist intervention principles, 91–93, 123–25, 156–62
      therapy relationship principles, 90–91, 122–23, 151–56
      treatment/provider moderating principles, 87–89, 120–21, 143–50
   social anxiety disorder comorbid with, 221–24, 260–63, 317–22
      case formulation and treatment plan, 257–59, 272–73, 315–17
      client process principles, 288–90
      client prognostic principles, 273–80
      compared to other social anxiety disorder cases, 263–66
      convergence and divergence in implementing principles, 326–27, 333–34, 336–37
      therapist intervention principles, 290–96
      therapy relationship principles, 290
      treatment/provider moderating principles, 280–88

person-centered approach. *See* nondirective psychotherapy
posttraumatic stress disorder (PTSD), 309, 313–14
practitioners. *See* clinicians
precontemplation stage of change, 21, 278. *See also* change readiness
preferences, matching clients to. *See* clients, matching to therapy preferences
preparation stage of change, 21, 277–78. *See also* change readiness
principle constructs, 194–97
principles of change, 167, 325, 365. *See also* clinical implementation of principles; *specific categories of principles; specific principles*
   alternative ways of organizing, 203
   categories of, 8, 365–66
   clinical helpfulness of, 183–94, 184*b*, 200*b*, 340–50, 341*b*, 369
   clinician and researcher experiences with, 370–73
   clinician reactions to, 6–7, 8–10, 97–98, 129–31, 162–65, 231–34, 269, 296–97, 299–300, 322–23
   coherence of, 126–27
   collaboration between clinicians and researchers, 3–5
   constructs featured in, 21–23
   convergence and divergence in implementation, 167–83, 325–40, 368–69
   deleted from list, 15–20, 19*b*, 199–202, 200*b*, 354–56, 355*b*
   and depression cases, 50–55
   final thoughts on, 202–10, 356–61
   fostering integration in clinical practice, 203, 205, 207–8
   future initiatives related to, 373–75
   future research directions, 198–202, 352–56, 370
   goals related to, 4–5
   possible combinations of, 194–97, 350–52, 369–70
   revised list, 6, 15, 16*b*
   revision process, 13–15
   and social anxiety disorder cases, 225–29
   suggested by clinicians, 198–99, 352–53
Principles of Therapeutic Change that Work (Castonguay & Beutler), 4–5, 13–14, 15
problematic experiences, assimilation of. *See* assimilation of problematic experiences
process principles. *See* client process principles

prognostic principles. *See* client prognostic principles
protocol-based treatments, 305–6
provider moderating principles. *See* treatment/provider moderating principles
psychoanalysis, 181, 231, 232
  general use of principles of change in, 232–34
  social anxiety disorder treatment
    with comorbid personality disorder, 257–63
    with comorbid substance abuse, 247–55
    comparisons between, 256–57, 263–66
    versus other therapy approaches, 326–40
    without co-morbidity, 234–47
psychodynamic interpretations (principles 29 and 30), 18*b*, 229. *See also* transference interpretations
  clinical helpfulness of principle, 188*b*, 192–93, 345*b*, 349
  convergence and divergence in implementation, 329, 330–32
  and depression treatment, 54
    CBASP application, 156
    with comorbid personality disorder, 91, 123, 156
    with comorbid substance abuse, 69, 77, 84, 114–16, 156
    convergence and divergence in implementation, 181
    without co-morbidity, 69, 73–74, 107–8, 156
  possible combinations of principles, 195
  quality of, defined, 23
  references supporting, 34–35
  and social anxiety disorder treatment, 290–92
    with comorbid personality disorder, 261, 266, 291–92, 319–20
    with comorbid substance abuse, 253–55, 291, 314–15
    comparisons between cases, 256–57
    without co-morbidity, 239–41, 242, 245–46, 290–92, 305, 306–7
psychodynamic therapy, 181, 314–15, 319–20
psychotherapy integration, 4–5, 6, 62, 126, 158–59. *See also* flexibility, therapist; principles of change; *specific principles of change*
Psychotherapy Relationships That Work (Norcross), 14, 15

quality of psychodynamic interpretations, defined, 23. *See also* psychodynamic interpretations

reactance, defined, 22. *See also* resistance/reactance
readiness for change. *See* change readiness
regard, therapist (principle 24), 18*b*, 228
  clinical helpfulness of principle, 187*b*, 344*b*
  convergence in implementation, 328–29
  and depression treatment, 54
    CBASP application, 154–56
    with comorbid personality disorder, 72–73, 90, 122–23
    with comorbid substance abuse, 77, 80–81, 113–14
    convergence and divergence in implementation, 169
    and depression treatment, 154–56
    without co-morbidity, 66–67, 105
  possible combinations of principles, 195
  references supporting, 33
  and social anxiety disorder treatment, 275–76, 282–83
    with comorbid personality disorder, 261–62, 266, 275–76, 316, 318–19
    with comorbid substance abuse, 251–52, 264–65, 275–76, 310–11, 312–13
    comparisons between cases, 256–57
    without co-morbidity, 239, 240–41, 242–43, 304, 306–7
relapse prevention plan, 313–14
relationship principles. *See* therapy relationship principles
religiously oriented psychotherapy (principle 14), 17*b*
  clinical helpfulness of principle, 185*b*, 190, 343*b*, 348
  for depression, 53
    CBASP application, 147
    with comorbid personality disorder, 88, 121, 147
    with comorbid substance abuse, 78, 111–12, 147
    without co-morbidity, 63–64, 103, 147
  references supporting, 30
  for social anxiety disorder, 227, 284
researchers
  collaboration between clinicians and, 3–5, 365–75
  unified landscape of science and practice, 10–11
resistance/reactance
  and benefits from psychotherapy (principle 22), 18*b*, 22, 277
    CBASP application, 150–51
    clinical helpfulness of principle, 187*b*, 344*b*

researchers (*cont.*)
    convergence and divergence in implementation, 174–75, 327
    depression with comorbid personality disorder, 53, 90, 120–21, 122, 150–51
    depression with comorbid substance abuse, 53, 80, 81, 82–83, 84–85, 113, 115–16, 150–51
    depression without co-morbidity, 53, 65, 71–72, 104–5, 150–51
    possible combinations of principles, 195, 351–52
    references supporting, 33
    social anxiety case comparisons, 256–57
    social anxiety with comorbid personality disorder, 228, 261, 262–63
    social anxiety with comorbid substance abuse, 228, 252, 264–65, 310–11
    social anxiety without co-morbidity, 228, 240, 304, 306
future initiatives related to, 374
and nondirective versus directive therapy (principle 11), 17*b*, 22
    CBASP application, 144–46
    clinical helpfulness of principle, 185*b*, 342*b*
    convergence and divergence in implementation, 326–27, 332
    depression with comorbid personality disorder, 52, 87–88, 120–21, 144–46
    depression with comorbid substance abuse, 52, 77–78, 80, 81, 111, 112, 144–45
    depression without co-morbidity, 52, 61–63, 71–72, 103, 145
    and motivation for change, 351–52
    possible combinations of principles, 351–52
    references supporting, 29
    social anxiety with comorbid personality disorder, 227, 258–59, 261, 262–63, 265–66, 282, 318–19
    social anxiety with comorbid substance abuse, 227, 232–33, 248–50, 251, 252, 281–82, 310
    social anxiety without co-morbidity, 227, 238, 239–40, 241, 282, 303–4
reverie process, 246–47
risk-containment strategies, 143–44
romantic relationships. *See* family relationships
rupture–repair episodes, therapeutic alliance (principle 27), 18*b*, 228
    clinical helpfulness of principle, 187*b*, 191–92, 344*b*
    convergence and divergence in implementation, 326, 333–34
    and depression treatment, 54
    CBASP application, 151–54
    with comorbid personality disorder, 90–91, 120, 121, 122–24, 152–54
    with comorbid substance abuse, 81, 112, 113–14, 152–53
    without co-morbidity, 65, 68, 105–6, 152–53
    references supporting, 34
    and social anxiety disorder treatment
    with comorbid personality disorder, 258–59, 261, 262–63, 285–86, 290, 319–21
    with comorbid substance abuse, 248–49, 254, 264–65, 314–15
    comparisons between cases, 256–57
    without co-morbidity, 243–44, 304–5, 306–7

secure attachment. *See* attachment
Seeking Safety protocol, 309
self-attributions, negative. *See* negative self-attributions
self-awareness, fostering. *See* externalizing coping styles; internalizing coping styles
self-disclosures, therapist (principle 28), 18*b*, 229
    clinical helpfulness of principle, 187*b*, 345*b*, 348–49
    convergence in implementation, 328–29
    and depression treatment, 54
    CBASP application, 154–56
    with comorbid personality disorder, 90, 122–23
    with comorbid substance abuse, 81, 114, 115–16
    without co-morbidity, 62, 67, 68–69, 72, 105–6
    references supporting, 34
    and social anxiety disorder treatment, 290
    with comorbid personality disorder, 261–62, 290, 319, 320
    with comorbid substance abuse, 251–52, 264–65, 290, 314–15
    without co-morbidity, 242, 244–45, 306–7
self-understanding, fostering (principle 35), 19*b*, 229, 290–91
    clinical helpfulness of principle, 188*b*, 346*b*
    convergence and divergence in implementation, 329, 331–32
    in depression treatment, 54
    CBASP application, 160–61

with comorbid personality disorder, 92,
    123–24, 125, 160–61
with comorbid substance abuse, 82, 111,
    115–16, 160–61
convergence and divergence in
    implementation, 171
without co-morbidity, 70, 71–72, 73–74,
    106–8, 160–61
in psychoanalytical therapy, 232–33
references supporting, 36
in social anxiety disorder treatment, 295
    with comorbid personality disorder, 260,
        261, 262–63, 265–66, 318–21
    with comorbid substance abuse, 248, 249–50,
        252, 254, 255, 311–12, 313–15
    without co-morbidity, 236–37, 238–39,
        240–42, 246, 304–6
SES. *See* socio-economic status, and
    psychotherapy benefits
short-term therapy. *See* baseline impairment:
    relation to length and intensity of
    therapy
situational analyses, in CBASP, 130–31, 140,
    142–43, 144, 146–47, 149, 152–53, 159,
    169–70, 174
skills training/behavioral rehearsal, 159–60
social anxiety disorder cases
    clinical implementation of principles
        clinical helpfulness of principles,
            340–50, 341*b*
        convergence and divergence in, 325–40
        final thoughts on, 356–61
        future research directions, 352–56
        possible combinations of principles, 350–52
    clinician reactions to writing about, 231–32,
        266–67, 299–300, 322–23
    with comorbid personality disorder, 221–24,
        260–63, 317–22
        case formulation and treatment
            plan, 257–59, 272–73, 315–17
        client process principles, 288–90
        client prognostic principles, 273–80
        compared to other social anxiety disorder
            cases, 263–66
        convergence and divergence in
            implementing principles, 326–27,
            333–34, 336–37
        therapist intervention principles, 290–96
        therapy relationship principles, 290
        treatment/provider moderating
            principles, 280–88
    with comorbid substance abuse, 219–21,
        249–55, 309–15

case formulation and treatment
    plan, 247–49, 271–72, 307–9
client process principles, 252, 288–90
client prognostic principles,
    250–51, 273–80
compared to other social anxiety disorder
    cases, 256–57, 263–66
convergence and divergence in
    implementing principles, 326–28,
    331–33, 335–36
therapist intervention principles,
    252–55, 290–96
therapy relationship principles,
    251–52, 290
treatment/provider moderating principles,
    251, 252, 280–88
comparisons between, 256–57, 263–66
overview, 215
principles of change related to, 225–29
therapist intervention principles in, 290–96
therapy relationship principles in, 290
without co-morbidity, 216–18,
    236–47, 303–7
    case formulation and treatment
        plan, 234–36, 269–71, 300–3
    client process principles, 239–41, 288–90
    client prognostic principles, 236–39,
        273–80, 303–4
    convergence and divergence in
        implementing principles, 328,
        330–31, 335
    therapist intervention principles, 239–40,
        245–47, 290–96
    therapy relationship principles,
        242–45, 290
    treatment/provider moderating principles,
        239–40, 241–42, 280–88
social needs, attention to. *See* impairment
    level, and attention to social or medical
    needs
socio-economic status (SES), and
    psychotherapy benefits
    (principle 7), 16*b*
clinical helpfulness of principle, 184*b*, 189,
    342*b*, 346–47, 357
and depression treatment, 52
    CBASP application, 141
    with comorbid personality disorder, 87,
        119, 141
    with comorbid substance abuse, 76–77,
        110, 141
    without co-morbidity, 61, 101–2, 141
references supporting, 27

socio-economic status (SES), and
psychotherapy benefits
(principle 7) (*cont.*)
and social anxiety disorder treatment,
226, 278–79
with comorbid personality disorder, 317
with comorbid substance abuse, 250–51,
278–79, 309
without co-morbidity, 241, 303
Socratic nondirective/directive methods, 144, 152
spiritually oriented psychotherapy
(principle 14), 17*b*
clinical helpfulness of principle, 185*b*, 190,
343*b*, 348
for depression, 53
CBASP application, 147
with comorbid personality disorder, 88,
121, 147
with comorbid substance abuse, 78,
111–12, 147
without co-morbidity, 63–64, 103, 147
references supporting, 30
for social anxiety disorder, 227, 284
spousal relationships. *See* family relationships
substance abuse, 6, 252
client, relation to therapist history of
(principle 20), 17*b*
CBASP application, 150
clinical helpfulness of principle, 186*b*,
190–91, 343*b*, 347–48
and depression with comorbid personality
disorder, 89, 150
and depression with comorbid substance
abuse, 53, 79, 83–84, 111–12, 150
and depression without co-morbidity,
63–64, 150
references supporting, 32
and social anxiety treatment, 228, 248–49,
288, 310
depression case comorbid with, 41,
45–47, 109–10
case formulation and treatment
plan, 74–75, 109–10, 132–33
client process principles, 79–80, 113, 150–51
client prognostic principles, 75–77,
110–11, 135–43
convergence and divergence in
implementing principles, 167–83
therapist intervention principles, 81–85,
114–17, 156–62
therapy relationship principles, 80–81,
113–14, 151–56
treatment/provider moderating principles,
77–79, 111–13, 143–50

social anxiety disorder comorbid with, 219–21,
249–55, 309–15
case formulation and treatment
plan, 247–49, 271–72, 307–9
client process principles, 252, 288–90
client prognostic principles,
250–51, 273–80
compared to other social anxiety disorder
cases, 256–57, 263–66
convergence and divergence in
implementing principles, 326–28,
331–33, 335–36
therapist intervention principles,
252–55, 290–96
therapy relationship principles, 251–52, 290
treatment/provider moderating
principles, 251, 252, 280–88
suicidality, 45, 47–48, 173, 219, 222–23, 258,
263–64, 311
supportive interventions, 336–37
supportive self-disclosures. *See* self-disclosures,
therapist
symptom reduction, focus on. *See* externalizing
coping styles; internalizing coping styles
Systematic Treatment Selection (STS), 41

TA (transactional analysis), 161–62
TFP (transference-focused psychotherapy),
316–17, 319–20, 337
TH (transference hypothesis), in CBASP, 141–42,
148, 156
therapeutic alliance. *See also specific related
principles*; therapy relationship principles
and adverse childhood events, 141–42
duality of nature of, 233
quality of, and benefits of psychotherapy
(principle 23), 18*b*, 54, 228, 233
CBASP application, 151–54
clinical helpfulness of principle, 187*b*, 344*b*
convergence and divergence in
implementation, 179, 326, 331,
332–33, 337–38
depression with comorbid personality
disorder, 90, 93, 122–23, 152–54
depression with comorbid substance
abuse, 80, 81, 93, 112–14,
115–16, 152–53
depression without co-morbidity, 65–66,
93, 103, 105, 152–53
references supporting, 33
social anxiety case comparisons, 256–57
social anxiety with comorbid personality
disorder, 258–59, 260–61, 262–63, 266,
272–73, 274–75, 277, 318

social anxiety with comorbid substance abuse, 248–49, 252, 253–54, 264–65, 271–72, 274–75, 310–11
social anxiety without co-morbidity, 236, 240–41, 242–43, 303–4, 306–7
rupture–repair episodes (principle 27), 18*b*, 54, 228
    CBASP application, 151–54
    clinical helpfulness of principle, 187*b*, 191–92, 344*b*
    convergence and divergence in implementation, 326, 333–34
    depression with comorbid personality disorder, 90–91, 120, 121, 122–24, 152–54
    depression with comorbid substance abuse, 81, 112, 113–14, 152–53
    depression without co-morbidity, 65, 68, 105–6, 152–53
    references supporting, 34
    social anxiety case comparisons, 256–57
    social anxiety with comorbid personality disorder, 258–59, 261, 262–63, 285–86, 290, 319–21
    social anxiety with comorbid substance abuse, 248–49, 254, 264–65, 314–15
    social anxiety without co-morbidity, 243–44, 304–5, 306–7
therapeutic change, principles of. *See* principles of change
therapeutic contracts, 252–53, 264–65
therapist demographics. *See* clients, matching to therapy preferences
therapist effects, 202, 204, 207, 208, 360
therapist intervention principles, 366.
    See also principles of change; *specific principles*
    clinical helpfulness of, 188–89*b*, 192–93, 345–46*b*, 349
    clinician reactions to, 95, 296–97
    convergence and divergence in implementation, 329
    defined, 8
    in depression treatment, 54–55
        CBASP application, 156–62
        with comorbid personality disorder, 91–93, 123–25, 156–62
        with comorbid substance abuse, 81–85, 114–17, 156–62
        convergence and divergence in implementation, 169, 170, 175–78, 179, 180–81
        without co-morbidity, 69–74, 106–9, 156–62

    references supporting, 34–37
    revised list, 18–19*b*
    in social anxiety disorder treatment, 229
        with comorbid personality disorder, 261–62, 290–96
        with comorbid substance abuse, 252–55, 290–96
        without co-morbidity, 239–40, 245–47, 290–96
    suggestions for implementing in practice, 95
therapist–patient demographics. *See* clients, matching to therapy preferences
therapist–patient relationship. *See* therapeutic alliance
therapists. *See* clinicians; *specific principles of change*
Therapy Process Rating Scale (TPRS), 42, 55–56, 215, 229–30
therapy relationship principles, 366. *See also* principles of change; *specific principles*
    clinical helpfulness of, 187*b*, 191–92, 344–45*b*, 348–49
    clinician reactions to, 95, 296–97
    convergence in implementation, 326, 328–29
    defined, 8
    in depression treatment, 54
        CBASP application, 151–56
        with comorbid personality disorder, 90–91, 122–23, 151–56
        with comorbid substance abuse, 80–81, 113–14, 151–56
        convergence and divergence in implementation, 169, 170, 175, 179
        without co-morbidity, 65–69, 105–6, 151–56
    references supporting, 33–34
    revised list, 18*b*
    in social anxiety disorder treatment, 228–29
        with comorbid personality disorder, 261–62, 290
        with comorbid substance abuse, 251–52, 290
        without co-morbidity, 242–45, 290
    suggestions for implementing in practice, 94
therapy roles, matching clients to. *See* clients, matching to therapy preferences
TOP (treatment outcome package), 157
TPRS (Therapy Process Rating Scale), 42, 55–56, 215, 229–30
training, implications of principles for, 203–4, 205–7, 357–60, 373–74
transactional analysis (TA), 161–62
transference-focused psychotherapy (TFP), 316–17, 319–20, 337

transference hypothesis (TH), in CBASP, 141–42, 148, 156
transference interpretations (principle 15), 17b
See also psychodynamic interpretations
  clinical helpfulness of principle, 186b, 190–91, 192–93, 343b, 347
  convergence and divergence in implementation, 181
  and depression treatment, 53
    CBASP application, 148
    with comorbid personality disorder, 88, 121, 123–24, 148
    with comorbid substance abuse, 78, 112, 148
    convergence and divergence in implementation, 181
    without co-morbidity, 63–64, 104, 105–6, 148
  possible combinations of principles, 196
  references supporting, 30–31
  and social anxiety disorder treatment, 227, 284–86
    with comorbid personality disorder, 258–59, 261–63, 285–86, 320
    with comorbid substance abuse, 248–49, 285, 310
    comparisons between cases, 256–57
    without co-morbidity, 238, 239–40, 284–85, 305
treatment outcome package (TOP), 157
treatment plans
  depression cases
    with comorbid personality disorder, 85–86, 117–18, 135
    with comorbid substance abuse, 74–75, 109–10, 133
    convergence and divergence in, 172–73
    without co-morbidity, 58–59, 99–100, 132
  social anxiety disorder cases
    with comorbid personality disorder, 257–59, 272–73, 315–17
    with comorbid substance abuse, 247–49, 271–72, 307–9
    without co-morbidity, 234–36, 269–71, 300–3
treatment/provider moderating principles, 366. *See also* principles of change; *specific principles*
  clinical helpfulness of, 185–86b, 190–91, 342–43b, 347–48
  clinician reactions to, 95, 296–97
  defined, 8
  in depression treatment, 52–53
    CBASP application, 143–50
    with comorbid personality disorder, 87–89, 120–21, 143–50
    with comorbid substance abuse, 77–79, 111–13, 143–50
    convergence and divergence in implementation, 171–72, 173–74
    without co-morbidity, 61–64, 102–4, 143–50
  references supporting, 29–32
  revised list, 16–17b
  in social anxiety disorder treatment, 227–28
    with comorbid personality disorder, 261–62, 280–88
    with comorbid substance abuse, 251, 252, 280–88
    without co-morbidity, 239–40, 241–42, 280–88
  suggestions for implementing in practice, 94
treatment type, matching clients to. *See* clients, matching to therapy preferences
12-step meetings, 81, 115
two-chair technique, 161–62

working alliance. *See* therapeutic alliance